BOLLINGEN SERIES XXXIII · 2

HUGO VON HOFMANNSTHAL

POEMS
and

VERSE PLAYS

BILINGUAL EDITION

Edited and introduced
by MICHAEL HAMBURGER

With a preface by T. S. ELIOT

BOLLINGEN SERIES XXXIII · 2
PANTHEON BOOKS

THIS IS VOLUME TWO
OF SELECTED WRITINGS OF HUGO VON HOFMANNSTHAL
CONSTITUTING NUMBER XXXIII IN BOLLINGEN SERIES
SPONSORED BY AND PUBLISHED FOR
BOLLINGEN FOUNDATION

The German texts are reprinted from two volumes, Gedichte
und lyrische Dramen *and* Dramen I, *in the* Gesammelte
Werke *of Hugo von Hofmannsthal, edited by Herbert
Steiner, with kind permission of the Editor and of the pub-
lishers, S. Fischer Verlag, Frankfurt a/M, Germany*

LIBRARY OF CONGRESS CATALOGUE CARD NO. 52–8758

MANUFACTURED IN THE UNITED STATES OF AMERICA
BY KINGSPORT PRESS, INC., KINGSPORT, TENN.
DESIGNED BY ANDOR BRAUN

Translators

JOHN BEDNALL
ARTHUR DAVIDSON
MICHAEL HAMBURGER
JOHN MANDER
CHRISTOPHER MIDDLETON
STEPHEN SPENDER
VERNON WATKINS

*The initials following each poem
are those of the translator.*

Contents

Contents

Contents

Preface

B Y MUSIC LOVERS the world over the name of Hugo von Hofmannsthal is identified as that of the author of the librettos of Richard Strauss's operas. To those visitors from America and England who have attended performances of *Jedermann* at Salzburg or elsewhere, Hofmannsthal is also known as a dramatist, though his other plays are little read, and seldom if ever performed, in English-speaking countries. But he was also a very fine poet, the less recognized as such abroad since the quantity of his lyric verse is small. Lastly, he wrote very distinguished prose. This volume contains a selection from Hofmannsthal's less-known work among his verse plays and lyric poetry.

I am tempted to contrast Hofmannsthal's verse plays with those of William Butler Yeats; and the inclusion here of several of them makes it possible for the English-speaking reader who knows no German to draw a comparison between the shorter plays of the two poets. Yeats in his early plays drew upon the pre-Christian folklore of Ireland; he used other sources in his *Plays for Dancers;* it is only in his short play on the Resurrection that he used Christian material (for apart from the name there is nothing Christian about his *Purgatory*). But the theme of the Resurrection play is one that Hofmannsthal would never have chosen. Yeats was very positively Irish and Protestant—his Christianity is what remained to him of a Protestant heritage. Hofmannsthal was equally positively Austrian and Catholic—his Christianity is that of a *practising* Catholic. (He was, I believe, a tertiary of the Franciscan Order.) I leave any further comparison or contrast to be developed by whoever will; my immediate purpose in linking the two names was to make the point that Hofmannsthal is worthy to stand with Yeats and with Claudel as one of the three men who did most, in the same age, to maintain and re-animate verse drama—in German, English, and French respectively.

T. S. ELIOT

Introduction

I

Hugo von Hofmannsthal published his first poem in June 1890, when he was a schoolboy of just over sixteen, his first playlet or "lyrical drama" in the following year. Though not unprecedented, this early emergence of a poet was extraordinary enough; and it was made more extraordinary by the emergence at the same time of the critic and man of letters—under the pseudonyms of Loris, Loris Melikow, Theophil Morren, or, in one case only, Archibald O'Hagan, B.A. From the autumn of 1890 onwards, this schoolboy poet and man of letters was also to be seen at the literary meeting-places of Vienna, such as the Café Griensteidl, at first in his father's company, later with older friends or alone. To say that he mixed on equal terms with established writers is an understatement; for he was accepted at once not merely as a youthful prodigy and a writer of the greatest promise, but as a master of his art. "Here at last," Hermann Bahr wrote of this first impact in a book published in 1894, "here at last was someone who contained the whole age, for all its thousand-fold contradictions and conflicts, within his mind."

This first, predominantly lyrical, phase of Hofmannsthal's working life lasted for roughly ten years, the last decade of the century. Though he continued to write poems after this period, he himself considered his lyrical vein exhausted and thought only five of his later poems worth preserving in book form. Much has been made of this apparent break in Hofmannsthal's development and of the crisis to which it was due. The majority of those who admired the lyrical poet neither understood nor forgave the change; they felt about it much as Rimbaud's admirers might have felt if he had lived to become a member of the Académie Française. Hofmannsthal's fame declined; it was said about him that if he had died at twenty-five he would have been a great poet. This epigram, as wrong and foolish as it was cruel, is quoted only because it sums up a superficial view of Hofmannsthal which not only prevailed during the greater part of his later life but persisted long after his death, in 1929, and has only recently been corrected by the publication in Germany of a fifteen-volume edition of his works, supplemented by several volumes of correspondence. The insight and researches of Hofmannsthal scholars like K. J. Naef, Richard Alewyn, and Martin Stern have also contributed to a reappraisal that is still in progress; and a collection of Hofmannsthal's posthumous works, soon to be published for the first time, should shed further light on one of the most complex and enigmatic minds of the half-century.

If one thing has already become clear, it is that the whole of Hofmannsthal's work, from the first poems, playlets, and stories to the last librettos, essays, and plays, is linked by strong, though bewilderingly subtle, threads. The present selection from the poetry of his first decade will be followed by a selection from the later plays and librettos; but I must be excused if I do not restrict my remarks to the early works. To treat the poems and lyrical plays in isolation would be to perpetuate the legend of Loris, of the "young prince," the "marvellous boy" of the *fin de siècle,* of whom it was also said that he dipped his hand into a bowl of precious stones while he wrote his "jewelled" verse. (The real Loris went to school, sailed, played tennis, and toured Italy on his bicycle; his parents were far from rich.) It will be necessary to stress not only

the uniqueness of the early poems and plays—and Hofmannsthal's abandonment of his first media has a significance not confined to his personal development—but their relation to the whole of his work. Had this legendary Loris really existed, his writings would still maintain their prominent place in German literature beside the contemporary work of Stefan George and Rilke: but for historical reasons, rather than for their enduring power to move and to disturb us.

The truth is that the early admirers of Loris saw only those facets of his poetry and prose which answered the requirements of the age; above all, they saw him as the belated representative in Austrian and German literature of that aesthetic movement whose progress they had followed in France and England. Hofmannsthal's early essays on the Pre-Raphaelites, Swinburne, Pater, Wilde, on Vielé-Griffin and Bourget, his translations from Maeterlinck and D'Annunzio, and his association with Stefan George's *Blätter für die Kunst* did point to a genuine affinity with an international movement opposed in various ways to mere Naturalism. What Hofmannsthal's contemporary readers and interpreters failed to see was that, however preoccupied with the reigning antinomy between art and life, even Loris, the real Loris, was as much intent on resolving the antinomy as the propagandists of a "consistent" Naturalism; but in a very different way. Even the critical essays of Loris bridge the gulf between aestheticism and Naturalism. Ibsen's plays are treated not as social documents, but as self-confessions; Barrès, on the other hand, is censured for lacking a "centre, style, form." Swinburne is praised for his "dionysian" fervour, but with this important reservation: "These artists, as I said, do not come out of life: what they produce does not enter into life." Throughout these early critical pieces Hofmannsthal shows only a half-hearted sympathy with the cult of decadence as such, much as he appre-

[xv]

ciates some of its artistic achievements. His marked preference
for the English aesthetic movement from Ruskin to Pater was
due to its habit of combining moral passion and social consciousness with the pursuit of beauty. Where these were
lacking, Hofmannsthal disapproved, though he was still unsure of the grounds of his disapproval. A passing addiction to
Nietzsche's vitalism is evident in several of the essays and re-
views, then again a concern with the forms of social life, style
in life rather than in art, pointing to Hofmannsthal's later
solution of the antinomy between art and life, introspection
and activity, individualism and community, in comedies at
once realistic and metaphysical, explorations of the symbolism
and mythology of manners.

If the critic was still unsure of his grounds—and this critic,
too, was predominantly lyrical, delighting in the leaps and
somersaults of the spontaneous *causerie*—the imaginative
writer was far less so. His very first verse play, *Gestern*, written when he was seventeen, was at once lyrical and didactic,
an expression of the moods of the age and a critique of the
self-centred hedonism that was one manifestation of contemporary aestheticism. In *Der Tor und der Tod*, written in 1893,
this critique goes farther and deeper—incomparably farther
and deeper, too, than any theoretical or polemical critique of
aestheticism, because it is a criticism from the inside. The
aesthetic man is revealed as the man who, ultimately, feels
nothing at all; and by placing him *in extremis*, face to face
with death, Hofmannsthal uncovers a much more radical
and universal paradox. Only one of his early verse plays, the
fragment *Der Tod des Tizian* of 1892, seems to lack the didactic sting of the other works, and only because it was left unfinished. But more of this later.

The paradox I am trying to indicate here is that it is the
early lyrical plays of Hofmannsthal, the very works that were

hailed as pure poetry in the sense defined by the French Symbolists and by Stefan George, which tended towards didacticism; and not even towards that didacticism into which the advocates of art for art's sake were apt to fall despite their creed—Villiers de L'Isle-Adam and George frequently did so —but towards one opposed to the creed itself. The richness and virtuosity of diction in these early plays, quite close at times to the freedom of Symbolist verse, make the contradiction not less, but more, acute. It is hardly suprising that Hofmannsthal could come to regard *Der Tor und der Tod* as the first in a series of morality plays continued much later by his *Jedermann* (1911) and *Das grosse Salzburger Welttheater* (1922). The paradox has something to do both with the "impasse of aestheticism"—Hofmannsthal's own phrase in an early letter—and with the predicament of verse drama in his time. *Das kleine Welttheater* is the outstanding exception; for, having come to recognize the lyrical nature of his playlets, Hofmannsthal no longer aimed at dramatic effects in this work; it is, as he called it, a puppet play, a sequence of very loosely interrelated monologues with no obvious moral framework and no dramatic interplay of characters. W. B. Yeats, who was faced with similar problems throughout his active life, was to resort to a related form in many of his later plays; but his *Plays for Dancers,* with their fusion of mime, music, mask, and the spoken word, offer a still more revealing parallel with Hofmannsthal's opera librettos and ballet scenarios of later years. Here it is important not to be misled by preconceptions about genres or by Hofmannsthal's greater readiness to affect an outward compromise with the requirements of the stage. In essence and conception, these works are as esoteric as those of Yeats, and both are late products of the Symbolist tradition. Hofmannsthal rightly emphasized the connection between his early lyrical plays and his librettos for *Die Frau ohne Schatten* (1913–14), *Ariadne auf Naxos* (1910 and 1916), and *Die ägyptische Helena* (1926).

To explain the transformation of the "pure" poet into the "mere" librettist of later years, the dramatist who did not disdain such "humble" tasks as the adaptation of plays by Sophocles, Calderón, Molière, Otway, and Jules Renard, the writing of scenarios for Diaghilev and even for a film about the life and work of Daniel Defoe, I must turn back to the beginning. Hofmannsthal's precocity was a real one. In reading his letters of the early period one is struck by his astonishing capacity for receiving and absorbing disparate experience, so that his attitudes never remain fixed for long, but are perpetually modified, corrected, and strengthened by self-criticism. His openness to external influences of every order—including the aura of persons, things, and places, of institutions, ways of life, ways of thinking and feeling—was such as to amount to a danger. To take only the most obvious of relationships, the personal, he was always in danger of being fascinated, overwhelmed, and abused by those whose strength lay in their monomania, the one kind of strength opposed to his own. This danger was inseparable from his strength; and the "magical" inspiration of his early work was nothing other than the presentiment or intuition of a multiplicity and underlying unity which his later work could only embody in a corresponding multiplicity of media, themes, and forms. The difference, as he said, lay between "pre-existence" and "existence," between potentiality and realization, between the homunculus in his bottle—endowed with prophetic and magical faculties as in Goethe's *Faust*—and the mature man's need to particularize, to separate, and to distinguish, a need inseparable from involvement in active life. Where Hofmannsthal's later works remain fragmentary or imperfectly realized, it is nearly always because the conception is too complex to be subordinated to the demands of the particular medium chosen, to be absorbed into the surface. So in the cases of his first prose comedy, *Silvia im Stern,* abandoned because too crowded with diverse characters and their intricate interactions, of the novel *Andreas,* the most tantalizingly enthralling of his many unfinished works, and, to a lesser extent, of his last tragedy, *Der Turm.*

All the hostility and misunderstandings to which Hofmannsthal's later work and person were subject arose from the prejudice that a writer so protean, so receptive, and so many-sided must be lacking in individuality and integrity. Yet even in the early poems and playlets Hofmannsthal's individuality had been nourished by his uncommon capacity for identification with what was not himself, whether experienced directly in his environment or indirectly in paintings, in the theatre, or in books. Unlike Yeats or Stefan George, he assumed no mask or anti-self, but relied on the social conventions to protect his privacy. "Manners," he noted, "are walls, disguised with mirrors"; and "manners are based on a profound conception of the necessity of isolation, while upholding—deliberately upholding—the illusion of contact." In the same way, Hofmannsthal could at once project and conceal his individuality by borrowing the artistic conventions of past ages; his refusal to draw a categorical line between "art" and "life," past and present, not only absolved him from the false dichotomies of his time but gave him a scope and a freedom that far exceeded the resources of direct self-expression. Needless to say, it also exposed him to the charge that he was a mere imitator of obsolete conventions, a receiver and renovator of stolen goods. Only the most minute attention reveals how much of himself he put even into adaptations of other men's works. His so-called translation of Molière's little comedy *Les Fâcheux* is a good instance; it is nothing less than a

preliminary sketch for Hofmannsthal's own comic master-
piece, *Der Schwierige.*

The escape of Loris from his legend and even the crisis recorded in the Chandos Letter were by no means the only
turning points in Hofmannsthal's development. His correspondence shows a marked change of style after the summer of
1892, when he left school to study law for a time, then Ro-
mance languages and literatures. If Loris ever existed, it was
only till July 1892, when Hofmannsthal was eighteen years
old. The affectation of *fin de siècle* languor—the French term
occurs in several earlier letters, like other modish phrases—of
sophistication, preciousness, and intellectual coquetry, hardly
appears after this early period. The analogy with Rimbaud, in
any case, is a far-fetched one. Hofmannsthal had never been a
rebel or a bohemian; as the only child of parents who approved
and fostered his interests, he had no cause to revolt. Though
he was to find it necessary at times to remind his father that he
was, after all, an artist—and an artist far more bizarre than
even his father knew—neither at this time nor at any time of
his life did Hofmannsthal wear his art on his sleeve. The more
sober tone after this summer had several causes; one of them is
too important to be omitted here.

In December 1891, Stefan George, who was staying in
Vienna, was introduced to Hofmannsthal in a café. The meeting was followed by others, by a hectic exchange of notes, and
by two poems written by Hofmannsthal, who was at once
flattered and repelled by George's impetuous demands for
friendship and loyalty. At one point George sent a bouquet of
roses into Hofmannsthal's classroom at school! His other presents included not only an inscribed copy of his early *Hymnen*
but a transcription in his own hand of Mallarmé's *L'Après-
midi d'un faune,* made in Paris with Mallarmé's permission. If
this was Hofmannsthal's introduction to the French poet's

work, the gift proved more than a token of his initiation into the Symbolist fraternity. But George's behaviour was not priestlike; in one letter he addressed Hofmannsthal as "my twin brother," and begged him to save him "from the road that leads to total nothingness." Hofmannsthal's replies became more and more stilted and evasive; another meeting in a café was cut short by Hofmannsthal, apparently because George had kicked and sworn at a dog. Hofmannsthal refused further meetings and returned some of the books sent to him by George, who accused Hofmannsthal of insulting him and even mentioned a possible challenge to a duel. Hofmannsthal offered a formal apology, but, when George renewed his appeals, could no longer cope with the situation and had to ask his father to intervene. All this within a month. A second, seemingly calmer, phase followed in May, when George returned to Vienna and persuaded Hofmannsthal to become a contributor to his periodical, *Blätter für die Kunst.* The two poets continued to correspond until 1906.

The shock of this early encounter with an artist diametrically opposed to him in temper and aims can be detected not only in Hofmannsthal's letters but in several of his later works, including his adaptation of Otway's *Venice Preserv'd* (1902–4), which he dedicated to George. Doubtless the shock was increased by the undercurrent of passionate courtship in George's first advances; but it was George's intellectual and moral demands—totally different from anything Hofmannsthal had known in his early friendships with Austrian writers like Arthur Schnitzler, Richard Beer-Hofmann, and Hermann Bahr—that left a deep imprint on his mind and work. Somehow George had succeeded in putting Hofmannsthal in the wrong; it was the younger man who appeared as the traitor, like Jaffier in *Venice Preserv'd,* enfeebled by that "molluscoid impressionability and lukewarm susceptibility" of which

George accused the Austrian artists of the time. "It was my firm belief," George complained in 1902, "that we—you and I—could have exercised a most beneficial dictatorship in our literature for many years." Hofmannsthal's failure to enter into this partnership—on condition, of course, of a complete acceptance of George's literary programme, which virtually excluded all contact with the *profanum vulgus* not dedicated to the aspirations of the Circle—was ascribed to Hofmannsthal's "rootlessness"; and, accustomed as he was to social relations governed not by imperious demands for allegiance, but by tact and at least the appearance of mutual tolerance, Hofmannsthal was not always capable of the firmness and bluntness needed to make his own position quite clear. The extent of George's power over him, never as great as George wished or Hofmannsthal sometimes seemed to concede, is most apparent in his choice for a time of the title *The Reflections, the Cut Stones, and the Speaking Masks* for the projected collection of his poems later published by George; this title, modelled on those of George's books, was reduced to the unpretentious *Selected Poems* before the collection appeared in 1903.

Another effect of the encounter with Stefan George, which assumed a kind of archetypal character for Hofmannsthal, as the first and extreme instance of several others that were to follow, was a gain in self-knowledge. Hofmannsthal began to understand his own need for an organic relationship with society, not for a dictatorship of the artist over his public, but a relationship essentially reciprocal. This need, he also recognized, was distinctly Austrian rather than German; and he became increasingly concerned with the distinction. "Was George stronger than I?" he reflected in a letter of 1919: "I don't know, there is too much that's artificial about him, *and*

he leaves out too much. In any case, since my eighteenth year
I have behaved quite consistently towards him, outwardly
placing myself—not him—at a distance, for I had no use for
the position of a *coadjutor sine jure succedendi* which he offered me pantomimically; all that was too German-fantastic
for my taste—too bourgeois, ultimately and deep down."

Hofmannsthal's humanism—quite different again from
George's ideal of an artistic élite, with its hierarchy of fastidi-
ously but arbitrarily selected exemplars—assumed the pecul-
iarly Austrian form of a desperate attempt to reconcile all the
component parts of a disintegrating culture, to re-integrate
them rather than subordinate them, and to find that centre
which alone could resist the tendency of things to "fall
apart." To that centre, difficult to define but easy to sense in
his writings, Hofmannsthal was committed with a fervour
and a constancy that survived all his defeats; but everything
was against him. In a centrifugal age the most fantastic and
monstrous progamme issued by any faction, sect, or party
was more likely to attract adherents. The influence of George's
exclusive circle radiated outwards, to the universities and the
youth movements and into political life, though with conse-
quences neither foreseen nor desired by its begetter. Hofmannsthal, one of the few writers of the time whose political
views were determined less by personal prejudice than by a
painstaking study of history, political theory, and current af-
fairs, had to be content to be the representative of a "society
that does not exist." At once liberal and mystical, because
rooted in his early intuition of the unity within all diversity, his
humanism lacked the appeal of those final solutions offered by
the extremists of every colour. Yeats summed up the dilemma
once and for all; but, though a gentleman according to Yeats's
definition of the gentleman as "a man whose principal ideas

are not connected with his personal needs and his personal success," Hofmannsthal did not "lack all conviction," only the "passionate intensity" of monomania.

This dilemma became more acute, and incomparably more painful, in Hofmannsthal's later years, especially during the first World War, when he undertook several missions of a semi-political kind, and in the post-war period; but his poetic crisis at the turn of the century had a social aspect touching on the dual function of language as self-expression and as a means of communication, and this linguistic crisis, too, was anticipated in many of Hofmannsthal's earlier works, both imaginative and critical. What he called his "word-scepticism" and "word-mysticism" are equally striking in an early book review, *Eine Monographie* (1895): "For people are tired of talk. They feel a deep disgust with words. For words have pushed themselves in front of things. Hearsay has swallowed the world. . . . This has awakened a deep love for all the arts that are executed in silence." So much for the "word-scepticism"; the "word-mysticism" is its corollary: "For usually it is not words that are in the power of men, but men who are in the power of words. . . . Whenever we open our mouths, ten thousand of the dead speak through us." Though a peculiar ambiguity characterized Hofmannsthal's attitude to the social function of language—and indeed to society in general—it is this social aspect of his linguistic crisis that lends it a more than personal significance. The difficult transition from the Romantic-Symbolist premises to a new classicism, or from individualism to a new impersonality, to put it differently, has confronted most of the major poet-dramatists of this century, from Claudel and Yeats to Eliot and Brecht; and the problem posed so succinctly and drastically in Hofmannsthal's Chandos Letter was an inescapable one.

It is a characteristic of Hofmannsthal's works of every period, even the social comedies, that the most crucial thoughts and feelings of his personages cannot be rendered in words, only intimated by gesture, music, or silence; the conventions of speech are masks that conceal more than they convey, or ciphers that must be translated into a medium other than words. "Form is mask, but without form neither giving nor taking from soul to soul," Hofmannsthal wrote; and he meant not only form in works of art but the conventions that govern speech, manners, and appearances in life, the phenomenalizing principle. In the early lyrical plays the problem is avoided more often than solved, because they represent characters who have not yet learnt to face it; Claudio, the closed man, is only the extreme instance of a total incapacity to give and take.

Poetry, of course, had once had the power to combine both functions of language; but while lyrical poetry "aspired to the condition of music," dramatic poetry—the public medium—had not evolved a satisfactory substitute for the rhetorical modes of past ages. After abandoning purely lyrical media, Hofmannsthal continued to experiment with adaptations of classical drama, both ancient and modern, before arriving at three distinct, or at least separable, solutions: the allegorical morality play, the fusion of words with music in opera, and the fusion of realistic dialogue with a concealed symbolism. Each of these solutions has its parallels in the practice of other poets—in Claudel's religious and Brecht's political drama, in Yeats's plays that draw on the Japanese Noh conventions, and in Eliot's comedies—and each is an attempt to arrive at a public medium as far removed from outmoded rhetoric as from the complacent trivialities of Naturalism.

"To introduce profundity into the mundane": thus an unpublished jotting defines the distinction at which Hofmannsthal aimed as a writer of comedies. His correspondence with Richard Strauss provides ample comment on the symbolism of

his librettos. Hofmannsthal, in fact, was a penetrating critic
and interpreter of his own works; and it may be that a writer
so complex could not hope to be understood without his own
help, which was largely withheld in his lifetime because he
loathed self-advertisement and put his faith only in what was
"formed." Certainly his part in the operas—that of a poet willing to sacrifice his immediate inspirations, though never his
basic conceptions, to the requirements of a highly specialized
and recalcitrant craft—was constantly belittled, if not despised
as a concession to the vulgar; and his practice of "concealing
the depth in the surface," the mystical core of his plays in their
social trappings, tended to perplex the mundane while an-
tagonizing the professedly profound. Yet to bridge the gulf between private vision and social involvement, the language of
ecstasy and the language of practical life, was no compromise
on Hofmannsthal's part; it was his primal need, and the necessary fulfilment of his lyrical pre-existence, to be achieved at
whatever cost to his happiness or his reputation. The Servant's
speech in *Das kleine Welttheater* prefigures the later course:

> *Mit dem ungeheueren Gemenge,*
> *Das er selbst im Innern trägt, beginnt er*
> *Nach dem ungeheueren Gemenge*
> *Äussern Daseins gleichnishaft zu haschen.*

> (With the vast and multitudinous tumult
> That's within him, he begins to clutch at
> All the vast and multitudinous tumult
> Of the outward world, its correspondence.)

II

Hofmannsthal's rejected title for his book of poems has the
merit of indicating something of their character; the exces-
sively precious "cut stones" rather less so than "reflections"

and "speaking masks." The last division, which he preserved in later editions under the heading "Figures," is the most telling of all; for, essentially lyrical though it is, his early work aspires to the condition of music or painting on the one hand, to the condition of drama on the other. Two influences on his early poetry mark the two directions: the musical lyrics of Verlaine, the dramatic monologues of Browning. Little more than its length distinguishes *Das kleine Welttheater* from the "speaking masks" or *personae* included among the poems, and indeed it is less dramatic than the brief *Idylle* of 1892. All the early playlets contain passages that could be printed as separate poems, even where they are not recognizable variants of short poems which Hofmannsthal wrote and published as such.

The significance of masks for Hofmannsthal, as for Wilde, Yeats, George, and other poets of the time, has already been touched upon. The development of the persona form by Yeats, Rilke, Ezra Pound, T. S. Eliot, and Gottfried Benn would yield further interesting comparisons. What is immediately clear is that the persona or dramatic monologue answered a need common to most of the major poets of the late Symbolist and post-Symbolist periods; and the one kind of poem not to be found in Hofmannsthal's various selections from his early work is the poem of direct self-confession. Hofmannsthal did, in fact, write such poems in the early years—the revealing *Für mich* of 1890 is a notable instance—but he never included them in any collection that appeared in his lifetime. Here the "molluscoid" Austrian proved more severe than the intransigent purist George, who did not exclude the literal "I" in the same way, though he also resorted to personae in many of his longer cycles. The difference is one not so much of subjectivity and objectivity—all lyrical poetry must combine both to succeed—as of the degree of empathy shown in the poet's projections of himself. In his capacity for self-identification, not only with the "figures" of his poems and verse plays but with things, situations, and atmospheres, Hofmannsthal was much closer to Rilke than to Stefan George.

Of the poems that aspire to the condition of music, none is more memorable than *Vorfrühling* (*Before Spring;* 1892). Since this had to be omitted from the present selection for lack of an adequate translation, I shall quote it here. A literal metaphrase—to use Dryden's valuable term for the most humble of his three kinds of verse translation—will serve to explain why such a poem cannot be rendered at once literally and poetically; and it will make amends for the poem's absence in the text.

Es läuft der Frühlingswind	The spring wind runs through
Durch kahle Alleen,	bare avenues; strange things
Seltsame Dinge sind	are in its blowing.
In seinem Wehn.	
Er hat sich gewiegt,	It has rocked itself where there
Wo Weinen war,	was weeping, and nestled in
Und hat sich geschmiegt	ruffled hair.
In zerrüttetes Haar.	
Er schüttelte nieder	It shook down acacia blossoms
Akazienblüten	and cooled the limbs which,
Und kühlte die Glieder,	breathing, glowed.
Die atmend glühten.	
Lippen im Lachen	Lips in their laughing it has
Hat er berührt,	touched, and scoured the soft
Die weichen und wachen	and awakened meadows.
Fluren durchspürt.	
Er glitt durch die Flöte	It slipped through the flute as
Als schluchzender Schrei,	a sobbing cry, and flew past
An dämmernder Röte	the red of twilight.
Flog er vorbei.	

Er flog mit Schweigen	In silence it flew through whis-
Durch flüsternde Zimmer	pering rooms and, descend-
Und löschte im Neigen	ing, extinguished the lamp's
Der Ampel Schimmer.	faint gleam.
Es läuft der Frühlingswind	The spring wind runs through
Durch kahle Alleen,	bare avenues; strange things
Seltsame Dinge sind	are in its blowing.
In seinem Wehn.	
Durch die glatten	Through the smooth, bare av-
Kahlen Alleen	enues its blowing drives pale
Treibt sein Wehn	shadows;
Blasse Schatten.	
Und den Duft	And the fragrance which it has
Den er gebracht,	brought from where it has
Von wo er gekommen	travelled since last night.
Seit gestern Nacht.	

In German, *Wind* is masculine; the English translator is faced at once with the alternative of neutering the wind or introducing an artificial personification. Yet the wind's sex is inherent in the conception—even deities and spirits are male or female—as is the analogy with the *pneuma* of inspiration and hence with the poet's mind, which touches on this and that, links one thing to another, gathers everything but retains nothing more substantial than a fragrance. The theme of the poem, in so far as it has a semantic theme, as distinct from a musical one, is the intuition of the multiplicity and unity of phenomena and of their correspondences; but these correspondences are established not by argument, as in Baudelaire's famous sonnet on the subject, the fountainhead of Symbolist poetry, but by Hofmannsthal's choice of the wind as the unifying factor, by the wind's passage through diverse phenomena, and by their organization into a pattern of rhythms and sounds. Alliteration and assonance, rather than similes, intimate the connections; by the recurrent *ü* sounds, for instance, of stanzas two and four, short in *zerrüttetes* and *schüttelte* (the ruffling and the shaking), long in *-blüten, kühlte, glühten, berührt,* and *gespürt.* To a very considerable extent, this poem was written by the German language itself; and, but for alliteration and assonance, quite a number of the epithets would not have occurred to the poet. Such effects cannot be rendered in another language, any more than the poem's lightness, that quality of happy improvisation exemplified by the change in its rhythm and rhyme scheme in the last two stanzas.

Not all the poems, of course, can be so easily classified. The *Lebenslied,* for example, can be read as a pure lyric like *Vorfrühling* or as a "reflection" rendered in a curious concatenation of symbols. Attempts to analyze and interpret these symbols have not convinced me that the poem as a whole has any but the vaguest meaning in rational terms. According to Dr. Carl J. Burckhardt, a close friend of Hofmannsthal's in his later years, Hofmannsthal pointed out to him that the lines

Der Flüsse Dunkelwerden
Begrenzt den Hirtentag

(The rivers' darkening shine
Binds up the shepherd's day)

are not an "incomprehensible ornament, but a perfectly straightforward observation of nature, familiar to every huntsman and farmer"—namely, that the surface of water remains bright when the rest of a landscape has grown dark—but went on to speak of the analogy between this phenomenon and a man's last thought, which "gathers all the light of day." This particular image, therefore, would seem to be related semantically to the references to death in the first stanza; and, in the notes and aphorisms which he called *Ad me Ipsum,* Hofmannsthal also commented on the special significance of evening in his early works, citing the conclusion of *Ballade des äusseren Lebens* and his playlet *Die Frau im Fenster*. Another of these notes is a comment on the last lines,

> *Die schwebend unbeschwerten*
> *Abgründe und die Gärten*
> *Des Lebens tragen ihn.*

> (The buoyant gulfs of blue
> And this life's gardens too
> Support him to the end.)

of which Hofmannsthal writes: "The meaning of the world is detachment. In worldly things nothing can be made fast. The world is a workshop, the place where things are shaped, the place of memory, change; it exists for the sake of the fulness of beauty, for the sake of love, etc." But here—as elsewhere in *Ad me Ipsum*—Hofmannsthal is reading later convictions into his early work. His Neoplatonic interpretation of the lines does not take account of the sheer arrogance which one can feel to be part of the gesture of this poem—the exuberant arrogance of the poet as magician. Nor did Hofmannsthal offer a detailed and comprehensive explanation of the poem as a whole, and I am not suggesting for a moment that he was under any obligation to do so. Though the poem undoubtedly says something about a certain attitude to the past, present, and future, to life and death, it is permissible to doubt that the eagle, lamb, and peacock have a strictly emblematic or heraldic function, or that Hofmannsthal attached an intelligible meaning to each of these animals. This is not to argue that others should not discover or invent such a meaning; but whatever current critical dogma may prescribe on the point, there is no compelling reason why a critic should know more about a poem's meaning than the poet knew. The degree of irrationality in a poem is one of its intrinsic and authentic qualities; it should be recognized and respected, not explained away.

As an imaginative gesture and a musical composition, the poem needs no justification; as an elaborate cryptogram, it will continue to provide the most strenuous exercises in ingenuity.

This brings me up against a vexed question which it would have been pleasant to leave alone: I mean the question of Hofmannsthal's mysticism in these early years. That he experienced uncommon states of exaltation, of communion with inanimate objects—very much like those which Rilke recorded in verse and prose—even of trance-like estrangement from his circumstantial self and kinship with the absent and the dead, proves that he had the disposition of a mystic; and his concern with the duality of phenomenon and essence, time and timelessness, flux and constancy, is the concern of mystics. Yet he himself was honest enough to distinguish between the disposition and the vocation, the poet's "magical" faculties and the mystic's dedication not to the state but to the object of communion. It was this honesty that compelled him to abjure his magic when he had come to regard his illuminations as a mere concomitant of the "lyrical state" (the term is his own), as a psychic, not a mystical condition. In a very early prose fantasy, *Gerechtigkeit* (1893?), the poet's feeling of kinship with the whole of creation is judged by an angel and dismissed as specious. According to *Ad me Ipsum,* the Chandos Letter describes "the situation of a mystic without a mystique" —an excellent description of all the poetic creeds, such as Rilke's, which base a metaphysical system on the poetic process itself.

How strongly Hofmannsthal was drawn to such a creed, and how desperately he resisted the attraction, is shown not only in the Chandos Letter but in many earlier and later works. The so-called "Chandos crisis," as I have suggested, was not confined to a brief period; it goes back to the beginning of Hofmannsthal's work, and recurred frequently to the

end. There is the splendid early story, *Das Märchen der 672.
Nacht* (1894), intimately related to the poems and the playlets, of the rich merchant's son estranged from his life of contemplation, idleness, and luxury, drawn despite himself into
the lives of his servants, into sordid and terrifying adventures,
and to his death. "Like the horror and the deathly bitterness of
a nightmare forgotten after waking, the weight of their lives,
of which they themselves knew nothing, dragged down his
limbs." It is not the servants' lives in themselves, but the young
man's projections on them, that destroy him, because he has
not found the bridge from his mode of existence to theirs.
(Bridges, like fountains, wells, and rivers, are among the recurrent symbols in Hofmannsthal's early work.) And this allegory points forward to *Die Frau ohne Schatten* of later years.
Everywhere the life of detached contemplation is contrasted
and linked with the life of active involvement, the two
modes of *Reiselied* and of *Manche freilich*.

> *Manche freilich müssen drunten sterben,*
> *Wo die schweren Ruder der Schiffe streifen,*
> *Andre wohnen bei den Steuer droben,*
> *Kennen Vogelflug und die Länder der Sterne.*
> . . .
> *Doch ein Schatten fällt von jenen Leben*
> *In die anderen Leben hinüber,*
> *Und die leichten sind an die schweren*
> *Wie an Luft und Erde gebunden:*

> (Many truly down below must perish
> Where the heavy oars of ships are passing;
> Others by the helm up there have dwelling,
> Know the flight of birds and starry countries.
> . . .
> Yet from their existence falls a shadow
> Reaching the existence of those others,
> And the easy are to the burdened
> Bound, as to earth and air, together:)

Introduction

In one of the early "speaking masks" not included in the present volume, *Der Jüngling und die Spinne* (1897), the two states are juxtaposed subjectively. The young man's ecstatic sense of being upborne by the cosmic powers is interrupted by his observation of a spider. What he felt to be communion with the whole of life now strikes him as a self-induced ὕβρις, the true nature of life being "to suffer pain, to inflict pain." As in many other crucial passages in Hofmannsthal's early work, it is an animal that works this change, so that even the conversion is brought about by an act of imaginative self-identification. If animals stand for the physical existence of men, their exposure to natural processes, the obtrusive reality of the spider has much the same function here as the "burdened" in the other poem. The arrogance of the lyrical state reaches its peak in the poem *Welt und ich;* and in *Der Jüngling in der Landschaft* it is contrasted with the religious life of service that was Hofmannsthal's alternative to it.

The purely subjective bridge over this dualism is empathy, that magical faculty which Hofmannsthal possessed to no less extraordinary a degree than Rilke. The Chandos Letter recapitulates the magical phase: "To sum up: In those days I, in a state of continuous intoxication, conceived the whole of existence as one great unit: the spiritual and physical worlds seemed to form no contrast, as little as did courtly and bestial conduct, art and barbarism, solitude and society; in everything I felt the presence of Nature, in the aberrations of insanity as much as in the utmost refinement of the Spanish ceremonial; in the boorishness of young peasants no less than in the most delicate of allegories; and in all expressions of Nature I felt myself." This empathy extended to animals and things: "A pitcher, a harrow abandoned in a field, a dog in the sun, a neglected cemetery, a cripple, a peasant's hut—all these can become the vessel of my revelation." Lord Chandos' feeling for

Introduction

the rats which he had ordered to be poisoned was "far more and far less than pity; an immense sympathy, a flowing over into these creatures, or a feeling that an aura of life and death, of dream and wakefulness, had flowed for a moment into them—but whence?" Yet the rats were poisoned all the same; and this is where Hofmannsthal's critique of poetic empathy links up with the linguistic crisis recorded in the same work. The cult of the merely aesthetic word—the word incapable of being translated into action and of "entering into life"—is rejected as altogether too easy. Only Hofmannsthal's later Platonism made it possible for him to come to terms with what he had come to regard as a pseudo-religion at best.

Hofmannsthal's own retrospective interpretation of his early work in *Ad me Ipsum* and elsewhere need not be taken as the last word on the subject; but since I am concerned with the whole of his development—in so far as it can be summed up at all in a brief study—even the more drastic of his later comments are relevant. The last persona to speak in *Das kleine Welttheater* is the Madman; and it seems that at the time of the Chandos Letter Hofmannsthal had already begun to consider the "lyrical state" in the light of psychopathology, and to relate it to the case histories recorded by the new psychological writers of various schools. His library contains the first edition of *Studien über Hysterie,* by Freud and Breuer (1895), works by the French psychologists Janet, Georges Dumas, Fulgence Raymond, and Gustave Le Bon, as well as many later works by Freud, Jung, Adler, and lesser-known writers on the subject. Two other books must be mentioned in this connection, because they were much marked and annotated by Hofmannsthal and served as sources for his own imaginative works: William James's *The Varieties of Religious Experience* (1902) and Morton Prince's *The Dissociation of a Personality* (1905). Hofmannsthal's most intense occupation with these and other psychological works falls into a later period, like that with the thought of Kierkegaard (though the three books by Kierkegaard extant in his library are German editions of 1886, 1890, and 1903 respectively); but, granted that the crisis did not begin and end in 1902, and considering that Hofmannsthal's friendship with Rudolf Kassner provided another contact with Kierkegaard's thought, both these influences must be taken into account. In *Ad me Ipsum* Hofmannsthal identifies the "word-magic" of his pre-existence with introversion and traces his gradual progress towards true existence in his own works. A comment on his poem *Weltgeheimnis* (1894) is almost startling in its psycho-analytical rigour. The poem begins:

> *Der tiefe Brunnen weiss es wohl,*
> *Einst waren alle tief und stumm,*
> *Und alle wussten drum.*
>
> *Wie Zauberworte, nachgelallt*
> *Und nicht begriffen in den Grund,*
> *So geht es jetzt von Mund zu Mund.*

(The deep well knows it still; once all were deep and dumb, and all knew about it.

Like magic formulae, babbled off parrot-wise and not fully grasped, now it passes from mouth to mouth.)

Hofmannsthal quotes the first line, and adds: "—in which the deep well is to be understood as the own ego." Amongst other things, the "Chandos crisis" was one akin to that rendered by W. B. Yeats in *The Circus Animals' Desertion*—a very late poem, fortunately for him and for his readers. Hofmannsthal, as a Viennese, could not easily escape the pervasive influence of depth psychology, which caused him to reduce the cosmic mystery of his poem to "the foul rag-and-bone shop of the heart."

Needless to say, Hofmannsthal did not fall into the narrow rationalism which his comment may suggest, any more than Yeats did; he grappled with the new science of the sub-conscious with the same open-mindedness with which he faced the facts of economics or biology, not in order to em-brace any simplifying orthodoxy—sex, money, or self-preser-vation as the *primum mobile*—but to correct and transcend his own inherited specialization, the deliberate irrationalism adopted in self-defence by a whole generation of poets at odds with the age. Hence the renunciation of a kind of poetry that was to become more and more deeply immured in its self-generated magic; a renunciation that can be judged as a loss of nerve or as a sacrifice, according to the point of view. What is important to note is that Hofmannsthal did not turn against this kind of art, or any other, but merely found its extreme developments unacceptable for himself. Whether we say that he feared for art or that he feared for society makes little difference; his fear, in any case, sprang from the aware-ness that the two are interdependent. With great patience and labour, Hofmannsthal proceeded to build his bridge from pre-existence—that "glorious but dangerous state," as he called it in *Ad me Ipsum*—to existence. The aesthetic man was not discarded in favour of the ethical or the religious man, as by Tolstoy in his anti-artistic fury at about the same time, but made to evolve, the whole man moving at once; and the true mysticism was sifted from the false. The sub-jective magic of the "lyrical state" now appeared to Hofmanns-thal not only as a prefiguration of the complexities and conflicts of active life—a stage to be passed, not forgotten or rejected—but as the revelation of a different order of reality above and beyond the scope of active life; and indeed the themes of his early poems and plays, stripped of their purely personal implications, reached their climax in the political conflicts of one of his last works, *Der Turm*.

Nor did Hofmannsthal retract his views on the nature of poetry. His *Gespräch über Gedichte,* a dialogue discussion of Stefan George's *Das Jahr der Seele* published after the Chandos Letter, in 1904, and read with deep admiration by Kafka at the time, still insists on empathy as the source and substance of lyrical verse, though on an empathy that truly grasps its object, instead of using it as a mere stimulus for introspection. "If we wish to find ourselves, we must not descend into our own inwardness; it is outside that we are to be found, outside." This is one of the many points of contact between Hofmannsthal's conception of art and his ethical convictions; his mystical affirmation of love in the later works rests on the same insight. "None of us possesses his own self: it is wafted at us from without, escapes us for long periods and returns to us in a breath. And self indeed! The word is so little more than a metaphor!" Then follows a definition that anticipates Rilke's more famous one, in his comments on the *Duino Elegies,* of men as the "bees of the Invisible," gathering the honey of the visible world to store it in "the great golden bee-hive of the Invisible." What Hofmannsthal says is: "We are no more than dove-cotes"; and he does not deceive himself or his readers by pretending that the doves are engaged in some transcendental business. "And from all its transformations, all its adventures, from all the abysses and gardens"—an echo of the *Lebenslied*—"poetry will bring back nothing more than the quivering breath of human feelings. . . . How, from any abyss of the worlds, could it bring back anything more than human feelings, when poetry itself is nothing more than the language of men!"

Neither here nor elsewhere was it Hofmannsthal's purpose to belittle poetry or expose its pseudo-mysticism as a kind of imposture; what he wanted was to recognize and praise it for what it is. His essay holds fast to the basic premise of his own early work, "that we and the world are not different things." Because this is so, he also defends the essential freedom of Symbolism, the freedom of image and metaphor: "Never does poetry put one thing in place of another, for it is poetry, above all, that feverously endeavours to put the thing itself. . . . That is why symbol is the very element of poetry, and that is why it never puts one thing in place of another: it utters words for the sake of words; that is its magic. For the sake of the magic power that words have to stir us bodily and to transform us incessantly." In defending the aesthetic function of poetry for its own sake, Hofmannsthal also makes it the agent of a transformation that cannot be exclusively aesthetic, because the human mind is not divided into hermetically sealed compartments.

Hofmannsthal's difference with the absolutists of aestheticism was not over the belief in the autonomy of the work of art—a belief inseparable from the practice of Symbolism, and thus from his own practice at every period—but over the belief in the autonomy of the artist. Though rarely formulated, this was a common assumption; and to Hofmannsthal it was one of those aberrations of individualism in contemporary life and literature which he had opposed ever since his early essays and playlets. Even the new depth psychology served him as a means of overcoming self-absorption. Yet for a long time his own psychological relativism weakened his criticism of the *mal du siècle,* as soon as he tried to formulate it in theory. His word-mysticism ("the word is mightier than he who speaks it," he wrote in 1919) and his growing indifference, if not hostility, to the cult of individual talent as an end in itself, did not become firmly grounded in metaphysical beliefs. *Ad me Ipsum* has an epigraph from St. Gregory of Nyssa: "He, the lover of highest beauty, believed what he had already seen to be only the faint copy of what he had not yet seen, and desired to enjoy the original itself." But even in *Ad me Ipsum*, as we have seen, Neo-Platonism and modern psychology entered into a somewhat precarious alliance.

Both the early work and the late rest on Hofmannsthal's presupposition that "we and the world are not different things"; yet there is a third factor missing in this identification, and it is this factor that distinguishes the early work from much of the later. The connecting link between ourselves and the world—a link indispensable in the early works—is named in one of the *Terzinen:*

Und drei sind Eins: ein Mensch, ein Ding, ein Traum.

(And three are one: a man, a thing, a dream.)

In pre-existence, it is the dream that affects the identification of the man with the thing; and the dreamlike quality of the early work—nowhere more immediate or more powerful than in the story of the merchant's son to which I have referred—made the identification incomparably easier than it became in those later works in which Hofmannsthal confronted the intricate realities of social life without the aid of a magical or fairy-tale convention.

One of the "reflections" included among the poems purports to deal with the "outer life," but it does so from the point of view of a man roused from his dream. The extraordinary weariness and detachment of its enumerations— admirably conveyed by the recurrent "and," with which the poem also begins—corresponds to the imagination's judgment on reality. In the *Ballade des äusseren Lebens* the identification of the man with the thing has broken down, at least in the opening stanzas; their treatment of the phenomena of the outer world shows the reverse side of Lord Chandos' "continuous intoxication," its hangover. Where the mediation of dream is withdrawn, the things of this world are emptied of all meaning. This is the general dilemma of Symbolist poetry; one thinks of Mallarmé's description of the outside world as a "brutal mirage."

Yet in Hofmannsthal's poem the meaninglessness is redeemed. From Novalis' *Hymns to Night* to Rilke's nocturnes, evening has been the time when dream replaces perception, the heart takes over from the head, to mend all that daylight has severed. As a comment on the line

> *Und dennoch sagt der viel, der »Abend« sagt*
>
> (Yet he says much who utters "evening")

Hofmannsthal refers to a passage from J. J. Bachofen's book on "mother-right" in the ancient world: "Hesperus who brings together all that Eos has divided (Sappho, fr. 95; Catullus 62. 20 ff.), who brings the chicks back to their mother, brings quiet to all the hill-tops (Demetrius, *De elocutione* 141); he shines to Sappho as the gentlest and loveliest of all the silver stars in the vault of heaven." But this does not exhaust the significance of evening in the poem; evening is also

> *Ein Wort, daraus Tiefsinn und Trauer rinnt*
> *Wie schwerer Honig aus den hohlen Waben.*
>
> (A word from which grave thought and sadness flow
> Like rich dark honey from the hollow combs.)

The time of day is also an age of man. If in *Vorfrühling* and another poem, *Vor Tag*, the season and the hour symbolize pre-existence in the sense of potential existence, here it is to its other, more truly mystical, aspect, the intuition of past experience, that the time of day alludes. The German word *altklug*—which Hofmannsthal used in an early letter to describe his first playlet—conveys the sense of "precocious" as an anticipation of the wisdom of old age. Psychologically, the two aspects of pre-existence are related in the way in which the premonition of life is related to the recollection of life. As Wilhelm Dilthey demonstrated in Hofmannsthal's lifetime, imagination and memory are very closely connected. Memory was the Mother of the Muses; and, at its most truly mystical, pre-existence approximates to Plato's anamnesis.

> *Erinnrung ists*
> *Die Götter aus uns macht—*
> *Ich fühls, so jung ich bin . . .*
>
> (It's memory
> That turns us into gods—
> Young though I am, I sense it . . .)

—Cesarino says in Hofmannsthal's play *Der Abenteurer und die Sängerin* (1899), opposing this intuition of his youthful pre-existence to the adventurer's belief that "the moment is all." Recollection and premonition have the same power to act as "bees of the Invisible" and fill the hollow honeycombs of outer life. To say that it is only the anticipation of life, or only the recollection of life, that gives meaning to it, amounts to much the same thing; the meaning of life, in either case, resides not in its phenomena but in what lies behind them —or in what our imagination makes of them. The difference is a crucial one; but Hofmannsthal's early works are open to either construction.

Even if we decide that it is not a Platonic idea, but a purely subjective state, that fills the hollow honeycombs of outer life, anticipation and recollection are the processes that characterize Hofmannsthal's pre-existence. From the point of view of non-involvement in life he could extend the same sympathy to the very old as to the very young; so to the grandmother figures in two of his playlets, and the persona of *Des alten Mannes Sehnsucht nach dem Sommer.* The very old, like the young, the Lunatic, the Lover, and the Poet of *Das kleine Welttheater,* stand at one remove from that transitory life which Hofmannsthal had not yet learnt to accept or to penetrate except in imagination, memory, and dream. To these Hofmannsthal was to oppose the "non-mystical way," "the way to the social as the way to one's higher self," as he put it in *Ad me Ipsum;* and he specified three means of attaining this higher self, "through deeds, through one's works, through one's children." Yet the sacrifice demanded by this way also entailed a danger: "To act is to give oneself up." Hofmannsthal's adventurers succumb to this danger. "The decisive factor," therefore, "lies not in action, but in loyalty. The identity of loyalty and destiny." The higher life must "come about through the proper fulfilment of one's destiny, not through dream or trance."

It was this dependence on the mediation of dream that Hofmannsthal came to regard as the predicament of the late Romantic-Symbolist generation to which he belonged.

> New dreams, new dreams; there is no truth
> Saving in thine own heart . . .

—W. B. Yeats wrote in his early *Song of the Happy Shepherd;*

> Dream, dream, for this is also sooth.

The poems in Yeats's *Crossways* (1889) and *The Rose* (1893) are poems of pre-existence precisely in Hofmannsthal's sense of the word. Where Yeats resorts to dialogue or persona forms in these early books, the resemblance to Hofmannsthal's poems and lyrical plays is especially close, as in these lines from *Anashuya and Vijaya:*

> . . . And, ever pacing on the verge of things,
> The phantom, Beauty, in a mist of tears . . .

[xliii]

Introduction

The dominant mood of Yeats' pre-existence is melancholy, as that of Hofmannsthal's is elation; but whether the phantom Beauty is captured through a mist of tears or through a haze of ecstasy, it can be captured nowhere but on "the verge of things." In Yeats's early work, too, the life of action and the life of imagination or contemplation are contrasted everywhere. Hofmannsthal's regal Gardener in *Das kleine Welttheater* has an exact counterpart in Fergus of Yeats's *Fergus and the Druid:*

DRUID: What would you, Fergus?

FERGUS: Be no more a king,
        But learn the dreaming wisdom that is yours. . . .
        A king is but a foolish labourer
        Who wastes his blood to be another's dream.

As in Hofmannsthal's *Ballade,* this dreaming wisdom opposes the flux whose symbol is the river or the road; and it matters little whether it is attributed to age or youth, since its essence is the same non-involvement in active life:

FERGUS: I see my life go drifting like a river
        From change to change; I have been many things . . .
        But now I have grown nothing, knowing all.

In images remarkably similar, both poets turn to

            . . . the loveliness
        That has long faded from the world;
        The jewelled crowns that kings have hurled
        In shadowy pools, when armies fled . . .

Both poets went on to resolve the dualism of life and art by means of an esoteric philosophy on the one hand, active involvement in life on the other, not without difficulties and ambiguities in either case. By resorting to an "anti-self"

[xliv]

and other deliberate constructions, Yeats succeeded in making the transition from pre-existence to existence in lyrical poetry, as Hofmannsthal did not. Yet *Des alten Mannes Sehnsucht nach dem Sommer,* one of the few later poems which Hofmannsthal included in his own selections, shows how close he was to the step which he did not take. Its colloquial diction—a characteristic, too, of some of the earlier poems, such as the *Ballade,* but to a lesser degree—and its realistic imagery point in the same direction as his dramatic work of the same period. Lyrical drama, as its paradoxical name implies, was even more inextricably trapped in the predicament which I have tried to outline. Lyrical poetry could, and did, survive even where it did not yield an inch of its esoteric ground; lyrical drama could survive as poetry, but not as drama. The fate of Yeats's verse plays on the English stage is the sad proof.

III

"My main incentive is not to let bygone ages be wholly dead, and to make people feel what is remote and alien as closely related to themselves," Hofmannsthal wrote to a friend about the Chandos Letter, intimate confession though it undoubtedly was; and it was one of his habits to make such detours in time or space in order to arrive at himself. His many borrowings from other writers served the same purpose. From the very start, the dramatist in Hofmannsthal was distinguished from the lyrical poet not only by his moral and social preoccupations, but by an uncommon capacity for grasping and rendering historical "ambiances," chiefly through his highly developed visual and pictorial sense. In the earliest playlets (not given in this selection) the function of the historical setting is little more than the incidental one of providing picturesque effects. "At the time of the great painters" is our significantly vague clue to the Renaissance background of *Gestern* (1891); but the scene is described in exact and elaborate detail, and the Savonarola-like figure Marsilio—an embodiment of the bad conscience of aesthetic hedonism, like many similar figures in contemporary works from Wilde's *Salomé* to Thomas Mann's *Gladius Dei* and *Fiorenza*—makes the choice of period less arbitrary than it would otherwise appear.

The setting of the next playlet is precisely dated only because it hinges on a historical event, the death of Titian in 1576; but, as it stands, this fragment is an aesthetic idyll in dialogue form, seemingly incapable of dramatic development because entirely lacking in conflict. The aged painter's last illness serves as a pretext for lyrical reflections on the beauty of landscape and art, on youth and old age, life, dream, and death. Much more than in *Gestern* or any other of the verse plays, one is conscious of the anachronism of the setting and characters. One can imagine these languorous, slightly hermaphroditic youths and maidens as part of the entourage of Beardsley, Böcklin, or Klimt, never of so robust an artist as Titian; or, more easily still, as members of Stefan George's circle, much given, as it was, to archaic fancy dress —and *Der Tod des Tizian* (1892) did, in fact, appear in George's *Blätter für die Kunst*. Yet, in a letter written shortly before his death, Hofmannsthal explained that his work on the play was cut short by his matriculation in the summer of 1892, and that he had planned to confront his characters with the plague; the missing conflicts were to be introduced with a vengeance. Unfortunately Hofmannsthal neither returned to this plan nor gave any indication of it in the many later editions. It was the fame of this fragment, the least

characteristic of Hofmannsthal's early works, that gave rise to
the total misapprehension of his aims. George, not Hofmannsthal, based all his early activities on the division of human
beings into "us" and "the others," the division made by Desiderio in a well-known lyrical passage of the play, an elabora-
tion of a poem that Hofmannsthal wrote in 1890:

Siehst du die Stadt, wie jetzt sie drunten ruht?
Gehüllt in Duft und goldne Abendglut
Und rosig helles Gelb und helles Grau,
Zu ihren Füssen schwarzer Schatten Blau,
In Schönheit lockend, feuchtverklärter Reinheit?
Allein in diesem Duft, dem ahnungsvollen,
Da wohnt die Hässlichkeit und die Gemeinheit,
Und bei den Tieren wohnen dort die Tollen;
Und was die Ferne weise dir verhüllt,
Ist ekelhaft und trüb und schal erfüllt
Von Wesen, die die Schönheit nicht erkennen
Und ihre Welt mit unsren Worten nennen . . .
Denn unsre Wonne oder unsre Pein
Hat mit der ihren nur das Wort gemein . . .
Und liegen wir in tiefem Schlaf befangen,
So gleicht der unsre ihrem Schlafe nicht:
Da schlafen Purpurblüten, goldne Schlangen,
Da schläft ein Berg, in dem Titanen hämmern—
Sie aber schlafen, wie die Austern dämmern.

(Calm lies the city; do you see her now?
Wrapped in her balm and golden evening glow
And rosy lucent yellows, lucent greys,
Blue of black shadows in deep alley-ways?
Her luring beauty, purity veiled in mist?
Yet in this fragrance fraught with premonitions
Vulgarity and ugliness exist,
The mad share lodgings with the brutish there;
And what the distance wisely has concealed
From you is loathsome, dully, drably filled
With creatures of all beauty unaware;

Introduction

Who yet to designate their world will borrow
The words we use . . . for only words we share
When we or they speak of "our joy," "our sorrow". . .
And though immersed in deepest sleep we lie
Our sleep from theirs still differs utterly:
Here crimson flowers are sleeping, golden snakes,
This hill, asleep, with hammering Titan's quakes—
They sleep much as the oysters live and die.)

Hofmannsthal's contemporary readers could not know that this speech foreshadows the linguistic crisis which Hofmannsthal was to resolve in favour less of the "we" than of the "they"; that it is a classical statement of the dilemma of pre-existence, confined by its own limitations to the beauty "on the verge of things"; or that the aesthete's awareness of the "mad and brutish" almost inevitably turns to fascination, as Rilke was to show in his poems of self-identification with them in his *Buch der Bilder,* and Hofmannsthal in his story of the merchant's son. Despite the evidence of Claudio's opening soliloquy in *Der Tor und der Tod (Death and the Fool)*—so closely and obviously akin to it—they read Desiderio's speech as though Hofmannsthal had been wholly on the side of the young artists on the terrace of Titian's villa, of which Antonio goes on to say:

Darum umgeben Gitter, hohe, schlanke,
Den Garten, den der Meister liess erbauen,
Darum durch üppig blumendes Geranke
Soll man das Aussen ahnen mehr als schauen.

(And that is why these railings, tall and fine,
Surround the park—the Master's own design,
And through lush-blossoming creepers trained between
The world without is guessed at more than seen.)

The overt irony is that Desiderio and Antonio do look down at Venice, and that their pre-existence is related to life outside, if only by a loathing more ambiguous than they say. What is more, Hofmannsthal's projected continuation of the play would have lent an almost macabre irony to Desiderio's lines on the fragrance and purity of the distant city—the kind of irony that pervades *Gestern* and *Der weisse Fächer* (1897), only more bitter. Whether or not he intended all these implications when he wrote the lines, very soon it was to be Hofmannsthal who was reprimanded for not keeping on the right side of the railings. In 1896 he asked Stefan George to meet an Austrian friend, Count Joseph Schönborn, who was travelling in Germany and wished to make the Master's acquaintance, though not himself an artist. George replied: "You write a sentence, my dear friend: 'he belongs to life, not to any of the arts,' which I would almost regard as a blasphemy. If a man belongs to no art, has he the right to claim that he belongs to life at all? What? At the most in semi-barbaric ages." This is the very attitude to which Hofmannsthal came to attribute the semi-barbarism of his own age.

As I have already suggested, Hofmannsthal's critique of aestheticism and of the hedonism that was its practical counterpart would be no less outmoded than contemporary tracts like Max Nordau's once-celebrated book if he had not been drawn to these creeds as strongly as he was repelled by them, or if he had not presented them poetically—that is, sympathetically, exhaustively, and in the round. Titian, who never appears in the fragment, is credited with the power to "create life" and to endow both the dreams and the waking perceptions of his pupils with the beauty lent to them by his soul; he is nothing less than a god, the god of the aesthetes. The near-blasphemy committed by Hofmannsthal in his letter to George was a blasphemy against this god, whose High Priest, if not whose very incarnation, George felt himself to be. That Titian should also be mortal, and that Hofmannsthal should have chosen the time of his death, are other implicit ironies which were to become more explicit in his next play, *Death and the Fool*.

The theme of *Gestern*—a lighter playlet that owes something to Musset's *comédies-proverbes,* as well as a great deal to Goethe's *Faust*—also illuminates these ironies. Andrea, its hero, is a practical aesthete; like the many adventurer and adventuress figures in Hofmannsthal's later plays, he believes in living in and for the moment, out of a scepticism close to nihilism:

> *Ohnmächtig sind die Taten, leer die Worte!*
> *Ergründen macht Empfinden unerträglich . . .*

> (Actions are impotent, and words are empty!
> Experience probed becomes unbearable . . .)

It is a vitalism begotten by despair, whose literary history is too long and tedious to be traced here. Once again words are called in doubt, as well as deeds. What is substituted for both is a Bergsonian continuum of activity and sensation, experience for the sake of experience, "life" for the sake of "life" as an escape from time and from the knowledge of an ultimate meaninglessness. That is why experience must not be probed—it had been probed out of existence by a long succession of literary auto-analysts. Hofmannsthal's horror of introversion was a horror of this void.

"Yesterday lies, and only today is true," Andrea asserts, at the beginning of *Gestern*. He is converted not by Death, like Claudio, or by the plague, but by the brief infidelity of Arlette. Though he can understand and forgive her whim in itself, as he is bound to do in the light of his own creed, the continuum of sensation is broken by her single act, and the continuum of time asserts itself. The true nature of time is that it is unredeemable; yesterday and today are no longer opposed, for the past has encroached on the present. Andrea learns that

Was einmal war, das lebt auch ewig fort.

(What once has been lives on eternally.)

The point is made a little blatantly, perhaps—Hofmannsthal was seventeen when he published the play—but it is made in terms of Andrea's own feelings and attitudes, not of a superimposed ethical code. Nor does Hofmannsthal use the machinery of the morality play to make the point, not even the moralizing prologue and epilogue of later playlets. Yet Andrea's condition is very close to Claudio's in *Death and the Fool;* the dividing line between comedy and tragedy is as thin in Hofmannsthal's early work as in Goethe's *Faust,* from which both plays derive. Claudio's pre-existence, like Andrea's, is characterized by a false relationship to time, and thus to reality. If Andrea initiates the succession of Hofmannsthal's adventurers, Faustian mystics of the moment, Casanova-like lyricists of the flesh, then Claudio is the man without a shadow, the potential man incapable of crossing the threshold into reality. Both resemble the Faust of the opening scenes of Part One of Goethe's play in their cult of sensation, their "word-scepticism," and their vain endeavours to become involved in life without committing themselves to temporal ties. That Claudio needs Death—a personified Death—to convert him, and that the claustrophobic mood and the prosody of this play recall the study scenes of *Faust,* does not make it more tragic, or even more serious, than *Gestern.* Andrea's conversion, too, has a counterpart in the Gretchen crisis of *Faust;* and the personification of death in the later playlet tends to turn the whole action into an allegory of an inward process, so that one can almost expect

Claudio to begin a new life when the curtain has fallen.

It may be that Goethe's play helped Hofmannsthal to crystallize his intuitive sense of the connection between the introverted and extroverted aesthete, the pseudo-mystic and the adventurer; but encyclopaedically as he borrowed from the literature and painting of the past, he borrowed what he could afford. The early nineteenth-century setting of *Death and the Fool* serves to veil, not to neutralize, the personal and topical urgency of the problem; and if we are tempted to dismiss the problem itself as a "literary" one, a little reflection will show that it was Hofmannsthal's outstanding achievement to have found the missing link between literary and existential problems in his time. The connection between the aesthete and the adventurer is one instance; a contemporary figure like D'Annunzio—whom Hofmannsthal knew and admired, though not without misgivings—was to show that the two can combine in a single individual. I have said that Claudio's predicament is that of the aesthete, but the aesthete is not necessarily an artist, and the artist is not necessarily an aesthete. Claudio's predicament can be understood in many different ways; amongst other things, he is a psychological type, a case of over-specialization, partial hypertrophy and partial atrophy. Hofmannsthal's ethic, in fact, is the ethic of integration: the integration of body and spirit, feeling and intellect, contemplation and action, the individual and the social man.

To a reader apt to equate morality with puritanism, it might even seem that the moral of *Gestern, Death and the Fool,* and *The Emperor and the Witch* is contradicted by that of *Der weisse Fächer*. Fortunio and Miranda in this playlet seem to stand for the very commitment to time against which Andrea, Claudio, and the Emperor offend. Their fidelity to their dead spouses, however, is a conventional

fixation, not a choice embraced by the whole of their natures.
What they are faithful to is not enough; they are too young,
and their married life was too brief, to have established a
continuum of time and experience that could sustain them
for the rest of their lives. It is made clear that the love between Fortunio and Miranda has deeper roots in the past
than their love for those whom they married; their faithful-
ness to the dead is as much an escape from reality as the
unfaithfulness of Claudio, the hedonism of Andrea, or the
Emperor's sensual addiction. Fortunio's widowed grandmother is introduced as a foil to Fortunio's pre-existence; she
proves to him that he knows as little about death as about
life when he mistakes the cry of a young rabbit killed by a
weasel for the cry of a bird. As in the poem *Der Jüngling
und die Spinne,* the animal world provides a corrective. To
the grandmother, who has known true bereavement and
pain, Fortunio is "like an actor who makes up his own part
as he goes along, and pays no attention to any cue"; and this
autonomy constitutes pre-existence. The paradox of a fidelity
that is a kind of infidelity is bound up with a paradox present in the whole of Hofmannsthal's work, that we cannot be
truly ourselves till we know how little of our selves is au-
thentically our own. Miranda's conversion, like Fortunio's,
springs from her discovery of the outside world; and because
her conversion entails an acceptance of the nature of time,
the most featherweight of all Hofmannsthal's early playlets
comes close to tragedy at this point:

> *morgen aber kommt*
> *Die Sonne, und vor ihr her läuft ein Wind*
> *Und trocknet alles.*
> > *Trocken sind die Finger!*
> *Welch eine Welt ist dies, wo böse Zeichen*
> *So schnell zu bannen sind?*

(but tomorrow comes
The sun, and ahead of it runs a wind
And dries all things.
                    The dew on my hands has dried!
O what a world is this, where evil omens
Can be so quickly banished?)

The mundane figure of the grandmother and the deliberate casualness with which the problem is posed relate this playlet to *Gestern* and the social comedies of later years, rather than to the most unsocial of all Hofmannsthal's plays, *Das kleine Welttheater* (*The Little Theatre of the World*) of the same year. In this work Hofmannsthal's pre-existence reached its culmination. The sub-title underlines the ecstasy which he experienced in that "glorious but dangerous state," whose climax in the play is the Madman's self-destructive frenzy. Despite the reservation that enabled Hofmannsthal to leave this state behind, and to go on writing when he had done so, this one work of his does almost permit comparison with the visionary poetry of Rimbaud. No one who knew Hofmannsthal's social self would have called him a "mystique à l'état sauvage," as Claudel called Rimbaud, but what makes Hofmannsthal more puzzling than any other great poet of his time is that this highly civilized and seemingly mundane figure contained just such a barbarous visionary. In a letter of 1918 to Rudolf Pannwitz, Hofmannsthal admitted that there was something almost monstrous about his ambition to encompass so much of history and of the human mind. He writes of "the really half naïve, but—if you look at its bad side—terribly arrogant, inmost tendency of my productive nature, towards this aim: to produce out of oneself a whole theatre, a whole repertory. Curiously Viennese, that —it is only lately that I've come to understand this myself." In the same correspondence, he admits "the bizarrerie of my nature generally." When Pannwitz criticized him for sacrificing too much of his individuality to social conventions, and becoming divorced from "the dionysian, ultimately productive" part of himself, Hofmannsthal went so far as to confess that his relation to society was "a much more nihilistic one than you may assume."

To co-ordinate his savagely primitive and his moral visions proved too much for Hofmannsthal at times. A series of dramatic projects that occupied him mainly between 1900 and 1904—the themes were Leda and the Swan, Jupiter and Semele, The Sons of Fortunatus, King Candaules, Pentheus, and Semiramis—are evidence of that element of "I-suppression" which Hermann Broch stressed in his interpretation of Hofmannsthal's development. The conception of all these abandoned works was more "dionysian," more daring in its confrontation of subconscious impulse than the completed works of even this period, the tragedies *Elektra* (1904) and *Ödipus und die Sphinx* (1906). It was in this tragic phase, between his pre-existence and the first of his prose comedies, that Hofmannsthal came closest to Freudian psychology.

Three transitional works are included in the present volume. *Das Bergwerk zu Falun (The Mine at Falun)* was a belated attempt on Hofmannsthal's part to return to the imaginative world of his pre-existence. Though he completed this play, only the first of its five acts is included here, in accordance with Hofmannsthal's own inclusion of the first act only among his lyrical plays. His dissatisfaction with the subsequent acts has to do with the theme, rather than the execution. Though the plot derived from a real event, it had been the subject of a tale by the Romantic writer E. T. A. Hoffmann, as well as of a more sober anecdote by J. P. Hebel. By the time he wrote the play, Hofmannsthal would have liked to reverse the implications of the story itself by liberating Elis from the pseudo-mystical cravings which Hofmannsthal had come to regard not romantically, but pathologically, as an extreme case of introversion and sub-conscious obsession; but every one of the sources, including the real event, demanded that Elis should fail in his attempt to marry and to come to terms with the outside world. It was only in *Die Frau ohne Schatten,* as Hofmannsthal remarked in *Ad me Ipsum,* that he succeeded in "reversing the theme of *The Emperor and the Witch* and the *Mine:* the love for a daemon is transmuted into love for a human being, instead of appearing as its antithesis." In this dilemma, too, Hofmannsthal was not alone; Yeats's play *The Shadowy Waters,* begun at about the same time but not completed to his satisfaction till 1911, presents a parallel so uncannily close that one is tempted to attribute both plays to the workings of an international *Zeitgeist.* Even in diction and syntax, Yeats's introductory lines to his play could have served for Hofmannsthal's:

> I had not eyes like those enchanted eyes,
> Yet dreamed that beings happier than men
> Moved round me in the shadows, and at night
> My dreams were cloven by voices and by fires;
> And the images I have woven in this story . . .
> Moved round me in the voices and the fires.

Yeats's Forgael, too, is a sailor, and he is related to his fellow sailors in exactly the same way as Hofmannsthal's Elis is to his, for exactly the same reasons. Forgael says to his companions:

> You've never known, I'd lay a wager on it,
> A melancholy that a cup of wine,
> A lucky battle, or a woman's kiss
> Could not amend.

[lvi]

Introduction

What sets Forgael and Elis apart is this:

> For it is love that I am seeking for,
> But of a beautiful, unheard-of kind
> That is not in the world.
>   . . . All would be well,
> Could we but give us wholly to the dreams,
> And get into their world that to the sense
> Is shadow . . .
>   . . . Fellow-wanderer,
> Could we but mix ourselves into a dream,
> Not in its image on the mirror!

Even the superficial difference that in Yeats's play it is the shadowy depth of the sea, in Hofmannsthal's the shadowy depth of a subterranean world, that symbolized dream and the subconscious, is suspended at one point of Yeats's play. "And she and I," Forgael says,

> Shall light upon a place in the world's core,
> Where passion grows to be a changeless thing,
> Like charmèd apples made of chrysoprase,
> Or chrysoberyl, or beryl, or chrysolite;
> And there, in juggleries of sight and sense,
> Become one movement, energy, delight . . .

Here Yeats's mineralogy evokes the very setting of Elis' transformation in the mine, just as Peter in Hofmannsthal's play evokes the bottom of the sea in his description of the tavern. A more significant difference is that Yeats managed to keep depth psychology out of his play, whereas Hofmannsthal—whether by design or intuition—went so far as to intimate a kind of mother-fixation on Elis' part; Elis' death-wish, therefore, could be understood as a recognizable symptom, and the mine as a recognizable symbol for pre-existence in a Freudian sense. The same fixation would explain Elis' ultimate failure to marry Anna (in the later acts of the play) and his curiously mixed feelings towards both her and her rival, the Queen of the Mountain. Such Freudian implications occur even in the earlier playlets, such as *The Emperor and the Witch* and *Death and the Fool*. Yeats avoided such implications; but his difficulties over *The Shadowy Waters* were not essentially different from Hofmannsthal's over *The Mine at Falun*. Both had reached a stage in their development at which their Romantic-Symbolist premises were challenged by their own mature experience and by the mental climate of their time. In Hofmannsthal's play the dichotomy is so stark that the realistic and symbolic scenes very nearly fail to fuse into a single action. In Yeats's play, the incongruity is apparent less in the action than in the diction, now colloquial, now erudite as in the mineralogical passage quoted above. Yeats had the obvious advantage of being able to draw on local traditions of supernatural lore, so that those of his characters who stand for the life of the imagination could be related more organically to their opposites; but, unlike Hofmannsthal, he was reluctant to enter sympathetically into the point of view of the pragmatic majority, as he could not help doing if he was to produce drama and sustain the tension on which both his and Hofmannsthal's plays depended. Yeats, one can never doubt for a moment, was on the side of his tragic visionaries, Forgael in *The Shadowy Waters* or Mary in *The Land of Heart's Desire* (1894). Hofmannsthal, on the other hand, would have liked his Elis to embrace the alternative to pre-existence which Maurteen vainly recommends to Mary in the early version of Yeats's play:

> When we are young
> We long to tread a way none trod before,
> But find the excellent old way through love,
> And through the care of children, to the hour
> For bidding Fate and Time and change goodbye.

Introduction

It has been held against Hofmannsthal that so much of his later commitment seems to be reducible to a commonplace of this order; but so is the commitment of many of those classical authors, such as Molière, whom he most admired. It is true that married love and the care of children assume a mystical significance in several of Hofmannsthal's later works, and that his own sudden death at the age of fifty-five occurred when he was about to leave for the funeral of his eldest son; but married love and the care of children are subjects no more commonplace in themselves than any other. If we consider them drab, it is our own drabness that makes them so. Hofmannsthal's ethic, as I have said, was the ethic of integration; and integration, like other "norms," is a state more easy to talk about than to attain, whether in art or in life. There is a mysticism of common experience, already hinted at in the Smith's speech in Hofmannsthal's *Idylle*:

Die ganze kenn ich, kennend meinen Kreis,
Massloses nicht verlangend, noch begierig ich,
Die flüchtge Flut zu ballen in der hohlen Hand.
Den Bach, der deine Wiege schaukelte, erkennen lern,
Den Nachbarbaum, der dir die Früchte an der Sonne reift
Und dufterfüllten lauen Schatten niedergiesst . . .
Das Haus begreif, in dem du lebst und sterben sollst,
Und dann, ein Wirkender, begreif dich selber ehrfurchtsvoll,
An diesen hast du mehr, als du erfassen kannst—

(I know the whole in knowing my own boundaries,
 Not yearning for the immeasurable, nor ever seeking
 To clench the fleeting flood within my hollow hand.
 The stream which rocked your cradle, that learn to know,
 The nearby tree ripening fruit for you in the sun,
 Casting down lukewarm shadows heavy with fragrance . . .
 Grasp the one house in which you must live and die,
 And then, as one accomplishing, grasp your own self with awe;
 These things alone are more than ever you'll comprehend.)

Introduction

This, according to Hofmannsthal, is a more truly religious attitude than the frantic reaching out for the cosmos in pre-existence; yet the tragic alternative, too, is present in his later work, just as the Smith's attitude is implicit in much of his early poetry. The Adventurer and the Gardener are the archetypes of the two modes, and both engaged Hofmannsthal's imagination and sympathy to the end.

Die Hochzeit der Sobeide (*The Marriage of Zobeide*) is the tragedy of a woman who just fails to attain integration through married love. Her tragedy is like that of the merchant's son in Hofmannsthal's earlier story in that her imagination resists her circumstances. The Oriental, Arabian Nights setting of both works has the function of permitting the greatest possible contrast of splendour and squalor, without resort to the supernatural as in *The Emperor and the Witch* or *The Mine at Falun*. Once again it is possible to read the work as a tract against the times—against free love, in this instance, if one chooses to blame the husband's indulgence—but Hofmannsthal's evolution as a dramatist had reached the point where his ethical ends had ceased to clash with his aesthetic means. A shorter and slighter play of 1897, *Die Frau im Fenster,* had exhausted the lyrical possibilities of a related theme, a woman's infidelity that is also a longing for death; there neither the lover nor the husband have an independent existence, for the play is dominated by Dianora's meditations. With the exception of *Der Abenteurer und die Sängerin* of 1898, *The Marriage of Zobeide* was the first of Hofmannsthal's plays to be conceived in terms of drama more than of poetry; and, though he was little more satisfied with it than with *The Mine at Falun,* and considered rewriting it in prose, the flaws in its motivation are outweighed by its tragic force. Tragedy, Hofmannsthal was to discover, was too dynamic, too monomaniacal a medium to permit that complexity

of structure, motive, and characterization which distinguished
his more realistic plays, from *Der Abenteurer und die Sängerin* onwards. Of all his dramatic works other than librettos
and the two morality plays now associated with the Salzburg
Festival, it is his comedy *Der Schwierige* (*The Man Who
Was Difficult;* 1918) that has established itself most securely
on the German and Austrian stage.

Since I have applied the word "realistic" to such works as
Der Schwierige, I must say again in conclusion that Hofmannsthal never broke with his past in any fundamental
regard. "The spirit seeks the real, the nonspirit clings to the
unreal," he wrote in his *Book of Friends;* but also: "Naturalism distorts Nature because by copying the surface it has to
neglect the wealth of inner relatedness—Nature's real mystery." His later realism could never be more than symbolic,
a realism of surfaces only, because he attributed no ultimate
reality to the institutions of this world. As the *Prologue to
"Antigone"* implies, it was the dreamlike nature of the stage,
and the stagelike nature of human life, that fascinated Hofmannsthal, and gave him the strength to grapple till the end
of his life with what Yeats cursed as

> plays
> That have to be set up in fifty ways . . .
> Theatre business, management of men,

though he also knew the sheer "fascination of what's difficult." *The Stage as Dream-Image* is the title of one of his
essays of 1903; and its theme is the "economy of dreams."
What he says there about the theatre holds good for all his
later works, whether their setting is contemporary, historical,
or mythical. "The man who designs a stage décor must
have lived and suffered through his eyes. He must have
vowed to himself a thousand times that the visible world

alone exists, and he must have asked himself a thousand times with a shudder whether it is not the visible world, of all things, that does *not* exist." The one dramatic subject that occupied Hofmannsthal throughout his working life is that of Calderón's *Life Is a Dream,* the subject on which he based his most ambitious play, *Der Turm* (*The Tower;* 1925 and 1927), the very play into which he put so much of his knowledge of past and present realities, so much of his hopes and fears for the future. Yet Claudio, the closed man of the early play, gives an intimation of this theme of life as a dream play when he dies on the threshold of existence.

Like his creator, the Messianic hero of *The Tower* is the representative of a society that does not exist, never has existed, and will only exist after a revolution not dreamed of in any current political philosophy. That is why Hofmannsthal could confess that, for all his public involvements, his relation to society was "a much more nihilistic one" than it appeared. What demanded his allegiance was not national or cultural institutions as such, but the ideas and principles of which they were the imperfect embodiment. Here again there is no rift between the early work and the later; and it is no less wrong to present the later Hofmannsthal as a conventional defender of the Austrian and European *status quo* —or *status quo ante,* as it had become by the time of his most intense concern with cultural and political issues—than to present Loris as a defender of *fin de siècle* aestheticism. Sigismund in *The Tower* is at once a prince and the lowest of outcasts, condemned to live like a caged animal, and his cause is that of the poor and the oppressed.

The totality of Hofmannsthal's work is as open to misunderstandings as Goethe's. Like Goethe, and unlike most of his contemporaries, he attempted that most difficult thing— difficult enough in Goethe's time, much more in Hofmannsthal's—to extend an essentially personal and esoteric vision to the most diverse spheres, to cut across established divisions and specializations, to make connections everywhere, and produce not only works, but a literature. That Hofmannsthal, as an Austrian, inherited a different culture did not make his task basically different from Goethe's; in trying to produce a literature, "a whole repertory," as he said, he drew not only on a national heritage, but on whatever seemed most congenial to him in ancient, mediaeval, and modern, European and Oriental tradition—Goethe's *Weltliteratur.* Goethe, too. "dabbled" in every branch of literature, including the writing of librettos; nothing was too small for him to attempt, nothing too great. Both denied an ultimate significance to transitory phenomena and institutions, yet applied themselves with intense devotion to their study and service. A century and a half of critical and scholarly industry has not exhausted Goethe's work, or made it widely accessible as a whole, because its diversity is more palpable than its unity. *Mutatis mutandis*—and it is their kind, not their stature, that makes the two writers comparable—the same is likely to be true of Hofmannsthal's work. Every new reading of any one of his works in the light of another reveals new inter-relations, new intricacies of texture and allusion, new seeming contradictions and paradoxes. "Man is a manifold person," Hofmannsthal wrote, and few men were more manifold than he. Because of his unceasing endeavour to grasp and shape this multiplicity, rather than to suppress it for the sake of an easy victory, even his failures remain interesting and admirable.

MICHAEL HAMBURGER

POEMS

Erlebnis

Mit silbergrauem Dufte war das Tal
Der Dämmerung erfüllt, wie wenn der Mond
Durch Wolken sickert. Doch es war nicht Nacht.
Mit silbergrauem Duft des dunklen Tales
Verschwammen meine dämmernden Gedanken,
Und still versank ich in dem webenden,
Durchsichtgen Meere und verliess das Leben.
Wie wunderbare Blumen waren da
Mit Kelchen dunkelglühend! Pflanzendickicht,
Durch das ein gelbrot Licht wie von Topasen
In warmen Strömen drang und glomm. Das Ganze
War angefüllt mit einem tiefen Schwellen
Schwermütiger Musik. Und dieses wusst ich,
Obgleich ichs nicht begreife, doch ich wusst es:
Das ist der Tod. Der ist Musik geworden,
Gewaltig sehnend, süss und dunkelglühend,
Verwandt der tiefsten Schwermut.
                                        Aber seltsam!
Ein namenloses Heimweh weinte lautlos
In meiner Seele nach dem Leben, weinte,
Wie einer weint, wenn er auf grossem Seeschiff
Mit gelben Riesensegeln gegen Abend
Auf dunkelblauem Wasser an der Stadt,
Der Vaterstadt, vorüberfährt. Da sieht er
Die Gassen, hört die Brunnen rauschen, riecht
Den Duft der Fliederbüsche, sieht sich selber,
Ein Kind, am Ufer stehn, mit Kindesaugen,
Die ängstlich sind und weinen wollen, sieht

An Experience

Silver-grey fragrance filled the vale of twilight
As when the moon's light trickles through the clouds.
And yet it was not night. In the dark valley's
Silver-grey fragrance my dim thoughts were merged,
And silently I drowned in the translucent,
Light-weaving ocean and left life behind me.
What marvellous flowers were there, with calyxes
Darkly glowing! A thicket of wild shrubs
Through which a radiance red and yellow as
Of topazes poured gleaming, in warm streams.
The whole was filled with a deep ebb and flow
Of melancholy music. This I knew,
Although I cannot grasp it, yet I knew it:
This must be death. Transmuted into music,
Intensely yearning, sweet and darkly glowing,
Akin to deepest sadness.
                        But how strange!
A nameless longing after life now wept
Within my spirit silently; it wept
As one would weep who on a massive ship
With yellow giant sails on dark-blue water
At evening time were sailing past his town,
His native town. There he would see the streets,
Would hear the fountains plashing, breathe the fragrance
Of lilac bushes and would see himself,
A child, stand on the shore with childish eyes
Timid and close to tears, and looking through

[3]

Hugo von Hofmannsthal

Durchs offne Fenster Licht in seinem Zimmer—
Das grosse Seeschiff aber trägt ihn weiter
Auf dunkelblauem Wasser lautlos gleitend
Mit gelben fremdgeformten Riesensegeln.

An Experience

An open window see his room lit up—
But the vast ocean-going ship moves on,
Noiselessly gliding on the dark-blue water
With yellow, strangely fashioned giant sails.

M. H.

Welt und ich

Geh hin, mein Lied, zum Riesen Atlas, der
Den Bau der Welt mit Arm und Nacken stützt,
Und sag: «Du magst ins Hesperidenland
Jetzt gehn und Äpfel pflücken, wenn dirs nützt.

Mein Herr will untertreten deiner Last,
Wie einer eine leichte Laute hält,
Die murmelnde, wie eine Schüssel Obst,
So trägt er auf den Armen diese Welt.

Das tiefe Meer mit Ungeheuern drin,
Die alles Lebens dumpfe Larven sind;
Die Bäume, deren Wurzel dunkel saugt
Und deren Krone voller Duft und Wind;
Und Mondlicht, das durch Laub zur Erde trieft,
Und Rasen, drauf der Schlaf die Menschen legt,
Gleich stummen Krügen, jeder angefüllt
Mit einer ganzen Welt:
                        . . . das alles trägt
Mein Herr auf seinen Armen dir zu Dienst
Und zittert nicht und hält es gerne gut,
So wie ein Silberbecken, angefüllt
Mit leise redender, lebendger Flut.»

Tritt hin, mein Lied, zum Atlas, sag ihm dies,
Und wenn der Riese Atlas dir nicht glaubt,
Sprich: «Wie ertrüg er sie im Arme nicht,
Mein Herr, da er sie lächelnd trägt im Haupt?»

[6]

World and Self

Go forth, my song, to giant Atlas who
Supports the world's mass on his neck and shoulders,
And say: "Be off to the Hesperides,
There to pick apples, if you like such labours.

My lord will take upon him your great burden
As he might hold the slenderest of lutes,
One gently murmuring, or like a dish of fruit
Will bear the whole world's weight upon one hand.

The bottomless sea with swimming monsters in it,
Amorphous parodies of all that lives;
And trees whose roots suck in obscurity,
Whose crests are full of heady scent and wind;
And moonlight dripping through their lower leaves,
And lawns where sleep has laid men down to rest
Like silent pitchers, each filled to the brim
With a whole world:
                    . . . these things my lord
Within one hand shall bear in serving you,
And will not tremble and will hold it gladly
As 't were a silver bowl, filled to the brim
With the soft speech of ever-living water."

Go forth, my song, to Atlas. Tell him this.
And if the giant Atlas doubts your offer, say:
"How should he not support it in his arms,
My lord, who bears it in his head and smiles?"

                                                J. M.

[7]

Der Beherrschte

Auf einem hohen Berge ging ich, als
Mir Kunde ward, sie hätten dich gefunden
Und mir zur Beute dich mit Laubgewind
Am Turm in meinem Garten festgebunden.

Ich nahm den Heimweg mit gehaltnem Schritt,
Wie eine Flamme mir zur Seite flog
Das Spiegelbild von deinem offnen Haar
Und deinem Mund, der sich im Zürnen bog.

Wie eine Flamme. Aber ich war stolz,
Und ruhig schreitend spähte ich im Weiher
Das Spiel des Fisches, der das Dunkel sucht,
Und überm Wald den Horst von einem Geier.

The Self-Controlled

High on a mountain I was walking when
They brought me word that, found and caught at last,
My booty and my pleasure, with green withes
Bound to my garden tower, they held you fast.

I made for home with slow and measured pace,
Though ever like a flame beside me whirled
The mirrored image of your flowing hair
And of your lips that scorn and fury curled.

Flew like a flame beside me. But I was proud,
Calmly strode on and at the pond-side stood
To glimpse the play of fishes that seek the dark
And glimpse the buzzard's eyrie above the wood.

M. H.

Reiselied

Wasser stürzt, uns zu verschlingen,
Rollt der Fels, uns zu erschlagen,
Kommen schon auf starken Schwingen
Vögel her, uns fortzutragen.

Aber unten liegt ein Land,
Früchte spiegelnd ohne Ende
In den alterslosen Seen.

Marmorstirn und Brunnenrand
Steigt aus blumigem Gelände,
Und die leichten Winde wehn.

Traveller's Song

To engulf us waters eddy,
Down the boulders roll, to crush,
And to bear us off already
Birds on powerful pinions rush.

But a landscape lies below
In its ageless lakes reflecting
Mellow fruit unendingly.

Brim of well and marble brow
Gleaming rise from flowery meadows,
And the gentle breezes blow.

M. H.

Hirtenknabe singt

Am Waldesrand im Gras
Hab ich geschlafen;
Goldne Sonnenpfeile,
Dicke, heisse, trafen
Meine Augenlider,
Meine kühlen Glieder.

Hatte an meinen Arm
Angeschmiegt Stirn und Wang,
Träumte so, tief und lang,
Träumte so, warm und bang:
Und ich war nicht allein,
Zu meiner Schläfen Blut
Rauschte ein fremd Geräusch
Leise herein.

Meint, ich läg im Arme
Der Geliebten da,
Still dem leisen Fliessen
Ihrer Adern nah,
Hörte mit geduckten
Und gespannten Sinnen
Ihres Lebens Leben
Leise rauschend rinnen.

Kühler Wind weckte mich,
Doch Rauschen blieb
Und Traum und Blut
Zu Kopf mir trieb.

Shepherd Boy's Song

At wood's edge in grass,
I lay down sleeping.
The sun's golden arrows
Thickly, hotly, meeting
My closed eyelids
And my cool limbs.

Pressed close against my arm
Brow and cheek rested.
This I dreamed, long and deep,
This I dreamed, warm and afraid.
And I was not alone,
Into my blood's sleep
Distant murmur whispered
Gently in.

That I lay in arms
Of the loved one there,
Quiet the gentle flowing
Of her veins near,
Heard I with such humble
And excited passion,
Living of her life
As its whispering ran on.

Cooling wind awoke me,
But murmuring stayed
And dream and blood
Drove through my head.

Hugo von Hofmannsthal

Heiss sprang ich auf
Und liess den Ort,
Doch leises Rauschen
Umgab mich fort.

Aber allein! und kalt!
Unter dem dunklen Wald
Rauschte mit fernem Schwall
Leise der Wasserfall,
Leise empor
Jetzt wie zuvor . . .

Was ich an mich gedrückt,
Was mich so warm beglückt,
Lässt mich im weiten Raum
Schauernd allein.
Lässt mich und weiss von nichts,
Scholl in mein Leben
Fremde hinein.

Shepherd Boy's Song

Hotly I sprang up
And left the place
But the soft murmuring
Round me stayed.

But quite alone! And cold!
Under the darkening wold
Murmured with distant swell
Softly the waterfall,
Softly afar
Now as before.

What I pressed close to me,
What brought such warmth to me
Leaves me in a distant place
Trembling alone,
Leaves me not knowing how
Pealed into my life
That stranger gone.

S. S.

Lebenslied

Den Erben lass verschwenden
An Adler, Lamm und Pfau
Das Salböl aus den Händen
Der toten alten Frau!
Die Toten, die entgleiten,
Die Wipfel in dem Weiten—
Ihm sind sie wie das Schreiten
Der Tänzerinnen wert!

Er geht wie den kein Walten
Vom Rücken her bedroht.
Er lächelt, wenn die Falten
Des Lebens flüstern: Tod!
Ihm bietet jede Stelle
Geheimnisvoll die Schwelle;
Es gibt sich jeder Welle
Der Heimatlose hin.

Der Schwarm von wilden Bienen
Nimmt seine Seele mit;
Das Singen von Delphinen
Beflügelt seinen Schritt:
Ihn tragen alle Erden
Mit mächtigen Gebärden.
Der Flüsse Dunkelwerden
Begrenzt den Hirtentag!

Song of Life

On eagle, lamb, and peacock
The heir may freely spend
The precious cruse of ointment
From the dead old woman's hand!
The dead that glide away,
Far treetops where they sway,
He counts as light as they
Were steps the dancers weave.

As one who fears no power
That threatens from behind,
He walks; although Life's wrinkles
Breathe "Death!" he smiles to find
A welcome everywhere,
Each house gives secret cheer;
As homeless as the air
He yields to every wave.

The swarm of wild bees hurries
His soul along with them;
The singing of the dolphins
Plumes his light feet with flame;
The powers of earth combine
To aid him with a sign;
The rivers' darkening shine
Binds up the shepherd's day.

[17]

Hugo von Hofmannsthal

Das Salböl aus den Händen
Der toten alten Frau
Lass lächelnd ihn verschwenden
An Adler, Lamm und Pfau:
Er lächelt der Gefährten.—
Die schwebend unbeschwerten
Abgründe und die Gärten
Des Lebens tragen ihn.

Song of Life

The precious cruse of ointment
From the dead old woman's hand
On eagle, lamb, and peacock
The smiling heir may spend:
He laughs at such a crew.—
The buoyant gulfs of blue
And this life's gardens too
Support him to the end.

A. D.

Dein Antlitz . . .

Dein Antlitz war mit Träumen ganz beladen.
Ich schwieg und sah dich an mit stummem Beben.
Wie stieg das auf! Dass ich mich einmal schon
In frühern Nächten völlig hingegeben

Dem Mond und dem zuviel geliebten Tal,
Wo auf den leeren Hängen auseinander
Die magern Bäume standen und dazwischen
Die niedern kleinen Nebelwolken gingen

Und durch die Stille hin die immer frischen
Und immer fremden silberweissen Wasser
Der Fluss hinrauschen liess—wie stieg das auf!

Wie stieg das auf! Denn allen diesen Dingen
Und ihrer Schönheit—die unfruchtbar war—
Hingab ich mich in grosser Sehnsucht ganz,
Wie jetzt für das Anschaun von deinem Haar
Und zwischen deinen Lidern diesen Glanz!

Your face . . .

Your face was wholly laden down with dreams.
Trembling I looked at you, without a word.
How it came back! That once before already
In earlier nights long past I had surrendered

My whole self to the moon, the valley loved
Too much, where on the empty slopes, divided,
The lean trees loomed and in the space between
The little, low clouds of the mist moved on

And through the stillness, silver-white, there glided
The ever new, the ever alien waters
The whispering river sent—how it came back!

How it came back! For to these things, each one,
And to their beauty—which was fruitless there—
I quite surrendered, vainly, vastly yearning,
As I do now for gazing at your hair
And for this gleam between your eyelids burning.

M. H.

Wir gingen einen Weg . . .

Wir gingen einen Weg mit vielen Brücken,
Und vor uns gingen drei, die ruhig sangen.
Ich sage dies, damit du dich entsinnst.
Da sagtest du und zeigtest nach dem Berg,
Der Schatten trug von Wolken und den Schatten
Der steilen Wände mit unsicheren Pfaden,
Du sagtest: «Wären dort wir zwei allein!»
Und deine Worte hatten einen Ton
So fremd wie Duft von Sandelholz und Myrrhen.
—Auch deine Wangen waren nicht wie sonst.—
Und mir geschah, dass eine trunkene Lust
Mich fasste, so wie wenn die Erde bebt
Und umgestürztes prunkvolles Gerät
Rings rollt und Wasser aus dem Boden quillt
Und einer taumelnd steht und doppelt sieht:
Denn ich war da und war zugleich auch dort,
Mit dir im Arm, und alle Lust davon
War irgendwie vermengt mit aller Lust,
Die dieser grosse Berg mit vielen Klüften
Hingibt, wenn einer ruhig wie der Adler
Mit ausgespannten Flügeln ihn umflöge.
Ich war mit dir im Arm auf jenem Berg,
Ich hatte alles Wissen seiner Höhe,
Der Einsamkeit, des nie betretnen Pfades
Und dich im Arm und alle Lust davon . . .
Und als ich heut im Lusthaus beim Erwachen
An einer kühlen Wand das Bild der Götter
Und ihrer wunderbaren Freuden sah:

We went along a way . . .

We went along a way of many bridges,
And three went on before us, quietly singing.
I tell you this to call to mind that moment.
You said then—pointing to the mountain mass
Checked by dark shadows from the clouds, and shadows
From the steep slopes with their uncertain paths—
You said: "O that we two were there alone!"
And your words at that moment had a ring
As strange as scent of sandalwood and myrrh.
—Even your cheeks were not as otherwise.—
It seemed as if a sudden drunken rapture
Possessed me, as when earth's surface quakes
And splendid ornaments turned upside down
Tumble around and water gushes forth
And he sees double who is standing there:
For I was *here* and at the same time *there,*
You in my arms and all the rapture of it
Somehow alloyed with all the rapture that
This mountain here with manifold ravines
Might yield to one who like an eagle softly
Flew round its mass, his wings at their full stretch.
We stood there and embraced upon the mountain;
I had full knowledge of its soaring height,
Its solitude, its never-trodden paths,
You in my arms and all the rapture of it . . .
And as today I woke in a summer-house
I saw the image painted on a wall
Of the Greek gods and their Elysian joys,

Hugo von Hofmannsthal

Wie sie mit leichtem Fusse, kaum mehr lastend,
Vom dünnen Dache weinumrankter Lauben
Ins Blaue tretend aufzuschweben schienen,
Wie Flammen ohne Schwere, mit dem Laut
Von Liedern und dem Klang der hellen Leier
Emporgeweht; da wurde es mir so,
Als dürft ich jenen letzten, die noch nah
Der Erde schienen, freundlich ihr Gewand
Anrühren, wie ein Gastfreund tuen darf
Von gleichem Rang und ähnlichem Geschick:
Denn ich gedachte jenes Abenteuers.

We went along a way . . .

How—light of foot and weightless seemingly—
From the slight roof of a vine-covered bower
They glided upwards into the blue sky,
Ethereal as flames, and with the noise
Of song and the sound of the bright lyre
Swept towards higher regions. And I felt
That I might touch the garments' folds of such
As seemed still close to earth—as might a friend,
A guest of theirs, of equal rank and fate:
For I had our adventure still in mind.

J. M.

Unendliche Zeit

Wirklich, bist du zu schwach, dich der seligen Zeit zu
    erinnern?
Über dem dunkelnden Tal zogen die Sterne herauf,
Wir aber standen im Schatten und bebten. Die riesige Ulme
Schüttelte sich wie im Traum, warf einen Schauer herab
Lärmender Tropfen ins Gras: Es war keine Stunde
    vergangen
Seit jenem Regen! Und mir schien es unendliche Zeit.
Denn dem Erlebenden dehnt sich das Leben: es tuen sich
    lautlos
Klüfte unendlichen Traums zwischen zwei Blicken ihm
    auf:
In mich hätt ich gesogen dein zwanzigjähriges Dasein
—War mir, indessen der Baum noch seine Tropfen behielt.

Infinite Time

Are you truly too weak to remember the time that seemed
  blessèd?
Over the darkening vale slowly the stars climbed the sky—
Yet in the shadow we stood and were trembling. The tower-
  ing elm-tree
Shuddered as in a dream, scattered a shower of drops
Pattering down on the grass: yet hardly an hour had gone
  by since
We heard that rain! And to me it seemed an infinite time.
For to the man who is living it, life seems to stretch: in the
  silence
Chasms of infinite dream open between two brief looks:
I had absorbed within me your twenty-year-old existence
While—so it seemed—still the tree held all its raindrops un-
  shed.

M. H.

Terzinen

I
Über Vergänglichkeit

Noch spür ich ihren Atem auf den Wangen:
Wie kann das sein, dass diese nahen Tage
Fort sind, für immer fort, und ganz vergangen?

Dies ist ein Ding, das keiner voll aussinnt,
Und viel zu grauenvoll, als dass man klage:
Dass alles gleitet und vorüberrinnt.

Und dass mein eignes Ich, durch nichts gehemmt,
Herüberglitt aus einem kleinen Kind
Mir wie ein Hund unheimlich stumm und fremd.

Dann: dass ich auch vor hundert Jahren war
Und meine Ahnen, die im Totenhemd,
Mit mir verwandt sind wie mein eignes Haar,

So eins mit mir als wie mein eignes Haar.

II

Die Stunden! wo wir auf das helle Blauen
Des Meeres starren und den Tod verstehn,
So leicht und feierlich und ohne Grauen,

Stanzas in Terza Rima

I
On Transitoriness

Still on my cheek I feel their warm breath fall:
How can it be that these near days are spent,
Past, wholly past, and gone beyond recall?

This is a thing that mocks the deepest mind
And far too terrifying for lament:
That all flows by us, leaving us behind.

And that unhindered my own self could flow
Out of a little child whom now I find
Remote as a dumb dog, and scarcely know.

Then: that in lives a century old I share
And kinsmen laid in coffins long ago
Are yet as close to me as my own hair,

Are no less one with me than my own hair.

II

Those hours! when long we stare into the sea
All blue and clear, when death does not amaze,
Grave without awe we stare, as fearlessly

Wie kleine Mädchen, die sehr blass aussehn,
Mit grossen Augen, und die immer frieren,
An einem Abend stumm vor sich hinsehn

Und wissen, dass das Leben jetzt aus ihren
Schlaftrunknen Gliedern still hinüberfliesst
In Bäum und Gras, und sich matt lächelnd zieren

Wie eine Heilige, die ihr Blut vergiesst.

III

Wir sind aus solchem Zeug wie das zu Träumen,
Und Träume schlagen so die Augen auf
Wie kleine Kinder unter Kirschenbäumen,

Aus deren Krone den blassgoldnen Lauf
Der Vollmond anhebt durch die grosse Nacht.
. . . Nicht anders tauchen unsre Träume auf,

Sind da und leben wie ein Kind, das lacht,
Nicht minder gross im Auf- und Niederschweben
Als Vollmond, aus Baumkronen aufgewacht.

Das Innerste ist offen ihrem Weben;
Wie Geisterhände in versperrtem Raum
Sind sie in uns und haben immer Leben.

Und drei sind Eins: ein Mensch, ein Ding, ein Traum.

Stanzas in Terza Rima

As little girls who pale in the light haze
Feeling the chill of dusk, wide-eyed and slim,
Dumbly one evening stand still and gaze,

Knowing that life now from each drowsy limb
To trees and grasses travels like a flood,
While faintly smiling they look proud and prim

Like a young martyr shedding her saintly blood.

III

We are such stuff as dreams are made on: these
Our dreams as suddenly open wide their eyes
As little children under cherry-trees

Out of whose crests the full moon mounts the skies
On her pale golden course through the great night.
. . . No differently our dreams emerge and rise,

Live like a laughing child for our delight,
And are as great in rising and in leaving
As the full moon when treetops frame her light.

Our inmost life is open to their weaving;
Like ghostly hands in a locked room they teem
Within us, always living and conceiving.

And three are one: a man, a thing, a dream.

M. H.

Ballade des äusseren Lebens

Und Kinder wachsen auf mit tiefen Augen,
Die von nichts wissen, wachsen auf und sterben,
Und alle Menschen gehen ihre Wege.

Und süsse Früchte werden aus den herben
Und fallen nachts wie tote Vögel nieder
Und liegen wenig Tage und verderben.

Und immer weht der Wind, und immer wieder
Vernehmen wir und reden viele Worte
Und spüren Lust und Müdigkeit der Glieder.

Und Strassen laufen durch das Gras, und Orte
Sind da und dort, voll Fackeln, Bäumen, Teichen,
Und drohende, und totenhaft verdorrte . . .

Wozu sind diese aufgebaut? und gleichen
Einander nie? und sind unzählig viele?
Was wechselt Lachen, Weinen und Erbleichen?

Was frommt das alles uns und diese Spiele,
Die wir doch gross und ewig einsam sind
Und wandernd nimmer suchen irgend Ziele?

Was frommts, dergleichen viel gesehen haben?
Und dennoch sagt der viel, der «Abend» sagt,
Ein Wort, daraus Tiefsinn und Trauer rinnt

Wie schwerer Honig aus den hohlen Waben.

Ballad of the Outer Life

And children grow with deeply wondering eyes
That know of nothing, grow a while and die,
And every one of us goes his own way.

And bitter fruit will sweeten by and by
And like dead birds come hurtling down at night
And for a few days fester where they lie.

And always the wind blows, and we recite
And hear again the phrases thin with wear
And in our limbs feel languor or delight.

And roads run through the grass, and here and there
Are places full of lights and pools and trees,
And some are threatening, some are cold and bare . . .

To what end were they built? With differences
No less innumerable than their names?
Why laughter now, now weeping or disease?

What does it profit us, and all these games,
Who, great and lonely, ever shall be so
And though we always wander seek no aims?

To see such things do travellers leave their homes?
Yet he says much who utters "evening,"
A word from which grave thought and sadness flow

Like rich dark honey from the hollow combs.

M. H.

Manche freilich . . .

Manche freilich müssen drunten sterben,
Wo die schweren Ruder der Schiffe streifen,
Andre wohnen bei dem Steuer droben,
Kennen Vogelflug und die Länder der Sterne.

Manche liegen immer mit schweren Gliedern
Bei den Wurzeln des verworrenen Lebens,
Andern sind die Stühle gerichtet
Bei den Sibyllen, den Königinnen,
Und da sitzen sie wie zu Hause,
Leichten Hauptes und leichter Hände.

Doch ein Schatten fällt von jenen Leben
In die anderen Leben hinüber,
Und die leichten sind an die schweren
Wie an Luft und Erde gebunden:

Ganz vergessener Völker Müdigkeiten
Kann ich nicht abtun von meinen Lidern,
Noch weghalten von der erschrockenen Seele
Stummes Niederfallen ferner Sterne.

Viele Geschicke weben neben dem meinen,
Durcheinander spielt sie alle das Dasein,
Und mein Teil ist mehr als dieses Lebens
Schlanke Flamme oder schmale Leier.

Many truly . . .

Many truly down below must perish
Where the heavy oars of ships are passing;
Others by the helm up there have dwelling,
Know the flight of birds and starry countries.

Many lie with heavy limbs remaining
Near the roots of life obscurely tangled;
There are chairs meanwhile set up for others
Near to sibyls, queens for their companions,
And they sit there as at home contented,
Easy in their heads, in their hands easy.

Yet from their existence falls a shadow
Reaching the existence of those others,
And the easy are to the burdened
Bound, as to earth and air, together.

I can never cast off from my eyelids
Lassitudes of long-forgotten peoples,
Nor from my astounded soul can banish
Soundless fall of stars through outer distance.

Many destinies with mine are woven;
Living plays them all through one another,
And my part is larger than this slender
Life's ascending flame or narrow lyre.

v. w.

Ein Traum von grosser Magie

Viel königlicher als ein Perlenband
Und kühn wie junges Meer im Morgenduft,
So war ein grosser Traum—wie ich ihn fand.

Durch offene Glastüren ging die Luft.
Ich schlief im Pavillon zu ebner Erde,
Und durch vier offne Türen ging die Luft—

Und früher liefen schon geschirrte Pferde
Hindurch und Hunde eine ganze Schar
An meinem Bett vorbei. Doch die Gebärde

Des Magiers—des Ersten, Grossen—war
Auf einmal zwischen mir und einer Wand:
Sein stolzes Nicken, königliches Haar.

Und hinter ihm nicht Mauer: es entstand
Ein weiter Prunk von Abgrund, dunklem Meer
Und grünen Matten hinter seiner Hand.

Er bückte sich und zog das Tiefe her.
Er bückte sich, und seine Finger gingen
Im Boden so, als ob es Wasser wär.

Vom dünnen Quellenwasser aber fingen
Sich riesige Opale in den Händen
Und fielen tönend wieder ab in Ringen.

A Dream of Great Magic

More regal far than pearls to fillet bound
And bold as a young sea in morning scent
Was a majestic dream—this dream I found.

Through open doors of glass the breezes went.
I slept in the pavilion, near the ground,
And through four open doors the breezes went—

Yet harnessed horses earlier had run
Through there, and hounds, a pack of them in line
Rushed past my bed. But suddenly between one

Wall and myself there was the mighty sign,
The Great Magician, foremost of them all:
His regal hair, nod haughty and benign.

And now behind him I could see no wall:
Wide pomp of chasms, of nocturnal sea,
Green pasture-land behind his hand grew tall.

He stooped and drew the deep in easily.
He stooped and plunged his fingers in the floor
As though it were water and their progress free.

But from the thin stream water his hands upbore
Gigantic opals formed there, briefly clung,
And, tinkling, fell in circles on the floor.

[37]

Dann warf er sich mit leichtem Schwung der Lenden—
Wie nur aus Stolz—der nächsten Klippe zu;
An ihm sah ich die Macht der Schwere enden.

In seinen Augen aber war die Ruh
Von schlafend- doch lebendgen Edelsteinen.
Er setzte sich und sprach ein solches Du

Zu Tagen, die uns ganz vergangen scheinen,
Dass sie herkamen trauervoll und gross:
Das freute ihn zu lachen und zu weinen.

Er fühlte traumhaft aller Menschen Los,
So wie er seine eignen Glieder fühlte.
Ihm war nichts nah und fern, nichts klein und gross.

Und wie tief unten sich die Erde kühlte,
Das Dunkel aus den Tiefen aufwärts drang,
Die Nacht das Laue aus den Wipfeln wühlte,

Genoss er allen Lebens grossen Gang
So sehr—dass er in grosser Trunkenheit
So wie ein Löwe über Klippen sprang.

. . . .

Cherub und hoher Herr ist unser Geist—
Wohnt nicht in uns, und in die obern Sterne
Setzt er den Stuhl und lässt uns viel verwaist:

Doch Er ist Feuer uns im tiefsten Kerne
—So ahnte mir, da ich den Traum da fand—
Und redet mit den Feuern jener Ferne

Und lebt in mir wie ich in meiner Hand.

A Dream of Great Magic

Then lightly, for mere pride it seemed, he swung
His hips and leapt upon a near cliff's brow;
Defeating gravity, on that sheer face he hung.

Yet in his eyes there was that stillness now
Which in rare gems one finds, alive though sleeping.
And he sat down, addressing such a "Thou"

To days long vanished beyond memory's keeping
That they thronged back to him, mournful and great:
This moved him both to laughter and to weeping.

Dreamlike he felt the whole of human fate
As his own self he felt in every limb,
Nothing was near or distant, small or great.

And as the earth grew cool deep under him,
Night snatched away the warmth the treetops kept,
Darkness welled up from craters dank and dim,

Such was his joy in the great rhythm kept
By all of life that in great drunkenness
Like a young lion over rocks he leapt.

.   .   .   .

Cherub and haughty lord our spirit is—
Dwells not in us, but in some upper star
Appoints his chair and leaves us fatherless:

Yet He is fire within our deepest core—
So I divined when the same dream I found—
And holds great converse with those fires afar,

And lives in me as I live in my hand.

M. H.

[39]

Der Jüngling in der Landschaft

Die Gärtner legten ihre Beete frei,
Und viele Bettler waren überall
Mit schwarzverbundnen Augen und mit Krücken—
Doch auch mit Harfen und den neuen Blumen,
Dem starken Duft der schwachen Frühlingsblumen.

Die nackten Bäume liessen alles frei:
Man sah den Fluss hinab und sah den Markt,
Und viele Kinder spielen längs den Teichen.
Durch diese Landschaft ging er langsam hin
Und fühlte ihre Macht und wusste—dass
Auf ihn die Weltgeschicke sich bezogen.

Auf jene fremden Kinder ging er zu
Und war bereit, an unbekannter Schwelle
Ein neues Leben dienend hinzubringen.
Ihm fiel nicht ein, den Reichtum seiner Seele,
Die frühern Wege und Erinnerung
Verschlungner Finger und getauschter Seelen
Für mehr als nichtigen Besitz zu achten.

Der Duft der Blumen redete ihm nur
Von fremder Schönheit—und die neue Luft
Nahm er stillatmend ein, doch ohne Sehnsucht:
Nur dass er dienen durfte, freute ihn.

The Youth in the Landscape

The gardeners were at work setting their beds
And many beggars could be seen abroad
With eyes thick-swathed in blackness and with crutches—
But also with their harps and the new flowers,
The potent breath of the frail blooms of Spring.

The naked trees let all reveal itself.
One saw the river's reach and saw the market,
And many children played beside the ponds.
Through this same landscape he went slowly on
And felt the power of its appeal, and knew—
That the world's destinies were his by kinship.

So now to those strange children he went up
And was prepared upon an unknown threshold
To let a new life pass away in service.
Nor did it once occur to him to rate
The riches he had found in his own soul,
Those ways he earlier took and recollection
Of fingers interlocked and souls exchanged
As more now than a negative possession.

The breath of flowers spoke to him, but only
Of alien beauty—and in silence he
Breathed in the pristine air, but without longing:
Only the need of serving made him glad.

                                        v. w.

Ein Knabe

I

Lang kannte er die Muscheln nicht für schön,
Er war zu sehr aus einer Welt mit ihnen,
Der Duft der Hyazinthen war ihm nichts
Und nichts das Spiegelbild der eignen Mienen.

Doch alle seine Tage waren so
Geöffnet wie ein leierförmig Tal,
Darin er Herr zugleich und Knecht zugleich
Des weissen Lebens war und ohne Wahl.

Wie einer, der noch tut, was ihm nicht ziemt,
Doch nicht für lange, ging er auf den Wegen:
Der Heimkehr und unendlichem Gespräch
Hob seine Seele ruhig sich entgegen.

II

Eh er gebändigt war für sein Geschick,
Trank er viel Flut, die bitter war und schwer.
Dann richtete er sonderbar sich auf
Und stand am Ufer, seltsam leicht und leer.

Zu seinen Füssen rollten Muscheln hin,
Und Hyazinthen hatte er im Haar,
Und ihre Schönheit wusste er, und auch
Dass dies der Trost des schönen Lebens war.

A Boy

I

For long he did not think of shells as fair:
He was too much out of one world with those;
The scent of hyacinths was nothing to him
And nothing his own image in the glass.

But all his days were open, as it were
A harp-shaped valley waiting on his joys
In which he was at once servant and lord
Of the white life and was exempt from choice.

Like one who still does what befits him ill,
Yet not for long, he went upon his walks,
And calmly his soul raised itself to meet
The next homecoming and the endless talks.

II

Before life yet had tamed him for his fate
Much of the heavy, bitter flood he drank.
Then curiously he drew himself erect
And stood there, strangely light, upon the bank.

Shells at his feet were rolling to their rest
And he had hyacinths about his hair,
And he discerned their beauty, and he knew
They brought life comfort as they made it fair.

[43]

Hugo von Hofmannsthal

Doch mit unsicherm Lächeln liess er sie
Bald wieder fallen, denn ein grosser Blick
Auf diese schönen Kerker zeigte ihm
Das eigne unbegreifliche Geschick.

A Boy

Yet with a smile of hesitation he
Soon let them fall again, for now a great
Look at those lovely prisons showed to him
His own inscrutably decided fate.

V. W.

Des alten Mannes Sehnsucht nach dem Sommer

Wenn endlich Juli würde anstatt März,

Nichts hielte mich, ich nähme einen Rand,
Zu Pferd, zu Wagen oder mit der Bahn
Käm ich hinaus ins schöne Hügelland.

Da stünden Gruppen grosser Bäume nah,
Platanen, Rüster, Ahorn oder Eiche:
Wie lang ists, dass ich keine solchen sah!

Da stiege ich vom Pferde oder riefe
Dem Kutscher: Halt! und ginge ohne Ziel
Nach vorwärts in des Sommerlandes Tiefe.

Und unter solchen Bäumen ruht ich aus;
In deren Wipfel wäre Tag und Nacht
Zugleich, und nicht so wie in diesem Haus,

Wo Tage manchmal öd sind wie die Nacht
Und Nächte fahl und lauernd wie der Tag.
Dort wäre Alles Leben, Glanz und Pracht.

Und aus dem Schatten in des Abendlichts
Beglückung tret ich, und ein Hauch weht hin,
Doch nirgend flüsterts: «Alles dies ist nichts.»

Das Tal wird dunkel, und wo Häuser sind,
Sind Lichter, und das Dunkel weht mich an,
Doch nicht vom Sterben spricht der nächtige Wind.

[46]

The Old Man's Longing for Summer

If only March would turn into July!

Nothing would keep me; resolute as before,
On horseback or by carriage or by train
I should go out to see the hills once more.

Great trees in groups quite close to me I'd find,
Old elm or oak, plane-tree or sycamore:
How long since last I saw one of that kind!

Then quickly I should dismount or else call out
Stop! to the coachman, and soon without a goal
Deep in the summer country stroll about.

And, resting, long beneath the trees I'd stay;
In their high crests it would be day and night
At once, and not as in this house where day

Too often is as desolate as night
And nights are black and louring as the days.
There all would be alive, glorious and bright.

And from the shade I step into the sphere
Of joy the late sun grants; a breath wafts by.
But nowhere "All this is nothing" is whispered here.

The valley darkens; where there are cottages
Lone lights appear, the darkness breathes on me:
But not of dying speaks the nocturnal breeze.

[47]

Hugo von Hofmannsthal

Ich gehe übern Friedhof hin und sehe
Nur Blumen sich im letzten Scheine wiegen,
Von gar nichts anderm fühl ich eine Nähe.

Und zwischen Haselsträuchern, die schon düstern,
Fliesst Wasser hin, und wie ein Kind, so lausch ich
Und höre kein «Dies ist vergeblich» flüstern!

Da ziehe ich mich hurtig aus und springe
Hinein, und wie ich dann den Kopf erhebe,
Ist Mond, indes ich mit dem Bächlein ringe.

Halb heb ich mich aus der eiskalten Welle,
Und einen glatten Kieselstein ins Land
Weit schleudernd, steh ich in der Mondeshelle.

Und auf das mondbeglänzte Sommerland
Fällt weit ein Schatten: dieser, der so traurig
Hier nickt, hier hinterm Kissen an der Wand?

So trüb und traurig, der halb aufrecht kauert
Vor Tag und böse in das Frühlicht starrt
Und weiss, dass auf uns beide etwas lauert?

Er, den der böse Wind in diesem März
So quält, dass er die Nächte nie sich legt,
Gekrampft die schwarzen Hände auf sein Herz?

Ach, wo ist Juli und das Sommerland!

The Old Man's Longing for Summer

I walk across the churchyard, and there I see
Nothing but flowers that sway in the last gleam,
And feel no other thing's proximity.

And between hazel shrubs already blear
Water flows by, and like a child I listen
And yet no whispered "This is vain" I hear.

Then, quick, I strip and jump; when next I look,
Raising my head again, the moon is out,
And I am wrestling with the little brook.

Then from the icy ripples raise my hand,
Straighten my back and toss a smooth round pebble
And in the radiant moonlight tall I stand.

And on the moonlit summer country falls
A shadow far and wide: his, who so sadly
Nods here, propped up with cushions, caged in walls?

Who sad and dreary draws himself up in jerks
Long before dawn and glowers at the pale light,
Knowing that for us both an enemy lurks?

His, who this March is cheated of his rest
By evil winds, so that he sits all night,
Black hands clamped down upon his heart and breast?

Oh, where is that July and the summer country!

M. H.

Verse auf ein kleines Kind

Dir wachsen die rosigen Füsse,
Die Sonnenländer zu suchen:
Die Sonnenländer sind offen!
An schweigenden Wipfeln blieb dort
Die Luft der Jahrtausende hangen,
Die unerschöpflichen Meere
Sind immer noch, immer noch da.
Am Rande des ewigen Waldes
Willst du aus der hölzernen Schale
Die Milch mit der Unke dann teilen?
Das wird eine fröhliche Mahlzeit,
Fast fallen die Sterne hinein!
Am Rande des ewigen Meeres
Schnell findest du einen Gespielen:
Den freundlichen guten Delphin.
Er springt dir ans Trockne entgegen,
Und bleibt er auch manchmal aus,
So stillen die ewigen Winde
Dir bald die aufquellenden Tränen.
Es sind in den Sonnenländern
Die alten, erhabenen Zeiten
Für immer noch, immer noch da!
Die Sonne mit heimlicher Kraft,
Sie formt dir die rosigen Füsse,
Ihr ewiges Land zu betreten.

Verses on a Small Child

Your rose-coloured feet you were given
To look for the lands of the sun.
The lands of the sun are all open!
In the silence of treetops for ever
The air of millennia lies prisoned,
And inexhaustible oceans
Remain there, remain for you still.
At the edge of immutable forests
From the bowl carved of wood will you drink then
The milk to be shared with the toad?
No merrier meal I could wish you,
The stars very nearly fall in!
At the edge of immutable ocean
Quite soon you'll discover a playmate:
The dolphin, good-natured and kind.
He'll leap to the dry land to meet you,
And if he should not come at times,
Before long the immutable breezes
Will drive back your tears as they well.
Held fast in those lands of the sun,
The ancient, the loftier ages
Remain there, remain for you still!
The sun with mysterious power
Your rose-coloured feet ever fashions
To tread his immutable land.

M. H.

[51]

Der Kaiser von China spricht

In der Mitte aller Dinge
Wohne Ich, der Sohn des Himmels.
Meine Frauen, meine Bäume,
Meine Tiere, meine Teiche
Schliesst die erste Mauer ein.
Drunten liegen meine Ahnen:
Aufgebahrt mit ihren Waffen,
Ihre Kronen auf den Häuptern,
Wie es einem jeden ziemt,
Wohnen sie in den Gewölben.
Bis ins Herz der Welt hinunter
Dröhnt das Schreiten meiner Hoheit.
Stumm von meinen Rasenbänken,
Grünen Schemeln meiner Füsse,
Gehen gleichgeteilte Ströme
Osten-, west- und süd- und nordwärts,
Meinen Garten zu bewässern,
Der die weite Erde ist.
Spiegeln hier die dunkeln Augen,
Bunten Schwingen meiner Tiere,
Spiegeln draussen bunte Städte,
Dunkle Mauern, dichte Wälder
Und Gesichter vieler Völker.
Meine Edlen, wie die Sterne,
Wohnen rings um mich, sie haben
Namen, die ich ihnen gab,
Namen nach der einen Stunde,
Da mir einer näher kam,

The Emperor of China Speaks

At the heart of all creation
I, the Son of Heaven, dwell;
With my wives and with my trees,
With my animals and ponds,
Which the inmost wall encloses:
Down below my ancestors
Lie in state with all their weapons,
And their crowns upon their heads;
Every one as it is fitting
Dwells in his allotted vault.
Far into the world's deep centre
My majestic tread resounds.
From these green and grassy banks,
Footstools rounded for my comfort,
Silently four equal rivers
East and west and north and south
Flow to irrigate my garden,
Every corner of the world.
Here they mirror the dark eyes,
Gaudy wings of my tame creatures,
Further out, the mottled cities,
Forests wide and dense, dark walls,
Faces of my various peoples.
But my nobles, like the stars,
Dwell around me bearing names
Which I gave to each in token
Of the one and solemn hour
When he rose into my presence,

[53]

Hugo von Hofmannsthal

Frauen, die ich ihnen schenkte,
Und den Scharen ihrer Kinder;
Allen Edlen dieser Erde
Schuf ich Augen, Wuchs und Lippen,
Wie der Gärtner an den Blumen.
Aber zwischen äussern Mauern
Wohnen Völker meine Krieger,
Völker meine Ackerbauer.
Neue Mauern und dann wieder
Jene unterworfnen Völker,
Völker immer dumpfern Blutes,
Bis ans Meer, die letzte Mauer,
Die mein Reich und mich umgibt.

The Emperor of China Speaks

Wives who were my gifts to them
And their multitude of children;
All the nobles of this earth
Owe their eyes and lips and stature
To my care, a gardener's care.
But between the outer walls
Dwell my peoples, warrior peoples,
Others too that till the fields.
New walls follow and within them
Subjects lately quelled, of ever
Dimmer and more torrid blood,
To the sea, the ultimate wall
That surrounds my realm and me.

M. H.

Inschrift

Entzieh dich nicht dem einzigen Geschäfte!
Vor dem dich schaudert, dieses ist das deine:
Nicht anders sagt das Leben, was es meine,
Und schnell verwirft das Chaos deine Kräfte.

Inscription

Do not evade the one task which to mention
Fills you with fear and trembling: it is yours.
By this alone you learn of life's intention,
And quickly Chaos will reject your powers.

M. H.

Drei Sinngedichte

Dichtkunst

Fürchterlich ist diese Kunst! Ich spinn aus dem Leib mir
    den Faden,
Und dieser Faden zugleich ist auch mein Weg durch die
    Luft.

Spiegel der Welt

«Einmal schon kroch ich den Weg,» im Mund eines
    schlafenden Königs
Sprachs der gesprenkelte Wurm.—«Wann?»—«In des
    Dichters Gehirn.»

Erkenntnis

Wüsst ich genau, wie dies Blatt aus seinem Zweige
    herauskam,
Schwieg ich auf ewige Zeit still: denn ich wüsste genug.

Three Epigrams

The Art of Poetry

Perilous, terrible art! This thread I spin out of my body
And at the same time the thread serves as my path through
the air.

Mirror of the World

"Once before I have crawled this way," in the mouth of a
sleeping monarch
Whispered the small speckled worm.—"When?"—"In the
poet's brain."

Knowledge

If I knew just how this leaf rose from its bough into daylight,
Lifelong my silence would be: I should have knowledge
enough.

M. H.

Prolog zu dem Buch «Anatol»

Hohe Gitter, Taxushecken,
Wappen nimmermehr vergoldet,
Sphinxe, durch das Dickicht schimmernd . . .
. . . Knarrend öffnen sich die Tore.—
Mit verschlafenen Kaskaden
Und verschlafenen Tritonen,
Rokoko, verstaubt und lieblich,
Seht . . . das Wien des Canaletto,
Wien von siebzehnhundertsechzig . . .
. . . Grüne, braune stille Teiche,
Glatt und marmorweiss umrandet,
In dem Spiegelbild der Nixen
Spielen Gold- und Silberfische . . .
Auf dem glattgeschornen Rasen
Liegen zierlich gleiche Schatten
Schlanker Oleanderstämme;
Zweige wölben sich zur Kuppel,
Zweige neigen sich zur Nische
Für die steifen Liebespaare,
Heroinen und Heroen . . .
Drei Delphine giessen murmelnd
Fluten in ein Muschelbecken . . .
Duftige Kastanienblüten
Gleiten, schwirren leuchtend nieder
Und ertrinken in den Becken . . .
. . . Hinter einer Taxusmauer
Tönen Geigen, Klarinetten,
Und sie scheinen den graziösen

Prologue to "Anatol"

Lofty railings, formal hedges,
Coats of arms, their gilt long faded,
Sphinxes shimmering through the thicket . . .
. . . Gratingly the gates swing open:
Sleepy waterfalls cascading,
Sleepy groups of sculptured tritons,
Dusty charm of the Rococo—
Look . . . the Vienna of Canaletto,
Vienna of the seventeen-sixties . . .
. . . Greens and browns of silent fishponds
Smoothly edged in gleaming marble,
In the water-nymphs' reflections
Gold and silver fish are playing . . .
On the close-cut lawns lie shadows,
Dainty, even-stemmed, and slender,
Cast by oleander-bushes;
Cupolas of vaulting branches,
Niches twined from dipping branches
Frame unbending pairs of lovers,
Stony heroines and heroes . . .
Water from a trio of dolphins
Murmurs in a shell-like basin . . .
Falls of fragrant chestnut-blossom
Glide and flutter gleaming earthwards,
Sinking, drowning in the basins . . .
. . . Sounds come through a wall of yew trees,
Clarinets and fiddles playing,
And it seems as if they issue

Amoretten zu entströmen,
Die rings auf der Rampe sitzen,
Fiedelnd oder Blumen windend,
Selbst von Blumen bunt umgeben,
Die aus Marmorvasen strömen:
Goldlack und Jasmin und Flieder . . .
. . . Auf der Rampe, zwischen ihnen
Sitzen auch kokette Frauen,
Violette Monsignori . . .
Und im Gras, zu ihren Füssen
Und auf Polstern, auf den Stufen
Kavaliere und Abbati . . .
Andre heben andre Frauen
Aus den parfümierten Sänften . . .
Durch die Zweige brechen Lichter,
Flimmern auf den blonden Köpfchen,
Scheinen auf den bunten Polstern,
Gleiten über Kies und Rasen,
Gleiten über das Gerüste,
Das wir flüchtig aufgeschlagen.
Wein und Winde klettert aufwärts
Und umhüllt die lichten Balken,
Und dazwischen farbenüppig
Flattert Teppich und Tapete,
Schäferszenen, keck gewoben,
Zierlich von Watteau entworfen . . .

Eine Laube statt der Bühne,
Sommersonne statt der Lampen,
Also spielen wir Theater,
Spielen unsre eignen Stücke,
Frühgereift und zart und traurig,
Die Komödie unsrer Seele,

Prologue to "Anatol"

From the graceful amoretti
Sitting perched around the ramp there,
Playing fiddles, winding garlands,
Gaily framed themselves in flowers
Pouring forth from marble vases:
Wallflowers, jasmine, lilac-blossoms . . .
. . . All along the ramp between them
Sit and chat coquettish ladies,
With them violet monsignori . . .
At their feet, on grass reclining,
And upon the steps, on cushions,
Cavaliers sit and abbati . . .
Some are helping other ladies
To descend from perfumed litters . . .
Rays of light which pierce the branches
Glint on heads of dainty fairness,
Shine upon the coloured cushions,
Glide along the grass and gravel,
Glide across the wooden framework
We have fleetingly erected.
Vines and creepers climbing upwards
Shroud the light-wood beams and rafters,
And between, a mass of colour,
Silks and tapestries flap gaily,
Pastoral idylls boldly woven,
Delicate designs by Watteau . . .

For our stage we have an arbour,
Summer sun instead of footlights;
This is how we act our parts out,
Acting plays of our own making,
Early-ripe and sad and tender,
The commedia of our spirit,

Hugo von Hofmannsthal

Unsres Fühlens Heut und Gestern,
Böser Dinge hübsche Formel,
Glatte Worte, bunte Bilder,
Halbes, heimliches Empfinden,
Agonien, Episoden . . .
Manche hören zu, nicht alle . . .
Manche träumen, manche lachen,
Manche essen Eis . . . und manche
Sprechen sehr galante Dinge . . .
. . . Nelken wiegen sich im Winde,
Hochgestielte weisse Nelken,
Wie ein Schwarm von weissen Faltern,
Und ein Bologneserhündchen
Bellt verwundert einen Pfau an.

Prologue to "Anatol"

What we feel as time slips by us,
Ugly facts in pretty guises,
Smooth-tongued speeches, coloured pictures,
Half-felt feelings sensed in secret,
Agonies and episodes . . .
Some are listening, some don't bother . . .
Some are dreaming, some are laughing,
Some are eating ices . . . others
Utter very gallant sayings . . .
. . . In the wind, carnations swaying,
Flocks of long-stemmed white carnations
Like butterflies with white wings fluttering,
And the tiniest of lap-dogs
Yaps in wonder at a peacock.

J. B.

Zum Gedächtnis des Schauspielers Mitterwurzer

Er losch auf einmal aus so wie ein Licht.
Wir trugen alle wie von einem Blitz
Den Widerschein als Blässe im Gesicht.

Er fiel: da fielen alle Puppen hin,
In deren Adern er sein Lebensblut
Gegossen hatte; lautlos starben sie,
Und wo er lag, da lag ein Haufen Leichen,
Wüst hingestreckt: das Knie von einem Säufer
In eines Königs Aug gedrückt, Don Philipp
Mit Caliban als Alp um seinen Hals,
Und jeder tot.

Da wussten wir, wer uns gestorben war:
Der Zauberer, der grosse, grosse Gaukler!
Und aus den Häusern traten wir heraus
Und fingen an zu reden, wer er war.
Wer aber war er, und wer war er nicht?

Er kroch von einer Larve in die andre,
Sprang aus des Vaters in des Sohnes Leib
Und tauschte wie Gewänder die Gestalten.

Mit Schwertern, die er kreisen liess so schnell,
Dass niemand ihre Klinge funkeln sah,
Hieb er sich selbst in Stücke: Jago war
Vielleicht das eine, und die andre Hälfte
Gab einen süssen Narren oder Träumer.

In Memory of the Actor Mitterwurzer

He went out suddenly like any light.
And we all bore a pallor on our faces
Like the reflection of a lightning flash.

He fell: then all the puppets collapsed with him
Into whose veins he'd poured his own life-blood.
Now speechlessly they died; and where he lay
There also lay stretched out a heap of corpses
In wreck and ruin: knee of a drunkard
Pressed into a king's eye; Don Philip
With Caliban a nightmare round his neck,
All of them dead.

Then we knew whom death had taken from us:
The sorcerer, the great great conjurer,
And we came from our houses, gathered round
And so began to talk of what he was.
Who was he though, and who else was he not?

He crept out of one mask into another,
Sprang from the father's into the son's body
And changed his shape as though it were his clothes.

On swords, which he crossed and uncrossed so quickly
That no one saw the gleaming of the blades,
He hewed himself in pieces. Iago was
Perhaps one half of him, the other was
A dreamer or a sweet and bitter fool.

Hugo von Hofmannsthal

Sein ganzer Leib war wie der Zauberschleier,
In dessen Falten alle Dinge wohnen:
Er holte Tiere aus sich selbst hervor:
Das Schaf, den Löwen, einen dummen Teufel
Und einen schrecklichen, und den, und jenen,
Und dich und mich. Sein ganzer Leib war glühend,
Von innerlichem Schicksal durch und durch
Wie Kohle glühend, und er lebte drin
Und sah auf uns, die wir in Häusern wohnen,
Mit jenem undurchdringlich fremden Blick
Des Salamanders, der im Feuer wohnt.
Er war ein wilder König. Um die Hüften
Trug er wie bunte Muscheln aufgereiht
Die Wahrheit und die Lüge von uns allen.
In seinen Augen flogen unsre Träume
Vorüber, wie von Scharen wilder Vögel
Das Spiegelbild in einem tiefen Wasser.

Hier trat er her, auf ebendiesen Fleck,
Wo ich jetzt steh, und wie im Tritonshorn
Der Lärm des Meeres eingefangen ist,
So war in ihm die Stimme alles Lebens:
Er wurde gross. Er war der ganze Wald,
Er war das Land, durch das die Strassen laufen.
Mit Augen wie die Kinder sassen wir
Und sahn an ihm hinauf wie an den Hängen
Von einem grossen Berg: in seinem Mund
War eine Bucht, drin brandete das Meer.

Denn in ihm war etwas, das viele Türen
Aufschloss und viele Räume überflog:
Gewalt des Lebens, diese war in ihm.
Und über ihn bekam der Tod Gewalt!

In Memory of the Actor Mitterwurzer

His entire body was a magic veil
Within whose many folds everything dwells.
He reached for animals out of himself,
The sheep, the lion, and a stupid devil,
And one who terrified, and this, and that,
And you and me. His whole body glowed
With inward fate shining through and through
Like burning coals, and he lived therein
And looked at us, us who dwelt in our houses,
Looked with that strange impenetrable gaze
Of a salamander who inhabits fire.
He was a savage king. Around his loins
He wore like coloured shells strung on a thread
The truth and the lie about us all.
Within his eyes our dreams were flying past
Like flocks of wild birds mirrored in deep water.

Here he stepped on, upon these very boards,
Where I now stand, and as the murmuring sea
Is imprisoned within Triton's shell
So were there in him voices of all life:
He became vast. He was the mighty forest.
He was the landscape through which the roads run.
With eyes as wide as children's we would sit
And gaze at him as upon the slopes
Of an enormous mountain: in his mouth
There was a bay, into which surged the sea.

For within him was something which unlocked
Many doors and flew through many rooms:
The power of living, there was that in him.
And over him now death has come to power!

Blies aus die Augen, deren innrer Kern
Bedeckt war mit geheimnisvollen Zeichen,
Erwürgte in der Kehle tausend Stimmen
Und tötete den Leib, der Glied für Glied
Beladen war mit ungebornem Leben.

Hier stand er. Wann kommt einer, der ihm gleicht?
Ein Geist, der uns das Labyrinth der Brust
Bevölkert mit verständlichen Gestalten,
Erschliesst aufs neu zu schauerlicher Lust?
Die er uns gab, wir konnten sie nicht halten
Und starren nun bei seines Namens Klang
Hinab den Abgrund, der sie uns verschlang.

In Memory of the Actor Mitterwurzer

Blown the light from his eyes, whose inner core
Was covered over with such secret signs,
Throttled within the throat a thousand voices,
And killed the body, that which limb from limb
Was laden with so many unborn lives.

He stood here. When will come another like him?
Spirit who populates the labyrinth of our breasts
With intelligible forms, unlocks
Anew for us such terrifying joy?
These men he gave to us we could not keep.
We stare now, at the echo of his name,
Down the abyss which swallowed them from us.

S. S.

Idylle

Der Schauplatz im Böcklinschen Stil. Eine offene Dorf-
schmiede. Dahinter das Haus, im Hintergrunde ein Fluss.
Der Schmied an der Arbeit, sein Weib müssig an die Türe
gelehnt, die von der Schmiede ins Haus führt. Auf dem
Boden spielt ein blondes kleines Kind mit einer zahmen
Krabbe. In einer Nische ein Weinschlauch, ein paar frische
Feigen und Melonenschalen.

DER SCHMIED

Wohin verlieren dir die sinnenden Gedanken sich,
Indes du schweigend mir das Werk, feindselig fast,
Mit solchen Lippen, leise zuckenden, beschaust?

DIE FRAU

Im blütenweissen kleinen Garten sass ich oft,
Den Blick aufs väterliche Handwerk hingewandt,
Das nette Werk des Töpfers: wie der Scheibe da,
Der surrenden im Kreis, die edle Form entstieg,
Im stillen Werden einer zarten Blume gleich,
Mit kühlem Glanz des Elfenbeins. Darauf erschuf
Der Vater Henkel, mit Akanthusblatt geziert,
Und ein Akanthus-, ein Olivenkranz wohl auch
Umlief als dunkelroter Schmuck des Kruges Rand.
Den schönen Körper dann belebte er mit Reigenkranz

[72]

Idyll

AFTER A PICTURE ON AN ANCIENT VASE: CENTAUR
WITH WOUNDED WOMAN AT THE EDGE OF A RIVER

*Scene in the style of Böcklin. A village smithy. Behind it, the
house, in the background, a river. The smith is at his work,
his wife leans idly at the door which leads from the smithy
into the house. On the floor a blond child plays with a tame
crab. In the niche, a wineskin, a couple of fresh figs, and
melon rinds.*

THE SMITH

Where does your pensive mind go lost and wandering
While, glowering almost, in silence you watch my work,
With lips like those I see now, slightly quivering?

THE WOMAN

I often sat in the small white-flowering garden
With gaze directed at my father's handiwork,
The potter's meticulous craft: watched how, from the wheel,
Susurring circle-wise, the noble form emerged,
In quietness of growth more like some delicate flower,
With the cool gleam of ivory. Whereupon he made
The handle ornamented with acanthus leaf
And an acanthus, or perhaps an olive wreath
Ran round the jug's edge, a dark red decoration;
Then with a dancing round enlivened that lovely bulk,

[73]

Der Horen, der vorüberschwebend lebenspendenden.
Er schuf, gestreckt auf königliche Ruhebank,
Der Phädra wundervollen Leib, von Sehnsucht matt,
Und drüber flatternd Eros, der mit süsser Qual die Glieder
Gewaltgen Krügen liebte er ein Bacchusfest   füllt.
Zum Schmuck zu geben, wo der Purpurtraubensaft
Aufsprühte unter der Mänade nacktem Fuss
Und fliegend Haar und Thyrsusschwung die Luft erfüllt.
Auf Totenurnen war Persephoneias hohes Bild,
Die mit den seelenlosen, toten Augen schaut
Und, Blumen des Vergessens, Mohn, im heiligen Haar,
Das lebenfremde, asphodelische Gefilde tritt.
Des Redens wär kein Ende, zählt ich alle auf,
Die göttlichen, an deren schönem Leben ich
—Zum zweiten Male lebend, was gebildet war—,
An deren Gram und Hass und Liebeslust
Und wechselndem Erlebnis jeder Art
Ich also Anteil hatte, ich, ein Kind,
Die mir mit halbverstandener Gefühle Hauch
Anrührten meiner Seele tiefstes Saitenspiel,
Dass mir zuweilen war, als hätte ich im Schlaf
Die stets verborgenen Mysterien durchirrt
Von Lust und Leid, Erkennende mit wachem Aug,
Davon, an dieses Sonnenlicht zurückgekehrt,
Mir mahnendes Gedenken andern Lebens bleibt
Und eine Fremde, Ausgeschlossne aus mir macht
In dieser nährenden, lebendgen Luft der Welt.

DER SCHMIED

Den Sinn des Seins verwirrte allzuvieler Müssiggang
Dem schön gesinnten, gern verträumten Kind, mich dünkt.
Und jene Ehrfurcht fehlte, die zu trennen weiss,
Was Göttern ziemt, was Menschen! Wie Semele dies,

Idyll

A dance of Hours, the hovering givers of life.
He modelled stretched out on her regal couch of rest
Phaedra's wonderful body wearied with yearning,
Eros fluttering above who fills our limbs with sweet pain.
On mighty vases he loved as adornment
A bacchanalia where the purple grape-juice
Spurted out under the naked feet of Maenads
And flying hair and swaying thyrsi filled the air.
Persephone's high image was on funeral urns
She who gazed out from her eyes dead and without soul,
Flowers of oblivion, poppies, in her sacred hair,
Who trod the fields of asphodel, strangers to life.
There'd be no end of telling if I counted all
The godly ones out of whose beautiful life I
—Experiencing vicariously what was portrayed—
Enjoyed in this way a portion, I, a child, of their
Lament and hate and passionate lust of loving,
And varying experiences of every kind.
The breath of these half-comprehended emotions
Stirred within my soul the deepest chords like a harp.
So it was at times as though in my sleep I had
Roamed through the maze of ever-hidden mysteries
Of joy and grief, an open-eyed initiate,
And later too, when I had turned back to this sunlight
Vague memories of the other life remained with me,
Making me now a stranger, never quite at home
Within this nourishing vital air of the world.

THE SMITH

It seems to me that too much idleness confused
This beauty-loving child, too easily lost in dreams.
Also, that reverence was missing which can distinguish
What fits gods from that fitting men: Like Semele

Die töricht fordernde, vergehend erst begriff.
Des Gatten Handwerk lerne heilig halten du,
Das aus des mütterlichen Grundes Eingeweiden stammt
Und, sich die hundertarmig Ungebändigte,
Die Flamme, unterwerfend, klug und kraftvoll wirkt.

DIE FRAU

Die Flamme anzusehen, lockts mich immer neu,
Die wechselnde, mit heissem Hauch berauschende.

DER SCHMIED

Vielmehr erfreue Anblick dich des Werks!
Die Waffen sieh, der Pflugschar heilige Härte auch,
Und dieses Beil, das wilde Bäume uns zur Hütte fügt.
So schafft der Schmied, was alles andre schaffen soll.
Wo duftig aufgeworfne Scholle Samen trinkt
Und gelbes Korn der Sichel dann entgegenquillt,
Wo zwischen stillen Stämmen nach dem scheuen Wild
Der Pfeil hinschwirrt und tödlich in den Nacken schlägt,
Wo harter Huf von Rossen staubaufwirbelnd dröhnt
Und rasche Räder rollen zwischen Stadt und Stadt,
Wo der gewaltig klirrende, der Männerstreit
Die hohe liederwerte Männlichkeit enthüllt:
Da wirk ich fort und halt umwunden so die Welt
Mit starken Spuren meines Tuens, weil es tüchtig ist.

Pause

DIE FRAU

Zentauren seh ich einen nahen, Jüngling noch,
Ein schöner Gott mir scheinend, wenn auch halb ein Tier,
Und aus dem Hain, entlang dem Ufer, traben her.

Idyll

Who, foolishly demanding, only when dying grasped it.
Learn then to hold holy thy husband's handiwork
Which, rooted in dark entrails of maternal depths,
Yet can subdue the hundred-armed, the untamed flame,
And strongly, cunningly can bend it to his will.

THE WOMAN

Watching the flames fascinates me ever anew,
The mutable, intoxicating with hot breath.

THE SMITH

Far better delight your eyes with the sight of work!
See the weapons, sacred hardness of the ploughshares
And this axe which hews the wild trees to be our huts.
So does the smith make that which makes all other things,
Where the odorous turned-up clod drinks up the seeds
And where the yellow corn billows towards the sickle,
Where between silent stems the arrow leaps forward
At timid game, bringing death when it meets the neck,
Where the hard hooves of horses pound, throwing up dust,
And rushing wheels roll between a town and a town,
Where the overpowering clatter of men in battle
Proves manhood noble, and worthy of being sung:
There I work on, and in that way entwine the world
With the strong traces of my toil, which never slackens.

Pause

THE WOMAN

I see a centaur drawing near, a young one, yet
He seems to me a beautiful god though but half-beast,
Trotting out of the coppice along the river here.

Hugo von Hofmannsthal

DER ZENTAUR

einen Speer in der Hand, den er dem Schmied hinhält

Find ich dem stumpfgewordnen Speere Heilung hier
Und neue Spitze der geschwungnen Wucht? Verkünd!

DER SCHMIED

Ob deinesgleichen auch, dich selber sah ich nie.

DER ZENTAUR

Zum ersten Male lockte mir den Lauf
Nach eurem Dorf Bedürfnis, das du kennst.

DER SCHMIED

                          Ihm soll
In kurzem abgeholfen sein. Indes erzählst
Du, wenn du dir den Dank der Frau verdienen willst,
Von fremden Wundern, die du wohl gesehn, wovon
Hieher nicht Kunde dringt, wenn nicht ein Wandrer
    kommt.

DIE FRAU

Ich reiche dir zuerst den vollen Schlauch: er ist
Mit kühlem säuerlichem Apfelwein gefüllt,
Denn andrer ist uns nicht. Das nächste Dürsten stillt
Wohl etwa weit von hier aus bessrer Schale dir
Mit heisserm Safte eine schönre Frau als ich.

Sie hat den Wein aus dem Schlauch in eine irdene Trink-
schale gegossen, die er langsam schlürft.

DER ZENTAUR

Die allgemeinen Strassen zog ich nicht und mied
Der Hafenplätze vielvermengendes Gewühl,
Wo einer leicht von Schiffern bunte Mär erfährt.

Idyll

THE CENTAUR

a spear in his hand, which he holds out to the smith

Do I find healing here for the spear become blunt,
And a new point for hurling of my fury? Tell me!

THE SMITH

Those of your kind I've seen, but never you.

THE CENTAUR

For the first time my step was summoned by this need
Of which you know, towards your village.

THE SMITH

                                    It shall
In a short while be satisfied. Meanwhile, if you
Wish to earn the gratitude of my wife, relate
The strange encounters you must have met with, whereof
No news reaches here unless some wanderer come.

THE WOMAN

But first I offer you this wineskin full: it is
Filled with a cool tart cider: we have no other
Wine here. Next time you thirst you will be satisfied
Far from this place perhaps, from a better vessel
With fierier juice by a woman more lovely than I.

*She has poured the cider out of the wineskin into an earthen-
ware cup, from which he slowly laps.*

THE CENTAUR

I did not take the most frequented road, and shunned
The jostling crowds and turmoil of the harbour squares,
Where the traveller hears strange stories told by sailors.

Hugo von Hofmannsthal

Die öden Heiden wählte ich zum Tagesweg,
Flamingos nur und schwarze Stiere störend auf,
Und stampfte nachts das Heidekraut dahin im Duft,
Das hyazinthne Dunkel über mir.
Zuweilen kam ich wandernd einem Hain vorbei,
Wo sich, zu flüchtig eigensinnger Lust gewillt,
Aus einem Schwarme von Najaden eine mir
Für eine Strecke Wegs gesellte, die ich dann
An einen jungen Satyr wiederum verlor,
Der, syrinxblasend, lockend wo am Wege sass.

DIE FRAU

Unsäglich reizend dünkt dies Ungebundne mir.

DER SCHMIED

Die Waldgebornen kennen Scham und Treue nicht,
Die erst das Haus verlangen und bewahren lehrt.

DIE FRAU

Ward dir, dem Flötenspiel des Pan zu lauschen? Sag!

DER ZENTAUR

In einem stillen Kesseltal ward mirs beschert.
Da wogte mit dem schwülen Abendwind herab
Vom Rand der Felsen rätselhaftestes Getön,
So tief aufwühlend wie vereinter Drang
Von allem Tiefsten, was die Seele je durchbebt,
Als flög mein Ich im Wirbel fortgerissen mir
Durch tausendfach verschiedne Trunkenheit hindurch.

DER SCHMIED

Verbotenes lass lieber unberedet sein!

[80]

Idyll

I chose the desolate heath for my day's journeyings
Where only flamingoes and the black steer shifted.
All night I trampled heather, breathed the scent of heather,
The hyacinthine darkness covering me.
At times in my wanderings I passed through a coppice
Where one of a troop of Naiades, determined on
Wilful and fleeting pleasure, kept me company
For a stretch of the journey; whom later I
Would lose again to some young satyr who, syrinx-blowing,
Seductively waited somewhere along the path.

THE WOMAN

Unspeakably charming is this wilderness to me.

THE SMITH

Those bred in the woods know nothing of shame and faith
Which only houses teach us to desire and uphold.

THE WOMAN

Did it happen to you to hear the pipes of Pan?

THE CENTAUR

This was vouchsafed to me in a deep silent valley.
Most mysterious sound with the hot evening wind
Swayed from the edge of the high rocks, as deeply stirring
As the confluent surge of all the deepest powers,
The utmost that the soul is ever shaken by,
As though in a whirlpool caught my self flew out of me
Through more than a thousand forms of drunkenness.

THE SMITH

Rather let forbidden things not be spoken of!

[81]

Hugo von Hofmannsthal

DIE FRAU

Lass immerhin, was regt die Seele schöner auf?

DER SCHMIED

Das Leben zeitigt selbst den höhern Herzensschlag,
Wie reife Frucht vom Zweige sich erfreulich löst.
Und nicht zu andern Schauern sind geboren wir,
Als uns das Schicksal über unsre Lebenswelle haucht.

DER ZENTAUR

So blieb die wunderbare Kunst dir unbekannt,
Die Götter üben: unter Menschen Mensch,
Zu andern Zeiten aufzugehn im Sturmeshauch,
Und ein Delphin zu plätschern wiederum im Nass
Und ätherkreisend einzusaugen Adlerlust?
Du kennst, mich dünkt, nur wenig von der Welt, mein
    Freund.

DER SCHMIED

Die ganze kenn ich, kennend meinen Kreis,
Massloses nicht verlangend, noch begierig ich,
Die flüchtge Flut zu ballen in der hohlen Hand.
Den Bach, der deine Wiege schaukelte, erkennen lern,
Den Nachbarbaum, der dir die Früchte an der Sonne reift
Und dufterfüllten lauen Schatten niedergiesst,
Das kühle grüne Gras, es trats dein Fuss als Kind.
Die alten Eltern tratens, leise frierende,
Und die Geliebte trats, da quollen duftend auf
Die Veilchen, schmiegend unter ihre Sohlen sich;
Das Haus begreif, in dem du lebst und sterben sollst,
Und dann, ein Wirkender, begreif dich selber
    ehrfurchtsvoll,
An diesen hast du mehr, als du erfassen kannst—

Idyll

THE WOMAN

Let him go on! What stirs the soul more delightfully?

THE SMITH

Life itself sets the time of the heart's high beating
As the ripened fruit gladly frees itself from the bough.
And we are not born to fearful revelations
Other than those that fate breathes on our wave of being.

THE CENTAUR

Did, then, the marvellous art which the gods exercise
Remain unknown to you: among men, a man,
At other times to merge in the breath of gales
And as a dolphin to splash again in waters,
And circling in the sky drink the joy of eagles?
I think you know but little of the world, my friend.

THE SMITH

I know the whole in knowing my own boundaries,
Not yearning for the immeasurable, nor ever seeking
To clench the fleeting flood within my hollow hand.
The stream which rocked your cradle, that learn to know,
The nearby tree ripening fruit for you in the sun,
Casting down lukewarm shadows heavy with fragrance,
The cool green grass your foot trod when you were a child.
Your aged parents trod it, shivering slightly,
And the beloved one trod it: fragrant, there swelled up
The violet, meekly bending under their soles.
Grasp the one house in which you must live and die,
And then, as one accomplishing, grasp your own self with
    awe;
These things alone are more than ever you'll comprehend.

[83]

Den Wanderliebenden, ich halt ihn länger nicht, allein
Der letzten Glättung noch bedarfs, die Feile fehlt,
Ich finde sie und schaffe dir das letzte noch.

Er geht ins Haus.

DIE FRAU

Dich führt wohl nimmermehr der Weg hieher zurück.
Hinstampfend durch die hyazinthne Nacht, berauscht,
Vergissest meiner du am Wege, fürcht ich, bald,
Die deiner, fürcht ich, nicht so bald vergessen kann.

DER ZENTAUR

Du irrst: verdammt von dir zu scheiden wärs,
Als schlügen sich die Gitter dröhnend hinter mir
Von aller Liebe dufterfülltem Garten zu.
Doch kommst du, wie ich meine, mir Gefährtin mit,
So trag ich solchen hohen Reiz als Beute fort,
Wie nie die hohe Aphrodite ausgegossen hat,
Die allbelebende, auf Meer und wilde Flut.

DIE FRAU

Wie könnt ich Gatten, Haus und Kind verlassen hier?

DER ZENTAUR

Was sorgst du lang, um was du schnell vergessen hast?

DIE FRAU

Er kommt zurück, und schnell zerronnen ist der Traum!

DER ZENTAUR

Mitnichten, da doch Lust und Weg noch offensteht.
Mit festen Fingern greif mir ins Gelock und klammre dich,
Am Rücken ruhend, mir an Arm und Nacken an!

[84]

Idyll

This lover of journeys I'll detain no longer: only,
The burnishing is not done: the file is missing,
I go to find it, and put the last touch to my work.

He goes into the house.

THE WOMAN

Your way will never lead you to this place again.
Trampling on drunken through the hyacinthine night,
I fear that soon you will forget me utterly,
Who for a long time yet, I fear, shall not forget you.

THE CENTAUR

You err: I should be cursed to separate from you
As though the trellises of all love's fragrance-filled
Gardens were now to close behind me with a clash.
But if you come, as I believe, as my companion,
I take such high charm away with me as booty
As never high Aphrodite, the all-quickening,
Poured forth, over the ocean and the wild flood.

THE WOMAN

How could I forsake husband, house, and child left here?

THE CENTAUR

Why worry long over what you will soon forget?

THE WOMAN

He is coming back: how quickly the dream is dispelled.

THE CENTAUR

Not at all: for joy and path still stand here open.
With firm fingers grasp my hair and climb up on me,
Lie resting on my back with arm clasped round my neck.

[85]

Hugo von Hofmannsthal

Sie schwingt sich auf seinen Rücken, und er stürmt hell schreiend zum Fluss hinunter, das Kind erschrickt und bricht in klägliches Weinen aus. Der Schmied tritt aus dem Haus. Eben stürzt sich der Zentaur in das aufrauschende Wasser des Flusses. Sein bronzener Oberkörper und die Gestalt der Frau zeichnen sich scharf auf der abendlich vergoldeten Wasserfläche ab. Der Schmied wird sie gewahr; in der Hand den Speer des Zentauren, läuft er ans Ufer hinab und schleudert, weit vorgebeugt, den Speer, der mit zitterndem Schaft einen Augenblick im Rücken der Frau steckenbleibt, bis diese mit einem gellenden Schrei die Locken des Zentauren fahrenlässt und mit ausgebreiteten Armen rücklings ins Wasser stürzt. Der Zentaur fängt die Sterbende in seinen Armen auf und trägt sie hocherhoben stromabwärts, dem andern Ufer zuschwimmend.

Idyll

She swings on to his back, and he rushes, whinnying, down to the river. The child shrieks and bursts into cries of lamentation. The smith comes out of the house. At the same moment, the centaur leaps into the hurrying water of the river. The bronze of the upper part of his body and the shape of the woman are revealed clearly against the gilded evening waves of the water. The smith sees them there: with the centaur's spear in his hand, he runs up the river bank and bending far forward, hurls the spear, which, with quivering shaft, remains for a moment fixed in the woman's back. With a terrible cry she lets go of the centaur's hair, and with arms spread out, falls backwards into the river. The centaur takes the dying woman up in his arms and carries her on high upstream, swimming towards the farther shore.

S. S.

VERSE PLAYS

DEATH AND THE FOOL

Translated by

MICHAEL HAMBURGER

Der Tor und der Tod

DER TOD

CLAUDIO, *ein Edelmann*

SEIN KAMMERDIENER

CLAUDIOS MUTTER

EINE GELIEBTE DES CLAUDIO ⎫ *Tote*

EIN JUGENDFREUND ⎭

Claudios Haus.

Kostüm der zwanziger Jahre des vorigen Jahrhunderts.

Studierzimmer des Claudio, im Empiregeschmack. Im Hintergrund links und rechts grosse Fenster, in der Mitte eine Glastüre auf den Balkon hinaus, von dem eine hängende Holztreppe in den Garten führt. Links eine weisse Flügeltür, rechts eine gleiche nach dem Schlafzimmer, mit einem grünen Samtvorhang geschlossen. Am Fenster links steht ein Schreibtisch, davor ein Lehnstuhl. An den Pfeilern Glaskasten mit Altertümern. An der Wand rechts eine gotische, dunkle, geschnitzte Truhe; darüber altertümliche Musikinstrumente. Ein fast schwarzgedunkeltes Bild eines italienischen Meisters. Der Grundton der Tapete licht, fast weiss; mit Stukkatur und Gold.

Death and the Fool

DEATH

CLAUDIO, *a nobleman*

HIS SERVANT

CLAUDIO'S MOTHER

A MISTRESS OF CLAUDIO } *Dead*

A FRIEND

Claudio's house.

Costume of the eighteen-twenties.

Claudio's study, Empire style. In the background, left and right, large windows, in the centre a glass door opening on to the balcony, from which a suspended wooden staircase leads to the garden. A white double door left, another right, leading to the bedroom, a green plush curtain in front of it. By the window, left, a writing-desk, an arm-chair in front of it. On the walls, glass cases containing bric-a-brac. Against the wall, right, a dark, carved Gothic chest, above it old-fashioned musical instruments. A picture by an Old Master, Italian, almost black with age. Wallpaper light in colour, almost white, with stucco and gilt decorations.

Hugo von Hofmannsthal

CLAUDIO *allein*

Er sitzt am Fenster. Abendsonne.

Die letzten Berge liegen nun im Glanz,
In feuchten Schmelz durchsonnter Luft gewandet.
Es schwebt ein Alabasterwolkenkranz
Zuhöchst, mit grauen Schatten, goldumrandet:
So malen Meister von den frühen Tagen
Die Wolken, welche die Madonna tragen.
Am Abhang liegen blaue Wolkenschatten,
Der Bergesschatten füllt das weite Tal
Und dämpft zu grauem Grün den Glanz der Matten;
Der Gipfel glänzt im vollen letzten Strahl.
Wie nah sind meiner Sehnsucht die gerückt,
Die dort auf weiten Halden einsam wohnen
Und denen Güter, mit der Hand gepflückt,
Die gute Mattigkeit der Glieder lohnen.
Der wundervolle wilde Morgenwind,
Der nackten Fusses läuft im Heidenduft,
Der weckt sie auf; die wilden Bienen sind
Um sie und Gottes helle, heisse Luft.
Es gab Natur sich ihnen zum Geschäfte,
In allen ihren Wünschen quillt Natur,
Im Wechselspiel der frisch und müden Kräfte
Wird ihnen jedes warmen Glückes Spur.
Jetzt rückt der goldne Ball, und er versinkt
In fernster Meere grünlichem Kristall;
Das letzte Licht durch ferne Bäume blinkt,
Jetzt atmet roter Rauch, ein Glutenwall
Den Strand erfüllend, wo die Städte liegen,
Die mit Najadenarmen, flutenttaucht,
In hohen Schiffen ihre Kinder wiegen,
Ein Volk, verwegen, listig und erlaucht.

[94]

Death and the Fool

He is sitting by the window. Evening sunlight.

Now the last mountains lie in gleaming shrouds,
Clothed in the moistened glow of sun-steeped air.
There hangs a wreath of alabaster clouds
Above, here rimmed with gold, grey shadows there:
So once did Masters of past centuries
Paint clouds which bear Our Lady through the skies.
Down on the slope some blue cloud-shadows lie,
The shadows of high mountains fill the valley,
Matting the meadows to a greenish grey;
The summit glistens in the last full ray.
How near to my deep longing have they grown
Who there on the wide pastures live alone,
Whose weariness of limb is well rewarded
By wealth which their own hands have plucked and hoarded.
The morning wind, the wonderful and wild,
That travels barefoot in the scent of heather,
Wakes them each day; around them wild bees build,
Fill with their humming God's pellucid air.
Nature has lent herself to be their ploy,
In all their wishes Nature wells each day,
Rest renews vigour, and in that interplay
All of this life's warm pleasures they enjoy.
Now moves the golden ball, now it inclines
Towards green crystal of the farthest seas;
Through distant trees the dying radiance shines.
Now red smoke breathes, a wall of glowing haze
Fills the sea-shore where all the cities are
Whose naiad arms, emerging from the tide,
In tall ships rock their children, cradled there,
A people reckless, cunning, full of pride.

Hugo von Hofmannsthal

Sie gleiten über ferne, wunderschwere,
Verschwiegne Flut, die nie ein Kiel geteilt,
Es regt die Brust der Zorn der wilden Meere,
Da wird sie jedem Wahn und Weh geheilt.
So seh ich Sinn und Segen fern gebreitet
Und starre voller Sehnsucht stets hinüber,
Doch wie mein Blick dem Nahen näher gleitet,
Wird alles öd, verletzender und trüber;
Es scheint mein ganzes so versäumtes Leben,
Verlorne Lust und nie geweinte Tränen,
Um diese Gassen, dieses Haus zu weben
Und ewig sinnlos Suchen, wirres Sehnen.

Am Fenster stehend

Jetzt zünden sie die Lichter an und haben
In engen Wänden eine dumpfe Welt
Mit allen Rausch- und Tränengaben
Und was noch sonst ein Herz gefangenhält.
Sie sind einander herzlich nah
Und härmen sich um einen, der entfernt;
Und wenn wohl einem Leid geschah,
So trösten sie . . . ich habe Trösten nie gelernt.
Sie können sich mit einfachen Worten,
Was nötig zum Weinen und Lachen, sagen.
Müssen nicht an sieben vernagelte Pforten
Mit blutigen Fingern schlagen.

Was weiss denn ich vom Menschenleben?
Bin freilich scheinbar drin gestanden,
Aber ich hab es höchstens verstanden,
Konnte mich nie darein verweben.
Hab mich niemals daran verloren.
Wo andre nehmen, andre geben,

Death and the Fool

Across the marvellous ocean, silent, far
As keel has never ventured yet, they glide;
Stirred by the fury of the savage main,
Their breasts are healed of folly and of pain.
Thus I see sense and blessings everywhere
And, full of yearning, stare across at them;
But when my gaze approaches what is near
All things grow bleak, offensive, dull, and dim.
Just as though all my missed and wasted days,
With their lost joys and tears unshed, were thronging
Around these streets, this house—my life a maze,
A search for ever vain, and aimless longing.

Going up to the window

But now they light the lamps and so confine
A shapeless world within their narrow walls,
Complete with all the liquors, tears, and wine
And other stuff that interests or enthralls.
They are so intimately near
And grieve for someone who is far away;
And if a man has suffered here
They comfort him . . . with words I cannot say.
In simple words they can convey
All that is wanted for laughter or tears,
Need not beat with bleeding fingers all day
At the seven nailed-up doors.

What do I know about human life?
True, I appeared to stand inside it,
But, at the most, I studied it,
Never was caught, but held aloof,
Never lost myself but, alien, eyed it.
Where others give and others take

Hugo von Hofmannsthal

Blieb ich beiseit, im Innern stummgeboren.
Ich hab von allen lieben Lippen
Den wahren Trank des Lebens nie gesogen,
Bin nie, von wahrem Schmerz durchschüttert,
Die Strasse einsam, schluchzend, nie! gezogen.
Wenn ich von guten Gaben der Natur
Je eine Regung, einen Hauch erfuhr,
So nannte ihn mein überwacher Sinn,
Unfähig des Vergessens, grell beim Namen.
Und wie dann tausende Vergleiche kamen,
War das Vertrauen, war das Glück dahin.
Und auch das Leid! zerfasert und zerfressen
Vom Denken, abgeblasst und ausgelaugt!
Wie wollte ich an meine Brust es pressen,
Wie hätt ich Wonne aus dem Schmerz gesaugt:
Sein Flügel streifte mich, ich wurde matt,
Und Unbehagen kam an Schmerzes Statt . . .

Aufschreckend

Es dunkelt schon. Ich fall in Grübelei.
Ja, ja: die Zeit hat Kinder mancherlei.
Doch ich bin müd und soll wohl schlafen gehen.

Der Diener bringt eine Lampe, geht dann wieder.

Jetzt lässt der Lampe Glanz mich wieder sehen
Die Rumpelkammer voller totem Tand,
Wodurch ich doch mich einzuschleichen wähnte,
Wenn ich den graden Weg auch nimmer fand
In jenes Leben, das ich so ersehnte.

Vor dem Kruzifix

Zu deinen wunden, elfenbeinern' Füssen,

Death and the Fool

I stood aside, my inmost centre dumb.
From all those charming lips I did not suck
The true, essential potion, life by name,
Have never been pierced and shaken with true pain
And never, sobbing, walked the streets alone.
If ever I felt a feeble breath or stir
Of natural emotion or desire,
At once my conscious mind, which never yet
Has learnt to sleep or to forget,
Would leap awake to meddle in the game
And kill the urge by giving it a name.
When thousands of comparisons occurred,
Then faith was gone and bliss an empty word.
And suffering, too! All shredded, torn, devoured
With too much thinking, faded, wrung and scoured!
Yet how I yearned to clasp it to my breast,
From pain and sorrow yearned to suck delight:
His wing soon grazed me, and I wanted rest,
Instead of pain, discomfort was my plight. . . .

Starting

Night falls. These are vain questions, vain retorts.
No doubt: the age has children of all sorts.
But I am tired and ought to go to bed.

The Servant brings a lamp, then goes out again.

Now in the brightness that the lamp has shed
I see the lumber-room, full of bric-a-brac,
By which I still had hoped to creep or crawl
Into the life I long for, though I lack
The straight and open highway walked by all.

In front of the Crucifix

Down here beneath your wounded ivory feet,

[99]

Hugo von Hofmannsthal

Du Herr am Kreuz, sind etliche gelegen,
Die Flammen niederbetend, jene süssen,
Ins eigne Herz, die wundervoll bewegen,
Und wenn statt Gluten öde Kälte kam,
Vergingen sie in Reue, Angst und Scham.

Vor einem alten Bild

Gioconda, du, aus wundervollem Grund
Herleuchtend mit dem Glanz durchseelter Glieder,
Dem rätselhaften, süssen, herben Mund,
Dem Prunk der träumeschweren Augenlider:
Gerad so viel verrietest du mir Leben,
Als fragend ich vermocht dir einzuweben!

Sich abwendend, vor einer Truhe

Ihr Becher, ihr, an deren kühlem Rand
Wohl etlich Lippen selig hingen,
Ihr alten Lauten, ihr, bei deren Klingen
Sich manches Herz die tiefste Rührung fand,
Was gäb ich, könnt mich euer Bann erfassen,
Wie wollt ich mich gefangen finden lassen!
Ihr hölzern, ehern Schilderwerk,
Verwirrend, formenquellend Bilderwerk,
Ihr Kröten, Engel, Greife, Faunen,
Phantastche Vögel, goldnes Fruchtgeschlinge,
Berauschende und ängstigende Dinge,
Ihr wart doch all einmal gefühlt,
Gezeugt von zuckenden, lebendgen Launen,
Vom grossen Meer emporgespült,
Und wie den Fisch das Netz, hat euch die Form gefangen!
Umsonst bin ich, umsonst euch nachgegangen,
Von eurem Reize allzusehr gebunden:
Und wie ich eurer eigensinngen Seelen

Death and the Fool

O Lord upon the Cross, many have lain,
Praying that those high flames, so pure and sweet,
Descend to their own hearts and enter in again,
And if, instead of heat, grey coldness came
They were consumed with dread, remorse and shame.

In front of an old picture

Gioconda, shining in the marvellous gloom,
With limbs that with the soul's suffusion gleam,
With sweet and bitter lips for ever dumb,
Splendour of eye-lids weighted with a dream:
Just so much life you have revealed to me
As, questioning, I lent your secrecy.

Turning away, in front of a chest

You cups to whose cool metal rim
How many mouths most blissfully have clung,
You ancient lutes whose music, when you rang,
Moved many hearts most deeply for a time,
If only I could live in servitude
To your old spell, how readily I would!
You ancient emblems, carved or cast,
Confusing, rich in images made to last,
You toads and angels, gargoyles, fauns,
Fantastic birds and gilded fruit in rings,
Intoxicating, terrifying things,
You, too, must have been felt before,
Conceived by twitching nerves, internal storms,
By the great ocean washed ashore
And, just as nets catch fish, so you were caught in forms!
In vain I have pursued you, all in vain,
Too much addicted to your curious charms:
By feeling through your masks, I could attain

Jedwede, wie die Masken, durchempfunden,
War mir verschleiert Leben, Herz und Welt,
Ihr hieltet mich, ein Flatterschwarm, umstellt,
Abweidend, unerbittliche Harpyen,
An frischen Quellen jedes frische Blühen . . .
Ich hab mich so an Künstliches verloren,
Dass ich die Sonne sah aus toten Augen
Und nicht mehr hörte als durch tote Ohren:
Stets schleppte ich den rätselhaften Fluch,
Nie ganz bewusst, nie völlig unbewusst,
Mit kleinem Leid und schaler Lust
Mein Leben zu erleben wie ein Buch,
Das man zur Hälft noch nicht und halb nicht mehr
    begreift,
Und hinter dem der Sinn erst nach Lebendgem schweift—
Und was mich quälte und was mich erfreute,
Mir war, als ob es nie sich selbst bedeute,
Nein, künftgen Lebens vorgeliehnen Schein
Und hohles Bild von einem vollern Sein.
So hab ich mich in Leid und jeder Liebe
Verwirrt mit Schatten nur herumgeschlagen,
Verbraucht, doch nicht genossen alle Triebe,
In dumpfem Traum, es würde endlich tagen.
Ich wandte nich und sah das Leben an:
Darinnen Schnellsein nicht zum Laufen nützt
Und Tapfersein nicht hilft zum Streit; darin
Unheil nicht traurig macht und Glück nicht froh;
Auf Frag ohn Sinn folgt Antwort ohne Sinn;
Verworrner Traum entsteigt der dunklen Schwelle,
Und Glück ist alles, Stunde, Wind und Welle!
So schmerzlich klug und so enttäuschten Sinn
In müdem Hochmut hegend, in Entsagen
Tief eingesponnen, leb ich ohne Klagen
In diesen Stuben, dieser Stadt dahin.

Death and the Fool

Each of your obstinate souls at last; but then
My life, my heart, the world were overcast
And, an encircling swarm, you held me fast,
Inexorable harpies who devour
All that new sources water, the new flower. . . .
Too much attracted to mere artifice,
I saw the very sun with eyes long dead
And through dead ears drew sounds into my head:
Not wholly conscious, nor free from consciousness,
My sufferings petty and my joys gone stale,
Always I dragged along that awful curse
Which made my life a book, some twice-told tale
Partly not yet intelligible, partly no longer so,
And which, to grasp the living truth, we must
    reverse—
Whatever hurt or pleased me did not seem
To represent its proper meaning—no!
It was some future life's projected beam,
Void image of some richer life to come.
So in my cares and loves I did no more
Than brawl with shadows, dizzy on the verge,
Exhausting, not enjoying, every urge,
Dreaming of dawn, and the untrodden shore.
I turned about and contemplated life:
In which the runner does not gain by speed,
Nor courage help the fighter in his strife,
Misfortune need not sadden, nor luck lead
To happiness; vain question, vain reply;
From the dark threshold rises a tangled dream,
And all is chance: the hour, the wind, the stream.
Hiding such painful cleverness behind
My languid pride, a disenchanted mind
Spun deep into renunciation, I
Live uncomplaining in these rooms, this city.

Die Leute haben sich entwöhnt zu fragen
Und finden, dass ich recht gewöhnlich bin.

*Der Diener kommt und stellt einen Teller Kirschen auf den
Tisch, dann will er die Balkontüre schliessen.*

CLAUDIO

Lass noch die Türen offen . . . Was erschreckt dich?

DIENER

Euer Gnaden glauben mirs wohl nicht.

Halb für sich, mit Angst

Jetzt haben sie im Lusthaus sich versteckt.

CLAUDIO

Wer denn?

DIENER

Entschuldigen, ich weiss es nicht.
Ein ganzer Schwarm unheimliches Gesindel.

CLAUDIO

Bettler?

DIENER

Ich weiss es nicht.

CLAUDIO

So sperr die Tür,
Die von der Gasse in den Garten, zu,
Und leg dich schlafen und lass mich in Ruh.

Death and the Fool

People have ceased to trouble me with their pity,
Ask me no questions and think I'm of their kind.

*Enter the Servant, who sets a plate of cherries on the table,
then is about to close the door to the balcony.*

CLAUDIO

Leave the doors open . . . Well, what's frightening you?

SERVANT

I fear you won't believe me, your lordship.

Half to himself, afraid

Now they've hidden in the pavilion, sir.

CLAUDIO

Who has?

SERVANT

Excuse me, your lordship, I don't know.
A whole pack of uncanny fellows, sir.

CLAUDIO

Beggars?

SERVANT

I don't know.

CLAUDIO

                    Then lock the door,
The one that leads from the garden to the street;
And go to bed, and leave me alone: good night.

[105]

DIENER

Das eben macht mir solches Graun. Ich hab
Die Gartentür verriegelt. Aber . . .

CLAUDIO

Nun?

DIENER

Jetzt sitzen sie im Garten. Auf der Bank,
Wo der sandsteinerne Apollo steht,
Ein paar im Schatten dort am Brunnenrand,
Und einer hat sich auf die Sphinx gesetzt.
Man sieht ihn nicht, der Taxus steht davor.

CLAUDIO

Sinds Männer?

DIENER

Einige. Allein auch Frauen.
Nicht bettelhaft, altmodisch nur von Tracht,
Wie Kupferstiche angezogen sind.
Mit einer solchen grauenvollen Art,
Still dazusitzen und mit toten Augen
Auf einen wie in leere Luft zu schauen,
Das sind nicht Menschen. Euer Gnaden sei'n
Nicht ungehalten, nur um keinen Preis
Der Welt möcht ich in ihre Nähe gehen.
So Gott will, sind sie morgen früh verschwunden;
Ich will—mit gnädiger Erlaubnis—jetzt
Die Tür vom Haus verriegeln und das Schloss
Einsprengen mit geweihtem Wasser. Denn
Ich habe solche Menschen nie gesehn,
Und solche Augen haben Menschen nicht.

Death and the Fool

SERVANT

That's just what frightens me so, your lordship.
I *have* locked the garden door, but . . .

CLAUDIO

Well, but what?

SERVANT

Now they're sitting on the garden seat,
Just next to where the sandstone Apollo stands,
A few of them in the shade, on the fountain's edge,
And one of them has sat down on the sphinx.
He can't be seen, the yew-tree's just in front.

CLAUDIO

Are they men?

SERVANT

Well, some of them are. But women too.
Not like beggars, only old-fashioned in dress,
Wearing such clothes as you'd find on old engravings,
With such a gruesome way of sitting still
And staring at you with eyes that look dead,
Eyes that seem lost in space—they can't be human.
Please don't be angry, your lordship, but not
For anything in the world would I go
Too near to them. God willing, they may be gone
Early tomorrow morning, or sooner still.
Now—with your kind permission, sir—I'll go
And bolt the main door of the house, then sprinkle
The lock with holy water, to keep them out.
For never have I looked upon such humans,
And never has a human had such eyes.

[107]

Hugo von Hofmannsthal

CLAUDIO

Tu, was du willst, und gute Nacht.

*Er geht eine Weile nachdenklich auf und nieder. Hinter der
Szene erklingt das sehnsüchtige und ergreifende Spiel einer
Geige, zuerst ferner, allmählich näher, endlich warm und voll,
als wenn es aus dem Nebenzimmer dränge.*

Musik?
Und seltsam zu der Seele redende!
Hat mich des Menschen Unsinn auch verstört?
Mich dünkt, als hätt ich solche Töne
Von Menschengeigen nie gehört . . .

Er bleibt horchend gegen die rechte Seite gewandt.

In tiefen, scheinbar langersehnten Schauern
Dringts allgewaltig auf mich ein;
Es scheint unendliches Bedauern,
Unendlich Hoffen scheints zu sein,
Als strömte von den alten, stillen Mauern
Mein Leben flutend und verklärt herein.
Wie der Geliebten, wie der Mutter Kommen,
Wie jedes Langverlornen Wiederkehr,
Regt es Gedanken auf, die warmen, frommen,
Und wirft mich in ein jugendliches Meer:
Ein Knabe stand ich so im Frühlingsglänzen
Und meinte aufzuschweben in das All,
Unendlich Sehnen über alle Grenzen
Durchwehte mich in ahnungsvollem Schwall!
Und Wanderzeiten kamen, rauschumfangen,
Da leuchtete manchmal die ganze Welt,
Und Rosen glühten, und die Glocken klangen,
Von fremdem Lichte jubelnd und erhellt:
Wie waren da lebendig alle Dinge,

Death and the Fool

Do as you please; good night.

*For a while he walks up and down, pensive. Behind the
scenes the nostalgic and moving strains of a violin are heard,
more distant at first, then gradually closer, finally warm and
full, as if they came from the next room.*

Can this be music?
And music by which the soul is strangely stirred!
Has that man's raving then unhinged me, too?
Such tones I never yet have heard
Coming from human violins. . . .

He stands listening, facing right.

In shuddering and long-awaited gusts
Most mightily this music thrusts
At me: unending hope it seems
And infinite regret, that streams
As if from all these ancient, silent walls
My life, transformed, were flowing back to me.
As when a mother or a loved one calls,
Like the return of anything long lost,
It stirs up thoughts, warm, pious ones, a host
Of thoughts that beckon like a youthful sea:
So once, a boy, I stood in gleaming spring
Feeling that I could float and melt in air,
Transcend the bounds of matter—anything,
Such fervent longing I experienced there!
Then came the roaming years; when without wine
I was so drunk, the whole world seemed to shine,
Bells pealed and roses glowed; all things were bright,
Radiant and jubilant with alien light:
How full of life created things were then,

[109]

Hugo von Hofmannsthal

Dem liebenden Erfassen nahgerückt,
Wie fühl ich mich beseelt und tief entzückt,
Ein lebend Glied im grossen Lebensringe!
Da ahnte ich, durch mein Herz auch geleitet,
Den Liebesstrom, der alle Herzen nährt,
Und ein Genügen hielt mein Ich geweitet,
Das heute kaum mir noch den Traum verklärt.
Tön fort, Musik, noch eine Weile so
Und rühr mein Innres also innig auf:
Leicht wähn ich dann mein Leben warm und froh,
Rücklebend so verzaubert seinen Lauf:
Denn alle süssen Flammen, Loh an Loh
Das Starre schmelzend, schlagen jetzt herauf!
Des allzu alten, allzu wirren Wissens
Auf diesen Nacken vielgehäufte Last
Vergeht, von diesem Laut des Urgewissens,
Den kindisch-tiefen Tönen angefasst.
Weither mit grossem Glockenläuten
Ankündigt sich ein kaum geahntes Leben,
In Formen, die unendlich viel bedeuten,
Gewaltig-schlicht im Nehmen und im Geben.

Die Musik verstummt fast plötzlich.

Da, da verstummt, was mich so tief gerührt,
Worin ich Göttlich-Menschliches gespürt!
Der diese Wunderwelt unwissend hergesandt,
Er hebt wohl jetzt nach Kupfergeld die Kappe,
Ein abendlicher Bettelmusikant.

Am Fenster rechts

Hier unten steht er nicht. Wie sonderbar!
Wo denn? Ich will durchs andre Fenster schaun . . .

Death and the Fool

How near to the beholder's loving mind,
How overjoyed I was, how rapt to find
Myself a link in life's encircling chain!
And, guided by the heart, I soon divined
The stream of love that nourishes all hearts,
Yet by a strange sufficiency retained
Such peace as hardly dreaming now imparts.
Music, play on, continue for a while
So to stir up my darkest memories:
My life grows warm and joyful by degrees
As now, I live it backwards, mile by mile:
For all the sweetest flames, blaze after blaze,
Melting my frozen past, rise and defile;
And that great load of twisted facts, conferred
Upon my shoulders, knowledge old and stale,
These tones remove, sound of the primal word,
Childishly deep, that heals when it is heard.
From far away, amidst the clang of bells,
Great news has been announced, news which foretells
No less than this: a different way of living,
Simple, yet strong in taking and in giving.

The music stops almost abruptly.

But now the music that so moved me ends,
In which the human with the godlike blends.
He who, unknowing, sent it on this mission
Will now be holding out his hat for coins,
A beggarly, belated street musician.

At the right-hand window

How very strange! No sign of him down here.
Where, then? I'd better try the other window. . . .

Hugo von Hofmannsthal

Wie er nach der Türe rechts geht, wird der Vorhang leise zurückgeschlagen, und in der Tür steht der Tod, den Fiedelbogen in der Hand, die Geige am Gürtel hängend. Er sieht Claudio, der entsetzt zurückfährt, ruhig an.

Wie packt mich sinnlos namenloses Grauen!
Wenn deiner Fiedel Klang so lieblich war,
Was bringt es solchen Krampf, dich anzuschauen?
Und schnürt die Kehle so und sträubt das Haar?
Geh weg! Du bist der Tod. Was willst du hier?
Ich fürchte mich. Geh weg! Ich kann nicht schrein.

Sinkend

Der Halt, die Luft des Lebens schwindet mir!
Geh weg! Wer rief dich? Geh! Wer liess dich ein?

DER TOD

Steh auf! Wirf dies ererbte Graun von dir!
Ich bin nicht schauerlich, bin kein Gerippe!
Aus des Dionysos, der Venus Sippe,
Ein grosser Gott der Seele steht vor dir.
Wenn in der lauen Sommerabendfeier
Durch goldne Luft ein Blatt herabgeschwebt,
Hat dich mein Wehen angeschauert,
Das traumhaft um die reifen Dinge webt;
Wenn Überschwellen der Gefühle
Mit warmer Flut die Seele zitternd füllte,
Wenn sich im plötzlichen Durchzucken
Das Ungeheure als verwandt enthüllte,
Und du, hingebend dich im grossen Reigen,
Die Welt empfingest als dein eigen:
In jeder wahrhaft grossen Stunde,
Die schauern deine Erdenform gemacht,

Death and the Fool

As he walks to the door, right, the curtain is pulled aside
gently, and in the doorway stands Death, the bow of his
violin in one hand, the violin hanging from his belt. He looks
at Claudio, calmly, but Claudio recoils in horror.

What senseless, nameless horror can this be?
Why, when your violin's music was so sweet,
Now does your aspect freeze and shatter me,
Tighten my throat, make all my pulses beat?
Away! You're Death. What is your business here?
I am afraid. Away! I cannot scream.

Swooning

My foothold and the breath of life are gone.
Away! Who called you? Go! Who let you in?

DEATH

Get up! Cast off hereditary fear!
I am not gruesome, am no skeleton.
As a great god of the soul I now appear,
To Dionysos, Venus most akin.
When in the stillness of a summer evening
Through warm and golden air a leaf came down,
My wafted breath was in your shuddering,
My breath which to ripe things adheres; and when
A brimming-over and uprush of feeling
In a warm torrent flooded your trembling soul;
Or when a sudden spasm was revealing
Your kinship with the vast and the unknown,
And you, abandoned to the cosmic dance,
Received the whole world's rhythm as your own:
In every hour pregnant with more than chance
Experienced fully in your earthly station,

[113]

Hab ich dich angerührt im Seelengrunde
Mit heiliger, geheimnisvoller Macht.

CLAUDIO

Genug. Ich grüsse dich, wenngleich beklommen.

` *Kleine Pause*

Doch wozu bist du eigentlich gekommen?

DER TOD

Mein Kommen, Freund, hat stets nur einen Sinn!

CLAUDIO

Bei mir hats eine Weile noch dahin!
Merk: eh das Blatt zu Boden schwebt,
Hat es zur Neige seinen Saft gesogen!
Dazu fehlt viel: Ich habe nicht gelebt!

DER TOD

Bist doch, wie alle, deinen Weg gezogen!

CLAUDIO

Wie abgerissne Wiesenblumen
Ein dunkles Wasser mit sich reisst,
So glitten mir die jungen Tage,
Und ich hab nie gewusst, dass das schon Leben heisst.
Dann . . . stand ich an den Lebensgittern,
Der Wunder bang, von Sehnsucht süss bedrängt,
Dass sie in majestätischen Gewittern
Auffliegen sollten, wundervoll gesprengt.
Es kam nicht so . . . und einmal stand ich drinnen,
Der Weihe bar, und konnte mich auf mich
Und alle tiefsten Wünsche nicht besinnen,

Death and the Fool

'Twas I who touched your very soul's foundation
With power most holy, fraught with mystery.

CLAUDIO

Enough. I greet you, though with a troubled heart.

Short pause

But tell me: for what purpose have you come?

DEATH

My coming, friend, never has more than *one*.

CLAUDIO

Oh, as for *that*, I'll wait. I've just begun.
Mark this: before the leaf glides to the ground,
Much heavy sap prepares it for its falling.
I'm far from that: I've scarcely felt the sun.

DEATH

Like other men, you have pursued your calling.

CLAUDIO

As meadow flowers, uprooted, flow
In dark flood water, driven on,
So my young days have passed and gone;
If that was really life, I never called it so.
Then . . . then I stood behind the gate of life,
Awed by its wonders, full of deep desire
That mighty storms should blast it with lightning's fire,
Cut every bar as with a marvellous knife.
It would not happen . . . but I stood inside,
Bereft of grace, and could not recollect
Even myself or my most fervent wishes,

[115]

Von einem Bann befangen, der nicht wich.
Von Dämmerung verwirrt und wie verschüttet,
Verdriesslich und im Innersten zerrüttet,
Mit halbem Herzen, unterbundnen Sinnen
In jedem Ganzen rätselhaft gehemmt,
Fühlt ich mich niemals recht durchglutet innen,
Von grossen Wellen nie so recht geschwemmt,
Bin nie auf meinem Weg dem Gott begegnet,
Mit dem man ringt, bis dass er einen segnet.

DER TOD

Was allen, ward auch dir gegeben,
Ein Erdenleben, irdisch es zu leben.
Im Innern quillt euch allen treu ein Geist,
Der diesem Chaos toter Sachen
Beziehung einzuhauchen heisst
Und euren Garten draus zu machen
Für Wirksamkeit, Beglückung und Verdruss.
Weh dir, wenn ich dir das erst sagen muss!
Man bindet und man wird gebunden,
Entfaltung wirken schwül und wilde Stunden;
In Schlaf geweint und müd geplagt,
Noch wollend, schwer von Sehnsucht, halbverzagt,
Tiefatmend und vom Drang des Lebens warm . . .
Doch alle reif, fallt ihr in meinen Arm.

CLAUDIO

Ich bin aber nicht reif, drum lass mich hier.
Ich will nicht länger töricht jammern,
Ich will mich an die Erdenscholle klammern,
Die tiefste Lebenssehnsucht schreit in mir.
Die höchste Angst zerreisst den alten Bann;
Jetzt fühl ich—lass mich—dass ich leben kann!

Death and the Fool

Bound by a spell that froze and petrified.
Half-blind in twilight, buried beneath the rubble,
Half-hearted and my senses stupefied,
Shattered and dazed, it seemed, in my deep trouble,
Held back from every kind of wholeness, tied,
I never felt the authentic glow within;
Never could feel quite flooded by the tide,
Never on all my ways could meet the God
With whom one wrestles till He blesses one.

DEATH

What all men have, you, too, were given:
An earthly life, to be lived in earthly fashion.
Inside you all a faithful spirit dwells
Who to this chaos of dead matter
Can lend significance and tells
Each one to make his garden so
That, in it, joys and cares and work may grow.
And woe to you, if *I* must tell you this!
A man binds others and is bound,
In wild, in tedious hours much gain is found;
Crying yourselves to sleep, worn out with toil,
Still hoping, full of longing, brave or timid,
Or breathing deeply, clinging to life's charms . . .
No matter—*ripe,* you fall into my arms.

CLAUDIO

But ripe is what I'm not, so leave me here.
No longer foolishly I shall complain,
But gladly to my little plot adhere,
Avid for life, its pleasure and its pain.
The wildest fear rips up the ancient curse,
At last I feel that I can live—and *must!*

[117]

Hugo von Hofmannsthal

Ich fühls an diesem grenzenlosen Drängen:
Ich kann mein Herz an Erdendinge hängen.
Oh, du sollst sehn, nicht mehr wie stumme Tiere,
Nicht Puppen werden mir die andern sein!
Zum Herzen reden soll mir all das Ihre,
Ich dränge mich in jede Lust und Pein.
Ich will die Treue lernen, die der Halt
Von allem Leben ist . . . Ich füg mich so,
Dass Gut und Böse über mich Gewalt
Soll haben und mich machen wild und froh.
Dann werden sich die Schemen mir beleben!
Ich werde Menschen auf dem Wege finden,
Nicht länger stumm im Nehmen und im Geben,
Gebunden werden—ja!—und kräftig binden.

Da er die ungerührte Miene des Todes wahrnimmt, mit
steigender Angst

Denn schau, glaub mir, das war nicht so bisher:
Du meinst, ich hätte doch geliebt, gehasst . . .
Nein, nie hab ich den Kern davon erfasst,
Es war ein Tausch von Schein und Worten leer!
Da schau, ich kann dir zeigen: Briefe, sieh,

Er reisst eine Lade auf und entnimmt ihr Pakete geordneter
alter Briefe.

Mit Schwüren voll und Liebeswort und Klagen;
Meinst du, ich hätte je gespürt, was die—
Gespürt, was ich als Antwort schien zu sagen?!

Er wirft ihm die Pakete vor die Füsse, dass die einzelnen
Briefe herausfliegen.

Da hast du dieses ganze Liebesleben,
Daraus nur ich und ich nur widertönte,

Death and the Fool

I know it by this boundless urge, this lust:
Oh, you shall see! No mere dumb animal
Or lifeless doll the others will remain,
I shall be moved by that which moves them all,
Plunge into every pleasure, every pain.
Faith I shall learn, and loyalty, the foundation
On which all being rests . . . Soon I shall know
Both good and evil and their domination,
Be wild and cheerful—I will have it so!
Then soon these lifeless patterns will be living
And on my way men, women will be found,
I'll not be dumb in taking and in giving,
But strongly bind and—yes!—be strongly bound.

*Seeing the unmoved expression on Death's face, with
mounting terror*

For, look, believe me, it wasn't so before:
You think that I *did* love, that I *did* hate . . .
No, never did I dream of such a state.
It was all words and lies and metaphor!
Look here. I'll show you: letters, sent to me.

He tears open a drawer and takes out a bundle of old letters.

Full of endearments, oaths, entreaties, sighs;
Do you think I ever felt as much as *they*—
Felt what I seemed to say in my replies?

*He throws the bundle at Death's feet, so that some letters
fly out.*

There, now you have it all, my love-life's essence
In which myself and only I resided,

[119]

Wie ich, der Stimmung Auf- und Niederbeben
Mitbebend, jeden heilgen Halt verhöhnte!
Da! da! und alles andre ist wie das:
Ohn Sinn, ohn Glück, ohn Schmerz, ohn Lieb, ohn Hass!

DER TOD

Du Tor! Du schlimmer Tor, ich will dich lehren,
Das Leben, eh dus endest, einmal ehren.
Stell dich dorthin und schweig und sieh hierher
Und lern, dass alle andern diesen Schollen
Mit lieberfülltem Erdensinn entquollen,
Und nur du selber schellenlaut und leer.

*Der Tod tut ein paar Geigenstriche, gleichsam rufend. Er steht
an der Schlafzimmertüre, im Vordergrund rechts, Claudio an
der Wand links, im Halbdunkel. Aus der Tür rechts tritt die
Mutter. Sie ist nicht sehr alt. Sie trägt ein langes schwarzes
Samtkleid, eine schwarze Samthaube mit einer weissen
Rüsche, die das Gesicht umrahmt. In den feinen blassen Fin-
gern ein weisses Spitzentaschentuch. Sie tritt leise aus der
Tür und geht lautlos im Zimmer umher.*

DIE MUTTER

Wie viele süsse Schmerzen saug ich ein
Mit dieser Luft. Wie von Lavendelkraut
Ein feiner toter Atem weht die Hälfte
Von meinem Erdendasein hier umher:
Ein Mutterleben, nun, ein Dritteil Schmerzen,
Eins Plage, Sorge eins. Was weiss ein Mann
Davon?

An der Truhe

Die Kante da noch immer scharf?
Da schlug er sich einmal die Schläfe blutig;

Death and the Fool

And leaving nothing sacred underided
I foamed with every passing effervescence.
There! There! And all the others are the same:
Void of all sense, and love, and hate, and shame!

DEATH

You fool! Pernicious fool, I'll teach you yet
To honour life—before you part with it.
Stand over there, keep quiet, look this way
And learn that all the others from their birth
With soul and senses loved their native earth,
And you alone were different—hollow clay.

Death plays a few notes on his violin, as if calling. He stands near the bedroom door, in the foreground, right, Claudio by the wall, left, in semi-darkness. From the door, right, enter the Mother. She is not very old. She wears a long black velvet dress, a bonnet to match, with a white ruche, in which her face is framed. A small lace handkerchief in her slender, white fingers. She steps from the door softly and walks about, silently.

THE MOTHER

How many dear, sweet sorrows I inhale
Together with this air. Like fine dead breath
Of dried, old lavender, one half of all
My life on earth wafts at me in this room:
A mother's life, a third of which is pain,
One trouble, grief the last. What does a man
Know of such things?

Near the chest

The corner there still sharp?
There once he struck his temple, made it bleed;

[121]

Freilich, er war auch klein und heftig, wild
Im Laufen, nicht zu halten. Da, das Fenster!
Da stand ich oft und horchte in die Nacht
Hinaus auf seinen Schritt mit solcher Gier,
Wenn mich die Angst im Bett nicht länger litt,
Wenn er nicht kam, und schlug doch zwei, und schlug
Dann drei und fing schon blass zu dämmern an . . .
Wie oft . . . Doch hat er nie etwas gewusst—
Ich war ja auch bei Tag hübsch viel allein.
Die Hand, die giesst die Blumen, klopft den Staub
Vom Kissen, reibt die Messingklinken blank,
So läuft der Tag: allein der Kopf hat nichts
Zu tun: da geht im Kreis ein dumpfes Rad
Mit Ahnungen und traumbeklommenem,
Geheimnisvollem Schmerzgefühle, das
Wohl mit der Mutterschaft unfasslichem
Geheimem Heiligtum zusammenhängt
Und allem tiefstem Weben dieser Welt
Verwandt ist. Aber mir ist nicht gegönnt,
Der süss beklemmend, schmerzlich nährenden,
Der Luft vergangnen Lebens mehr zu atmen.
Ich muss ja gehen, gehen . . .

Sie geht durch die Mitteltüre ab.

CLAUDIO

Mutter!

DER TOD

Schweig!
Du bringst sie nicht zurück.

CLAUDIO

Ah! Mutter, komm!

[122]

Death and the Fool

Of course, he was young then, impatient, wild
In his movements, headstrong. And the window, there!
Often I stood there, listening into the night
For his dear footfall, listening with such greed,
When fear and worry drove me from my bed;
When it struck two, then three, and when already
A pale dawn rose—and still he did not come . . .
How often . . . yet next day he never knew—
And in the daytime, too, I was much alone.
This hand: it waters flowers, beats the dust
From cushions, rubs brass handles bright and clean—
So the day passes; but the head has nothing
To do: all day a padded wheel revolves,
With premonitions, nightmare anxieties,
Mysterious feelings of unwarranted pain,
Connected, I suppose, with the obscure,
Unfathomable sacrament of motherhood
Which is akin to all the deepest workings
Of this world. But no longer I am allowed
To breathe the sweet, oppressive, painfully
Nourishing air of a life that's past and gone.
I must be leaving, leaving. . . .

Exit by the middle door.

CLAUDIO
Mother!

DEATH
Quiet!

You'll never bring her back.

CLAUDIO
O Mother, stay!

[123]

Lass mich dir einmal mit den Lippen hier,
Den zuckenden, die immer schmalgepresst,
Hochmütig schwiegen, lass mich doch vor dir
So auf den Knieen . . . Ruf sie! Halt sie fest!
Sie wollte nicht! Hast du denn nicht gesehn?!
Was zwingst du sie, Entsetzlicher, zu gehn?

DER TOD

Lass mir, was mein. Dein war es.

CLAUDIO

Ah! und nie
Gefühlt! Dürr, alles dürr! Wann hab ich je
Gespürt, dass alle Wurzeln meines Seins
Nach ihr sich zuckend drängten, ihre Näh
Wie einer Gottheit Nähe wundervoll
Durchschauert mich und quellend füllen soll
Mit Menschensehnsucht, Menschenlust—und -weh?!

Der Tod, um seine Klagen unbekümmert, spielt die Melodie eines alten Volksliedes. Langsam tritt ein junges Mädchen ein; sie trägt ein einfaches grossgeblümtes Kleid, Kreuzbandschuhe, um den Hals ein Stückchen Schleier, blosser Kopf.

DAS JUNGE MÄDCHEN

Es war doch schön . . . Denkst du nie mehr daran?
Freilich, du hast mir weh getan, so weh . . .
Allein was hört denn nicht in Schmerzen auf?
Ich hab so wenig frohe Tag gesehn,
Und die, die waren schön als wie ein Traum!
Die Blumen vor dem Fenster, meine Blumen,
Das kleine wacklige Spinett, der Schrank,
In den ich deine Briefe legte und
Was du mir etwa schenktest . . . alles das

Death and the Fool

For once with trembling lips—the very same
Which, always tightly pressed, haughtily dumb,
Could not relax—here, on my knees with shame,
Oh, let me . . . Call her back! Don't let her go!
She did not want to go! Didn't you see?
Why do you force her to, Monstrosity?

DEATH

Leave me what's mine. Once it *was* yours.

CLAUDIO

Yet never
Felt to be so. But withered, all was withered.
When did I ever feel that all the roots
Of my life cried out for her? Or that her nearness
Filled me with awe like some great godhead's nearness,
As it was meant to do, miraculously
Filled me with human longing, joy and grief?

*Death, unmoved by this lamentation, plays the tune of an old
popular song. Slowly a young girl enters wearing a flowered
dress, very simple, cross-laced shoes, wisp of a veil about her
neck, her head bare.*

THE YOUNG GIRL

Yes, it was lovely . . . Have you quite forgotten?
It's true, you hurt me, hurt me, oh, so much . . .
But, after all, what doesn't end in pain?
I've known so very few untroubled days,
And these were lovely, lovely as a dream!
The flowers in front of my window, my own flowers,
The little rickety virginal, the cupboard
In which I put your letters and the things
You used to give to me at first . . . all this—

—Lach mich nicht aus—das wurde alles schön
Und redete mit wachen lieben Lippen!
Wenn nach dem schwülen Abend Regen kam
Und wir am Fenster standen—ah, der Duft
Der nassen Bäume!—Alles das ist hin,
Gestorben, was daran lebendig war!
Und liegt in unsrer Liebe kleinem Grab.
Allein es war so schön, und du bist schuld,
Dass es so schön war. Und dass du mich dann
Fortwarfest, achtlos grausam, wie ein Kind,
Des Spielens müd, die Blumen fallen lässt .   .
Mein Gott, ich hatte nichts, dich festzubinden.

Kleine Pause

Wie dann dein Brief, der letzte, schlimme, kam,
Da wollt ich sterben. Nicht um dich zu quälen,
Sag ich dir das. Ich wollte einen Brief
Zum Abschied an dich schreiben, ohne Klag,
Nicht heftig, ohne wilde Traurigkeit;
Nur so, dass du nach meiner Lieb und mir
Noch einmal solltest Heimweh haben und
Ein wenig weinen, weils dazu zu spät.
Ich hab dir nicht geschrieben. Nein. Wozu?
Was weiss denn ich, wieviel von deinem Herzen
In all dem war, was meinen armen Sinn
Mit Glanz und Fieber so erfüllte, dass
Ich wie im Traum am lichten Tage ging.
Aus Untreu macht kein guter Wille Treu,
Und Tränen machen kein Erstorbnes wach.
Man stirbt auch nicht daran. Viel später erst,
Nach langem, ödem Elend durft ich mich
Hinlegen, um zu sterben. Und ich bat,
In deiner Todesstund bei dir zu sein.

Death and the Fool

Don't laugh at me—all this grew beautiful
And spoke to me with dear and eloquent lips.
When after sultry evenings there was rain,
We stood at the open window together—
Oh, the fragrance of trees in the rain!—All that
Is gone, and what was living in it, dead.
All buried in the little grave of our love.
Yet it was beautiful, too, and you're to blame
That it *was* so beautiful; and that afterwards
You threw me away, unthinkingly cruel,
Like a child who, tired of playing, drops his flowers . . .
God knows I had nothing to hold you with.

Short pause

But when your letter, the last, the bad one, came
I wanted to die. Not to torment you now
Do I tell you this. I wanted to write
A farewell letter, gentle, uncomplaining,
Quite without bitterness or unbridled grief;
Only so that for my love and for myself
One day you might feel some longing and weep
A little, knowing it was too late for tears.
I did not write to you. Why should I write?
How can I know how much of your own heart
Was in it all—all that had filled my mind
And senses with such radiance, such a fever
That as though dreaming I walked in brightest day.
Good will can never cure unfaithfulness,
And tears can never waken what has died.
Nor does one die of it. Only much later,
After much long and lonely wretchedness,
I was allowed to die. Then I requested
That I might join you at your dying hour;

Nicht grauenvoll, um dich zu quälen nicht,
Nur wie wenn einer einen Becher Wein
Austrinkt und flüchtig ihn der Duft gemahnt
An irgendwo vergessne leise Lust.

Sie geht ab; Claudio birgt sein Gesicht in den Händen.
Unmittelbar nach ihrem Abgehen tritt ein Mann ein. Er hat
beiläufig Claudios Alter. Er trägt einen unordentlichen, be-
staubten Reiseanzug. In seiner linken Brust steckt mit her-
ausragendem Holzgriff ein Messer. Er bleibt in der Mitte der
Bühne, Claudio zugewendet, stehen.

DER MANN

Lebst du noch immer, Ewigspielender?
Liest immer noch Horaz und freuest dich
Am spöttisch-klugen, nie bewegten Sinn?
Mit feinen Worten bist du mir genaht,
Scheinbar gepackt von was auch mich bewegte . . .
Ich hab dich, sagtest du, gemahnt an Dinge,
Die heimlich in dir schliefen, wie der Wind
Der Nacht von fernem Ziel zuweilen redet . . .
O ja, ein feines Saitenspiel im Wind
Warst du, und der verliebte Wind dafür
Stets eines andern ausgenützter Atem,
Der meine oder sonst. Wir waren ja
Sehr lange Freunde. Freunde? Heisst: gemein
War zwischen uns Gespräch bei Tag und Nacht,
Verkehr mit gleichen Menschen, Tändelei
Mit einer gleichen Frau. Gemein: so wie
Gemeinsam zwischen Herr und Sklave ist
Haus, Sänfte, Hund, und Mittagstisch und Peitsche:
Dem ist das Haus zur Lust, ein Kerker dem,
Den trägt die Sänfte, jenem drückt die Schulter
Ihr Schnitzwerk wund; der lässt den Hund im Garten

Death and the Fool

Not horribly, not to torment you now,
Only as when one drinks a glass of wine
And for a moment its taste or smell recalls
Some long-forgotten place or dim delight.

*Exit; Claudio covers his face with his hands. Immediately
after her exit, enter a man. He is of about Claudio's age, wears
an untidy, dusty travelling suit. The wooden grip of a knife
sticks out from his chest, over his heart. He remains in the
middle of the stage, facing Claudio.*

THE MAN

What, still alive, still always playing at life?
Still reading Horace and still taking pleasure
In mocking, clever, unimpassioned things?
With your fine words you came quite close to me,
Seemingly gripped by that which moved me, too . . .
You said I had reminded you of things
That, latent in you, slept, as the night wind
Will speak of destinations out of mind . . .
Oh yes, a fine Aeolian harp you were,
And always the love-sick wind that made it play
Was another's exploited breath, my own
Or someone else's. Friends we called ourselves
For quite some time. Yes, friends indeed! That means
We talked together daily and late at night,
Knew the same people, flirted and played about
With the same woman, shared our lives. We shared
As slave and master share a single house,
One litter, dinner table, dog, and whip:
To one the house means pleasure, jail to the other;
One rides aloft, the other's shoulder smarts,
Cut by the litter's carvings; one delights
To see the dog jump through a lifted hoop

[129]

Durch Reifen springen, jener wartet ihn! . . .
Halbfertige Gefühle, meiner Seele
Schmerzlich geborne Perlen, nahmst du mir
Und warfst sie als dein Spielzeug in die Luft,
Du, schnellbefreundet, fertig schnell mit jedem,
Ich mit dem stummen Werben in der Seele
Und Zähne zugepresst, du ohne Scheu
An allem tastend, während mir das Wort
Misstrauisch und verschüchtert starb am Weg.
Da kam uns in den Weg ein Weib. Was mich
Ergriff, wie Krankheit über einen kommt,
Wo alle Sinne taumeln, überwach
Von allzu vielem Schaun nach einem Ziel . . .
Nach einem solchen Ziel, voll süsser Schwermut
Und wildem Glanz und Duft, aus tiefem Dunkel
Wie Wetterleuchten webend . . . Alles das,
Du sahst es auch, es reizte dich! . . . «Ja, weil
Ich selber ähnlich bin zu mancher Zeit,
So reizte mich des Mädchens müde Art
Und herbe Hoheit, so enttäuschten Sinns
Bei solcher Jugend.» Hast du mirs denn nicht
Dann später so erzählt? Es reizte dich!
Mir war es mehr als dieses Blut und Hirn!
Und sattgespielt warfst du die Puppe mir,
Mir zu, ihr ganzes Bild vom Überdruss
In dir entstellt, so fürchterlich verzerrt,
Des wundervollen Zaubers so entblösst,
Die Züge sinnlos, das lebendge Haar
Tot hängend, warfst mir eine Larve zu,
In schnödes Nichts mit widerlicher Kunst
Zersetzend rätselhaften süssen Reiz.
Für dieses hasste endlich ich dich so,
Wie dich mein dunkles Ahnen stets gehasst,

Death and the Fool

Down in the park; the other serves the dog! . . .
Half-completed feelings, pearls of my soul
Painfully born, you took away from me
And juggled with them, toys you thought your own,
You, quick to make new friends and quick to drop them,
I, with a dumb devotion in my soul,
Teeth tightly clenched; you, touching everything,
Devoid of shame, while, diffident, unsure,
The word I groped for withered on the way.
A woman crossed our path. What pounced on me
And penetrated as an illness does
In which the senses, over-wakeful, swoon
With too much concentration on one aim. . . .
For such an aim, which tender gloom surrounds,
A lovely scent and lustre that seem woven
Out of deep darkness and sheet-lightning. . . . This
You, too, observed, and it excited you! . . .
"Oh yes, because at times I feel the same,
The weary, languid manner of this girl,
Her hard and bitter haughtiness excited me—
So disillusioned, yet so young." These were
Your very words to me. Excited you!
More than this blood and brain she meant to me!
And, sick of the game, you threw the doll to me,
To me, when her whole image was defaced
By your own surfeit, horribly distorted,
Stripped of her spell by your satiety,
Her features meaningless, her living hair
Dead where it hung—threw me an empty mask,
Reducing sweet and enigmatic charm
To nothing with abominable art.
For this, at last, I hated you as much
As my forebodings always hated you,

Und wich dir aus.

    Dann trieb mich mein Geschick,
Das endlich mich Zerbrochnen segnete
Mit einem Ziel und Willen in der Brust—
Die nicht in deiner giftgen Nähe ganz
Für alle Triebe abgestorben war—
Ja, für ein Hohes trieb mich mein Geschick
In dieser Mörderklinge herben Tod,
Der mich in einen Strassengraben warf,
Darin ich liegend langsam moderte
Um Dinge, die du nicht begreifen kannst,
Und dreimal selig dennoch gegen dich,
Der keinem etwas war und keiner ihm.

     Er geht ab.

CLAUDIO

Wohl keinem etwas, keiner etwas mir.

   Sich langsam aufrichtend

Wie auf der Bühn ein schlechter Komödiant—
Aufs Stichwort kommt er, redt sein Teil und geht,
Gleichgültig gegen alles andre, stumpf,
Vom Klang der eignen Stimme ungerührt
Und hohlen Tones andre rührend nicht:
So über diese Lebensbühne hin
Bin ich gegangen ohne Kraft und Wert.
Warum geschah mir das? Warum, du Tod,
Musst du mich lehren erst das Leben sehen,
Nicht wie durch einen Schleier, wach und ganz,
Da etwas weckend, so vorübergehen?
Warum bemächtigt sich des Kindersinns
So hohe Ahnung von den Lebensdingen,

And shunned you.
>   But my fate, which even then
Blessed me, the broken-down, with adamant will,
With resolution and a conscious end—
Even your poisonous proximity
Had not quite killed all passion, every urge—
My fate, I say, in a high cause impelled me
To meet this murderous blade and virile death;
But, cast into a ditch and lying there,
Rotting away, still I had time to think
Of things that you will never understand,
Still thrice as blessed, as fortunate as you,
The utterly unloving and unloved.

>   *Exit.*

CLAUDIO

Indeed unloving and indeed unloved.

>   *Slowly drawing himself up*

As on the stage a bad comedian passes—
He enters on his cue, recites his part
And, deaf to all that's not himself, walks off,
Not even moved by hearing his own voice,
Nor, ringing hollow, able to move others—
So, too, across this larger stage of life
I passed, without conviction, strength or worth.
Why was this done to me? Why, tell me, Death,
Did I need *you* to teach me to see life
Not only through a veil, but clear and whole,
And, rousing up so much, must you move on?
Why is the childish mind so richly blessed
With high presentiment of earthly things,

Dass dann die Dinge, wenn sie wirklich sind,
Nur schale Schauer des Erinnerns bringen?
Warum erklingt uns nicht dein Geigenspiel,
Aufwühlend die verborgne Geisterwelt,
Die unser Busen heimlich hält,
Verschüttet, dem Bewusstsein so verschwiegen,
Wie Blumen im Geröll verschüttet liegen?
Könnt ich mit dir sein, wo man dich nur hört,
Nicht von verworrner Kleinlichkeit verstört!
Ich kanns! Gewähre, was du mir gedroht:
Da tot mein Leben war, sei du mein Leben, Tod!
Was zwingt mich, der ich beides nicht erkenne,
Dass ich dich Tod und jenes Leben nenne?
In eine Stunde kannst du Leben pressen,
Mehr als das ganze Leben konnte halten,
Das schattenhafte will ich ganz vergessen
Und weih mich deinen Wundern und Gewalten.

Er besinnt sich einen Augenblick.

Kann sein, dies ist nur sterbendes Besinnen,
Heraufgespült vom tödlich wachen Blut,
Doch hab ich nie mit allen Lebenssinnen
So viel ergriffen, und so nenn ichs gut!
Wenn ich jetzt ausgelöscht hinsterben soll,
Mein Hirn von dieser Stunde also voll,
Dann schwinde alles blasse Leben hin:
Erst, da ich sterbe, spür ich, dass ich bin.
Wenn einer träumt, so kann ein Übermass
Geträumten Fühlens ihn erwachen machen,
So wach ich jetzt, im Fühlensübermass,
Vom Lebenstraum wohl auf im Todeswachen.

Er sinkt tot zu den Füssen des Todes nieder.

Death and the Fool

Why do those very things, once realized,
Grant only faint, remembered whisperings?
Why does your violin not sound its tune
And so stir up the hidden world of spirits
Which secretly the heart inherits,
But buries it so far from consciousness,
As flowers are buried under sliding stone?
If I could stay where you alone are heard,
Untroubled by the vain and trivial word!
I can! Now grant me that with which you threatened:
Since all my life was dead, Death, be my life!
Admitting neither, I can save my breath:
Need not call past things life, nor call you Death.
Into one hour you can compress more life
Than once the whole of life had space to hold.
All that is dim and vague I shall forget,
Into your powers and miracles enrolled.

He reflects for a moment.

All this, it may be, is mere dying thought
Raised by the throbbing blood so nearly spent,
Yet never have my living senses caught
And grasped so much; therefore I am content.
If now, extinguished, I must pass away,
My brain replete with this last ecstasy,
This poor and faded life will not be missed:
Dying, at last I feel that I exist.
When a man sleeps, often his dream will break
With too much dreamed emotion, dream's excess;
So from the dream of life I now may wake,
Cloyed with emotion, to death's wakefulness.

He falls dead at Death's feet.

[135]

Hugo von Hofmannsthal

DER TOD

indem er kopfschüttelnd langsam abgeht

Wie wundervoll sind diese Wesen,
Die, was nicht deutbar, dennoch deuten,
Was nie geschrieben wurde, lesen,
Verworrenes beherrschend binden
Und Wege noch im Ewig-Dunkeln finden.

Er verschwindet in der Mitteltür, seine Worte verklingen.

*Im Zimmer bleibt es still. Draussen sieht man durchs Fenster
den Tod geigenspielend vorübergehen, hinter ihm die Mutter,
auch das Mädchen, dicht bei ihnen eine Claudio gleichende
Gestalt.*

Death and the Fool

DEATH

as he slowly leaves the stage, shaking his head

Strange are these creatures, strange indeed,
Who what's unfathomable, fathom,
What never yet was written, read,
Knit and command the tangled mystery
And in the eternal dark yet find a way.

Exit by the middle door; his words fade away.

The room remains silent. Outside, through the window, we see Death pass by, playing his violin; behind him the Mother, also the Girl and, close to them, a figure resembling Claudio.

THE EMPEROR AND THE WITCH

Translated by

CHRISTOPHER MIDDLETON

Der Kaiser und die Hexe

DER KAISER PORPHYROGENITUS

DIE HEXE

TARQUINIUS, *ein Kämmerer*

EIN VERURTEILTER

EIN ARMER MENSCH

EIN URALTER BLINDER

Der oberste Kämmerer, der Grossfalkonier, der Präfekt des Hauses und andere Hofleute. Ein Hauptmann. Soldaten.

Eine Lichtung inmitten der kaiserlichen Jagdwälder. Links eine Quelle. Rechts dichter Wald, ein Abhang, eine Höhle, deren Eingang Schlingpflanzen verhängen. Im Hintergrund das goldene Gitter des Fasanengeheges, dahinter ein Durchschlag, der hügelan führt.

DER KAISER

tritt auf, einen grünen, goldgestickten Mantel um, den Jagdspiess in der Hand, den goldenen Reif im Haar

Wohl, ich jage! ja, ich jage!
Dort der Eber, aufgewühlt
Schaukelt noch das Unterholz,
Hier der Speer! und hier der Jäger!

The Emperor and the Witch

THE EMPEROR PORPHYROGENITUS

THE WITCH

TARQUINIUS, *a chamberlain*

A CONDEMNED MAN

A POOR MAN

AN OLD BLIND MAN

The Lord Chamberlain, the Grand Falconer, the Chief Almoner, and other members of the Court. A Captain. Soldiers.

A clearing in the middle of the Imperial forests. Left, a spring. Right, thick woodland, a slope, a cave with its entrance overhung with creepers. In the background, the golden trellis of the pheasant covert, behind it a pathway leading uphill.

EMPEROR

enters, a green gold-embroidered cloak around him, his hunting spear in his hand, the gold circlet crown in his hair

The hunt is up! And I the huntsman!
There the wild boar, roused and raging,
Shakes the bushy undergrowth.
Here the spear, and here the huntsman!

[141]

Hugo von Hofmannsthal

Er schaudert, lässt den Speer fallen.

Nein, ich bin das Wild, mich jagt es,
Hunde sind in meinem Rücken,
Ihre Zähne mir im Fleisch,
Mir im Hirn sind ihre Zähne.

Greift sich an den Kopf

Hier ist einer, innen einer,
Unaufhörlich, eine Wunde,
Wund vom immer gleichen Bild
Ihrer offnen weissen Arme . . .
Und daneben, hart daneben,
Das Gefühl von ihrem Lachen,
Nicht der Klang, nur das Gefühl
Wie ein lautlos warmes Rieseln . . .
Blut? . . . Mein Blut ist voll von ihr!
Alles: Hirn, Herz, Augen, Ohren!
In der Luft, an allen Bäumen
Klebt ihr Glanz, ich muss ihn atmen.
Ich will los! Die Ohren hab ich
Angefüllt mit Lärm der Hunde,
Meine Augen bohr ich fest
In das Wild, ich will nichts spüren
Als das Keuchen, als das Flüchten
Dieser Rehe, dieser Vögel,
Und ein totenhafter Schlaf
Soll mir nachts mit Blei versiegeln
Diese Welt . . . doch innen, innen
Ist die Tür, die nichts verriegelt!
Keine Nacht mehr! Diese Nächte
Brechen, was die Tage schwuren.

Er rüttelt sich an der Brust.

The Emperor and the Witch

He shudders, and lets his spear fall.

No, I am the prey myself,
At my back the hounds pursue,
In my flesh their teeth are buried,
And their teeth tear at my brain.

With both hands to his head

Here is one, here's one within me,
Unremittingly, a wound
Cut by the same ceaseless image
Of her white extended arms . . .
And beside it, close beside it,
Is the feeling of her laughter,
Not its sound, the feeling only,
Like a warm and soundless flowing . . .
Blood? My blood is filled with her!
All of me: brain, heart, eyes, ears!
In the air, to all the trees
Her radiance clings and I must breathe it.
To be free from her! My ears
I have filled with these hound voices,
Drilled the quarry with my eyes,
And I desire to feel no more
Than the panting, than the running
Of these deer, this flight of birds,
And each night may sleep, like death,
Affix a leaden seal between
The world and me. But O, within me
Is the door no power can close!
No more night! These nights betray
The secrets that the days have sworn!

He tears at his breast.

[143]

Steh! es wird ja keine kommen,
Sieben sind hinab, vorbei . . .
Sieben? Jetzt, nur jetzt nichts denken!
Alles schwindelnd, alles schwach,
Jagen und nur immer jagen,
Nur bis diese Sonne sank,
Diesen Taumel noch ertragen!
Trinken hier, doch nicht besinnen.

DIE HEXE

*jung und schön, in einem durchsichtigen Gewand, mit
offenem Haar, steht hinter ihm*

Nicht besinnen? nicht auf mich?
Nicht auf uns? nicht auf die Nächte?
Auf die Lippen nicht? die Arme?
Auf mein Lachen, auf mein Haar?
Nicht besinnen auf was war?
Und auf was, einmal verloren,
Keine Reue wiederbringt . . . ?

DER KAISER

Heute, heute ist ein Ende!
Ich will dirs entgegenschrein:
Sieben Jahre war ich dein,
War ein Kind, als es begann,
End es nun, da ich ein Mann!
Wusstest du nie, dass ichs wusste,
Welches Mittel mir gegeben,
Abzureissen meinem Leben
Die Umklammrung deiner Arme
Sichrer als mit einem Messer?

[144]

The Emperor and the Witch

Stop! No more are left to follow,
Seven have fallen, passed away . . .
Seven? Now only think of nothing!
All things reel and waver round me;
Hunt, and think of hunting only,
Only till this sun has set,
Bear till then this giddiness!
Drink you may, but not remember.

THE WITCH

*young and beautiful in a transparent cloak, with unbound
hair, stands behind him*

Not remember, even me?
Not ourselves? And not the nights?
Not the lips, and not the arms?
Not my laughter, not my hair?
Not remember all that was,
Not remember what, once lost,
No repentance can recover?

EMPEROR

Today the end has come, today!
And I shall cry it in your teeth:
Yours for seven years I was,
Was a child, when it began,
And now I end it, grown to man!
Did you ever think my life
Could not be cut from your embrace
By means I all along possessed
More finally than with a knife?

[145]

Hugo von Hofmannsthal

Verwirrt

Sieh mich nicht so an . . . ich weiss nicht,
Du und ich . . . wie kommt das her?
Alles dreht sich, alles leer!

Sich ermannend

Wusstest du nie, dass ichs wusste?
Immerhin . . . ich will nicht denken,
Welch verschlungnen Weg dies ging,
Fürchterlich wie alles andre . . .
Ich steh hier! dies ist das Innre
Eines Labyrinths, gleichviel
Wo ich kam, ich weiss den Weg,
Der hinaus ins Freie! Freie! . . .

Er stockt einen Moment unter ihrem Blick, dann plötzlich
sehr laut

Sieben Tage, wenn ich dich
Nicht berührt! Dies ist der letzte!
Diese Sonne dort im Wipfel,
Nur so wenig muss sie fallen,
Nur vom Wipfel bis zum Boden,
Und hinab in ihren Abgrund
Reisst sie dich, und ich bleib hier!
Sieben Tag und sieben Nächte
Hab ich deinen Leib nicht anders
Als im Traum berührt—der Traum
Und der Wahnsinn wacher Träume
Steht nicht in dem Pakt!—mit Händen
Und mit Lippen nicht den Leib,
Nicht die Spitzen deiner Haare

The Emperor and the Witch

Confused

Do not look upon me so . . .
I cannot tell . . . and you and I . . .
What is this? All things are turning,
Turning empty, round and round.

Mastering himself

Did you never think I knew?
Yet now I have no will to think
Of the bewildering way I took,
As terrible as all things else . . .
Here I stand! This is the centre
Of a labyrinth, no matter
How I came here, now I know
Which way shall lead to freedom, freedom!

He falters a moment as her eyes rest on him, then, suddenly,
very loud

Seven days, in which I have not
Touched you once, this is the last!
Look, the sun, up in the treetop,
Has to descend a little distance
From the treetop to the ground,
But once it sets, then it will drag you
Into its abyss, and I,
I shall still be standing here.
Seven days and seven nights
I have touched your body only
In my dreams—and neither dreams
Nor madness of my waking dreams
Come within the pact! My hands,
And my lips, they have not touched
Your body, have not touched your hair

Hugo von Hofmannsthal

Hab ich angerührt in sieben
Tag . . . und Nächten . . . Traum ist nichts! . . .
Wenn die Sonne sinkt, zerfällst du:
Kröte! Asche! Diese Augen
Werden Schlamm, Staub wird dein Haar,
Und ich bleibe, der ich war.

DIE HEXE *sanft*

Ist mein Haar dir so verhasst,
Hast doch in das End davon
Mit den Lippen einen Knoten
Dreingeknüpft, wenn wir dort lagen,
Mund auf Mund und Leib auf Leib,
Und ein Atemholen beide
Hob und senkte, und der Wind
Über uns im Dunkel wühlte
In den Bäumen.

DER KAISER

Enden, enden
Will ich dieses Teufelsblendwerk!

DIE HEXE

Wenn du aufwachst in der Nacht
Und vor dir das grosse schwere
Dunkel ist, der tiefe Schacht,
Den kein Schrei durchläuft, aus dem
Keine Sehnsucht mich emporzieht,
Wenn du deine leeren Hände
Hinhältst, dass ich aus der Luft
Niederflieg an deine Brust,
Wenn du deine Hände bebend
Hinhältst, meine beiden Füsse
Aufzufangen, meine nackten

[148]

The Emperor and the Witch

For seven days and seven nights . . .
And my dreams—they are as nothing.
Come the sunset, you shall vanish:
Reptile! Ashes! These your eyes
Will turn to mud, to dust your hair,
And I remain, just as before.

WITCH *softly*

You may say you hate my hair,
Yet your lips once tied a knot
In the tips of it, we lay
Mouth to mouth, body to body,
And we shared one breath between us,
Rising, falling, overhead
The wind into the darkness burrowed,
In the trees.

EMPEROR

    And now it ends,
Ends, this devilish delusion!

WITCH

If you wake up in the night
And before you find the huge
And heavy darkness, its deep shaft
Which no cry can penetrate,
No longing can invoke me from,
If you hold out empty hands,
Hoping that I may descend
Out of the air and fly to you,
If you hold your hands out, trembling,
Hope to catch my naked feet,

Füsse, schimmernder und weicher
Als der Hermelin, und nichts
Schwingt sich aus der Luft hernieder,
Und die beiden Hände beben
Leer und frierend? Nicht die goldne
Weltenkugel deines Reiches
Kann sie füllen, nicht die Welt
Füllt den Raum, den meine beiden
Nackten Füsse schimmernd füllten!

DER KAISER

Welch ein Ding ist diese Welt!
Sterne, Länder, Menschen, Bäume:
Ein Blutstropfen schwemmt es fort!

DIE HEXE

Jeden Vorhang hebst du auf,
Windest dich in den Gebüschen,
Streckst die Arme in die Luft,
Und ich komme nie mehr! Stunden
Schleppen hin! die Tage leer,
Leer die Nächte! und den Dingen
Ihre Flamme ausgerissen,
Jede Zeit und jeder Ort
Tot, das Glühen alles fort . . .

DER KAISER
die Hand vor den Augen

Muss ich denn allein hier stehen!
Gottes Tod! ich bin der Kaiser,
Meine Kämmrer will ich haben,
Meine Wachen! Menschen, Menschen!

The Emperor and the Witch

Feet more shimmering and softer
Than the ermine, but then nothing
Hovers downward from the air,
And your hands begin to tremble,
Empty, freezing? Not your empire's
Very orb can make them full,
Not the very world itself
Can fill the space that my two naked
Shimmering feet before had filled!

EMPEROR

What a thing it is, the world!
Stars and lands and men and trees,
A drop of blood sweeps all away!

WITCH

Every curtain you may raise,
Squeeze your way among the bushes,
Stretch your arms into the air—
I shall not return! The hours
Drag on slowly; empty days,
And nights all empty; and the flame
Is torn clean from the heart of things,
Every time and every place
Dead, the glow of living gone . . .

EMPEROR

shading his eyes with his hand

Well and good, I stand alone!
God's death! I am Emperor,
Call my chamberlains, my court,
Guards! Let human beings come!

[151]

Hugo von Hofmannsthal

DIE HEXE

Brauchst die Wachen, dich zu schützen,
Armer Kaiser, vor dir selber?
Droh ich dir, rühr ich dich an?
Nein, ich gehe, und wer will,
Kommt mir nach und wird mich finden.
Armer Kaiser!

Sie biegt die Büsche auseinander und verschwindet.

DER KAISER

Nicht dies Lachen!
Einmal hat sie so gelacht . . .
Was dann kam, ich wills nicht denken!
Hexe, Hexe, Teufelsbuhle,
Sehn! Ich will dich sehn, ich will nicht
Stehn wie damals vor dem Vorhang.
Gottes Tod, ich wills nicht denken!
Faune, ekelhafte Faune
Küssen sie! die weissen Hände
Toter, aus dem Grab gelockter
Heiden sind auf ihr, des Paris
Arme halten sie umwunden:
Ich ertrag es nicht, ich reisse
Sie hinweg!

TARQUINIUS

aus dem Hintergrunde rechts auftretend

Mein hoher Herr!

DER KAISER

Was? und was? wer schickt dich her?

The Emperor and the Witch

WITCH

Do you need your guards to save you
From your self, poor Emperor?
Do I threaten, do I touch you?
No, I leave you, and who will
May follow after me and find me,
My poor Emperor!

She parts the bushes and vanishes.

EMPEROR

That laughter!
Once she laughed that selfsame way!
What ensued, I dare not think it.
Witch, a witch, a devil's bawd—
Look! I want to see you, stand
No longer as before a curtain.
God's death! But I dare not think it!
Fauns, disgusting filthy fauns
Kiss her! Dead men's pallid hands
And hands of heathens she's enchanted
From the grave are on her, arms
Of Paris now embrace her, hold her:
It's too much to bear, I'll force her
Free from them!

TARQUINIUS

entering from upstage, right

Your Majesty!

EMPEROR

What is it? Who sent you here?

Hugo von Hofmannsthal

TARQUINIUS

Herr, es war, als ob du riefest
Nach den Kämmrern, dem Gefolge.

DER KAISER *nach einer langen Stille*

Rief ich und du hörtest, gut.

Er hört ins Gebüsch.

Hier ist alles still, nicht wahr?

TARQUINIUS

Herr, die Jagd zog dort hinunter,
Jenseits des Fasangeheges.

DER KAISER

Lass die Jagd! Du hörst hier nichts?
Nichts von Flüstern, nichts von Lachen?
Wie? *In Gedanken verloren, plötzlich*
Abblasen lass die Jagd!
Ich will meinen Hof um mich:
Meine Frau, die Kaiserin,
Soll hierher, mein Kind soll her,
Um mich her mein ganzer Hof,
Ringsum sollen Wachen stehen,
Und so will ich liegen, liegen,
Auf den Knien die heilige Fahne.
Zugedeckt, so will ich warten,
Bis die Sonne . . . wohin gehst du?

TARQUINIUS

Herr, zu tun, was du befahlst,
Deinen Hof hierher zu rufen.

DER KAISER *halblaut*

Wenn sie kommt vor meinen Hof,

[154]

The Emperor and the Witch

TARQUINIUS

Sire, I thought I heard you calling
For your chamberlains and court.

EMPEROR *after a long pause*

I called you, and you heard me. Good.

He listens towards the undergrowth.

Not a sound, not one, you'd say?

TARQUINIUS

Sire, the hunt has ridden further,
Past the pheasant covert there.

EMPEROR

Forget the hunt! Can you hear nothing,
Not a whisper? No one laughing?
Can you?
       Lost in thought, suddenly
    Call the huntsmen back!
I want my court around me now:
My wife as well, the Empress, let her
Come to me, and bring my child,
Gather round me all my court,
Place my guards to watch around me,
Thus I want to lie, to lie,
The holy banner on my knees.
Blanketed, thus I shall wait
Until the sun . . . Where are you going?

TARQUINIUS

Sire, to do what you command,
To tell your court to gather here.

EMPEROR *half aloud*

If the court's here when she comes

[155]

Sich zu mir hinschleicht und flüstert
Und die Scham hält mich, ich muss
Ihren Atem fühlen, dann
Wird es stärker sein als ich!
Bleib bei mir, es kommen andre.
Du bleib da. Ich will mit dir
Reden, bis die andern kommen.

*Er geht auf und ab, bleibt schliesslich dicht vor dem
Kämmerer stehen.*

Bist der jüngste von den Kämmrern?

TARQUINIUS *auf ein Knie gesunken*

Nicht zu jung, für dich zu sterben,
Wenn mein Blut dir dienen kann!

DER KAISER

Heisst?

TARQUINIUS

Tarquinius Morandin.

DER KAISER *streng*

Niemands Blut kann niemand dienen,
Es sei denn sein eignes.

TARQUINIUS
Herr,
Zürn mir nicht, die Lippen brennen,
Einmal dirs herauszusagen.

DER KAISER
Was?

Creeping to me, whispering,
And my shame controls me, I must
Feel her breath, then it will be
Far stronger than I am myself.
Soon others will be here, you stay,
Stay here beside me. I would like
To talk with you until they come.

He walks up and down, finally stopping in front of the Chamberlain.

Are you the youngest chamberlain?

TARQUINIUS *on one knee*

Not too young to die for you,
If my blood can do you service!

EMPEROR

Name?

TARQUINIUS

Tarquinius Morandin.

EMPEROR *severely*

No man's blood can serve another;
That alone his own can do.

TARQUINIUS

Sire, do not be angry with me.
My lips burn to speak one thing.

EMPEROR

What is that?

[157]

Hugo von Hofmannsthal

TARQUINIUS
steht verwirrt.

DER KAISER *gütig*

Nun was?

TARQUINIUS
Gnädiger Herr,
Dass ich fühle, wie du gut bist,
So mit Hoheit und mit Güte,
Wie ein Stern mit Licht beladen.

DER KAISER
Kämmerer, du bist ein Kind . . .
Wenn du nicht ein Schmeichler bist!
Junge Menschen sind nicht gut,
Und ob älter auch wie du,
Bin ich jung. Nimm dich in acht;
Ich weiss nichts von dir, weiss nicht,
Wie du lebst, nur Seele seh ich,
Die sich so aus deinen Augen
Lehnt, wie aus dem Kerkerfenster
Ein Gefangner nach der Sonne;
Nimm du dich in acht, das Leben
Hat die rätselhafte Kraft,
Irgendwie von einem Punkt aus
Diesen ganzen Glanz der Jugend
Zu zerstören, blinden Rost
Auszustreun auf diesen Spiegel
Gottes . . . wie das alles kommt?

Halb für sich

Anfangs ists in einem Punkt,

The Emperor and the Witch

TARQUINIUS
stands confused.

EMPEROR *kindly*
Well? Won't you tell me?

TARQUINIUS
Majesty, my lord and master:
That I feel how good you are,
Rich with majesty and goodness
As a star is rich with light.

EMPEROR
Chamberlain, you are a child . . .
Unless you are a flatterer!
Young men are not good at all,
Older no doubt I am than you,
But still young. You must watch yourself;
I know nothing of you, know not
How you live, but see alone
How the soul leans from your eyes
As a prisoner seeks the sun
From the window of his dungeon;
You must watch yourself; for life
Possesses the mysterious power
Somehow from any given point
To take youth's radiance entire
And to annihilate it, scatter
Opaque rust upon this mirror
That is God's . . . How can this be?

Half to himself

First it happens at one point,

[159]

Doch dann schiebt sichs wie ein Schleier
Zwischen Herz und Aug und Welt,
Und das Dasein ist vergällt;
Bist du aussen nicht wie innen,
Zwingst dich nicht, dir treu zu sein,
So kommt Gift in deine Sinnen,
Atmests aus und atmests ein,
Und von dem dir gleichen Leben
Bist du wie vom Grab umgeben,
Kannst den Klang der Wahrheit hören,
So wie Hornruf von weither,
Doch erwidern nimmermehr;
Was du sprichst, kann nur betören,
Was du siehst, ist Schattenspiel,
Magst dich stellen, wie du willst,
Findest an der Welt nicht viel,
Wandelst lebend als dein Grab,
Hexen deine Buhlerinnen . . .
Kehr dich nicht an meine Reden,
Wohl! wenn du sie nicht verstehst.
Denk nur eins: ich will dir Gutes!
Nimms, als käm es dir von einem,
Den du sterbend wo am Wege
Liegen findest; nimms an dich,
Drücks an dich wie eine Lampe,
Wenn dich Finsternis umschlägt;
Merk dir: jeder Schritt im Leben
Ist ein tiefrer. Worte! Worte!
Merk dir nichts als dies, Tarquinius:
Wer nicht wahr ist, wirft sich weg!

The Emperor and the Witch

But then it penetrates, a veil
Dividing heart and eye and world,
And then existence turns to gall;
If you are not outwardly
The same as inwardly you are,
If you do not have the power
To be to your own being true,
Then poison sure will enter you,
Enter your senses and the breath
You breathe inhaling and exhaling,
And by a life that's like yourself,
A very grave, you are encircled;
Hear perhaps the sound of truth
Like a horn blast blown from far,
But you can answer nevermore;
All you say can but deceive,
All you see is shadow-play,
Face whichever way you choose,
The world will seem of small account,
And you will walk, a living grave,
With witches come to take your love . . .
Pay no attention to my words;
Best if you do not understand them.
Think only this: I wish you well!
Take it as if it came from one
Whom you found lying on the road
And near to death; and take it to you,
Press it to you like a lantern
When the darkness falls around you;
And remark: each step in life
Goes deeper, deeper. Words, O words!
Think only this, Tarquinius:
The untrue man discards himself!

Hugo von Hofmannsthal

. . . Doch vielleicht begreifst du dies
Erst, wenn es zu spät ist; merk
Dies allein: nicht eine einzige
Stunde kommt zweimal im Leben,
Nicht ein Wort, nicht eines Blickes
Ungreifbares Nichts ist je
Ungeschehn zu machen, was
Du getan hast, musst du tragen,
So das Lächeln wie den Mord!

Nach einer kleinen Pause

Und wenn du ein Wesen liebhast,
Sag nie mehr, bei deiner Seele!
Als du spürst. Bei deiner Seele!
Tu nicht eines Halms Gewicht
Mit verstelltem Mund hinzu:
Dies ist solch ein Punkt, wo Rost
Ansetzt und dann weiterfrisst.
Dort am Durchschlag hör ich Stimmen:
Jäger sind es wohl, die kommen,
Aber hier ist alles still . . .
Oder nicht? . . . Nun geh nur, geh,
Tu, wie ich dir früher sagte.

TARQUINIUS

Hierher ruf ich das Gefolge.

DER KAISER

Ja! was noch?

TARQUINIUS

Du hast befohlen.

Geht.

[162]

The Emperor and the Witch

. . . Yet you may come to understand
Only when it's too late; remark
This thing alone: no single hour
Comes twice in life, no single word,
No single insignificant
Intangible glance can be undone,
What you have done, that you must bear,
It may be murder, or a smile.

After a short pause

And if you love another being,
Never, by your soul, allow
Your words to overtake your feelings.
By your soul! Nor let your mouth
Speak credulous hypocrisy:
There is the point where rust intrudes,
Begins to gnaw, and does not stop.
From that pathway I hear voices:
Huntsmen, they are coming nearer.
But here everything is quiet;
Or is it quiet? Go now, go,
And do what I have told you to.

TARQUINIUS

I'll tell them to come to you.

EMPEROR

Yes! What else?

TARQUINIUS
Those were your orders.

Exit.

[163]

Hugo von Hofmannsthal

DER KAISER

Irgendwo ist Klang der Wahrheit
Wie ein Hörnerruf von weitem,
Doch ich hab ihn nicht in mir;
Ja, im Mund wird mir zur Lüge,
Was noch wahr schien in Gedanken.
Schmach und Tod für meine Seele,
Dass sie in der Welt liegt wie ein
Basilisk, mit hundert Augen,
Die sich drehen, nach den Dingen
Äugend! dass ich Menschenschicksal
So gelassen ansehn kann
Wie das Steigen und Zerstäuben
Der Springbrunnen! dass ich meine
Eigne Stimme immer höre,
Fremd und deutlich wie das Schreien
Ferner Möwen! Tod! mein Blut
Ist verzaubert! Niemand, niemand
Kann mir helfen, und doch bin ich
Stark, mein Geist ist nicht gemein,
Neugeboren trug ich Purpur,
Diesen Reif, bevor die Schale
Meines Kopfs gehärtet war . . .

Er reisst sich den Reif vom Kopf.

Und er schliesst das Weltall ein:
Diese ganze Welt voll Hoheit
Und Verzweiflung, voll von Gräbern
Und von Äckern, Bergen, Meeren,
Alles schliesst er ein . . . was heisst das?
Was ist mir dies alles? welche
Kraft hab ich, die Welt zu tragen?
Bin ich mir nicht Last genug!

The Emperor and the Witch

Surely the sound of truth is somewhere,
Like a horn blast blown from far,
Yet in myself I cannot hear it;
In my mouth what even seemed
So true in thought is turned to falsehood.
Death and perdition seize my soul
That lounges like a basilisk
Within the world and with a hundred
Swivelling eyes seeks all things out,
Seize it for watching destinies
Of men with no less nonchalance
Than one might watch a fountain rise
And then disintegrate! For hearing
Always my own voice as if it
Were as alien and clear as
Far gulls' crying! There's a spell
Works in my blood! And no one, no one
Can assist me; yet I'm strong,
My spirit knew no common birth,
A new-born babe I wore this purple,
And I wore this crown before
The cupped bones of my skull had settled.

He tears off his crown.

And it contains the universe:
This whole world that's full of doubt
And majesty, is full of graves,
Full of ploughland, mountains, seas,
For all things it contains . . . The meaning?
What does all this mean to me?
What strength have I to bear the world,
Who to myself am such a burden?

Hugo von Hofmannsthal

Er zerbricht den Reif, wirft die Stücke zu Boden und atmet
wild.

DIE STIMME DER HEXE
aus dem Gebüsch.

DER KAISER
horcht vorgebückt.

DIE STIMME

Komm, umschling mich mit den Armen,
Wie du mich so oft umschlungen!
Fühlst du nicht, wie meine Schläfen
Klopfen, fühlst dus mit den Lippen?

DER KAISER
sich zurückwerfend, mit emporgestreckten Armen

Redet sie zu mir? zu einem
Andern? ich ertrag es nicht!
Hat sie alles noch mit andern,
Wie mit mir? Dies ist so furchtbar,
Dass es mich zum Wahnsinn treibt . . .
Alles ist ein Knäul, Umarmung
Und Verwesung einerlei,
Lallen von verliebten Lippen
Wie das Rascheln dürrer Blätter,
Alles könnte sein, auch nicht . . .

Die Arme sinken ihm herunter, seine Augen sind starr zu
Boden gerichtet. Er rafft sich auf und schreit

Menschen, Menschen, ich will Menschen!

DIE DREI SOLDATEN
mit dem Verurteilten treten von rückwärts auf. Der Kaiser
läuft auf sie zu.

The Emperor and the Witch

He breaks the crown, throws the pieces to the ground, and pants wildly.

THE WITCH'S VOICE
from the undergrowth.

EMPEROR
leans forward, listening.

VOICE

Come, and with your arms embrace me
As you have embraced me often!
Can't you feel, feel with your lips,
The pulses beating in my temples?

EMPEROR
throws himself back with arms raised high

Is it to me she's speaking? Or
Is it another? I can't bear it!
Is she the same when she's with others
As with me? O terrifying
Thought that lures me into madness!
All things in a knot, embrace
And rottenness are all the same,
The murmur from loved lips the same
As sifting sounds the dry leaves make;
All this could be, or could not be . . .

*His arms drop, his eyes are fixed rigidly on the ground. Then
he straightens himself and shouts*

I want human, human kind!

THE THREE SOLDIERS
*advance from upstage with the Condemned Man. The Em-
peror runs towards them.*

[167]

Hugo von Hofmannsthal

DER KAISER

Ihr seht aus wie Menschen. Hierher
Tretet! hier!

EIN SOLDAT
Was will der Mensch?

ZWEITER

Still, das ist ein Herr vom Hof!
Tu, was er uns heisst.

DER KAISER

Diesen hier macht frei! die Ketten
Sind für mich! in mir ist einer,
Der will dort hinein, er darf nicht
Stärker werden! gebt die Ketten!

Allmählich beruhigter

Zwar mich dünkt, nun ist es still . . .
Und die Sonne steht schon tief! . . .
. . . Welch ein Mensch ist dies, wohin
Führt ihr ihn?

ERSTER
Zu seinem Tod.

DER KAISER

Warum muss er sterben?

DER SOLDAT
Herr,
Lydus ist es.

DER KAISER
Lydus?

[168]

The Emperor and the Witch

EMPEROR

You seem to be human: here!
Come here!

FIRST SOLDIER

What can he want with us?

SECOND SOLDIER

Quietly! He's from the court!
Do what he says.

EMPEROR

Set this man here free. The chains
Are rightly mine! There's someone in me
Wants to go in *there,* he must
Be chained before he grows much stronger!

Gradually becoming more composed

Truly things are now more still . . .
And the sun is low already . . .
Who is this man? And, tell me, where
Have you to take him?

FIRST SOLDIER

To his death.

EMPEROR

Why does he have to die then?

FIRST SOLDIER
Sir,

This is Lydus.

EMPEROR
Lydus?

[169]

Hugo von Hofmannsthal

DER SOLDAT

Herr,
Wenig weisst du, was im Land,
Was sich im Gebirg ereignet,
Wenn du nichts von diesem weisst.
Dieser ist der Fürchterliche,
Der ein ganzes Land verbrannte,
Feuer warf in dreizehn Städte,
Sich Statthalter Gottes nannte
Und der Ungerechten Geissel,
Selbst ein ungerecht Begehren
Wie ein Rad von Blut und Feuer
Durch das Land des Friedens wälzend.

DER KAISER

Doch die Richter?

DER VERURTEILTE *den Blick am Boden*

Einen Richter,
Der das Recht bog, wollt ich hängen,
So fing alles an.

DER KAISER

Der Kaiser?
Der doch Richter aller Richter?

DER SOLDAT

Herr, der Kaiser, der ist weit.

Eine kleine Stille

DER HAUPTMANN
kommt gelaufen

Hier ist nicht der Weg. Wir müssen

[170]

The Emperor and the Witch

FIRST SOLDIER

Sir,
If you do not know this man
You can't know much of what goes on
Round hereabouts, and in these hills.
This is the man they're all afraid of,
For he fired whole tracts of land
And then burned thirteen cities down,
Called himself Viceroy of God
And the Scourge of the Unrighteous,
Yet his own unrighteousness
Rolled a wheel of fire and blood
Through all this quiet peaceful land.

EMPEROR

But his judges?

CONDEMNED MAN *looking down*

Once I tried
To hang a judge who twisted justice,
So it began.

EMPEROR

The Emperor?
The judge who stands above all judges?

FIRST SOLDIER

Sir, the Emperor's miles away.

Brief silence

THE CAPTAIN
comes running

You've taken the wrong path, be quick

[171]

Hugo von Hofmannsthal

Weg von hier. Des Kaisers Jagd
Kommt bald hier vorbei.

Erkennend

Der Kaiser!

Kniet nieder, sogleich auch die drei Soldaten.

DER KAISER
zum Verurteilten

Stehst du, Mensch? die andern knien.

DER VERURTEILTE *den Blick am Boden*

Diese Spiele sind vorüber;
Morgen knie ich vor dem Block.

DER KAISER

Mensch, bei Gott, wie fing dies an?
Wie der erste Schritt davon?

DER VERURTEILTE
hebt seinen Blick

Mensch, bei Gott, mit einem Unrecht.

DER KAISER

Das du tatest?

DER VERURTEILTE
immer die Augen auf ihn geheftet

Das ich litt!

DER KAISER

Und was weiter kam?

And leave this place. The Emperor's hunt
Will soon ride by.

Recognizing

The Emperor!

Kneels and the Three Soldiers follow suit.

EMPEROR
to the Condemned Man

Man: you stand? The rest are kneeling.

CONDEMNED MAN *looking down*

I have given up these games;
I'll kneel tomorrow at the block.

EMPEROR

Man, by God, how did it start?
And how begin, to come to this?

CONDEMNED MAN
raises his eyes

Man, by God, with an injustice.

EMPEROR

Which you committed?

CONDEMNED MAN
still gazes at him

Which I suffered!

EMPEROR

And what followed?

[173]

Hugo von Hofmannsthal

DER VERURTEILTE
Geschick.

DER KAISER
Und die Toten?

DER VERURTEILTE
Gut verstorben.

DER KAISER
Und was morgen kommt?

DER VERURTEILTE
Das Ende,
Das höchst nötige gerechte
Ende.

DER KAISER
Doch gerecht?

DER VERURTEILTE *ruhig*
Jetzt wohl.

DER KAISER
*geht auf und ab. Endlich nimmt er seinen Mantel ab, hängt
ihn dem Verurteilten um, winkt den Soldaten, aufzustehen.*

TARQUINIUS
zurückkommend, verneigt sich.

DER KAISER
Kämmrer, schliess dem Mann den Mantel
Und mach ihm die Hände frei!
Es geschieht.

[174]

CONDEMNED MAN
Was my fate.

EMPEROR
And the dead?

CONDEMNED MAN
Good riddance to them.

EMPEROR
And what of tomorrow?

CONDEMNED MAN
Finish,
The most just and necessary
Finish of it.

EMPEROR
Just?

CONDEMNED MAN *calmly*
Yes, now.

EMPEROR
*walks up and down. At length takes off his cloak, puts it on
the Condemned Man, and motions the Soldiers to stand.*

TARQUINIUS
returning, bows.

EMPEROR
Chamberlain, make sure this cloak
Is safely fastened. Free his hands.
This is done.

[175]

Hugo von Hofmannsthal

DER VERURTEILTE

blickt unverwandt, mit äusserster Aufmerksamkeit, beinahe mit Strenge den Kaiser an.

DER KAISER

Tarquinius zu sich, nach rechts vorne, heranwinkend

Die Galeeren nach Dalmatien,
Die Seeräuber jagen sollen,
Warten, weil ich keinen Führer
Noch genannt. Ich nenne diesen,
Diesen Lydus. Wer sich selber
Furchtbar treu war, der ist jenseits
Der gemeinen Anfechtungen.
Als ich in der Wiege lag,
Trug ich Purpur, um mich her
Stellten sie im Kreise Männer,
Und auf wen mit unbewusstem
Finger ich nach Kindesart
Lallend deutete, der war
Über Heere, über Flotten,
Über Länder zum Gebieter
Ausgewählt. Ein grosses Sinnbild!
Auf mein ungeheures Amt
Will ich Kaiser mich besinnen:
Meine Kammer ist die Welt,
Und die Tausende der Tausend
Sind im Kreis um mich gestellt,
Ihre Ämter zu empfangen.
Ämter! darin liegt noch mehr!
Kämmrer, führ den Admiral!
Lydus heisst er, Lydus, merk.
Sonst ist nichts vonnöten, geh.

The Emperor and the Witch

CONDEMNED MAN

looks steadily, with intense concentration, almost severely, at
the Emperor.

EMPEROR

motioning Tarquinius to come with him, moves forward, right

Those galleys ordered to Dalmatia
With intent to punish pirates
Are at anchor still. I have not
Found an admiral for them. But now,
Now I appoint this man, this Lydus.
For the man who to himself
Is true so terribly, must be
Beyond temptation's common reach.
When I was lying in the cradle,
I wore purple; round about me
Men were gathered in a circle,
And whomever I might point to
With unwitting childish finger,
Babbling, then that man became
Elect commander over armies,
Fleets, and regions. Great example!
I now recall as Emperor
The duties my dread office holds:
For my throne-room is the world,
Thousands upon thousands gather
Round me in a circle; each
Receives his office from my hands.
Offices! Far more is meant!
Lead my admiral, chamberlain!
Lydus, mark it, is his name.
No more is necessary: go.

Hugo von Hofmannsthal

*Sie gehen ab, noch im Weggehen heftet der Mann seinen
ernsten, beinahe strengen Blick auf den Kaiser.*

Doch . . . wie eitel ist dies alles,
Und wie leicht, daran zu zweifeln,
Wie so leicht, es wegzuwerfen!
Dieses Hauchen lauer Luft
Saugt mir schon die Seele aus!
Kommt nicht irgend etwas näher?
Schwebt es nicht von oben her
Unbegreiflich sanft und stark?
Meinem Blut wird heiss und bang . . .
Wie soll dies aus mir heraus?
Nur mit meinen Eingeweiden!
Denn ich bin darin verfangen
Wie der Fisch, der allzu gierig
Eine Angel tief verschlang.
Sklave! Hund! was steh ich hier?
Weiss, dass sie mich nehmen will,
Steh ihr selbst am Kreuzweg still!
Dies muss sein! Ich will mich selber
An den Haaren weiterschleppen
Bis zum Sinken dieser Sonne!
Jagen! Jagd ist alles! Schleichen
Auf den Zehen, mit dem Spiess
Eigne Kraft in eines fremden
Lebens Leib so wie der Blitz
Hineinschleudern . . . Eine Taube!
Wie sie an den Zweigen hinstreift,
Trunken wie ein Abendfalter,
Kreise zieht um meinen Kopf!
Wo der Spiess? Doch hier der Dolch!
Hier und so!

The Emperor and the Witch

*The others leave, and the Condemned Man's earnest, almost
severe gaze, rests, as he is leaving, on the Emperor.*

Yet . . . How empty such things are!
How easily one doubts them all,
How easily casts them aside!
My soul is even now sucked out
By this warm breath of evening air.
Is there something coming nearer?
Something hovering from the air,
Gentle, and strong, beyond belief?
My blood is hot, and much afraid . . .
How shall this emerge from me?
Only with my very body!
For I am imprisoned there,
Like a fish that all-too-greedy
Took and ate the angler's hook.
Slave! And dog! Why should I stand,
Knowing that she would possess me,
At this crossroads, motionless?
This must be! And I shall drag
Myself along by my own hair
Until the setting of this sun.
Hunt! The hunt is all! And creep
On tiptoe with the ready spear,
Hurl one's strength hard like a stroke
Of lightning deep into the flesh
Of other bodies . . . Look! A dove!
How it flutters in the branches,
Drunken like an evening moth,
Drawing circles round my head!
Where's my spear? No, take the dagger!
Here; and now!

Hugo von Hofmannsthal

Er wirft den Dolch nach der Taube. Die Hexe, angezogen wie ein Jägerbursch, taumelt hervor. Sie presst die Hände auf die Brust und sinkt am Rand eines Gebüsches rechts nieder.

DIE HEXE
O weh! getroffen!

DER KAISER
Trug und Taumel! wessen Stimme?
Vogel wars! Die Taube flog!

In der Nähe, aufschreiend

Was für Augen, welche Lippen!

Kriecht auf den Knien der Hingesunkenen näher.

DIE HEXE *sanft wie ein Kind*
Lieber, schlägst du mir mit Eisen
Rote Wunden, blutig rote
Neue Lippen? Dort wo deine
Lippen lagen oft und oft!
Weisst du alles das nicht mehr?
So ist alles aus? Leb wohl,
Aber deiner nächsten Freundin,
Wenn ich tot bin, sei getreuer,
Und bevor du gehst und mich
Hier am Boden sterben lässest,
Deck mir noch mit meinen Haaren
Meine Augen zu, mir schwindelt!

DER KAISER
hebt die Hände, sie zu berühren. In diesem Augenblick über-schüttet die dem Untergang nahe Sonne den ganzen Wald-rand mit Licht und den rötlichen Schatten der Bäume. Der

The Emperor and the Witch

*He throws his dagger at the dove. The Witch, dressed as a
young huntsman, tumbles from the undergrowth. She presses
her hands to her breast and sinks down by the edge of the
bushes, right.*

WITCH

Ah! I am hit!

EMPEROR

Ghouls and phantoms! What's that voice?
It was a bird! A dove flew out!

Nearer, he cries out

But what eyes, and O, what lips!

Crawls on his knees closer to the prone figure.

WITCH *gentle as a child*

Dearest, would you cut red wounds
With iron in me, lips all red
And bloody, there where your own lips
Have rested often, O so often?
Can this mean nothing to you now?
Can everything be past? Farewell,
But to your next sweetheart be,
When I am dead, O be more true;
And before you go and leave me
Dying here upon the ground,
Close my eyes and cover them
With my hair, for I am faint.

EMPEROR

*raises his hands to touch her. At this moment the setting sun
floods the whole forest edge with light; the trees cast reddish
shadows. The Emperor shudders, stands there, slowly walks*

[181]

Hugo von Hofmannsthal

Kaiser schaudert zurück, richtet sich auf, geht langsam, die
Augen auf ihr, von ihr weg; sie liegt wie tot.

Tot! was ist für diese Wesen
Tot? die Sonne ist nicht unten,
Dunkel flammt sie, scheint zu drohen.
Soll ich sie hier liegen sehen?
Sollen Ameisen und Spinnen
Über ihr Gesicht hinlaufen
Und ich sie nicht anrührn? ich,
Der mit zehnmal so viel Küssen
Ihren Leib bedeckt hab, als
Das Gewebe ihres Kleides
Fäden zählt, wie? soll ich sie
Liegen lassen, dass mein Hof,
Meine Diener ihr Gesicht
Mir betasten mit den Blicken?
Ich ertrüg es nicht, ich würfe
Mich auf sie, sie zuzudecken!
Dort! ein Mensch, der Stämme schleppt,
Abgeschälte schwere Stämme.
Hier ist eine schönre Last.

Er tritt in eine Lichtung und winkt.

Du, komm her! komm hierher! hier!
Zwar, womit den Menschen lohnen?
Auf den Gold- und Silberstücken
Ist mein Bild, doch hab ich keines!
Doch, der Reif, den ich zerbrach:
Wenn die Krone auch zerschlagen
Da und dort am Boden rollt,
Ist sie doch noch immer Gold.

Er bückt sich und hebt ein paar Stücke auf. Er betrachtet die
Stücke, die er in der Hand hält.

[182]

away from her, looking at her; she lies there as if dead.

Dead? Does dead mean anything
To such a creature? Still the sun
Has not gone down, flames darkly, seems
To threaten. Should I watch her lie there?
Should the ant and spider come
To scramble over her fair face
And I not touch her? Who have clothed
Her body with ten times more kisses
Than the threads that weave her dress?
What? And let her lie and let
My court, my servants, touch her face
With curious glances? No, I could not
Bear such things; upon her body
I would throw myself to hide her!
Over there! There's someone coming,
Dragging barked and heavy tree-trunks.
He has a lovelier load to bear.

He steps into a clearing and makes a sign.

You, come here! Come here! Come nearer!
Yet how can I pay this man?
My image, it is struck on gold
And silver pieces, yet I've none.
But no, where is the crown I broke?
Even if I broke my crown
And fragments of it rolled away,
Still those fragments are of gold.

*He stoops and picks up some fragments of the crown, holds
them in his hand, and looks at them.*

[183]

Wohl, solange du geformt warst,
Warst du viel. Dein blosses Blinken
Konnte ungeheure Heere
Lenken wie mit Zauberwinken.
Krone, brauchtest nur zu leuchten,
Nur zu funkeln, nur zu drohn . . .
Kaum die Dienste eines Knechtes
Zahlt dein Stoff, der Form entflohn.

Eine kleine Stille

Mitten drunter kann ich denken,
Ruhig denken, sonderbar.

DER ARME MENSCH
*in Lumpen, ein junges, entschlossenes Gesicht und eine un-
scheinbare, gebückte Haltung*

Herr, was riefst du, dass ich tun soll?

DER KAISER
steht vor der Leiche abgewandt

Diesen Toten . . .

DER MENSCH
Herr, ein Weib!

DER KAISER
Frag nicht, schaff sie fort!

DER MENSCH
Wohin?
Fort? Wohin?

DER KAISER
Gleichviel! ins Dickicht.
Wo sie keiner sieht, wo ich

[184]

The Emperor and the Witch

You were much, when you had form;
How strange. Your very glittering
Directed as with magic signs
Gigantic armies. O poor crown,
A little gleam was all you needed,
Or a threat, a little glint . . .
The stuff you're made of can at most
Pay off a slave, now form is lost.

A short pause

Yet I can think, in spite of it,
And calmly think: that is most strange.

THE POOR MAN

*in rags, with young and resolute face, his bearing stooped and
diffident*

Sir, what would you have me do?

EMPEROR

stands by the corpse, turned away

This dead man . . .

POOR MAN

Sir, it's a woman!

EMPEROR

No questions. Take her!

POOR MAN

Take her?

Where?

EMPEROR

Anywhere. Into the bushes.
Where no one can see her, where

[185]

Sie nicht sehe! später dann . . .
Hier ist Gold für deine Arbeit.

DER MENSCH
steht starr

Dies? dafür? für nichts als das?

DER KAISER

Nicht genug? komm später wieder.

DER MENSCH

Nicht genug? es wär genug,
Mir mein Leben abzukaufen.
Herr, wer bist du? um dies Gold
Stoss ich dir am hellen Tag,
Wen du willst von deinen Feinden,
Während er bei Tisch sitzt, nieder . . .
Um dies Gold verkauft dir meine
Schwester ihre beiden Töchter!

Er richtet sich gross auf, mit ausgestreckten Armen.

DER KAISER

Später dann, wenns dunkel ist,
Kommst du wieder und begräbst sie,
Gräbst im Dunkeln ihr ein Grab,
Aber so, dass auch kein Wiesel
Davon weiss und je es aufspürt;
Hüte dich!

DER MENSCH

Ich will es graben,
Dass ich selber morgen früh
Nicht den Ort zu sagen wüsste:

The Emperor and the Witch

I cannot see her! Later then . . .
Here is gold; I'll pay your work.

POOR MAN

stands rigidly

This? For that, just that, no more?

EMPEROR

Not enough? But more can follow.

POOR MAN

Not enough? It is enough
To buy my life, if you should want it.
Sir, who are you? For this gold
I would destroy for you whichever
Enemy of yours you chose,
And in broad daylight, as he ate
His dinner; for this gold my sister
Would even sell you her two daughters!

He stands drawn up to his full height, with arms outstretched.

EMPEROR

Later then, when it is dark,
You will come and bury her,
Dig her in the dark a grave,
But so that not a weasel even
Knows of it or sniffs it out;
Watch yourself!

POOR MAN

I'll dig the grave
So that, myself, tomorrow morning,
I'll not know where it was dug:

[187]

Hugo von Hofmannsthal

Denn mit diesem Leib zugleich
Werf ich in die dunkle Grube
Meinen Vater, meine Mutter,
Meine Jugend, ganz beschmutzt
Mit Geruch von Bettelsuppen,
Mit Fusstritten feiger Lumpen!

DER KAISER

Geh nun, geh! Doch hüte dich,
Dass du sie nicht anrührst, nicht
Mehr als nötig, sie zu tragen.
Ich erführ es, sei versichert,
Ich erführs, und hinter dir
Schickte ich dann zwei, die grüben
Schneller dir ein Grab im Sand,
Schneller noch und heimlicher,
Als du diese wirst begraben.

*Er winkt ihm, Hand anzulegen, setzt sich selbst auf einen
Baumstrunk und schlägt die Hände vors Gesicht.*

DER MENSCH
schleppt den regungslosen Leib ins Gebüsch.

Lange Stille

DER KAISER
aufstehend, umherschauend

Ist sie fort, für immer fort? . . .
Und die Sonne doch noch da? . . .
Zwar nicht Tag, nicht schöner Tag,
Vielmehr Nacht mit einer Sonne.
Und ich tat es wirklich, tat es?
Unsre Taten sind die Kinder

[188]

The Emperor and the Witch

For the grave that takes this body
Takes my father too, my mother
And my youth, with all its filth
Of stinking beggar soups and with
The kicks I've got from craven cheapsters.

EMPEROR

Go now, go! But watch yourself,
See you do not touch her more
Than's needed when you carry her.
I'll know if you do, be sure,
I'll know, and shall send behind you
Two more men to dig your grave,
A sandy one, more secretly
And quickly than you dig her grave.

*He motions him to lift the body, sits on a tree-stump, and
covers his face with his hands.*

POOR MAN

drags the motionless body into the undergrowth.

Long silence

EMPEROR

standing, looking about him

Has she gone? For ever gone? . . .
And the sun not even set? . . .
Not quite day, not lovely day,
Rather the night a sun has lit.
And I really did it? Really?
All our deeds are children of

[189]

Hugo von Hofmannsthal

Eines Rauchs, aus rotem Rauch
Springen sie hervor, ein Taumel
Knüpft, ein Taumel löst die Knoten.
Meine Seele hat nicht Kraft,
Sich zu freun an dieser Tat!
Diese Tat hat keinen Abgrund
Zwischen mich und sie getan,
Ihren Atem aus der Luft
Mir nicht weggenommen, nicht
Ihre Kraft aus meinem Blut!
Wenn ich sie nicht noch einmal
Sehen kann, werd ich nie glauben,
Dass ich mich mit eignem Willen
Von ihr losriss; dies noch einmal
Sehen! dies, was eine Hand
Zudeckt, dieses kleine Stück
Ihres Nackens, wo zur Schulter
Hin das Leben sich so trotzig
Und so weich, so unbegreiflich
Drängt, nur dieses eine sehen!
Sehen und freiwillig nicht—
Nicht!—berühren . . . Aber wo?
Fort! er trug sie . . . ich befahl,
Schuf mir selber diese Qual.
Aber dort die grünen Ranken
Seh ich, spür ich nicht? sie beben!
Frag ich viel, obs möglich ist!
Spür ich nicht dahinter Leben?

Er reisst die Ranken weg, die den Eingang der Höhle ver-
hängen.

EIN URALTER BLINDER

tritt ängstlich hervor, weit mit einem dürren Stecken vor sich
hintastend. Sein ganzes Gewand ist ein altes linnenes Hemd.

The Emperor and the Witch

A plume of smoke, from that red smoke
Full-grown they spring, and one delusion
Ties the knots that others untie.
Gratification from this deed,
My soul's too weak for it! Between
Myself and her it has not set
A chasm, and has not removed
Her breath from air that I must breathe,
Nor drained her power from my blood.
If I never, face to face,
See her again, I'll not believe
That by my will alone I tore
Myself from her; and just to see it—
What a single hand could hide,
This tiny portion of her neck
Where life runs down so stubbornly,
Incredible, so delicate,
To meet the shoulder: just to see it!
See and voluntarily
Not to touch, to touch . . . but where?
Gone! He carried her . . . I told him,
And am the cause of all my torment.
But—those green sprays over there,
Can I see, and sense? They're trembling!
Yes or no, what do I care!
Can it be life I sense behind them?

He tears away the branches blocking the entrance to the cave.

A BLIND OLD MAN

*enters timidly, tapping the ground a good distance in front of
him with a thin stick. He is wearing only an old linen garment.*

[191]

Hugo von Hofmannsthal

DER KAISER

hinter sich tretend

Wie, hier auch ein Mensch! Dies feuchte
Loch noch immer Raum genug
Für ein Leben? Ists damit,
Dass ich sehen soll, welch ein Ding
Herrschen ist, dass mir der Wald
Und die Strasse, ja das Innre
Eines Berges nichts wie Menschen
Heut entgegenspein? Heisst dies,
Kaiser sein: nicht atmen können,
Ohne mit der Luft ein Schicksal
Einzuschlucken?

DER GREIS

War es Sturm, der meine Türe
Aufriss? Weh, es ist nicht Nacht!
Nicht das kleine Licht der Sterne
Rieselt auf die Hände nieder . . .
Schwere Sonne! schwacher Wind!

DER KAISER *für sich*

Diese Stirn, die riesenhaften,
Ohnmächtigen Glieder, innen
Ist mir, alles dieses hab ich
Schon einmal gesehen! wann?
Kindertage! Kindertage!
Hier ist irgendein Geheimnis,
Und ich bin darein verknüpft,
Fürchterlich verknüpft . . .

[192]

The Emperor and the Witch

EMPEROR

retreating from him

How, how can a man be here, this
Hollow, damp, be space enough
For something living? By these tokens
Am I to learn what thing it is
To be a ruler, that the road,
The forest too, and, yes, the inside
Of a mountain spew at me
Nothing today but living beings?
Is this what Emperor can mean:
You cannot draw a single breath
But swallow with the air a human
Destiny?

OLD MAN

Was it the wind that made my door
Fall open? Ah, it's not yet night!
Not the tiniest starlight falls
Trickling down upon my hands . . .
Heavy sun! A feeble wind!

EMPEROR *to himself*

This man's brow, these powerless
And giant limbs, I have somehow
A feeling I have seen all this
Before already once, but when?
Childhood days! O childhood days!
Here some secret lies, and I
Am linked with it, most terribly
Am linked with it . . .

[193]

Hugo von Hofmannsthal

DER GREIS

Dort! es steht! es atmet jung!

Pause

Wie ein junges Tier!

Pause

Ein Mensch!

Er zittert

Hab Erbarmen! ich bin blind!
Lass mich leben! leben! leben!

DER KAISER

Alter Mann, ich tu dir nichts.
Sag mir deinen Namen.

DER GREIS

Lass mich leben, hab Erbarmen!

DER KAISER

Fühl, ich habe leer Hände!
Sag mir, wer du bist.

Lange Pause

DER GREIS
seine Hände anfühlend

Ring!

DER KAISER
Den Namen, sag den Namen!

DER GREIS

Was für Stein?

[194]

The Emperor and the Witch

OLD MAN

There! It's upright! Fresh and breathing!

Pause

Like a young animal!

Pause

A man!

He trembles

Have mercy on me! I am blind!
Let me live, live, let me live!

EMPEROR

I'll do no harm to you, old man.
Tell me your name.

OLD MAN

Let me live, have mercy on me!

EMPEROR

Feel my hands. My hands are empty.
Tell me who you are.

Long pause

OLD MAN

feeling the Emperor's hands

Ring!

EMPEROR

Your name, tell me your name!

OLD MAN

What stone there?

Hugo von Hofmannsthal

DER KAISER

Ein grüner.

DER GREIS

Grüner?

Grosser grüner?

DER KAISER

Deinen Namen!

Er fasst ihn an, der Greis schweigt. Im Hintergrunde sammelt sich der Hof. Sie geben ihre Spiesse an die Jäger ab. Links rückwärts wird ein purpurnes Zelt aufgeschlagen. Unter den anderen steht der Verurteilte, er trägt ein rotseidenes Gewand, darüber den Mantel des Kaisers, in der herabhängenden Hand einen kurzen Stab aus Silber und Gold.

TARQUINIUS

kniend

Herr! die allergnädigste
Kaiserin lässt durch mich melden,
Dass sie sich zurückgezogen,
Weil die Zeit gekommen war
Für das Bad der kaiserlichen
Kinder.

DER KAISER

ohne aufzumerken, betrachtet den Greis, wirft dann einen flüchtigen Blick auf seinen Hof, alle beugen ein Knie.

Decken!

Man bringt purpurne Decken und Felle und legt sie in die Mitte der Bühne.

[196]

The Emperor and the Witch

EMPEROR

It's a green one.

OLD MAN

Green one?

Green one. Big?

EMPEROR

Tell me your name!

He places his hands on the Old Man's shoulders. In the background the court gathers. They give their spears to the huntsmen. Left, upstage, a purple tent is pitched. Among the others stands the Condemned Man. He wears a robe of red silk, over it the Emperor's cloak; in his hand, which hangs at his side, a short staff of silver and gold.

TARQUINIUS

kneeling

Sire, her most gracious Majesty
The Empress bids me tell you that
She has gone back, for it was time
To bathe the royal children.

EMPEROR

without noticing Tarquinius, looks at the Old Man, then glances at the court; all bow on one knee.

Rugs!

Purple rugs and skins are brought and laid in the middle of the stage.

[197]

Hugo von Hofmannsthal

Der Kaiser führt den Blinden hin und lässt ihn setzen. Er
sitzt wie ein Kind, die Füsse gerade vor sich. Die weichen
Decken scheinen ihn zu freuen.

DER KAISER
von ihm wegtretend

Grossfalkonier! ich habe diesen Menschen
Im kaiserlichen Forst gefunden. Wer
Ist das? Kannst du mir sagen, wer das ist?

Tiefe Stille

Grosskämmerer, wer ist der Mann? mich dünkt,
Ich seh ihn heute nicht zum erstenmal.

Stille

Präfekt des Hauses, wer ist dieser Mensch?

Stille

Grosskanzler, wer?

Stille

Grossdragoman, wer ist das?

Stille

Die Kapitäne meiner Wachen! wer?

Stille

Du, Tarquinius, bist zu jung
Um mich anzulügen, hilf mir!

TARQUINIUS
um den Blinden beschäftigt

Herr, er trägt ein Band von Eisen
Um den Hals geschmiedet, einen
Schweren Ring mit einer Inschrift.

[198]

The Emperor and the Witch

The Emperor leads the Old Man to them and seats him among them. He sits like a child, his feet straight in front of him. He seems to enjoy such soft rugs.

EMPEROR

moving away from him

Grand Falconer! I found this person living
In the Imperial forests. Who is he?
This person, can you tell me who he is?

Complete silence

Lord Chamberlain! Who is this man?
It's not the first time I have seen him.

Silence

Chief Almoner! Who is this man?

Silence

Lord Chamberlain . . . ?

Silence

General, who is this man?

Silence

Captains of the Guard, who is he?

Silence

You, Tarquinius, are too young
To tell me lies, so help me now.

TARQUINIUS

who is looking after the Old Man

Sire, he wears a heavy iron
Band around his neck; a ring
That seems to carry an inscription.

[199]

Hugo von Hofmannsthal

DER KAISER
winkt ihm zu lesen. Tiefe Stille.

TARQUINIUS
liest

Ich, Johannes der Pannonier,
War durch dreiunddreissig Tage
Kaiser in Byzanz.

Pause. Tiefe Stille

Geblendet
Bin ich nun und ausgestossen
Als ein Frass der wilden Tiere
Auf Befehl . . .

DER KAISER *sehr laut*

Lies weiter, Kämmrer!

TARQUINIUS
liest weiter

Auf Befehl des höchst heiligen, höchst
Weisen, des unbesiegbarsten, erlauchtesten
Kindes . . .

Stockt.

DER KAISER *sehr laut*

Kindes . . . lies!

TARQUINIUS

Dein Name, Herr!

Lange Stille

[200]

The Emperor and the Witch

EMPEROR
motions him to read it. Complete silence.

TARQUINIUS
reads

I, John the Pannonian,
Was for three and thirty days
Emperor of Byzantium.

Pause. Complete silence

Now I am blinded and cast out
As scraps to feed wild animals,
By the command . . .

EMPEROR *very loud*
Read, Chamberlain!

TARQUINIUS
continues reading

By the command of the most holy,
Wise, unconquerable, illustrious
Child . . .

Stops.

EMPEROR *very loud*
Read on!

TARQUINIUS
Sire, it's your name.

Long silence

[201]

Hugo von Hofmannsthal

DER KAISER *mit starker Stimme*

Grosskämmerer! wie alt war ich, der Kaiser,
Als dies geschah?

DER GROSSKÄMMERER
kniend

Drei Jahre, hoher Herr.

Lange Stille

DER KAISER
mit halber Stimme, nur zu Tarquinius

Kämmrer, schau, dies war ein Kaiser!
Zu bedeuten, das ist alles!

Nach einem langen Nachdenken

Ja, den Platz, auf dem ich stehe,
Gab mir ungeheurer Raub,
Und mit Schicksal angefüllt
Ist die Ferne und die Nähe.
Von viel buntern Abenteuern,
Als ein Märchen, starrt die Welt,
Und sie ist der grosse Mantel,
Der von meinen Schultern fällt.
Überall ist Schicksal, alles
Fügt sich funkelnd ineinander
Und unlöslich wie die Maschen
Meines goldnen Panzerhemdes.
Denn zu unterst sind die Fischer
Und Holzfäller, die in Wäldern
Und am Rand des dunklen Meeres

The Emperor and the Witch

EMPEROR *firmly*

Lord Chamberlain, what age was I,
The Emperor, when this was done?

LORD CHAMBERLAIN
kneeling

Three years of age, Your Majesty.

Long silence

EMPEROR
half aloud, only to Tarquinius

Look, an Emperor, Chamberlain!
All of power is in the seeming.

After long reflection

Yes, the place on which I stand
Was given me by monstrous theft,
And with destiny are filled
The distances and places near.
With many various adventures,
Like a fairy-tale, the world
Bristles, and is like the cloak
Unfurling from my shoulders. Look,
And destiny is everywhere;
All things glittering join together,
Never sundered, like the meshes
Of my golden shirt of mail.
Lowest come the fishermen
And woodsmen, who in forests and
Upon the edge of dark seas breathe,

[203]

Hugo von Hofmannsthal

Atmen und ihr armes Leben
Für die Handvoll Gold dem ersten,
Der des Weges kommt, verkaufen.
Und dann sind die vielen Städte . . .
Und in ihnen viele Dinge:
Herrschaft, Weisheit, Hass und Lust,
Eins ums andere feil, zuweilen
Eines mit dem andern seine
Larve tauschend und mit trunknen
Augen aus dem ganz verkehrten
Antlitz schauend. Und darüber
Sind die Könige, zuoberst
Ich: von dieser höchsten Frucht
Fällt ein Licht zurück auf alles
Und erleuchtet jede tiefre
Stufe; jede: auf den Mörder
Fällt ein Strahl, Taglöhner, Sklaven
Und die Ritter und die Grossen,
Mir ist alles nah; ich muss das
Licht in mir tragen für den,
Der geblendet ward um meinet-
Willen, denn ich bin der Kaiser.
Wunderbarer ist mein Leben,
Ungeheurer aufgetürmt
Als die ungeheuren Dinge,
Pyramiden, Mausoleen,
So die Könige vor mir
Aufgerichtet. Ich vermag
Auf den Schicksalen der Menschen
So zu thronen, wie sie sassen
Auf getürmten toten Steinen.
Und so ungeheure Kunde,
Wer ich bin und was ich soll,

The Emperor and the Witch

And who will sell their pauper lives
To please the first who comes along,
For gold, a handful. Then the cities . . .
And in these are many things:
Power, wisdom, pleasure, hate,
All are exchangeable for gold,
And sometimes interchange their masks
And stare out of their drunken eyes
With crooked faces. Higher still
Above them are the kings, and over
These myself: this highest fruit
Sheds back a light on all things else,
Illuminating each receding
Deeper level; each: a ray
Falls on assassins, labourers,
On slaves and knights and men of fame,
All equidistant from me; I must
Bear that light within myself
For him they blinded for my sake,
Since I indeed am Emperor.
My life is much more marvellous,
More terribly towered up, than all
The terrible things, the pyramids,
The mausoleums which those kings
Built up before me. And I can
Enthrone myself on destinies
Of men as those kings once were seated
On the dead and towering stones.
And this terrible decree
That tells me what I do and am

Hugo von Hofmannsthal

Brachte diese eine Stunde,
Denn ihr Mund war übervoll
Von Gestalten . . .

DER GREIS

*wendet sich mit heftiger Unruhe und einem leisen Wimmern
nach dem Hintergrunde.*

TARQUINIUS

Herr, es ist, er riecht die Speisen,
Die sie hinterm Zelt bereiten,
Und ihn hungert.

DER KAISER

Bringt zu essen.

*Es kommen drei Diener mit goldenen Schüsseln. Den ersten
und zweiten beachtet der Greis nicht, nach der Richtung, wo
der dritte steht, begehrt er heftig. Tarquinius nimmt dem
dritten die Schüssel aus der Hand, kniet vor dem Greis hin
und reicht ihm die Schüssel.*

TARQUINIUS
bei dem Greis kniend

Er will nur von dieser Speise:
Süsses ist es.

*Tarquinius will ihm die Schüssel wieder wegnehmen, der
Greis weint. Er stellt die Schüssel hin.*

DER GREIS

*winkt mit der Hand, alle sollen wegtreten, versichert sich,
dass er die Schüssel hat, richtet sich gross auf, streckt die
Hand, an der des Kaisers Ring steckt, gebieterisch aus—der
Arm zittert heftig—und ruft schwach vor sich hin*

Ich bin der Kaiser!

*Sogleich setzt er sich wieder hin wie ein Kind, isst die
Schüssel leer.*

The Emperor and the Witch

This single hour has brought to me;
Indeed the mouth of this one hour
Was crammed with images . . .

OLD MAN

turns with violent agitation and whimpers weakly towards the background.

TARQUINIUS

Sire, he seems to smell the food
They are preparing there, behind
The tent. He's hungry.

EMPEROR

Bring some food.

Three servants come with golden dishes. The Old Man ignores the first and second, but looks most anxiously towards the third. Tarquinius takes the dish from the hands of the third, kneels before the Old Man, and holds the dish out to him.

TARQUINIUS

kneeling close to the Old Man

This is the only food he wants.
It's sweet.

Tarquinius makes as if to take the dish away, the Old Man weeps. Tarquinius puts the dish down.

OLD MAN

motions everyone to withdraw, makes sure the dish is by him, stands to his full height, stretches out an imperious hand, on which the Imperial ring can be seen—his arm trembles violently—and calls in a weak voice

I am the Emperor!

Quickly he sits down again like a child, and eats the dish clean.

Hugo von Hofmannsthal

DER KAISER

rührt ihn sanft an

Du, du hast aus meiner Schüssel
Jetzt gegessen; komm, ich geb dir
Jetzt mein Bett, darin zu schlafen.

DER GREIS

*nickt, der Kaiser stützt und führt ihn in das Zelt. Der Hof
zieht sich nach links rückwärts zurück. Man sieht sie zwischen
den Bäumen lagern und essen. Rechts rückwärts geht eine
Wache auf und ab. Die Sonne steht nun in dem Wald-
durchschlag, dem Rande des Hügels sehr nahe.*

DER KAISER

aus dem Zelt zurückkommend, neben ihm Tarquinius

Immer noch dieselbe Sonne!
Geht mirs doch wie jenem Hirten,
Der, den Kopf im Wasserschaff,
Meinte, Welten zu durchfliegen.

Er setzt sich links vorne auf einen Stumpf.

Ich bin heiterer, mein Lieber,
Als ich sagen kann . . . gleichviel,
Denk nicht nach! . . . Es ist der neue
Admiral, der mich so freut.
Sieh, ein Schicksal zu erfinden,
Ist wohl schön, doch Schicksal sein,
Das ist mehr; aus Wirklichkeit
Träume baun, gerechte Träume,
Und mit ihnen diese Hügel
Und die vielen weiten Länder
Bis hinab ans Meer bevölkern

The Emperor and the Witch

EMPEROR

touches him gently

Now you have eaten from my dish,
Come, you can sleep upon my bed.

OLD MAN

*nods. The Emperor supports him, leads him into the tent. The
court moves back, left, and then can be seen sitting and eating
among the trees. Upstage, right, a guard is walking up and
down. The sun is now seen in the pathway opening between
the trees, very near the brow of the hill.*

EMPEROR

returns from the tent with Tarquinius beside him

Always still the same sun shines!
I am indeed like that poor shepherd
Who with his head immersed in water
Seemed to himself to fly through worlds!

Sits on a tree-stump, front, left.

My friend, now I am happier
Than I can say . . . but, nonetheless,
Let's not be thinking of it. Our
New admiral delights me so.
It is a fine thing to create
A destiny, but something more
To be one; from reality
To build up dreams, and rightful dreams,
And populate with them these hills
And all the many lands that spread
Down to the seashore, and to watch them

[209]

Und sie vor sich weiden sehn,
Wie der Hirt die stillen Rinder . . .

Eine kleine Pause

Grauenhaftes, das vergangen,
Gibt der Gegenwart ein eignes
Leben, eine fremde Schönheit,
Und erhöht den Glanz der Dinge
Wie durch eingeschluckte Schatten.

TARQUINIUS

Die Kaiserin!

Er springt zurück.

Von hinten her ist mit leisen Schritten die Hexe herangetreten. Sie trägt das Gewand der Kaiserin, in dessen untersten Saum grosse Saphire eingewebt sind. Über das Gesicht fällt ein dichter goldner Schleier. In der Hand trägt sie eine langstielige goldne Lilie.

DER KAISER *ohne aufzustehen*

So kommst du
Doch! Man hat mir was gemeldet . . .
Doch du kommst, so sind die Kinder
Wohl gebadet, Helena.
Lass uns von den Kindern reden!
Zwar du redest von nichts anderm . . .
In der Kammer, wo sie schlafen,
Wohnt die Sonne, Regenbogen,
Mond, die schönen klaren Sterne,
Alles hast du in der Kammer,
Nicht? Mich dünkt, du lächelst nicht!
Lächelst doch so leicht: zuweilen

The Emperor and the Witch

Grazing as a cowherd might
His quiet animals.

Short pause

Horror, past,
Endows the present with a life
That's all its own, a beauty, strange,
And magnifies the shine of things
As by a swallowing of shadows.

TARQUINIUS

The Empress!

He jumps back.

*From behind him the Witch has silently emerged. She is
wearing the regalia of the Empress, with enormous sapphires
stitched into the lowest hem. A thick golden veil falls over her
face. In her hand she carries a long-stemmed golden lily.*

EMPEROR *without standing up*

Ah! So after all
You've come! They told me . . . but no matter,
You have come, the children safely
Bathed and happy, Helena.
Now let's talk of them! As if
You ever talked of other things . . .
In their bedroom, where they sleep,
There lives the rainbow, and the sun,
Moon, and the beautiful bright stars,
You've furnished it with everything;
Or have you? Now! And not a smile?
You smile so easily: at times

Bin ich blass vor Zorn geworden,
Wenn ich sah, wie leicht dir dieses
Lächeln kommt, wenn ich bedachte,
Dass ein Diener, der dir Blumen
Bringt, den gleichen Lohn davon hat
Wie ich selber . . . es war unrecht!
Heut begreif ichs. Über alle
Worte klar begreif ichs heute:
Welch ein Kind du bist, wie völlig
Aus dir selbst dies Kinderlächeln
Quillt. Ich bin so froh, zu denken,
Dass . . . ich mein, dass du es bist,
Die mir Kinder auf die Welt bringt.
Meine Kinder, Helena— . . .
Wie von einer kleinen Quelle
Hergespült, wie aufgelesen
Von den jungen grünen Wiesen,
Die Geschwister ahnungsloser,
Aus dem Nest gefallner kleiner
Vögel sind sie, Helena,
Weil es deine Kinder sind!
Keine Antwort? und den Schleier
Auch nicht weg? Wir sind allein!

DIE HEXE
schlägt den Schleier zurück.

DER KAISER
aufspringend

Hexe du und Teufelsbuhle,
Stehst du immer wieder auf?

DIE HEXE
indem sie sich halb wendet, wie ihn fortzuführen

Komm, Byzanz! Wir wollen diese

The Emperor and the Witch

I have gone pale with wrath to see
Those easy smiles you give, to think
That any servant, who might bring
Some flowers to you, earned the same
Reward as I . . . it was not right!
Today I understand. Beyond all
Words I understand it clearly:
What a child you are, and how
Entirely from your own sweet childish
Being flows that smile. I am
So glad to think this . . . no, I mean:
Glad that you can give me children,
Give me children, Helena— . . .
Just as if they all had brimmed
From a small spring, and had been picked
Out of a stream by green young willows.
They're the brothers and the sisters
Of small thoughtless birds that tumble
From their nests, my Helena,
Because they are your children too!
You do not answer? Do not even
Draw your veil? We are alone!

THE WITCH

throws back the veil.

EMPEROR

jumps to his feet

O foul witch, you devil's bawd,
Will you walk the earth for ever?

WITCH

half turning, as if to lead him away

Come, Byzantium! Forget

Schäferspiele nun vergessen!
Miteinander wieder liegen
In dem goldnen Palankin,
Dessen Stangen deine Ahnherrn,
Julius Cäsar und die andern
Tragen.

DER KAISER
lacht.

DIE HEXE *mit ausgebreiteten Armen*

Ich kann nicht leben
Ohne dich!

DER KAISER
Geh fort von mir!

DIE HEXE
Sieben Jahre!

DER KAISER
Trug und Taumel!
Sieben Tage brachen alles!

DIE HEXE
Hör mich an!

DER KAISER
Vorbei! vorbei!

DIE HEXE
Keine Stunde! Deine Lippen
Beben noch.

DER KAISER
Gott hats gewendet!
Jeden Schritt von deinen Schritten
Gegen dich! Aus allen Klüften,

The Emperor and the Witch

Your pastorals and let us lie
Again together in the golden
Palanquin whose poles are carried
By your ancestors—that
Julius Caesar and the rest!

EMPEROR
laughs.

WITCH *with arms outstretched*
              I cannot live without you!

EMPEROR

Go!

WITCH
For seven years . . .

EMPEROR
            All phantoms!
Seven days destroyed them all!

WITCH
But listen to me!

EMPEROR
        Finished, finished!

WITCH
No, not finished! For your lips,
They're trembling!

EMPEROR
       God has tipped the scales!
Every step that you may take
Now goes against you. Out of every

Hugo von Hofmannsthal

Von der Strasse, aus den Wäldern,
Von dem Boden, aus den Lüften
Sprangen Engel, mich zu retten!
Wo ich hingriff, dich zu spüren,
Taten sich ins wahre Leben
Auf geheimnisvolle Türen,
Mich mir selbst zurückzugeben.

DIE HEXE

*schleudert ihre goldene Lilie zu Boden, die sogleich zu Qualm
und Moder zerfällt*

Hingest doch durch sieben Jahr
Festgebannt an diesen Augen
Und verstrickt in dieses Haar!
Völlig mich in dich zu saugen
Und in mir die ganze Welt;
Hexe denn! und Teufel du,
Komm! uns ziemt das gleiche Bette!

DER KAISER

Willst du drohen? sieh, ich stehe!
Sieh, ich schaue! sieh, ich lache!
Diese Flammen brennen nicht!
Aber grenzenlose Schwere
Lagert sich in dein Gesicht,
Deine Wangen sinken nieder,
Und die wundervollen Glieder
Werden Runzel, werden Grauen
Und Entsetzen anzuschauen.

DIE HEXE

zusammensinkend, wie von unsichtbaren Fäusten gepackt

Sonne! Sonne! ich ersticke!

The Emperor and the Witch

Cleft and road and forest glade,
From earth itself, and out of air,
Angels have sprung to rescue me!
When I held out hands to touch you,
Secret doors were opened to me,
On the true life opened, and they
Led me back to my true self.

WITCH

*throws down her golden lily. It disintegrates in vapour and
dust*

Yet you hung for seven years
In the enchantment of these eyes
And prisoned in this hair of mine;
Tried to suck me down inside you,
And the whole wide world down with me;
Witch, then! But a devil you!
Come! It's the same bed we share!

EMPEROR

Threaten as you will, I stand!
Look, I see you! Look, I laugh!
These flames cannot burn me now.
But an infinite heaviness
Is falling, falling on your face,
And your cheeks are shrivelling,
And your limbs, so exquisite,
Are ribbed with wrinkles, utterly
Abhorrent, O a loathsome sight!

WITCH

sinks slowly down, as if held by invisible fists

Sun! O sun! I cannot breathe!

[217]

Hugo von Hofmannsthal

Sie schleppt sich ins Gebüsch, schreit gellend auf und rollt im Dunkel am Boden hin. Die Sonne ist fort. Der Kaiser steht, die Augen starr auf dem Gebüsch. Eine undeutliche Gestalt, wie ein altes Weib, humpelt im Dickicht nach rückwärts.

DER KAISER

Gottes Tod! dies halten! haltet!
Wachen! Kämmrer! dort! dort! dort!

TARQUINIUS
kommt gelaufen

Hoher Herr!

DER KAISER
Die Wachen, dort!
Sollen halten!

Lange Pause

TARQUINIUS
kommt wieder

Herr, die Wachen
Schworen: niemand ging vorüber
Als ein runzlig altes Weib,
Eine wohl, die Beeren sammelt
Oder dürres Holz.

DER KAISER
ihn anfassend, mit einem ungeheuren Blick

Tarquinius!

Zieht ihn an sich, überlegt, schweigt eine Weile, winkt ihm wegzutreten, kniet nieder.

[218]

The Emperor and the Witch

She crawls into the undergrowth, shrieks, and rolls away in the dark across the ground. The sun has set. The Emperor stands looking rigidly towards the undergrowth. A vague shape, like an old woman's, hobbles retreating through the thicket.

EMPEROR

God's death! Stop her! Stop that thing!
Guards! Chamberlains! There, there, there!

TARQUINIUS

comes running

Your Majesty!

EMPEROR

Send guards! In there!
And stop her!

Long pause

TARQUINIUS

returns

Sire, the guards all swear
No one has gone that way except
An old, old wrinkled woman, who
Perhaps was gathering berries or
Dry firewood.

EMPEROR

grasps him, gazes overwhelmingly at him

Tarquinius!

Embraces him, reflects, is silent a while, then motions Tarquinius to stand aside, then kneels.

Hugo von Hofmannsthal

Herr, der unberührten Seelen
Schönes Erbe ist ein Leben,
Eines auch ist den Verirrten,
Denen eines, Herr, gegeben,
Die dem Teufel sich entwanden
Und den Weg nach Hause fanden.

Während seines Gebetes ist der Vorhang langsam gefallen.

The Emperor and the Witch

Lord, an inheritance of loveliness,
Their life, all virgin souls possess;
And all who into error come,
To them again the gift is made,
Who slip the snares the Devil laid,
And at long last find their way home.

During his prayer the curtain slowly falls.

THE LITTLE THEATRE
OF THE WORLD

Translated by

MICHAEL HAMBURGER

Das kleine Welttheater

ODER DIE GLÜCKLICHEN

Die Bühne stellt den Längsschnitt einer Brücke dar, einer gewölbten Brücke, so dass die Mitte höher liegt als links und rechts. Den Hintergrund bildet das steinerne Geländer der Brücke, dahinter der Abendhimmel und in grösserer Ferne die Wipfel einiger Bäume, die Uferlandschaft andeutend.

Der Gärtner trägt ein Gewand von weissem Linnen, eine blaue Schürze, blosse Arme, Schuhe von Stroh;

Der junge Herr einen dunkelgrünen Jagdanzug mit hohen gelben Stulpstiefeln;

Das junge Mädchen ein halblanges Mullkleid, mit blossen Armen, einen Strohhut in der Hand;

Der Dichter einen dunklen Mantel.

Alle im Geschmack der zwanziger Jahre des vorigen Jahrhunderts.

DER DICHTER

Ich blieb im Bade, bis der Widerschein
Des offnen Fensters zwischen meinen Fingern
Mir zeigte, dass der Glanz der tiefen Sonne
Von seitwärts in die goldnen Bäume fällt
Und lange Schatten auf den Feldern liegen.
Nun schreit ich auf und ab den schmalen Pfad,

The Little Theatre of the World

OR THE FORTUNATE ONES

---

*The stage presents a cross-section of a bridge, a vaulted bridge,
so that the middle is higher than the right and left. The background is formed by the stone parapet of the bridge, behind
it the evening sky and, farther away, the crests of a few trees,
indicating a river-bank landscape.*

*The Gardener wears a garment of white linen, a blue apron,
bare arms, shoes made of straw;*

*The Young Gentleman a dark-green hunting costume with
tall yellow top boots;*

*The Young Girl a half-length muslin dress, bare arms, a
straw hat in her hand;*

The Poet a dark cloak.

All in the style of the eighteen-twenties.

THE POET

I bathed, till by the open window's glare
Glancing between my fingers I could tell
That slantwise now the low sun's rays were falling
On golden trees, long shadows gloomed the fields.
Now up and down I pace the narrow path;

[225]

Von weitem einem Vogelsteller gleichend,
Vielmehr dem Wächter, der auf hoher Klippe
Von ungeheuren Schwärmen grosser Fische
Den ungewissen Schatten sucht im Meer:
Denn über Hügel, über Auen hin
Späh ich nach ungewissen Schatten aus:
Dort, wo ein abgebrochnes Mauerstück
Vom Park die Buchen dämmernd sehen lässt,
Dort hebt sichs an! Kehr ich die Schultern hin
Und wende mich, den hellen Fluss zu sehen:
Ich weiss drum doch, es regt sich hinter mir.
Mit leichten Armen teilen sie das Laub:
Gestalten! und sie unterreden sich.
O wüsst ich nur, wovon! ein Schicksal ists,
Und irgendwie bin ich dareinverwebt.
Mich dünkt, sie bücken sich, mich dünkt, die Riemen
Der Schuhe flechten sie für langen Weg . . .
Mir schlägt das Herz bei ihrem Vorbereiten:
Seh ich nun aber jenseits an den Hängen
Nicht Pilger mühsam wie Verzauberte
Hinklimmen und mit jeder Hecke ringen?
Und mit geheimnisvoll Ermüdeten
Ist jener Kreuzweg, sind die kleinen Wege
Durch die Weingärten angefüllt: sie lagern
Und bergen in den Händen ihr Gesicht . . .
Doch an den Uferwiesen, doch im Wasser!
Von Leibern gleicher Farbe wie das Erz
Sind funkelnd alle Wellen aufgewühlt;
Sie freuen sich im Bad, am Ufer liegen
Die schweren Panzer, die sie abgeworfen,
Und andre führen jetzt die nackten Pferde,
Die hoch sich bäumen, in die tiefe Welle.
Warum bewegen sich so fürchterlich

The Little Theatre of the World

Bird-catcher you would think me from a distance.
More like the watchman on some towering cliff
Who scans the sea for vague and shadowy blurs,
Shoals of great fishes; far across the hills
And pastures for vague shadows I look out:
There, where a gap in that old crumbling wall
Reveals the beech-trees' half-light in the park,
It begins now! Though I turn my shoulders
And look the other way towards the river,
Yet I know well, it stirs behind my back.
Light fingers part the foliage and white arms:
Shapes, apparitions! In grave conference.
Oh, if I knew the theme. A fate it is,
And in some way I'm interwoven with it.
It seems that they bend down, it seems they fasten
The buckles of their shoes for some long track . . .
Their preparations make my heart beat fast:
But now beyond them on the farther slopes
Are those not pilgrims clambering painfully,
As though bewildered, and grappling with each hedge?
And now the crossroads, and the little footpaths
That run through every vineyard are filled up,
Crowded with men mysteriously exhausted,
Prostrate, their faces hidden in their hands . . .
But on the river banks, but in the water!
Look! all the ripples are astir, and sparkle
With bodies metal-coloured, bright as ore;
They frolic in their bath, and on the banks
Their heavy armour lies, mail coats discarded.
And others now lead the unsaddled horses,
That rear and prance, down to the deepest pools.
But why so dreadfully do the willow clumps

Hugo von Hofmannsthal

Die Weidenbüsche? andre Arme greifen
Daraus hervor, mit jenen nackten Schultern
Seh ich gemischt Gepanzerte, sie kämpfen,
Von Badenden mit Kämpfenden vermengt
Schwankt das Gebüsch: wie schön ist diese Schlacht!

Er wendet sich.

Den Fluss hinab! da liegt der stille Abend.
Kaum ein verworrenes Getöse schwimmt
Herab mit Blut und golddurchwirkten Decken.
Nun auch ein Kopf: am Ufer hebt sich einer
Und misst mit einem ungeheuren Blick
Den Fluss zurück . . . Warum ergreifts mich so,
Den einen hier zu sehn? . . . Nun lässt er sich
Aufs neue gleiten, kein Verwundeter!
So selig ist er wie ein wilder Faun,
Und mit den Augen auf dem Wasser schwimmt
Er hin und fängt mit trunknen Blicken auf
Die feuchten Schatten, durcheinanderkreisend,
Der hohen Wolken und des stillen Goldes,
Das zwischen Kieseln liegt im Grund. Den Schwimmer
Trifft nur der Schatten riesenhafter Eichen,
Von einer Felsenplatte überhängend:
Er kann nicht sehn die Schöngekleideten,
Die dort versammelt sind . . . um was zu tun?
Sie knien nieder . . . einen zu verehren?
Vielmehr sie graben, alle bücken sich:
Ist eine Krone dort? ist dort die Spur
Von einem Mord verborgen? Doch der Schwimmer,
Die Augen auf die Wellen, gleitet fort.
Will er hinab, bis wo die letzten Meere
Wie stille leere Spiegel stehen? wird er,
Sich mit der Linken an die nackte Wurzel

Begin to sway and writhe? New arms emerge,
Clutching, and now amidst the naked shoulders
Mailed men I see; they mingle, and they fight.
The bushes bend with bathers and with warriors
Gripped in close combat: beautiful, this battle!

He turns away.

Downstream! There still the evening quiet reigns.
Faintly, a muted hum, that turmoil drifts
Down with the blood and gold-embroidered cloth.
Now a head also: someone scales the bank,
Rises and casts a long, mysterious glance
Back up the river . . . Why does it move me so
To see this one man here? Now, though unwounded,
Once more he lowers his body, and floats on.
As happy now, as glad as a wild faun
His eyes fixed on the water he swims on
And with his drunken and ecstatic eyes
Hunts the moist shadows, whirling, spiralling,
Of the high clouds and of the motionless gold
That lies between the pebbles on the bed.
Only the shadow of gigantic oaks
Falls on the swimmer from a ledge of rock:
He cannot see the beautiful attire
Of those forgathered there . . . but why forgathered?
I see them kneel . . . in homage to some man?
Rather they dig, their faces to the ground:
Is it a crown they seek, then? Or the trace
Of murder done in secret? But the swimmer,
His eyes fixed on the wavelets, still floats on.
To reach that far-off place where the last seas
Lie like blank mirrors—could that be his will?
And with his left hand clutching at the naked root

Hugo von Hofmannsthal

Des letzten Baumes haltend, dort hinaus
Mit unbeschreiblichem Erstaunen blicken?
Ich will nicht ihn allein, die andern will ich,
Die auf den Hügeln wiedersehn, und schaudernd
Im letzten Lichte spür ich hinter mir
Schon wieder neue aus den Büschen treten.
Da bebt der Tag hinab, das Licht ist fort,
Wie angeschlagne Saiten beb ich selber.

Die Bühne wird dunkler.

Nun setz ich mich am Rand des Waldes hin,
Wo kleine Weiher lange noch den Glanz
Des Tages halten und mit feuchtem Funkeln
Die offnen Augen dieser Landschaft scheinen:
Wenn ich auf die hinsehe, wird es mir
Gelingen, das zu fertigen, wofür
Der Waldgott gern die neue Laute gäbe
Aus einer Schildkrot, überspannt mit Sehnen:
Ich meine jenes künstliche Gebild
Aus Worten, die von Licht und Wasser triefen,
Worein ich irgendwie den Widerschein
Von jenen Abenteuern so verwebe,
Dass dann die Knaben in den dumpfen Städten,
Wenn sie es hören, schwere Blicke tauschen
Und unter des geahnten Schicksals Bürde,
Wie überladne Reben schwankend, flüstern:
«O wüsst ich mehr von diesen Abenteuern,
Denn irgendwie bin ich dareinverwebt
Und weiss nicht, wo sich Traum und Leben spalten.»

*Der Dichter geht ab, der Gärtner tritt auf. Er ist ein Greis mit
schönen, durchdringenden Augen. Er trägt eine Giesskanne
und einen kleinen Korb aus Bast.*

[230]

The Little Theatre of the World

Of the last tree, there will he stay and gaze
In inexpressible wonder? Not him alone,
The others too, those on the hills, I wish
To see again, and with a shiver now
Behind me in the last and dying light
I sense how more and more step from the bushes.
Day trembles to its close; the light is gone.
Like lute-strings lightly plucked, I too am trembling.

The stage darkens.

Now at the forest's edge I shall sit down
Where little ponds for some while yet will hold
The gleam of day and, moistly glittering,
This landscape's open eyes, will wake and peer.
If I look into them I shall succeed
In fashioning that for which the woodland god
Most willingly would barter his new lute
Made of a tortoise-shell and strung with sinews:
I mean that artifice, that rare creation
Formed out of words that drip with light and water
And into which in some strange way I weave
The mirrored image of the day's adventures
In such a way that boys who hear it later
In the close air of cities will exchange
Meaningful glances and, beneath the burden
Of the prefigured fate that will be theirs,
Swaying like overladen vines, will whisper:
"Oh, that I knew much more of these adventures,
For in some way I'm interwoven with them
And do not know where life and dream divide."

Exit the Poet. Enter the Gardener. He is an old man with fine, penetrating eyes. He carries a watering can and a little straw basket.

Hugo von Hofmannsthal

GÄRTNER

Ich trug den Stirnreif und Gewalt der Welt
Und hatte hundert der erlauchten Namen,
Nun ist ein Korb von Bast mein Eigentum,
Ein Winzermesser und die Blumensamen.

Wenn ich aus meinem goldnen Haus ersah
Das Blumengiessen abends und am Morgen,
Sog ich den Duft von Erd und Wasser ein
Und sprach: Hierin liegt grosser Trost verborgen.

Nun giess ich selber Wasser in den Mund
Der Blumen, seh es in den Grund gesogen
Und bin vom Schatten und gedämpften Licht
Der ruhelosen Blätter überflogen,

Wie früher von dem Ruhm und Glanz der Welt.
Der Boten Kommen, meiner Flotte Rauschen,
Die goldnen Wächter, Feinde, die erblassten:
Befreiung wars, dies alles umzutauschen

Für diese Beete, dieses reife Lasten
Der Früchte, halbverborgen an Spalieren,
Und schwere Rosen, drin die goldig braunen
Von Duft betäubten Bienen sich verlieren.

Noch weiss ich eines: Hier und Dort sind gleich
So völlig, wie zwei Pfirsichblüten sind,
In einem tiefen Sinn einander gleich:
Denn manches Mal, wenn mir der schwache Wind

Den Duft von vielen Sträuchern untermengt
Herüberträgt, so hab ich einen Hauch
Von meinem ganzen frühern Leben dran,
Und noch ein Grössres widerfährt mir auch:

The Little Theatre of the World

GARDENER

I wore the diadem and worldly power
And by a hundred glorious names was known;
Now a straw basket, vintner's pruning knife,
This handful of small seeds are all I own.

When from my golden house I saw the garden
Sprayed in the morning and at evening,
I drew in deep the scent of earth and water
And thought: From such a source great joy could
                                        spring.

Now it is I who feed the mouths of flowers
And see the water sucked into the ground.
I whom the shadows and the muted light
Of the wind-ruffled, restless leaves surround,

As once the fame and splendour of the world.
Messengers bustling, my fleet that swept the seas,
The gilded watchmen, the dying enemies:
More than relief it was to exchange all these

For my small flower-beds, this mellow weight
Of fruit half-hidden in the trellises,
These heavy roses and, lost within their petals,
Drunken and faint with fragrance, the brown bees.

Yet this I know: that Here and There are one,
As much alike as two peach blossoms are,
In a deep sense alike, and wholly so:
For often, when the soft wind from afar

Has borne the mingled scent of many shrubs
To where I stood, in one long breath I drew
My whole life's essence in, and all my past;
And something greater still befalls me too:

[233]

Hugo von Hofmannsthal

Dass an den Blumen ich erkennen kann
Die wahren Wege aller Kreatur,
Von Schwach und Stark, von Üppig oder Kühn
Die wahre Art, wovon ich früher nur

In einem trüben Spiegel Spuren fand,
Wenn ich umwölkt von Leben um mich blickte:
Denn alle Mienen spiegelten wie Wasser
Nur dies: ob meine zürnte oder nickte.

Nun aber webt vor meinen Füssen sich
Mit vielen Köpfen, drin der Frühwind wühlt,
Dies bunte Leben hin: den reinen Drang
Des Lebens hab ich hier, nur so gekühlt,

Wie grüne Kelche sich vom Boden heben,
So rein und frisch, wie nicht in jungen Knaben
Zum Ton von Flöten fromm der Atem geht.
So wundervoll verwoben sind die Gaben

Des Lebens hier: mir winkt aus jedem Beet
Mehr als ein Mund wie Wunden oder Flammen
Mit schattenhaft durchsichtiger Gebärde,
Und Kindlichkeit und Majestät mitsammen.

*Er tritt ab, der junge Herr tritt auf, langsam, sein Pferd am
Zügel führend.*

DER JUNGE HERR

Ich ritt schon aus, bevor der Tau getrocknet war.
Die andern wollten mich daheim zu ihrem Spiel,
Mich aber freut es so, für mich allein zu sein.
Am frühen Tage bin ich schon nicht weit von hier
Dem Greis begegnet, der mir viel zu denken gibt:
Ein sonderbarer Bettler, dessen stummer Gruss

The Little Theatre of the World

That by the flowers I can recognize
The secret ways of all created things,
The strong and weak, the sensual and the bold,
Know their true ways of which mere glimmerings

In a dim mirror once I could discern,
When, clouded over with life, I looked around;
Because like water then all faces mirrored
Only that mine smiled favour, or mine frowned.

But now, through heads in which the spring breeze plays,
Life weaves her strands unwound from many a spool
Wherever I go: pure life-urge now is mine
And seems to meet me everywhere, but as cool

As these green chalices rising from the ground,
More pure and fresh than is the breath that drifts
From boys who sing to flutes religiously.
So weirdly interwoven are life's gifts

Here in my garden; from every bed there beckons
More than a mouth like wounds or flames to me
With a mysterious, a transparent motion
Compact of innocence and majesty.

*Exit Gardener. Enter the Young Gentleman, slowly, leading
his horse by the bridle.*

THE YOUNG GENTLEMAN

I rode out early before the dew was dry.
The others wanted me to join them in their games,
But to roam freely and alone is what I like.
And soon, not far from here, I had a strange encounter,
One that has made me ponder: an old man it was,
A kind of beggarman, and yet his silent greeting

[235]

So war, wie ihn vielleicht ein Fürst besitzen mag
Von einer Art, wie ich von keinem freilich las:
Der schweigend seine Krone hinwürf und vor Nacht
Den Hof verliess und nie mehr wiederkäm.
Was aber könnte einen treiben, dies zu tun?
Ich weiss, ich bin zu jung, und kann die vielerlei
Geschicke nicht verstehn; vielmehr sie kommen mir
Wie Netze und Fussangeln vor, in die der Mensch
Hineingerät und fallend sich verfängt; ich will
So vielen einmal helfen, als ich kann. Schon jetzt
Halt ich mein Pferd vor jedem an, der elend scheint,
Und wenn sie wo im Felde mähen, bleib ich stehn
Und frage sie nach ihrem Leben, und ich weiss
Schon vielerlei, was meinen Brüdern völlig fremd.
Zu Mittag sass ich ab im dämmernden Gebüsch,
Von Brombeer und von wilden Rosen ganz umzäunt,
Und neben meinem Pferde schlief ich ein. Da fing
Ich gleich zu träumen an. Ich jagte, war der Traum:
Zu Fuss und mit drei grossen Hunden trieb ich Wild,
Gekleidet wie auf alten Bildern und bewaffnet
Mit einer Armbrust, und vor mir der dichte Wald
War angefüllt mit Leben, überschwemmt mit Wild,
Das lautlos vor mir floh. Nichts als das Streifen
Der Felle an den Bäumen und das flinke Laufen
Von Tausenden von Klauen und von leichten Hufen
Auf Moos und Wurzeln, und die Wipfel droben dunkel
Von stiller atemloser Flucht der Vögel. In getrennten,
Doch durcheinander hingemengten Schwärmen rauschten
Birkhähne schweren Flugs, das Rudern wilder Gänse,
Und zwischen Ketten der verschreckten Haselhühner
    schwangen
Die Reiher sich hindurch, und neben ihnen, ängstlich
Den Mord vergessend, hasteten die Falken hin.

The Little Theatre of the World

Was such as of a prince perhaps you would expect,
Yet such a prince as I have never read about:
One rather who would quietly throw his crown away,
Creep from his court at nightfall, and never return.
What could induce a prince to do so? That's the question.
Of course I know I'm still too young, and cannot grasp
The multiplicity of destinies; but rather
As treacherous nets and mantraps see them, into which
Men blunder and, falling, are ensnared. So now I want
To help as many of them as I can. Already
Wherever I see wretchedness I pull up my horse,
And when they're mowing in some meadow, I stop a while
To question them about their lives; and I've discovered
Much that my brothers neither know nor care to know.
At midday I dismounted in a copse,
Densely hedged round with briar and bramble creepers
And went to sleep beside my horse. At once
I fell into this dream: that I was hunting,
On foot, with three great hounds, was stalking deer,
Armed with a cross-bow, dressed as in old pictures,
In front of me the darkling forest, filled
With every kind of wild life, overflowing
With game that in mute panic fled from me.
No sound, but hairy pelts that brushed the trees,
The rapid pounding of a thousand claws,
Hoof-beat on roots, hoof-patter on the moss;
And up above me all the treetops dark
With the mute breathless flight of birds. In flocks
At once distinct and madly intermingled,
Heathcock flapped heavy wings, the wild geese paddled,
And between coveys of startled grouse the herons
Thrust their lone way, and next to them, forgetting
Murder in fear, scurried the sparrow-hawks.

Dies alles trieb ich vor mir her, wie Sturm ein schwarzes
Gewölk, und drängte alles einer dunklen Schlucht
Mit jähen Wänden zu. Ich war vom Übermass
Der Freude über diese Jagd erfüllt und doch
Im Innersten beklommen, und ich musste plötzlich
An meinen Vater denken, und mir war, als säh ich
Sein weisses Haar in einem Brunnen unter mir.
Da rührte sich mein Pferd im Schlaf und sprang auf einmal
Zugleich auf die vier Füsse auf und schnaubte wild,
Und so erwachte ich und fühlte noch den Traum
Wie dunkle Spinnweb um die Stirn mir hängen. Aber dann
Verliess ich diese dumpfe Kammer grüner Hecken, und
    mein Pferd
Ging neben mir, ich hatte ihm den leichten Zaum
Herausgenommen, und es riss sich kleine Blätter ab.
Da schwirrten Flügel dicht vor mir am Boden hin:
Ich bückte mich, doch war kein Stein im tiefen Moos,
Da warf ich mit dem Zaum der Richtung nach und traf:
Zwei junge Hühner lagen dort und eine Wachtel, tot,
In einem Wurf erschlagen mit der Trense. Sonderbar
War mir die Beute, und der Traum umschwirrte mich so
    stark,
Dass ich den Brunnen suchte und mir beide Augen schnell
Mit klarem Wasser wusch; und wie mir flüchtig da
Aus feuchtem Dunkel mein Gesicht entgegenflog,
Kam mir ein Taumel so, als würd ich innerlich
Durch einen Abgrund hingerissen, und mir war,
Da ich den Kopf erhob, als wär ich um ein Stück
Gealtert in dem Augenblick. Zuweilen kommt,
Wenn ich allein bin, solch ein Zeichen über mich:
Und früher war ich innerlich bedrückt davon
Und dachte, dass in meinem tiefsten Seelengrund
Das Böse läg und dies Vorboten wären, und
Erwartete mit leiser Angst das Kommende.

The Little Theatre of the World

All this I drove before me, as gales drive clouds,
And pressed it all into a gloomy chasm,
Walled with sheer rocks. Extremity of joy
The chase infused in me, and yet oppressed me,
And of my father suddenly made me think;
It seemed that in a well that opened up
Beneath me, I caught sight of his white hair.
Just then my horse moved in his sleep, and leapt
To his four feet at once and wildly snorted,
And so I woke and still could feel the dream
Cling like dark cobwebs to my forehead.
But quickly I left this cubby-hole of hedges,
My horse beside me, his light bridle loosed,
Free now to tear and munch at the small leaves.
Then, close to me, wings whirred along the ground;
I stooped, but found no stone in that deep moss,
So threw the bridle blindly, and struck home:
A brace of partridges lay there, and one young quail,
Killed at one blow of the snaffle. Weird indeed
That booty seemed to me; and the dream so loudly
Whirred round my head that for the well I searched
And washed both eyes; and when my face flew up
Briefly from that dank darkness, I experienced
A giddiness as though my inmost self
Were flung into a chasm, and when I raised
My head from it, I felt as though that moment
Had added to my age. Now such a sign
Comes to me sometimes when I'm left alone;
And formerly it oppressed me, and I thought
That deep within my soul lurked evil, brought
Into the open by these rare forebodings,
And, with faint dread, awaited things to come.

Nun aber ist durch einen Gruss ein solches Glück
In mich hineingekommen, dass ich früh und spät
Ein Lächeln durch die lichten Zweige schimmern seh,
Und statt die Brüder zu beneiden, fühl ich nun
Ein namenloses stilles Glück, allein zu sein:
Denn alle Wege sind mir sehr geheimnisvoll
Und doch wie zubereitet, wie für mich
Von Händen in der Morgenfrühe hingebaut,
Und überall erwarte ich den Pfad zu sehn,
Der anfangs von ihr weg zu vieler Prüfung führt
Und wunderbar verschlungen doch zu ihr zurück.

Er geht mit seinem Pferde ab. Nun ist völlige Dämmerung.
Der Fremde tritt auf; nach seiner Kleidung könnte er ein
geschickter Handwerker, etwa ein Goldschmied, sein. Er
bleibt auf der Brücke stehen und sieht ins Wasser.

DER FREMDE

Dies hängt mir noch von Kindesträumen an:
Ich muss von Brücken in die Tiefe spähen,
Und wo die Fische gleiten übern Grund,
Mein ich, Geschmeide hingestreut zu sehen,

Geschmeide in den Kieselgrund verwühlt,
Geräte, drin sich feuchte Schatten fangen.
Wie Narben an dem Leib von Kindern wuchs
Mit mir dies eingegrabene Verlangen!

Ich war zu klein und durfte nie hinab.
Nun wär ich stark genug, den Schatz zu heben,
Doch dieses Wasser gleitet stark und schnell,
Zeigt nicht empor sein stilles innres Leben.

Nur seine Oberfläche gibt sich her,
Gewaltig wie von strömendem Metalle.
Von innen treibt sich Form auf Form heraus
Mit einer Riesenkraft in stetem Schwalle.

But now a simple greeting has infused
Such joy in me that early and late I see
A smile light up between the bright-leaved boughs
And far from envying my brothers feel
Silent, ineffable joy in being on my own:
For every road is fraught with mystery
And yet as though prepared for me, as though
Built by strange hands for me at early morning,
And everywhere I wait to see the path
Which leads away from her at first, to many trials
And marvellously tortuous yet leads back to her.

*Exit with his horse. Now the dusk has deepened. Enter the
Stranger; his clothes suggest that he might be an artisan,
perhaps a goldsmith. He stops on the bridge and looks down
into the water.*

THE STRANGER

Still this adheres to me from childhood dreams:
From bridges to the deep my gaze must turn
And where the fishes glide above the bed
Jewelled and golden ornaments I discern.

Jewels and gold half buried in the pebbles,
Vessels that hide dark shadows from my view.
As I grew up, like scars on children's bodies,
In me this deep-embedded longing grew.

Then I was small, and not allowed to go.
Now I am strong enough to lift that treasure
But strongly, quickly too the waters flow
And keep their silent inner life submerged.

Only the surface yields. I cannot enter.
Mighty it flows, as though of molten metal.
Shape after shape thrusts outward from the centre
With protean power in never-ending motion.

Hugo von Hofmannsthal

Aus Krügen schwingen Schultern sich heraus,
Aus Riesenmuscheln kommt hervorgegossen
Ein knabenhafter Leib, ihm drängt sich nach
Ein Ungeheuer und ist schon zerflossen!

Lieblichen Wesen, Nymphen halb, halb Wellen,
Wälzt eine dunkle riesige Gewalt
Sich nach: mich dünkt, es ist der Leib der Nacht,
In sich geballt die dröhnende Gestalt:

Nun wirft sie auseinander ihre Glieder,
Und für sich taumelt jedes dieser wilden.
Mich überkommt ein ungeheurer Rausch,
Die Hände beben, solches nachzubilden,

Nur ist es viel zu viel, und alles wahr:
Eins muss empor, die anderen zerfliessen.
Gebildet hab ich erst, wenn ichs vermocht,
Vom grossen Schwall das eine abzuschliessen.

In einem Leibe muss es mir gelingen,
Das unaussprechlich Reiche auszudrücken,
Das selige Insichgeschlossensein:
Ein Wesen ists, woran wir uns entzücken!

Seis Jüngling oder Mädchen oder Kind,
Das lasse ich die schmalen Schultern sagen,
Die junge Kehle, wenn sie mir gelingt,
Muss jenes atmend Unbewusste tragen,

Womit die Jugend über Seelen siegt.
Und der ich jenes Atmen ganz verstehe,
Wie selig ich, der trinkt, wo keiner trank,

The Little Theatre of the World

Great shoulders rise from pitchers, and swing round.
From shells I see a boyish body pour,
But as I look a monster seems to gallop
In close pursuit of him, and is no more!

Delightful beings, half nymph, half ripple, flee
Some vast and gloomy thing, a rolling pall:
The body of Night I think this apparition,
Her thundering spaces clenched into a ball.

Now she unwinds her limbs; and now they throng,
Reel into wild and separate commotion.
A drunken urge possesses me: I long,
My fingers itch, to mould those images,

Yet there are far too many, and all true;
One rises up, the others melt away.
Never I'll hold that flux, until I learn
To isolate one shape and make it stay,

Within one body's lineaments compress
All this unspeakable wealth for ever fleeing,
Create a shape self-immanent, self-blessed.
What we delight in is a single being!

Whether it be a youth or girl or child,
This I shall let the narrow shoulders say,
The youthful throat, if well I model it,
That light unconscious breathing shall convey

Which lends to youth its power to conquer souls.
And I who wholly understand that breathing,
How happy I to drink where none has drunk

Hugo von Hofmannsthal

Am Quell des Lebens in geheimer Nähe,
Wo willig kühle unberührte Wellen
Mit tiefem Klang dem Mund entgegenschwellen!

Tritt ab. Das junge Mädchen tritt auf. Sie ist noch ein halbes
Kind. Sie geht nur wenige Schritte, setzt sich dann auf den
steinernen Brückenrand. Ihr weisses leichtes Kleid schimmert
durch das Dunkel.

DAS MÄDCHEN

Die Nacht ist von Sternen und Wolken schwer,
Käm jetzt nur irgendeiner daher
Und säng recht etwas Trauriges,
Indes ich hier im Dunkeln säss!

DIE STIMME EINES BÄNKELSÄNGERS
aus einiger Entfernung

Sie lag auf ihrem Sterbebett
Und sprach: Mit mir ists aus.
Mir ist zumut wie einem Kind,
Das abends kommt nach Haus.

Das Ganze glitt so hin und hin
Und ging als wie im Traum:
Wie eines nach dem andern kam,
Ich sterb und weiss es kaum!

Kein andrer war, wie der erste war:
Da war ich noch ein Kind,
Es blieb mir nichts davon als ein Bild,
So schwach, wie schwacher Wind.

Dem zweiten tat ich Schmerz und Leid
So viel an, als er mir.
Er ist verschollen: Müdigkeit,
Nichts andres blieb bei mir.

[244]

Close, though in secret, to the source of life,
Where pure and cool the willing wavelet dips
With a deep resonance towards my lips.

Exit. Enter the Young Girl. She is little more than a child.
She takes only a few paces, then sits down on the stone
parapet of the bridge. Her white dress shines faintly through
the darkness.

THE GIRL

The night is heavy with clouds and stars,
If only someone now would pass
And sing a ballad that's really sad
While I sit hidden here in the dark.

THE VOICE OF A MINSTREL

some distance away

Upon her death-bed she lay down
And said: It's my last goodnight.
What I feel like is a little child
Who walks home in the failing light.

All things moved by and moved away
And went as in a dream:
How each was linked to the one before
Even now I can hardly say.

No other man was like the first:
And I a foolish young thing.
Nothing remained of it all but a picture
Faint as a breeze in spring.

The second I gave both pain and distress,
As much as he gave me:
He left me and vanished: weariness
Is all that he left to me.

[245]

Den dritten zu denken, bringt mir Scham.
Gott weiss, wie manches kommt!
Nun lieg ich auf meinem Sterbebett:
Wenn ich nur ein Ding zu denken hätt,
Nur ein Ding, das mir frommt!

DAS MÄDCHEN
Es ist aufgestanden und spricht im Abgehen

Die arme Frau, was die nur meint?
Das ganze Lied ist dumm, mir scheint.
Schlaftrunken bin ich. Mir scheint, dort fällt
Ein Stern. Wie gross ist doch die Welt!
So viele Sachen sind darin.
Mir käm jetzt manches in den Sinn,
Wenn ich nur nicht so schläfrig wär . . .
Mir kann doch alles noch geschehn!
Jetzt aber geh ich schon ins Haus,
Ich ziehe mich im Dunkeln aus
Und lass die Läden offenstehn!
Nun schläft der Vogel an der Wand,
Ich leg den Kopf auf meine Hand
Und hör dem lang noch singen zu.
Ich hör doch für mein Leben gern
So traurig singen, und von fern.

Geht ab. Es ist völlig Nacht geworden. Der Wahnsinnige tritt auf, jung, schön und sanft, vor ihm sein Diener mit einem Licht, hinter ihm der Arzt. Der Wahnsinnige lehnt sich mit unbeschreiblicher Anmut an den Brückenrand und freut sich am Anblick der Nacht.

DER DIENER
Schicksal ist das Schicksal meiner Herrschaft,

To think of the third makes me feel ashamed,
God knows how it comes about!
Now on my death-bed I lie down
And wish that I had one single thought,
One thought to see me out.

THE GIRL

who has stood up, and says as she leaves

Poor soul. I wonder what she meant.
To me the whole song makes no sense.
I'm drunk with sleep. I think that over there
A star is falling. Yes, the world's immense.
So many things in it. I vow
If I were not so sleepy now
I'd have ideas in plenty, and to spare . . .
What could not happen to me still!
But I'll go home now nonetheless.
And in the dark I shall undress,
Leaving the shutters open. And,
Though on the wall the cage-bird sleeps,
I'll lay my head upon my hand
And long shall listen to his trill.
Because I dearly love to hear
Sad songs and ballads from afar.

Exit. It is quite dark now. Enter the Madman, young, hand-some, and gentle. In front of him his Servant with a light, behind him the Doctor. The Madman leans against the parapet of the bridge with indescribable grace and takes pleasure in gazing into the night.

THE SERVANT

Fate, I say, and mean my masters' only,

[247]

Von dem eignen sei mir nicht die Rede!
Dieser ist der Letzte von den Reichen,
Von den Mächtigen der Letzte, hilflos.
Aufgetürmten Schatz an Macht und Schönheit
Zehrte er im Tanz wie eine Flamme.
Von den Händen flossen ihm die Schätze,
Von den Lippen Trunkenheit des Siegers,
Laufend auf des Lebens bunten Hügeln!
Wo beginn ich, sein Geschick zu sagen?
Trug er doch gekrönt von wildem Feuer
Schon in knabenhafter Zeit die Stirne:
Und der Vater, der die Flüsse nötigt,
Auszuweichen den Zitronengärten,
Der die Berge aushöhlt, sich ein Lusthaus
Hinzubaun in ihre kühle Flanke,
Nicht vermag er, seinen Sohn zu bändigen.
Dieser dünkt sich Prinz und braucht Gefolge:
Mit den Pferden, mit den schönen Kleidern,
Mit dem wundervollen tiefen Lächeln
Lockt er alle Söhne edler Häuser,
Alles läuft mit ihm; den Papageien,
Den er fliegen lässt, ihm einzufangen,
Laufen aus den Häusern, aus den Gärten
Alle, jeder lässt sein Handwerk liegen
Und der lahme Bettler seine Krücke.
Und so wirft er denn aus seinem Fenster
Seines Vaters Gold mit beiden Händen:
Wenn das Gold nicht reicht, die goldnen Schüsseln,
Edle Steine, Waffen, Prunkgewebe,
Was ihr wollt! Wie eine von den Schwestern
Liebesblind, mit Fieberhänden schöpfend,
Von den aufgehäuften Hügeln Goldes
Alles gibt, die Wege des Geliebten

As for mine, it shall not be in question.
This one is the last of all the wealthy,
Of the mighty too the last, and helpless.
Heaped up treasure, hoards of might and beauty
Dancing he devoured, a ravenous fire.
From his hands the treasures poured uncounted,
From his lips the drunkenness of victors,
Running on life's many-coloured hilltops!
Where shall I begin to tell his story?
When in boyhood even crowned with arrogance,
Fire unquenchable, he bore his forehead.
And his father, who compels the rivers,
Forcing them to skirt the lemon orchards,
Hollows out the mountain-sides to build there
Palaces and mansions for his pleasure,
Never learned to tame so proud a spirit.
Prince, he thinks himself, and needs attendants:
With his horses, finery of dress,
With his deep, mysterious way of smiling,
Charms the sons of all the noble houses,
Makes them run for him; to catch the parrot
He, the prince, has just released on purpose,
Out of houses, gardens, streets they hurry.
All the tradesmen leave their work to serve him.
And the crippled beggar leaves his crutches.
Then again I see him at the window,
Happily throwing out his father's gold;
When the coins run out, the golden platters,
Precious stones, embroideries and weapons,
What you will! As one of his young sisters,
Blind with love, her feverish fingers grasping,
Gives away the heaped-up gold in handfuls,
All of it, so that her lover's path

Hugo von Hofmannsthal

Mit endloser Huldigung zu schmücken
—Fremd ist ihr die Scheu wie einer Göttin—,
Wie die andre Fürstengüter hingibt,
Sich mit wundervollen Einsamkeiten
Zu umgeben, Park und Blütenlaube
Einer starren Insel aufzulegen,
Mitten in den öden Riesenbergen
Eigensinnig solchen Prunk zu gründen:
ER vereinigt in den süssen Lippen,
In der strengen, himmelhellen Stirne
Beider Schönheit—, in der einen Seele
Trägt er beides: ungeheure Sehnsucht,
Sich für ein geliebtes zu vergeuden—
Wieder königliche Einsamkeit.
Beides kennend, überfliegt er beides,
Wie er mit den Füssen viele Länder,
Mit dem Sinn die Freundschaft vieler Menschen
Und unendliches Gespräch hindurchfliegt
Und der vielen Frauen Liebesnetze
Lächelnd kaum berührt und weiterrauscht.
Auf dem Wege blieben wie die Schalen,
Leere Schalen von genossnen Früchten,
Herrliche Gesichter schöner Frauen,
Lockig, mit Geheimnissen beladen,
Purpurmäntel, die um seine Schultern
Kühnerworbne Freunde ihm geschlagen.
Alles dieses liess er hinter sich!
Aber funkelnde Erfahrung legte
Sich um seiner Augen innre Kerne.
Wo er auftritt, bringen kluge Künstler
Ihm herbei ihr lieblichstes Gebilde;
Mit den Augen, den beseelten Fingern
Rührt ers an und nimmt sich ein Geheimnis,

Shall be bright, adorned with endless tributes—
Qualms are strange to her as to a goddess—
As the other spends whole princely fortunes
To surround herself with solitudes,
To establish on some arid island
Marvellous parks and arbours richly trellised,
In the midst of desolate mountain ranges
Obdurate, like splendours she imposes:
In the sweetness of his lips, the strictness
Of his radiant and unclouded forehead
He combines the beauties of both sisters—
Both in his one soul contains: vast longing
Out of love to squander his own person—
Then again for regal solitude.
Knowing both, he flies above them both.
Just as with his feet through many countries
With his mind through multitudes of friendships
Or unending discourse he will fly;
Smiling, hardly touches all the love-snares
Women lay for him, and rushes on.
On his way lie husks he left unheeded,
Empty husks of fruit enjoyed in passing.
Glorious faces of the loveliest women,
Framed in heavy curls and veiled with secrets,
Purple mantles which about his shoulders
Friends by daring won had wrapped in tribute.
This and more he left behind as litter!
Yet experience deeply sparkling gathered
Round the inmost kernel of his eyes.
Where he goes the most ingenious artists
Bring to him the best of their creations;
With his eyes, or with his soulful fingers
Grazing it, he takes its mystery in,

Das der Künstler selbst nur dunkel ahnte,
Nimmt es atmend mit auf seinem Wege.
.   .   .   .

Manches Mal an seinem Wege schlafend
Oder sitzend an den dunklen Brunnen,
Findet er die Söhne oder Töchter
Jener fremden Länder; neben ihnen
Ruht er aus, und mit dem blossen Atmen,
Mit dem Heben seiner langen Wimpern
Sind sie schon bezaubert, und er küsst sie
Auf die Stirn und freut sich ihres Lebens.
Denn er sieht ihr sanftes, stilles Leben,
Mit dem stillen Wehen grüner Wipfel
Sieht er es in ihren grossen Augen.
Sie umklammern seine Handgelenke,
Wenn er gehen will, und wie die Rehe
Schauen sie voll Angst, warum er forteilt.
Doch er lächelt; und auf viele Fragen
Hat er eine Antwort: mit den Augen,
Die sich dunkler färben, nach der Ferne
Winkend, sagt er mit dem strengen Lächeln:
"Wisst ihr nicht? Dies alles ist nur Schale!
Hab so viele Schalen fortgeworfen,
Soll ich an der letzten haftenbleiben?"
Und er treibt sein Pferd schon vorwärts wieder,
Wie ihn selbst die rätselvolle Gottheit.
Seine Augen ruhen auf der Landschaft,
Die noch nie ein solcher Blick getroffen:
Zu den schönsten Hügeln, die mit Reben
An die dunklen, walderfüllten Berge
Angebunden sind, zu schönen Bäumen,
Hochgewipfelt seligen Platanen,
Redet er: er will von ihnen Lächeln,
Von den Felsen will sein starker Wille

Though its maker scarcely had divined it,
Takes it breathing with him on his way.

. . . .

More than once asleep upon the wayside
Or beside a dark well sitting idly
He will come upon a son or daughter
Of those alien countries; and will linger
Near them for a while; by merely breathing,
By the lifting of his long eye-lashes
In a trice enchants them; and he kisses
Each cool brow, rejoices in their being.
For he sees their gentle, quiet being,
With the gentle swaying of green treetops,
Sees it mirrored in their great round eyes.
When he makes to go, they gently seize him
By his wrists, and gazing at him deer-like,
Wild gazelles, they plead in fear and wonder.
But he smiles; and to their many questions
Makes one answer: with his eyes, grown darker
Indicating distance, tells them smiling:
"Don't you know, then? This is only wrapping!
Having thrown away so many wrappings,
Should I let the very last detain me?"
And at once he urges on his horse,
He himself urged on by god or daemon.
Now his gaze reposes on the landscape
Never yet such eyes as his have looked on:
To the loveliest hillsides, linked by vine-shoots
To the dark and forest-laden mountain,
To the lovely bulk of elms and ashes,
To the high and happy crests of plane-trees,
Now he speaks: from them he wants their smiling.
Of the rocks his mighty will requires

Eine atmend wärmere Verkündung,
Alle stummen Wesen will er, flehend,
Reden machen, in die trunkne Seele
Ihren grossen Gang verschwiegnen Lebens,
Wie der Knaben und der Mädchen Leben,
Wie der Statuen Geheimnis haben!
Und er weint, weil sie ihm widerstehen.
Diese letzte Schale wegzureissen,
Einen unerhörten Weg zu suchen
In den Kern des Lebens, dahin kommt er.
In das einsamste von den Kastellen,
Nur ein Viereck von uralten Quadern,
Rings ein tiefer Graben dunklen Wassers,
Nistet er sich ein. Das ganze Leben
Lässt er draussen, alle bunte Beute
Eines grenzenlos erobernden
Jungen Siegerlebens vor dem Tore!
Nur die zaubermächtigen Geräte
Und die tief geheimnisvollen Bücher,
Die Gebildetes in seine Teile
Zu zerlegen lehren, bleiben da.
Unbegreiflich ungeheure Worte
Fängt er an zu reden und den Abgrund
Sich hinabzulassen, dessen obrer
Äussrer Rand an einer kleinen Stelle
Von des Paracelsus tiefsten Büchern
Angeleuchtet wird mit schwacher Flamme.
Und es kommen wundervolle Tage:
In der kahlen Kammer, kaum der Nahrung,
Die ein zahmer Vogel nimmt, bedürftig,
Wirft sich seine Seele mit den Flügeln,
Mit den Krallen kühner als ein Greife,
Wilder als ein Greife, auf die neue

Warmer and more vital revelation.
And beseeching every silent creature
Bids it speak to him, that he may share in
And contain within his drunken spirit
Life's ineffable and hidden movement
As he shares the life of boys and maidens,
Makes his own the mystery of statues!
And he weeps because they still resist him.
To tear off the last of all the wrappings,
Find a path unheard of and untrodden
To the core of life, no less he aims at.
In the most remote of all the castles,
Nothing but a cube of ancient freestone
Moated round with deep and murky water,
Finally he settles; leaves behind him
All of life and all the varied booty
Of a youth which well before the threshold
Was a victor's, limitless in conquest!
Potent instruments of magic only,
And those deep and esoteric volumes
In whose pages all created matter
Is reduced to elements, he retains.
Monstrous unintelligible phrases
Form upon his lips; and now commences
His descent to that abyss whose upper,
Outer edge is dimly, scantly charted
In the deepest works of Paracelsus.
Now a chain of marvellous days awaits him:
In his barely furnished cell, and needing
No more food than does a little cage-bird.
With its mighty pinions beating, talons
More relentless than a swooping griffin's,
Wilder than a griffin's too, his spirit

Hugo von Hofmannsthal

Schattengleiche, körperlose Beute.
Mit dem ungeheueren Gemenge,
Das er selbst im Innern trägt, beginnt er
Nach dem ungeheueren Gemenge
Äussern Daseins gleichnishaft zu haschen.
Tausend Flammen schlagen ihm entgegen
Da und da! in Leben eingekapselt;
Und vor ihm beginnt der brüderliche
Dumpfe Reigen der verschlungnen Kräfte
In der tiefsten Nacht mit glühendem Munde
Unter sich zu reden: Wunderliches,
Aus dem Herzblut eines Kindes quellend,
Findet Antwort in der Gegenrede
Eines Riesenblocks von dunklem Porphyr!

. . . .

Welcher Wahnsinn treibt mich, diesen Wahnsinn
Zu erneuern! Ja, dass ich es sage:
Wahnsinn war das wundervolle Fieber,
Das im Leibe meines Herren brannte! . . .
Nichts hat sich seit jenem Tag verändert,
Mit den süssen hochgezognen Lippen
Tauscht er unaufhörlich hohe Rede
Mit dem Kern und Wesen aller Dinge.
Er ist sanft, und einem Spiel zuliebe,
Meint er, bleibt er noch in seinem Leibe,
Den er lassen könnte, wenn er wollte . . .
Wie vom Rande einer leichten Barke
In den Strom hinab, und wenn er wollte,
In das Innre eines Ahornstammes,
In den Halm von einem Schilf zu steigen.
Nie von selber denkt er sich zu nähren,
Und er bleibt uns nicht an einem Orte:

Hurls itself upon its newly sighted
Shadowy and incorporeal booty.
With the vast and multitudinous tumult
That's within him, he begins to clutch at
All the vast and multitudinous tumult
Of the outward world, its correspondence.
Roaring flames by thousands meet his coming.
There! and there! Confined in living matter;
And before his eyes the vague fraternal
Round of all the interwoven powers
Dancing deep in night with lips like embers
Each to each begin to utter: marvels
Welling from the heart-blood of an infant
Find their answer in the weird rejoinder
Of a giant block of porphyry!

. . . .

But what madness leads me to renew this
Madness! Openly at last I'll name it:
Raving madness was that marvellous fever
Burning in the entrails of my master! . . .
Nothing since has altered his condition.
With his lips turned up, disdainful sweetness,
Endlessly he holds exalted discourse
With the core and essence of creation.
Gentle, for the sake of a mere game,
So he says, he stays within his body,
Able to discard it when he pleases . . .
Pass as from the rim of some light vessel
Down into the stream, and, if he cared to,
Penetrate a sycamore's trunk and enter,
Dwell within the stems of reeds and rushes.
Left alone, he never thinks of eating
Nor will stay for long where we have left him:

Denn er will die vielen seiner Brüder
Oft besuchen und zu Gast bei ihnen
Sitzen, bei den Flüssen, bei den Bäumen,
Bei den schönen Steinen, seinen Brüdern.
Also führen wir ihn durch die Landschaft
Flusshinab und hügelan, wir beide,
Dieser Arzt und ich, wie nicht ein Kind ist
Sanft und hilflos, diesen, dem die Schönen
Und die Mächtigen sich dienend bückten,
Wenn er hinlief auf des Lebens Hügeln,
Trunkenheit des Siegers um die Stirne.

DER ARZT

Ich sehe einen solchen Lauf der Welt:
Das Übel tritt einher aus allen Klüften;
Im Innern eines jeden Menschen hält
Es Haus und schwingt sich nieder aus den Lüften:
Auf jeden lauert eigene Gefahr,
Und nicht die Bäume mit den starken Düften
Und nicht die Luft der Berge, kühl und klar,
Verscheuchen das, auch nicht der Rand der See.
Denn eingeboren ist ihr eignes Weh
Den Menschen: ja, indem ich es so nenne,
Verschleir ich schon die volle Zwillingsnäh,
Mit ders dem Sein verwachsen ist, und trenne,
Was nur ein Ding: denn lebend sterben wir.
Für Leib und Seele, wie ich sie erkenne,
Gilt dieses Wort, für Baum und Mensch und Tier.
Und hier . . .

DER WAHNSINNIGE
*indem er sich beim Schein der Fackel in einem silbernen
Handspiegel betrachtet*

The Little Theatre of the World

Ever urged to see his many brothers,
As their guest to sit with them in converse,
Entertained by plants and trees and rivers,
By the inarticulate rocks, his brothers.
So we lead him slowly through the landscape.
Down the rivers, up the hills, his guardians,
This physician and myself; we lead him
Gentle now, more helpless than an infant.
Him to whom the beautiful and mighty
Bowed in homage once and longed to serve him
Running on life's many-coloured hilltops,
On his brow the drunkenness of victors!

THE DOCTOR

Such, as I see it, is the way of the world:
In every crevice evil has its lair,
Within the heart of every man lies curled
As in a nest, and pounces from the air.
To each, peculiar peril threatens death;
And not the trees, for all their balmy breath,
And not the mountain air, though cool and clear,
Can drive it off; nor yet the edge of the sea.
In each his own affliction is innate,
Congenital; but if I call it so
I veil the perfect twin-affinity
Of this and life itself, I separate
What always has been *one:* for living we die.
To soul and flesh, as all researches show,
These words apply, to man and beast and tree,
And here. . . .

THE MADMAN

*contemplating his reflection in a small silver mirror by the
light cast by the torch*

Hugo von Hofmannsthal

Nicht mehr für lange hält dieser Schein,
Es mehren sich schon die Stimmen,
Die mich nach aussen rufen,
So wie die Nacht mit tausend Lippen
Die Fackel hin und wider zerrt:
Ein Wesen immer gelüstet es nach dem andern!
Düstern Wegen und funkelnden nachzugehen,
Drängts mich auseinander, Namen umschwirren mich
Und mehr als Namen: sie könnten meine sein!
Ich bin schon kaum mehr hier!
Ich fühl schon auf der eigenen Stirn die Spur
Der eignen Sohle, von mir selber fort
Mich schwingend wie ein Dieb aus einem Fenster.
Hierhin und dorthin darf ich, ich bin hergeschickt,
Zu ordnen, meines ist ein Amt,
Des Namen über alle Namen ist.
Es haben aber die Dichter schon
Und die Erbauer der königlichen Paläste
Etwas geahnt vom Ordnen der Dinge,
Der ungeheuren dumpfen Kräfte
Vielfachen Mund, umhangen von Geheimnis,
Liessen sie in Chorgesängen erschallen, wiesen ihm
Gemessene Räume an, mit Wucht zu lasten,
Empor zu drängen, Meere abzuhalten,
Selbst urgewaltig wie die alten Meere.
Schicksal aber hat nur der einzelne:
Er tritt hervor, die ungewissen Meere,
Die Riesenberge mit grünem Haar von Bäumen,
Dies alles hinter ihm, nur so wie ein Gewebe,
Sein Schicksal trägt er in sich, er ist kühn,
Verfängt sich in Fallstricke und schlägt hin
Und vieles mehr, sein Schicksal ist zehntausendmal
Das Schicksal von zehntausend hohen Bergen:

The Little Theatre of the World

This illusion will not last much longer,
The voices multiply
That call me out of myself.
Just as the night with a thousand lips
Tugs at the torch this way and that:
Always one creature will lust after another!
To follow darkling paths and follow sparkling paths
I feel a dividing urge, and names whir around me,
And more than names: they could be my own!
As it is, I am scarcely here!
On my own forehead I feel the track
The soles of my own feet are leaving as I vault
Away from myself as a burglar vaults from the window.
Here I may go, and there, I have been sent,
To set all things in order, mine's a mission
Whose name is higher than all names.
Yet before me the poets and
The builders of royal palaces
Faintly foreknew the ordering of things
And made to sound in choral song
The manifold mouth hung round with mystery
Of powers vast, amorphous, and allotted
A measured space to it, now to exert its weight,
Now to surge up and hold great oceans back,
Themselves primevally powerfully as the ancient oceans,
But fate none but the single man possesses:
He ventures forth, and the uncertain oceans,
The towering mountains with the green hair of trees,
All these behind him, only like some frail web,
His fate he bears within him, he is bold,
Is caught in man-traps and crashes down,
And much besides, his fate ten thousand times
As great as of ten thousand towering mountains.

Hugo von Hofmannsthal

Der wilden Tiere Dreistigkeit und Stolz,
Sehnsüchtige Bäche, der Fall von hohen Bäumen,
Dies alles ist darin verkocht zehntausendmal.

Hier tritt der Mond vor die Wolken und erleuchtet das
Flussbett.

Was aber sind Paläste und die Gedichte:
Traumhaftes Abbild des Wirklichen!
Das Wirkliche fängt kein Gewebe ein:
Den ganzen Reigen anzuführen,
Den wirklichen, begreift ihr dieses Amt?
Hier ist ein Weg, er trägt mich leichter als der Traum.
Ich gleite bis ans Meer, gelagert sind die Mächte dort
Und kreisen dröhnend, Wasserfälle spiegeln
Den Schein ergossnen Feuers, jeder findet
Den Weg und rührt die andern alle an . . .
Mit trunknen Gliedern, ich, im Wirbel mitten,
Reiss alles hinter mir, doch alles bleibt
Und alles schwebt, so wie es muss und darf!
Hinab, hinein, es verlangt sie alle nach mir!

Er will über das Geländer in den Fluss hinab. Die beiden
halten ihn mit sanfter Gewalt. Er blickt, an sie gelehnt, und
ruft heiter, mit leisem Spott

Bacchus, Bacchus, auch dich fing einer ein
Und band dich fest, doch nicht für lange!

The Little Theatre of the World

The daring and the pride of savage beasts,
Nostalgic brooks, the falling of mighty trees,
Concocted in his fate ten thousand times.

Now the moon emerges from behind the clouds and lights up
the river-bed.

But what are palaces, and what are poems?
The dreamlike image of reality!
The real no mortal tracery can catch:
To lead the *whole* dance, the *whole* round,
The real, can you begin to grasp this task?
Here is a way to bear me yet more lightly than the dream.
I drift towards the sea, where all the powers forgather,
And, roaring, circle round where waterfalls reflect
The glow of fire poured forth, where each one finds
The way and touches all the others. . . .
And I with drunken limbs, I in the whirlpool's midst
Tear all along with me, yet all remains,
All hovers yet, as hover it may and must!
Down then! and into it! They long for me, each one!
Down, then!

He makes to leap over the parapet into the river. The two
guardians restrain him with gentle firmness. Leaning against
them, he calls out cheerfully, with faint scorn

Bacchus, Bacchus, you too were caught by someone,
Who bound you fast, but not for long!

THE MINE AT FALUN

(Act One)

Translated by

MICHAEL HAMBURGER

Das Bergwerk zu Falun

ELIS FRÖBOM

DER ALTE TORBERN

DIE BERGKÖNIGIN

DER KNABE AGMAHD

FRAU JENSEN, *Wirtin*

ILSEBILL

REGINE

KATHRINE

PETER

KLAUS   } *Matrosen*

PORTUGIESER

DER ALTE FISCHER

SEINE FRAU

SEIN SOHN

*Der Meeresstrand einer kleinen Hafenstadt. Rechts Fischer-
hütten. Zwischen ihnen Netze zum Trocknen ausgespannt.
Zur Linken eine ärmliche Matrosenschenke, davor Tische und
Bänke. Hie und da spärliches Buschwerk. Im Hintergrund ist
ein Fischerboot halb an den Strand gezogen. Jenseits der
Meeresbucht in der Ferne blaue Bergketten.*

The Mine at Falun

ELIS FRÖBOM

OLD TORBERN

THE QUEEN OF THE MOUNTAIN

THE BOY AGMAHD

MRS. JENSEN, *innkeeper*

ILSEBILL

REGINA

CATHERINE

PETER

CLAUS ⎱ *Seamen*

THE PORTUGUESE

THE OLD FISHERMAN

HIS WIFE

HIS SON

The beach of a small harbour. On the right, fishermen's shacks. Between them, nets hung up to dry. On the left, a dingy sailor's tavern with tables and benches in front of it. A few bushes here and there. In the background a fishing boat has been half drawn up on the beach. Beyond the bay, blue mountain ranges can be seen in the distance.

Hugo von Hofmannsthal

Der alte Fischer, nachher seine Frau, treten aus der vordersten Hütte.

DER FISCHER
tut ein paar Schritte gegen das Wirtshaus hin, murmelt

's ist niemand da.
Kehrt wieder um.

DIE FRAU *in der Tür ihrer Hütte stehend*
Nu, hast du ihrs gesagt?
Hast du sie angeredet um den Dienst?

FISCHER
Sie hat ja doch kein Mannsbild in der Wirtschaft.
Wir lassen ihn. Ist alles eins.

FRAU
Drei Mädel
Sind drin.

FISCHER
Kein Mensch!

FRAU
Drei junge starke Mädel,
Ich weiss doch! Jesus, geh doch, red sie an!

FISCHER
geht gegen die Schenke, kehrt wieder um

Von woher sollten denn drei Mädel da sein,
Wer sollten denn die sein?

FRAU
Zwei städtische,
Und eine ist die Ilsebill vom Schneider.

The Mine at Falun

The Old Fisherman comes out of the foremost cottage, followed by his Wife.

THE FISHERMAN
takes a few paces towards the inn, mumbles

There's no one in.
> *Turns back again.*

THE WOMAN *standing in the doorway of cottage*

Well, did you speak to her?
Did you go in and ask her if she'll do it?

FISHERMAN

Oh, but she hasn't got a man about the house.
We'll let it be. It's all the same.

WOMAN

Three girls

Live in that house.

FISHERMAN

No one!

WOMAN

Three strapping girls,
I know it! Heavens, man, go in and ask her!

FISHERMAN
goes up to the inn, turns back again

And how would three young girls come to be in there?
Who would they be, then?

WOMAN

Two girls from the town,
And one is Ilsebill, the tailor's girl.

[269]

FISCHER

Für was sind die daher?

FRAU

Na, Vater.

FISCHER

So.

Nu ja. Ei so. Mit Branntwein und mit Bier
Macht sie nicht viel Geschäft, die Jensen.

FRAU

Nein,

's ist gar zu abgelegen. Aber so,
Das bringt schon dann und wann Matrosen her.
Die trinken dann halt besser in Gesellschaft.
So bitt sie doch, jetzt ist die Luft so schön.
Er möchte besser atmen.

FISCHER

Das ist so

Das Ganze, was er hat: wenn das nicht wär,
So möcht man ihn grad in die Grube legen,
Und wär kein Mord. Denn wo kein Leben ist,
Ist auch kein Mord.

FRAU

Na, geh jetzt, Vater, geh,
Und red dich nicht hinein.

FISCHER
kehrt wieder um

Sie hat uns erst
Den Branntwein geben. Ich mag nicht schon wieder . . .

[270]

The Mine at Falun

FISHERMAN

But why? What business . . .

WOMAN

Can't you guess?

FISHERMAN

I see.
Oh, well. All right. You mean there's not much trade
In beer and brandy, at Mrs. Jensen's.

WOMAN

No.
It's too much out of the way. But thanks to them
A sailor or two drop in from time to time.
It's just that drink tastes better in company.
Go in and ask her; now the air's so fresh,
He'd like to breathe more freely.

FISHERMAN

That's about all
The lad's got left: if it weren't for that
They might as well just lay him in the pit.
And it wouldn't be murder. Where there's no life
There can be no murder.

WOMAN

Get along now, father,
And don't start talking deep.

FISHERMAN

turns back again

Only the other day
She gave us that brandy. I hate to ask her . . .

Hugo von Hofmannsthal

FRAU

So geh doch. Soll er ganz verkümmern drin
In der stinkigen Kammer? Und du bringst ihn
Doch nicht heraus mit deinem Arm.

FISCHER

               Du, Alte,
Was Glück ist so, das haben wir schon nicht:
Bei mir ein Tau, der halbe Arm . . . schön, schön!
Bei ihm die Rah . . . der Kopf. Da liegt er so,
Lebt nicht und stirbt nicht.

FRAU JENSEN
tritt aus der Schenke

          Nun, was macht der Sohn?

FISCHER

Der Sohn, der macht nicht viel. Er liegt halt so.
Wir möchten Sie schön bitten, wegen . . . weil
Ich ihn nicht tragen kann.

FRAU

        Wir möchten ihn
Ins Schiff hinlegen, dass er doch die Luft
Einatmet.

FISCHER
's ist das einzige, was er hat.

FRAU JENSEN

Wir tragen ihn heraus. Geh, Ilsebill,
Und eine von den Fischermädeln; welche
Ist denn die stärkere? . . .

The Mine at Falun

WOMAN

Go in, I say. Do you want him to perish
In that stinking room? And by yourself
You'll never carry him out, not with your arm.

FISHERMAN

You couldn't call us lucky, could you, Mother?
With me, a rope, and half my arm gone: Lovely!
With him the main yard . . . and his head. So there
He lies and neither lives nor dies.

MRS. JENSEN

comes out of the inn

                    How is he?

FISHERMAN

My son? He's nothing much. Just lying there.
We've come to ask you kindly to . . . because
His weight's too much for me.

WOMAN

                    We'd like to get him
Out in the boat, so he can breathe the air
At least.

FISHERMAN

That's all that's left for him to do.

MRS. JENSEN

We'll carry him out. Come on, then, Ilsebill.
And one of the two fishermen's girls; but which
Of you is the stronger?

Hugo von Hofmannsthal

EINE STIMME *aus dem Hause links*

Geh du!

ANDERE STIMME

Ich mag nicht!

ERSTE

Ich hab nicht Zeit!

ZWEITE

Ich kämme mir mein Haar!

ERSTE

Sie lügt, sie liegt im Bett!

ILSEBILL

tritt aus der Schenke. Sie ist blond und voll, noch jung, doch
mit Spuren des Verblühens. Sie geht hinüber gegen die
Fischerhütte. Ruft nach rückwärts

So kommt ihr doch!

DAS EINE MÄDCHEN *aus dem Fenster*

Hast du uns zu befehlen?

ILSEBILL
stampft zornig auf

Komm, du Hex!

Vor Mitleid aufgeregt

Er schaut aus wie ein Totes!

STIMME DER ZWEITEN *aus dem Haus*

Du, ich geh,

Ich möcht ihn sehn.

[274]

The Mine at Falun

A VOICE *from the house on the left*

You go!

SECOND VOICE

I don't want to go.

THE FIRST

I haven't time.

THE SECOND

And I'm just doing my hair!

THE FIRST

A lie! She's still in bed.

ILSEBILL

Comes out of the inn. She is blonde and buxom, still young, but with signs that she is past the bloom of youth. She walks over towards the Fisherman's cottage. Calls out to the back

Come on, you two!

FIRST GIRL *from the window*

Who's giving orders to us?

ILSEBILL

stamps her foot angrily

Come, you witch.

Excited with pity

Why, he looks like a dead thing.

VOICE OF THE SECOND GIRL
from the house

Hey, I'm going,
I want to see.

[275]

Hugo von Hofmannsthal

ERSTE
tritt vom Fenster zurück

Nein, ich!

ZWEITE *drinnen*

Jetzt will ich gehen!

ERSTE *drinnen, schreit*

Sie riegelt mir die Tür!

ZWEITE
Sie will mich schlagen!

ILSEBILL
an der Tür der Fischerhütte

Kommt ihr einmal! Wär ich ein Bursch, ich schlüg euch!

*Die beiden Mädchen, ziemlich hübsch, verwahrlost, treten
aus der Schenke, gehen hinüber.*

*Ilsebill und das grössere Mädchen tragen den Fischerssohn
aus der Hütte in das rückwärts liegende Boot. Das kleine
Mädchen geht neugierig hinterher. Der alte Fischer hilft mit
dem linken Arm tragen.*

DES FISCHERS FRAU
zu Frau Jensen; rechts vorne

Zehn Tag liegt er nun so: seit in der Früh
Am letzten Mittwoch.

The Mine at Falun

THE FIRST

stepping back from the window

No, me!

THE SECOND *inside*

Now I want to go!

THE FIRST *inside, shrieking*

She's locking me in!

THE SECOND

She's trying to hit me!

ILSEBILL

at the cottage door

Now come along! If only I were a man
I'd give you both a hiding!

*The two Girls, rather pretty, slovenly, come out of the inn,
walk across.*

*Ilsebill and the taller Girl carry the Fisherman's Son from the
cottage to the boat at the back. The shorter Girl follows them
inquisitively. The Old Fisherman helps them carry with his
left arm.*

THE FISHERMAN'S WIFE

to Mrs. Jensen; right front

Ten days he's been lying like that: since early
Last Wednesday morning.

[277]

Hugo von Hofmannsthal

FRAU JENSEN

Er steht schon noch auf.

FISCHERSFRAU

Zehn Tag, zehn Nächte liegt er so: kein Bissen
Im Mund, kein Tropfen Wasser durch die Kehle.
Sein Puls geht schwach, ein ungebornes Kalb
Im Mutterleibe drin hat stärkern Herzschlag.

FRAU JENSEN

Nu, schlägt doch fort.

FISCHERSFRAU

          Am Mittwoch in der Früh
Seh ich ihn stehn und reden: da genau,
Wo Ihr nun steht, mit einem fremden Herrn.
Mutter, sagt er, ich fahr den Herrn hinüber,
Und zeigt über die Bucht, dann geht der Fremde
Ein bissl weg, und er tritt her an 'n Zaun
Und sagt: muss ein Engländer sein, drei Taler
Krieg ich, sagt er und lacht, und geht zum Schiff
Und richtet dem ein Kissen her zum Sitzen.
's geht Landwind. Nun, was denn? vor Sonnenaufgang
Was soll da gehn? Er bückt sich: da auf einmal
Schlägt der Wind um und packt von draussen her
Das Segel wie mit Fäusten, schlägt die Rah
Ihm dröhnend auf den Schädel; ohne Taumeln,
Eh ich aufschreien kann, fällt er ins Schiff . . .

DER ALTE FISCHER
ist dazugetreten

Und seitdem geht der Wind vom Meer herein,

[278]

The Mine at Falun

MRS. JENSEN
He'll be up again.

FISHERMAN'S WIFE

Ten days, ten nights he's been lying like that:
Not a bite in his mouth, not a drop of water
Down his poor throat. His pulse is weak; why, an unborn
    calf
Inside its mother has a stronger heartbeat.

MRS. JENSEN

But beating still.

FISHERMAN'S WIFE
Early on Wednesday morning
I see him stand and talk: exactly where
You're standing now, and talking with a stranger.
Mother, he says, I'm taking this gentleman
Across, and points across the bay; the stranger
Walks round a bit, and he steps up to the fence
And says: must be an Englishman, I'm getting
Three crowns, he says and laughs, and goes to the boat
And puts a cushion down for him to sit on.
A land-breeze. And why not? What else would blow
Just before sunrise? He bends down: and all at once
The wind turns, grips the sail as though with fists
From the open sea, and brings the main yard down
On his head with a crack; without so much as a stagger,
Before I can even scream, he falls into the boat . . .

THE OLD FISHERMAN
who has joined them

And ever since it's blown in from the sea

[279]

Nicht eine Mütze voll geht umgekehrt,
Bald stark, bald schwach. Ich sitz an dreissig Jahr
Hier an dem Ufer, in den dreissig Jahren
Hab ich das nicht erlebt, Ihr merkt das nicht,
Ich merks, und was es ist . . . 's ist nicht natürlich!

*Der Fischer und seine Frau gehen in ihre Hütte, Frau Jensen
in die Schenke. Die Mädchen stehen im Hintergrund und
betrachten flüsternd den Regungslosen.*

*Von rechts her treten auf: der kurze Peter, der faule Klaus,
der Portugieser, einer hinter dem andern, dann Elis Fröbom.
Peter umschauend, Klaus tabakkauend, Elis den Blick starr
zu Boden gerichtet.*

PETER

Hier sind wir.

PORTUGIESER
Hier?

PETER
Zur Stelle.

*Frau Jensen tritt aus der Schenke. Peter geht auf sie zu,
schüttelt ihr die Hand. Die andern stehen hintereinander:
Klaus phlegmatisch, der Portugieser neugierig, Elis den Blick
zu Boden.*

FRAU JENSEN
knicksend

Vielleicht, die Herren treten hier herein,
Wenns so gefällig sein wird . . .

Die drei stehen verlegen.

[280]

Now strong, now faint, and not one hatful blows
The other way. The best part of thirty years
I've lived on this same shore, and never known
The like of it to happen. You don't notice
A thing like that; I do and know the meaning.
I'll tell you this: it isn't natural.

The Fisherman and his Wife go into their cottage, Mrs.
Jensen into the inn. The Girls stand about in the background,
looking at the motionless body and whispering.

From the right enter: Short Peter, Lazy Claus, the Portuguese,
one behind the other, then Elis Fröbom. Peter looking about
him. Claus chewing tobacco. Elis gazing fixedly at the ground.

PETER

We're there.

THE PORTUGUESE

What, here?

PETER

That's right. The very place.

Mrs. Jensen comes out of the inn. Peter goes up to her,
shakes her hand. The others stand one behind the other:
Claus, phlegmatic, the Portuguese inquisitive, Elis looking
down.

MRS. JENSEN

curtsying

Perhaps the gentlemen will step in here,
If they feel so disposed . . .

The three of them stand there embarrassed.

[281]

Hugo von Hofmannsthal

PETER

Geht! Die hol ich!

*Springt nach rückwärts zu den Mädchen. Er bringt die
Kathrine und Regine nach vorne. Indessen stehen Klaus und
der Portugieser unbeweglich.*

ELIS

*hat sich auf eine der Bänke vor dem Wirtshaus gesetzt, ohne
sonst auf jemand zu achten.*

PETER

bringt die beiden Mädchen zu den Matrosen.

KLAUS

nimmt Kathrine am Kinn.

KATHRINE

schlägt nach seiner Hand

Pfui, Tran!

FRAU JENSEN

weist auf Elis

Was ist mit dem? Gehört der nicht zu euch?

PETER *halblaut*

Das ist ein Neriker, lasst den in Ruh.
Wo der her ist, da scheint die Sonne nicht,
Da füllt ein blasses Licht, dem Mond vergleichbar,
Höhlichte Täler, dran das Elchwild äst,
Da sitzt der Nöck am Wassersturz und singt.
Schau sein Gesicht nur an, ists nicht so schleirig
Wie Eulen ihrs? Sein Vater war grad so,
War Steuermann und hatt ein zweit Gesicht
Und wanderte in Moor und Bergesklüften,

[282]

The Mine at Falun

PETER

Go in! I'll get them!

*Leaps to the back and joins the girls. He fetches Catherine
and Regina into the foreground. Meanwhile Claus and the
Portuguese stand motionless.*

ELIS

*has sat down on one of the benches in front of the inn, paying
no attention to anyone.*

PETER

takes the two girls up to the sailors.

CLAUS

chucks Catherine under the chin.

CATHERINE

strikes at his hand

Pooh, fish-oil!

MRS. JENSEN

pointing at Elis

What about him? Isn't he one of you?

PETER *softly*

He's melancholic, leave him out of it.
Where he comes from, the sun never shines,
There a pale light, paler than moonlight, fills
Cavernous valleys where the wild elks graze,
There by the waterfalls the sprite sits singing.
Just take a look at his face; is it not veiled,
Dim as a barn-owl's? His father was the same,
A helmsman with the gift of second sight,
Who roamed about the moors and mountain chasms

[283]

Indes sein Leib bei uns an Bord umherging.
Nun kommt er heim und findt die Mutter tot:
Das hat ihm ganz den schweren Mund verschlagen.

Sie wenden sich alle, ins Haus zu gehen.

PETER
*im Abgehen zu Frau Jensen, die inzwischen Elis einen Becher
auf den Tisch gesetzt hat*

Ach! neunzehn Wochen kein vernünftiger Hafen!

*Alle treten in die Schenke. Elis bleibt auf seinem Platz. Nach
einer Weile tritt Ilsebill geräuschlos aus dem Hause und stellt
sich vor Elis hin.*

ILSEBILL

Kennst mich noch, Elis?

ELIS
nickt

Bist die Ilsebill.

Da, trink.

ILSEBILL
Ich dank dir schön.

Setzt sich neben ihn, trinkt.

Pause

ELIS *gleichgültig*
Wie lebst?

ILSEBILL
schiebt den Becher zurück

Ich dank dir, gut.

The Mine at Falun

While in the flesh he worked with us on board.
Then this one goes home and finds his mother dead:
That finished it, and stopped his sullen tongue.

They all turn to go into the house.

PETER

as he goes in, to Mrs. Jensen, who meanwhile has put a beaker on the table for Elis

Oh, nineteen weeks without a decent port!

All go into the inn. Elis stays where he is. After a while Ilsebill comes quietly out of the house and stands in front of Elis.

ILSEBILL

Do you remember me, Elis?

ELIS

nods

You're Ilsebill.

Here, have a drink.

ILSEBILL

Oh, thank you.

Sits down next to him, drinks.

Pause

ELIS *indifferent*

Well, how's life?

ILSEBILL

pushing back the cup

I don't complain, thank you for asking me.

[285]

Steht auf

Ich stehl dir deine Zeit.

ELIS

Ich brauch sie nicht.
Ich wart auf einen, der ja so nicht kommt.
Auf Niels, den Sohn vom frühern Kirchspielschreiber.

ILSEBILL

Sagst du mit Fleiss den Namen da vor mir,
Damit du mir was tust? Dann geh ich fort.

ELIS

Was ist mir dir und dem?

ILSEBILL

Es ist gar nichts.
Es war nur was.

Mit abgewandtem Gesicht

Ein Kind hab ich gehabt
Von ihm. Der arme Wurm ist tot.
Ich leb. Und jetzt geht mich der Niels nichts an.

ELIS

So, so.

ILSEBILL

Es ist gar lang her, dass du fort warst.

ELIS
mit künstlicher Gelassenheit

Ja, ja. Die Mutter muss jetzt so was sein,
Wie da an meinem Stiefel hängt. Und ist
Nicht etwa schnell gestorben . . .

[286]

The Mine at Falun

Gets up

I'm taking up your time.

ELIS

                    I've no use for it.
I'm waiting for a man who'll never come.
For Niels, the son of the former parish clerk.

ILSEBILL

Is it on purpose you have spoken that name,
To hurt me? If you have, I must be going.

ELIS

What's between you and him?

ILSEBILL

                    Nothing at all.
But there *was* something.

Turning away her face

                    I had a child by him.
The poor little mite is dead. I'm still alive.
And now your Niels is no concern of mine.

ELIS

I see.

ILSEBILL

It's quite a time you've been away.

ELIS

pretending to be calm

Oh, yes. By now my mother must be something
Rather like that thing hanging from my boot;
And died no quick death either . . .

[287]

Hugo von Hofmannsthal

ILSEBILL

nickt

Deine Mutter.

ELIS

Und da wir gingen, war sie aus dem Zeug
Wie du und ich, nur besser. Ihre Augen
So rein, ihr Mund viel frischer wie der deine.
Drei Jahr sind freilich eine lange Zeit.

ILSEBILL

Und du hasts nicht gewusst?

ELIS

*anscheinend gleichmütig, mit der Ironie tiefsten
Schmerzes*

Nein, nein, o nein.
Erst beim Anklopfen. Erst hab ich gemeint,
Es ist ein falsches Haus. Es steht ein Ofen,
Wo sonst ihr Bette stand; und wo ihr Leib
Erkaltete im Tod, da wärmt ein Hund
Den seinen. Und dem Kirchspielschreiber Niels
Hab ich geschrieben, dass er mir das Amt
Ansagt, wo ich die Sachen holen kann,
Wenn was geblieben ist, wie man so schreibt:
Nach Abzug der Begräbniskosten.

Starrt vor sich hin.

ILSEBILL

wischt sich die Augen

Elis!
Lass deine Hand anschauen, nein, die andre.
Weisst du noch, was das ist?

The Mine at Falun

ILSEBILL

nods

Yes, your mother.

ELIS

And when we left she was of the same stuff
As you or me, only better. Her eyes so pure.
Her lips more fresh, more young than your lips are.
Yes, as you say, three years are quite a time.

ILSEBILL

And you never knew of it?

ELIS

seemingly indifferent, with the irony of deepest grief

No, no, oh no.
Not till I knocked. At first I thought I'd come
To the wrong house. Because there was a stove
Where her bed used to be; and where her body
Grew cold with death, a dog was warming his.
And then I wrote to Niels, the parish clerk,
To let me know where to collect the things,
If anything was left; you know the phrase:
After deduction of the funeral costs.

Stares in front of him.

ILSEBILL

wiping her eyes

Elis! Hold out your hand. No, no, the other.
Do you remember what that is?

[289]

Hugo von Hofmannsthal

ELIS

Die Narbe da?
Das ist ja alles nicht mehr wahr. Wann war das?

ILSEBILL

Elis, wir gingen aus der Sonntagsschule,
Da tratest du mir in den Weg.

ELIS

Ach ja . . .
Und fragte dich . . .

ILSEBILL

Du fragtest nicht, du sprachst:
Was ich jetzt tu, das tu ich zum Beweis,
Dass ich dich liebhab und damit dus glaubst:
Sonst will ich nichts.

ELIS

Und schnitt mich da hinein?

ILSEBILL

Du bücktest dich, da lag ein roter Scherben
Von hartem Ton, und damit fuhrst du dir
Wild über deine Hand, dass schweres Blut
Aufquoll.

ELIS

Ich schnitt beinah die Sehnen durch.

Lacht trocken.

ILSEBILL

*bückt sich auf den Tisch und drückt die Lippen auf seine
Hand.*

The Mine at Falun

ELIS

That scar?
All finished with, a lie. When did I do it?

ILSEBILL

Why, we were going home from Sunday school
And suddenly you made me stop.

ELIS

Oh, yes . . .

And asked you . . .

ILSEBILL

No, you didn't ask, you said:
What I'm about to do now is to prove
I'm fond of you, so you'll believe I mean it.
That's all I want.

ELIS

And cut my hand just there?

ILSEBILL

You stooped—there was a piece of earthenware,
Red like a flower-pot shard, you picked it up
And gashed your hand with it so hard, thick blood
Flowed out.

ELIS

I nearly cut the tendons through.

He gives a dry laugh.

ILSEBILL

*bends her head over the table and presses her lips on his
hand.*

[291]

ELIS

zieht die Hand weg, rückt mit dem Stuhl fort.

ILSEBILL

Zudringlich bin ich.

Pause

Elis!

ELIS

sieht sie an.

ILSEBILL *mit ängstlich flehendem Blick*

Gar nichts mehr?

ELIS

zuckt die Achseln, klopft seine Pfeife aus.

ILSEBILL *zögernd*

Wenn du nicht wüsstest, wo du wohnen solltest . . .
Weil ja die Mutter tot ist, hätt ich nur
Gemeint, du könntest ja bei mir . . .

ELIS

Schön Dank.

Ich schlaf an Bord.

ILSEBILL

sieht vor sich hin.

ELIS

*sucht in seinen Rocktaschen, nimmt ein buntes Tuch, zieht
aus der Geldkatze zwei Goldstücke, wickelt sie ins Tuch,
schiebt es hin, wo es ihre Hand berührt*

Das Tuch da nimm und trags,
Ist indisch Fabrikat. Wers kennt, erkennts.

The Mine at Falun

ELIS

withdraws it—pushes his chair back.

ILSEBILL

I'm pestering you.

Pause

Elis!

ELIS

looks at her.

ILSEBILL *with an imploring look*

It's all over then?

ELIS

shrugs his shoulders and knocks out his pipe.

ILSEBILL *hesitantly*

If you should happen to have nowhere to stay . . .
I mean, because your mother's dead, I thought
Perhaps you'd like to come . . .

ELIS

Thanks very much.

I sleep on board.

ILSEBILL

stares in front of her.

ELIS

rummages in his coat pockets, pulls out a coloured scarf, takes two gold coins out of his purse, wraps them in the scarf, pushes it to where it touches her hand

Here, have this scarf and wear it,
Real Indian—anyone who knows will tell you.

[293]

Hugo von Hofmannsthal

ILSEBILL

wickelt die Goldstücke aus und schiebt sie ihm wieder hin

Sei schön bedankt fürs schöne Tuch. Dein Geld
Behalt. Das will ich nicht. Das wär mir nichts,
Von dir Geld nehmen. Dein Geld brauch ich nicht.
Ich schwimm im Gelde, wie man spricht. Ich habs
Nicht nötig.

Lacht, näher dem Weinen.

DER PORTUGIESER
sieht aus dem Fenster der Schenke

Blas doch nicht immer Trübsal, Elis, trink
Und lass das Mädel trinken.

ELIS
*hält Ilsebill den Becher hin, sie schüttelt den Kopf; er trinkt
den Branntweinbecher aus, atmet tief auf und lehnt sich
zurück*

Schön warst du freilich. Nun ich trunken hab,
Kommt mirs zurück. Die Züge scharfgezackt
Wie die Korallen, die tief drunten wachsen,
Blass das Gesicht, allein so rot die Lippen . . .
So schön warst du, wo hast dus hingetan?
Hör auf mit Weinen. Kann auch sein, du bist
Nicht gar so anders. Ich hab andre Augen.
Den Star hat mirs gestochen, und mir kehrt
Das Leben wie ein Wrack sein Eingeweide zu.
Wenn ich dich anschau, fest, so seh ich deutlich
Zwei Augen, glasig Zeug, gefüllt mit Wasser,
Zwei Lippen, rund wie Egel, auch geformt,
Sich festzusaugen. Was steckt da dahinter,
Was denn für grosse Lust? und dann nachher

The Mine at Falun

ILSEBILL

unwraps the coins and pushes them back to him

Thanks for the lovely scarf. But keep your money.
It would seem foolish to me, and not right
To accept money from you. And I don't need it,
I'm rolling in it, as they say. So there's
No need.

Laughs, but feels more like weeping.

THE PORTUGUESE
looking out of the window of the inn

Stop spreading gloom around you, Elis; drink,
And let the poor girl drink.

ELIS
*holds out the glass of brandy to Ilsebill; she shakes her head.
He drains it, takes a deep breath and leans back*

Yes, you were lovely! Now the drink's in me,
It all comes back. Your features clean and clear
Like corals that grow deep down; your face was pale,
Only your lips that red. . . . You were so lovely—
What have you done with it? There, stop your crying.
It could be that you're not so very different.
I see with different eyes. They're opened now,
The film is off, and now life seems to show
Only its guts to me, like some old wreck.
Now when I look at you, hard, what I see clearly
Is two eyes, glassy stuff, all full of water,
Two lips, as round as leeches, shaped like them
To suck and cling. What's in it? What's behind it?
What marvellous delight? And afterwards

[295]

Was für ein Schmerz? was weiter für ein Schmerz?
Was ist daran so viel?

Schlägt sich an den Kopf

Wie konnt ich träumen
Und danach hungern, immerfort danach!
Es ist doch über alle Massen schal!

Er streift seine Ärmel auf

Da trag ich auch so was. Die küsste mich
Und bohrte ihre kleinen Zähne ein:
Ein javanesisches Geschöpf: ihr Reden
Verstand ich so, wie ich ein Tier versteh;
In ihren Augen war was Bittendes,
Wie Hunde bitten, und sie wollte immer,
Dass ihrer Zähne Spur mir nicht verginge—
Denn ihre Lippen freilich waren weich
Wie Blumenblätter—da brannt ich mir das
Als Zeichen ein, damit mirs immer bliebe.
Da lachte sie vor Freude . . . vor dem Spiegel
Hab ichs gemacht, mit Nadeln macht man das
Und reibts mit Pulver ein.

ILSEBILL
Das bleibt dir nun.

ELIS
Die Haut ist freilich zäh.

Nach einer Pause

Der arme Hund, das Mädchen, wollt ich sagen,
Von Java . . . einmal stiess ich so nach ihr,
Wie man nach Hunden stösst . . . denselben Abend

The Mine at Falun

What pain? And after that what other pain?
What does it all amount to?

Striking his forehead

                        How could I dream
Of it, and hunger for it, always that!
A thing more dreary, wretched than I can say!

He pulls back his sleeves

Look here's another. That one kissed me here
And dug her little teeth into my flesh.
A Javanese she was: as for her talk,
It was about as plain to me as an animal's;
There was a pleading look in her black eyes,
As in a dog's, and what she always wanted
Was that her teeth would leave a lasting mark—
Although her lips were soft and light as petals—
So I tattooed this as a sign, to keep
As a reminder. How she laughed for joy!
I used a mirror; you know, it's done with needles,
And then you rub a powder in.

                    ILSEBILL
                        So now
It's yours for good.

                      ELIS
                Of course the skin is tough.

              After a pause

Poor bitch, that girl, is what I meant to say,
The Javanese . . . Once I kicked out at her
As people kick at dogs . . . and that same night

Hugo von Hofmannsthal

Dacht ich an dich: mir war, der Unterschied
Wär riesengross: ich seh, es ist gar keiner:
So schal bist du mir nun wie damals die.

ILSEBILL
dumpf

Elis!

ELIS
Den Namen wusste die dort auch.

Denselben Abend . . .

Starrt vor sich.

ILSEBILL
Elis!

ELIS

      . . . ist mein Vater
Verbrannt. Allein der Hund blieb ganz gesund,
Der Schiffshund, ja. Er schlief mit ihm in einer
Kabine. Die Kabine brannte aus,
Mein Vater mit. Der Hund lief heil heraus,
Mein Vater schlief. Er hatte ein Gesicht
Drei Tage früher.

Starrt vor sich.

ILSEBILL *ängstlich*
Elis!

ELIS
in sehr hartem Ton, abweisend

Liebes Mädchen,

Verstehst du,

Er steht auf, geht auf und ab

[298]

The Mine at Falun

I thought of you: a world of difference
I saw between you: but now I see there's none.
You mean no more to me than she did then.

ILSEBILL

gasps out

Elis!

ELIS

She too could say that name.
And that same evening . . .

Stares in front of him.

ILSEBILL

Elis!

ELIS

. . . my poor father
Was burnt to death. Only the dog escaped
Unhurt, the ship's dog, though it used to sleep
Under his bunk. The cabin was burnt out,
My father with it. And the dog walked out
Unscathed; my father slept. Three days before
He'd had a vision.

Stares in front of him.

ILSEBILL anxiously

Elis!

ELIS

his voice very hard, warding her off

My dear girl,

You see,

Rises, walks up and down

[299]

Hugo von Hofmannsthal

meines Vaters Sohn zu sein,
Das war kein Kinderspiel. Er war nicht hart,
Allein sein Wandeln war stille Verzweiflung.
Tief war sein Sinn. Er lebte in der Furcht.
Er hatte ein Gesicht, ehdem er starb,
Und wusste seinen Tod drei Tage vorher,
Und ging so hin, der alte Mann, und schwieg. . . .
Gleich nachher kam die Sehnsucht über mich,
Nach ihm nicht, nach der Mutter!

Setzt sich wieder, flüstert

's war ein Auftrag
Von ihm, drum kams so plötzlich über mich:
Sie geben solchen Auftrag, die dort unten.
Mir fuhr das Schiff zu langsam: in den Adern
Quoll mir das Blut wie schweres glühndes Erz
Und drückte mich zur Nacht: da ward aus mir
Jedwede andre Sehnsucht ausgeglüht:
Dies einzige Verlangen frass die andern
Im Finstern auf; wär ich im Krampf erstarrt
Und so gestorben, auf den Lippen hätte,
Den starren, jedes Aug den Laut gelesen,
Mit dem du anhebst, wenn du Mutter sagst.

Er steht auf

Die war schon unten, als ich kam. Die Reden,
Die mir im voraus von den Lippen trieften,
Wie Wasser aus des gierigen Hundes Lefze,
Die schlugen sich nach innen. Mir ist übel,
Die Landluft widert mir, mir widert Seeluft.

Setzt sich wieder

Mir ist das Bett verleidet und der Becher;

The Mine at Falun

to be my father's son, that was
No child's play. Not that he was hard or strict.
But all his journeying was a dumb despair,
His mind was deep. He lived in constant fear.
Before he died he had a vision, seeing
His death three days before it came to him.
That's how the old man went, and still kept silent . . .
Immediately after that the longing took me,
But for my mother, not for him!

Sits down again, whispers

It was
A call from him, that's why it suddenly took me:
They put these calls on you, the ones down there.
The ship became too slow for me. My blood
Welled in my veins like heavy, molten ore
And weighed on me at night: then every other
Longing burned out inside me, and grew cold:
This one desire consumed them in the dark.
Devoured them all; if all convulsed I'd died then,
Rigid from top to toe, on my taut lips
All eyes would easily have read the sound
That you begin to form when you say "Mother."

He rises

But she was down below when I arrived.
The speeches dripping from my lips already,
Like warm saliva from a hungry dog's,
Turned back and went inside me. I feel sick,
Land air revolts me, and the sea air too.

Sits down again

I've come to loathe my bed and loathe my drink;

[301]

Hugo von Hofmannsthal

Wenn ich allein bin, bin ich nicht allein,
Und bei den andern bin ich doppelt einsam.

ILSEBILL
Dein Blut ist schwer. Dich hat der grosse Kummer
Tiefsinnig werden lassen. Geh mit mir.

ELIS
Ich könnte stundenlang auf meine Hände
Hinunterstarren und den fremden Mann
Mir träumen, dem die zwei gehören können.

ILSEBILL
legt ihr Gesicht auf seine Hände.

ELIS
seine Hände wegziehend, rauh
Hab ichs nicht schon gesagt, ich schlaf an Bord.

ILSEBILL
nickt unterwürfig, schleicht sich lautlos fort.

ELIS
sitzt allein.
Die andern drinnen lärmen und singen. Der faule Klaus
und der Portugieser kommen ans Fenster.

PORTUGIESER
beugt sich aus dem Fenster zu Elis
Wo bist du wieder?

ELIS
spricht über die Schulter, ohne sich umzusehen
Ich, ja, Portugieser,
Ich bin hinüber.

The Mine at Falun

And when I'm on my own, I'm not alone,
And with the others I feel twice as lonely.

ILSEBILL

Your blood's grown heavy. Your great grief has made
You melancholy. Elis, come with me.

ELIS

I could sit still for hours and merely stare
At my two hands, and dream of the strange man
Of whom those two strange hands might be a part.

ILSEBILL

laying her face on his hands.

ELIS

withdrawing his hands, roughly

Haven't I told you once: I sleep on board.

ILSEBILL

nods submissively, creeps noiselessly away.

ELIS

sits there alone.

*The others, inside, sing and bawl. Lazy Claus and the
Portuguese appear at the window.*

THE PORTUGUESE

leaning out of the window towards Elis

Where have you got to now?

ELIS

over his shoulder, without looking round

What, Portuguese,
Oh, yes. I've just crossed over.

[303]

Hugo von Hofmannsthal

PORTUGIESER

Was?

ELIS

Ei ja. Herum
Ums letzte Kap und schwimm mit nackten Masten
Und ohne Steuer in der grossen Drift,
Der grossen Drift, dort drunten, von woher
Kein Schoner wiederkommt und keine Brigg.

PORTUGIESER

Er redet wie ein Pfarrer!

KLAUS

Sauf und schweig!

Gehen vom Fenster weg.

ELIS *vor sich*

Ich bin herumgekommen. Ich war jung,
Da war mir nur ums Fahren. Einen Fusstritt
Gab meinem Kahn der Vater, und die Mutter
Blies ihren letzten Atem in die Leinwand,
Da kam ich gleich hinüber. Und da ist
Die Drift, die grosse, totenhafte Drift.

PORTUGIESER *wieder am Fenster*

Komm doch herein und iss jetzt einen Bissen!

Geht wieder weg.

ELIS *vor sich hin*

Sagt einer «guten Bissen,» so sag ich:
Den besten essen doch die Würmer, freilich . . .

The Mine at Falun

THE PORTUGUESE

Eh?

ELIS

That's right.
Rounded the last cape, and now I'm drifting
With the great current, rudderless, the masts
All bare—drifting with that great undercurrent
That never yet brought brig or schooner back.

THE PORTUGUESE

Oh listen to the parson!

CLAUS

Drink and shut up!

They leave the window.

ELIS *to himself*

I've come full circle. Now, when I was young
Sailing was all I cared for. With a kick
My father sped the boat off, and my mother
Sent her last breath to fill the sails for me,
So I could cross in no time. There I found
The current, oh, the great and deathly current.

THE PORTUGUESE *at the window again*

Why don't you come inside and have a bite?

Goes in again.

ELIS *to himself*

If a man says "a bite of something good"
I say: the best of all is what the worms eat . . .

[305]

Sagt einer: «Schau, das Mädel, schöne Brüste,»
Sag ich: ein Stein wär besser. Diese Steine,

Er stösst mit dem Fuss gegen den Erdboden

Die sind doch auch herum ums grosse Kap,
Die haben ausgespielt, die spüren nichts.

Er versinkt in ein finsteres Hinträumen. Die drinnen singen.
Der alte Fischer schleicht aus seiner Hütte zu dem Ohn-
mächtigen hin, betrachtet ihn traurig, geht mit gesenktem
Kopf wieder nach Hause.
Frau Jensen, die beiden Mädchen und der Peter kommen aus
der Tür herausgetanzt, einander umschlungen haltend.

KATHRINE

Wo ist dein Mann?

REGINE

Wo ist dein Mann?

ALLE DREI

So sind wir halt drei Witwen dann!

KATHRINE

Der meine wollte mich verkaufen
Und 's Geld versaufen,
Da bin ich fortgelaufen!

REGINE

Mir lief der meine selber fort!

FRAU JENSEN

Der meine sitzt an einem Ort,
Da möcht er gern und kann nicht fort.

And if he says: "Look at that girl—what breasts!"
I say: "I'd sooner have a stone." These stones,

He kicks the ground

They too have rounded the great cape, and reached
Their destination, and feel nothing now.

*He falls into gloomy brooding. Those inside the inn are sing-
ing. The Old Fisherman creeps out of his cottage to his
unconscious son, looks at him sadly, goes back with bowed
head.*
*Mrs. Jensen, the two Girls, and Peter come dancing out of
the inn door, their arms round one another.*

CATHERINE

Where's your husband gone?

REGINA

Where's your husband gone?

ALL THREE

Why, we're three widows, all alone!

CATHERINE

Mine tried to barter me, to pay
For drink enough to booze all day,
So, quick as lightning, I ran away.

REGINA

Mine did the running off, not I.

MRS. JENSEN

Mine never leaves a single spot,
Whether he likes it there or not.

[307]

Hugo von Hofmannsthal

ALLE DREI

Ach Gott, mir ist das Herz so schwer!
Wo nehm ich schnell einen andern her?

REGINE

setzt sich dicht zu Elis

Ich möcht einen Mann!

PETER

Eine Maultrommel nimm und marschier voran!

PORTUGIESER

*ist mit Klaus auch herausgetreten; sie stehen auf den
Türstufen*

Wo solls denn hin?

PETER

Meint ihr, wir verhocken den Abend hier?
Ich möcht ein bissl noch was andres haben
Als fades Bier und die paar Mädel da.
Ich weiss euch ein Lokal: ein Keller ists,
Hui, wenn du da hinabkommst, weisst du nicht,
Ob du nicht gar im Meer bist: nichts als Licht
Und Spiegel vorn und hinten, dass dich schwindelt.
Du schiebst dich weiter, und in eine Höhle
Trittst du, da ist kein Licht, kein Öl, nicht Kerzen;
Die ganzen Wände leuchten wie Karfunkel,
Und Bänke stehen drin von rotem Samt,
Da sitzen dir zwei, drei, die können singen!
Du meinst, es wäre künstlich, nicht natürlich!
Und wenn sie dann gesungen haben, wenn sie
Sich zu dir setzen, weisst du gar nicht erst,
Was du mit einer solchen reden sollst:

[308]

The Mine at Falun

ALL THREE

Ah me! I'm weary and undone.
Where shall I find another one?

REGINA

sitting down close to Elis

I want a man!

PETER

Then take your Jew's harp and march in the van.

THE PORTUGUESE

has come out with Peter; they stand on the doorstep

Where are we off to?

PETER

Why, do you think we'll waste the evening here?
If you ask me, I'm after something better
Than watery beer and these few bits of fluff.
I know a place worth going to, a cellar;
And when you get down there you'll feel you've reached
The bottom of the sea: nothing but light
And mirrors front and back, to make you giddy.
But you push on, and come into a cave
Where there's no light at all, no oil, no candles;
The whole walls are aglow like carbuncles
And there are benches with red velvet seats
And, on them, a few girls—but can they sing!
You think it can't be real, not natural!
And when they've finished singing, and sit down
Right next to you, it's more than you can do
Merely to think of words to say to such a girl.

Dir nimmts den Atem, wie sie nach Vanille
Und Rosenwasser riecht. Und willst du trinken,
Greifst in die Wand der Höhle, wo du willst,
So faul du kannst, das Mädel auf den Knien,
Drehst einen Hahn, hältst unter, rot und grün
Kommt ein Getränke, stark und süss zugleich,
Wie Feuersirup, und die Mädel, du . . .

  Geht auf Elis zu, schüttelt ihn an den Schultern

Du willst nicht mit? Du bist ja gar kein Seemann,
Hätt ich ein Schiff, mir tät es grausen, grausen,
Dich mitzunehmen, dich.

ELIS
sieht einen Augenblick ihm ins Gesicht, dann zu Boden

   Das kann wohl sein,
Dass ich kein Seemann mehr bin, kurzer Peter!

PETER
zornig, dass ihm Elis nicht widerspricht

Ein Maulwurf bist du, weiter nichts!

*Links vorne ist unscheinbar der alte Torbern aufgetreten.—
Er ist ein kräftiger, etwas gebeugter Mann, dem Ansehen nach
kaum siebzig. Trägt altertümliche Bergmannstracht, völlig
abgetragen und verschossen. Hat blutumränderte merkwür-
dige Augen. Steht dort in der linken Ecke, an den Zaun
gelehnt, von niemandem beachtet, und lässt seine Augen auf
Elis ruhen.*

ELIS
sieht Peter gross an

     Ja, Peter,

The Mine at Falun

It takes your breath away, the way she smells
Of roses and vanilla. If you're thirsty
You stretch your hand out, anywhere in the wall,
As lazy as you like, her on your knees,
Just turn a tap, hold out your glass, and out
It rushes, red and green, potent and sweet,
Like syrup mixed with fire. As for the girls . . .

> *Goes up to Elis, shakes him by the shoulders*

You won't come with us? Call yourself a seaman?
If someone asked me now to pick a crew
The very thought of having you on board would
Give me the creeps.

ELIS
*looking him in the face for a moment, then lowers his eyes to
the ground* .

       Well, Peter, you may be right:
Perhaps I'm not a sailor any more.

PETER
angry because Elis doesn't contradict him

A creeping mole, that's all you are!

*Old Torbern has entered quietly from the left foreground. He
is a sturdy, rather bent old man, who looks less than seventy.
He wears an old-fashioned miner's outfit, completely worn
out and faded. He has strange, red-rimmed eyes. He stands
there, in the left corner, leaning against the fence, unnoticed,
his eyes fixed on Elis.*

ELIS
staring at Peter, wide-eyed

       Yes, Peter,

Hugo von Hofmannsthal

Das kann schon sein. Mir ist, du hast ganz recht.
Das ist nicht dumm, was du da sagst. Mir wär
Sehr wohl, könnt ich mich in die dunkle Erde
Einwühlen. Ging es nur, mir sollt es schmecken,
Als kröch ich in den Mutterleib zurück.

*Er steht auf, fährt mit den Händen wie staunend an seinem
Leib herab*

Mir löst sichs jetzt, dass dieser hier mein Leib
Nur ein Geköch ist aus lebendigen Erden,
Verwandt den Sternen auch. Wär das nicht so,
Wär nicht gewaltsam nur die Nabelschnur
Zerrissen zwischen mir und den Geschöpfen,
Den andern, dumpfen, erdgebundenen:
Wie dränge mir ans Herz des Hirschen Schrei?
Wie möchte dann der Linde Duft mein Blut
Bewegen? wie verschlänge mich die Nacht
In schwere Träume? wie gelüstete
Mein Leib, die Gleichgeschaffnen zu berühren?

*Tut ein paar schwere, gleichsam gebundene Schritte nach
vorwärts; spricht gegen den Boden*

Du tiefes Haus, was streben wir von dir,
Wir sinnentblösst Wahnwitzigen aufs Meer,
Dem Lügensinn, dem Aug allein gehorchend,
Der uns vorspiegelt, was für ewig uns
Verborgen sollte sein, die bunte Welt,
Die wir doch nie besitzen!
                              Seht, die Unke,
Das tagblinde verborgene Geschöpf,
Ist strahlend gegen unsre Finsternis
Und winkt mir mit bediademtem Haupt:
Denn ihr ist noch Gemeinschaft mit der Erde!

[312]

The Mine at Falun

That may be so. I think you must be right.
You've hit on something. It would give me pleasure
To dig my way into the deep, dark earth;
If only it would work, I'd relish it
Like creeping back into my mother's womb.

He rises and passes his hands over his body
as if in wonder

And now it's dawned on me, that this, my body,
Is nothing but a compound and concoction
Of living substances akin to earth,
And to the stars as well. Were this not so,
And more than a cut navel-string between
Me and all other dull and earth-bound creatures,
How could a lime-tree's fragrance stir my blood,
Or the night's darkness drag me down into
Oppressive dreams? How could my body long
To touch the body of a fellow creature?

He takes a few heavy, dragging steps forward; and speaks to
the ground

O house deep down, why do we seek to flee you,
Senseless, demented, leave you for the sea,
Ruled by the one sense that deceives, our sight,
And what it shows us: the mirage of that
Which should be ever-hidden, the bright world
We never shall possess!
                    Think of the toad:
That creature day-blind, dark and secretive,
Beside our darkness is a radiant thing
And beckons to me with its diadem:
For still it knows communion with the earth!

[313]

Hugo von Hofmannsthal

REGINE

schreiend

Nimm dich in acht, es hört dir einer zu!

Springt weg, schlägt ein Kreuz über ihn.

TORBERN

ist einen Schritt näher getreten.

DIE ANDEREN

stehen rechts rückwärts beisammen, im Begriff, wegzugehen.

KLAUS

So war sein Vater, wenns ihn überfiel!

PETER

Lasst ihn allein. Nachher wird er wie immer.

Sie wenden sich zum Gehen.

ELIS

*an dem Busch, der vorne steht; immer gegen den Erdboden
sprechend*

Haus, tu dich auf! gib deine Schwelle her:
Ein Sohn pocht an! auf tu dich, tiefe Kammer,
Wo Hand in Hand und Haar versträhnt in Haar
Der Vater mit der Mutter schläft, ich komme!
Entblösst euch, ihr geheimnisvollen Adern,
Ausbluten lautlos sich die meinen schon!
Mein Haar sträubt sich vor Lust, bei euch zu sein,
Ihr Wurzeln, die ihr an dem Finstern saugt,
Euch funkelnd nährt aus jungfräulicher Erde!
Mein Herz will glühn in einem Saal mit euch,
Blutrote Funkelsteine, hocherlauchte,
Schlaflose Lampen, täuscht mich nicht, ich seh euch,

The Mine at Falun

REGINA

screaming

Be careful what you say. There's someone listening!
Runs away, making the sign of the cross over him.

TORBERN

has taken a step forward.

THE OTHERS

stand together in the background, left, ready to go.

CLAUS

That's how his father acted, when it took him.

PETER

Leave him alone. He'll soon be his old self.

They turn to go.

ELIS

next to the bush in the foreground; still talking to the ground

House, open up! Yield up your threshold to me:
It is a son who knocks! Open, deep vault
Where hand in hand and hair entwined in hair
Father and mother lie asleep. I'm here!
Strip yourself bare, all you mysterious veins!
Silently mine already shed their blood!
Longing for you sends shivers down my spine,
You roots that suck at darkness, burrowing
And, sparkling, feed upon the virginal earth!
My heart desires to glow in one great hall
With you, august and blood-red glittering jewels.
Unsleeping lamps, do not deceive me now.

Ich seh euch glühen wie durch fahles Horn,
Versinkt mir nicht, ich halt euch mit der Seele!

Tiefer gebückt, wild atmend.

DIE ANDEREN
sind fort.

TORBERN
steht vor ihm, hüllt ihn in seinen Blick.

ELIS
auffahrend, in völlig verändertem Ton

Wer bist du, der mir zuhört? Was hab ich
Geredet? Wer bist du? Die Worte brachen
Aus mir hervor . . .

Stark

Das hast du mir getan!

TORBERN
Und wie?

ELIS
ohne ihn anzusehen

Das frag ich mich. So warst dus nicht?
Du warsts! Du sprachst ein Zauberwort.

TORBERN *sehr laut*

Sprach ich?

Kleine Pause
Flüsternd

Bedurft es dessen auch? Entquoll den Lippen
Von selber nicht das rechte Wort? Entglomm
Dem Aug von selber nicht der starke Strahl?

[316]

The Mine at Falun

I see you, see you glow as through pale bone,
Do not escape me now, my spirit holds you!

Bending lower, panting wildly.

THE OTHERS
have gone.

TORBERN
stands before him, enveloping him in his gaze.

ELIS
starting up, in a wholly different tone of voice

Who are you, eavesdropping on me? What have
I said? Who are you? All those words gushed out
Of me unbidden . . .

Firmly

You did that to me!

TORBERN

How?

ELIS
without looking at him

That's what I'm wondering. Or wasn't it you?
It was. You spoke some magic formula.

TORBERN *very loudly*

Did I?

A short pause
Then, whispering

And did I need to? Was it not
That the right word was formed on your own lips,
The mighty radiance shone from your own eyes?

[317]

ELIS

Mir war, ich sähe in den Grund. Mein Blut
Macht mir was vor.

TORBERN

Du blöder Tor, gib acht.

ELIS

Zuerst so leise, nun so überlaut!
Willst du betrügen?

TORBERN *sehr leise*

      Meiner Stimme Klang
Bin ich entwöhnt.

ELIS

Wo kamst du her?

TORBERN

            Von dort.
Wo du hin willst.

ELIS
zurücktretend

Ich weiss nicht, was ich sprach.

TORBERN *leise*

Doch sinds der Seele tiefgeheimste Wünsche,
Die sich dem unbewussten Mund entringen.

ELIS

Wer seid denn Ihr?

[318]

The Mine at Falun

ELIS

I thought the earth had opened up. My blood
Is playing tricks on me.

TORBERN

You fool, be careful.

ELIS

At first your voice was low, and now you're shouting!
Could you be fooling me?

TORBERN *very softly*

I have forgotten
The sound of my own voice.

ELIS

Where have you come from?

TORBERN

From where you want to go.

ELIS

stepping back

I spoke unthinking.

TORBERN *softly*

Yet it's the inmost longings of the soul
That babbling lips reveal unwittingly.

ELIS

Who can you be?

[319]

Hugo von Hofmannsthal

TORBERN

Ein Bergmann. Hast du keinen noch gesehn?

ELIS

Der Mutter Vater war ein Bergmann auch.
Sein Kleid war ähnlich, doch auch wieder anders.
Was wollt Ihr von mir?

TORBERN

Nur den Weg dir zeigen.
Ich kam, weil du mich brauchst.

ELIS

Ich brauch dich nicht.

TORBERN

Du brauchst mich, wie ich dich.

ELIS

Ich bin ein Seemann . . .

TORBERN

lacht.

ELIS

stutzt; fährt dann fort

Zurück aus Indien und nehm nächstens Handgeld
Nach Grönland. Guten Abend.

Will gehen.

TORBERN

hält ihn sanft

Elis Fröbom . . .

The Mine at Falun

TORBERN

A miner. Have you never seen one, then?

ELIS

My mother's father was a miner too.
His clothes were much like yours, but not the same.
What do you want?

TORBERN

Only to show you the way.
I came because you need me.

ELIS

No, I don't.

TORBERN

You need me as I need you.

ELIS

But I'm a seaman . . .

TORBERN

laughs.

ELIS

is taken aback, then continues

Just back from India, and am taking ship
For Greenland soon. Goodnight.

About to go.

TORBERN

gently holds him back

Stay, Elis Fröbom . . .

[321]

Hugo von Hofmannsthal

ELIS

Wir haben miteinander nichts zu schaffen,
Als . . . etwa . . . da . . .

Will ihm Geld geben

Was hältst du meine Augen
Mit deinem Blick?

Macht sich los

Ei, geht und lasst mich gehn.

Er geht einige Schritte, wird langsamer, bleibt stehen.

TORBERN
sieht ihm nicht nach, bückt sich, betrachtet einen Kiesel

Ich halt Euch nicht.

ELIS
geht, wie gezogen, wieder zu ihm zurück.

TORBERN
richtet sich jäh auf.

ELIS

So ists ein Auftrag, den du hast an mich?

TORBERN

Nenns immer so. Mir ist es aufgetragen,
Dass ich den Weg dir zeig, und dir . . .

ELIS *fieberhaft*

Und mir?

TORBERN

Dass du ihn gehst.

[322]

The Mine at Falun

ELIS

Let go! We have no business with each other,
Unless . . . perhaps . . . have this . . .

Offering him money

Why do you hold
My eyes with yours?

Frees himself

Now go, and let me go.

He takes a few steps, slows down, stops.

TORBERN

does not look at him, stoops and picks up a pebble
I'm not detaining you.

ELIS

returns to him as though pulled back against his will.

TORBERN

suddenly straightens his back.

ELIS

So you have come to me with some charge or other?

TORBERN

Well, you could call it that. It is my charge
To show you where to go, and . . .

ELIS *feverishly*

Well, what else?

TORBERN

Make sure you take that way.

[323]

Hugo von Hofmannsthal

ELIS *wie verloren*

Ich wollte jetzt fortgehn.

TORBERN

Doch kamst du wieder.

ELIS

Wusstest dus voraus?

Pause

Womit bezwingst du mich?

TORBERN *rasch*

Mit deinem Willen.

ELIS

Der war, zu gehn!

TORBERN

Der ist: mit mir zu gehn
Nach Falun und ein Bergmann dort zu sein.

ELIS *tonlos*

Zu werden?

TORBERN

Keiner wird, was er nicht ist.

Eine starke Pause

ELIS

Was hält mich hier?

Er spricht mehr zu sich als zu dem andern

The Mine at Falun

ELIS *bewildered*

I was just going.

TORBERN

But you came back.

ELIS

And did you know I should?

Pause

How do you force my will?

TORBERN *quickly*

With your own will.

ELIS

Which was to go!

TORBERN

Which is to go with me
To Falun, and become a miner there.

ELIS *in a whisper*

Become?

TORBERN

No one becomes what he is not.

A pregnant pause

ELIS

What keeps me here?

Speaking more to himself than to the other

[325]

Hugo von Hofmannsthal

Was soll ich mir gewinnen
Und was der Preis, womit ichs zahlen soll?
Hier steh ich, Elis Fröbom, ein Matros
Und eine Waise: wenn dies hier die Falltür
Der Hölle ist, und der des Teufels Bote,
Und meine Seele das, worauf er ausgeht,
So gib mir du, an den mein Flehn sich klammert,
Ein Zeichen, dran ich mich ermannen kann!

Pause

Wenn ich mich zwingen wollte und es lügen:
Die Zunge bäumt sich gegen meinen Willen,
Und sie bekennt: in mir geht etwas vor!

Er befühlt sich

Was immer nun dies sei, ich kann nicht anders!
Die Knie werden schwer . . .

TORBERN
                    Denn es verlangt sie
Hinabzusteigen.

ELIS
          Wolken droben, Bäume,
Sie werden fahl . . .

TORBERN
          Dein Aug will Schönres sehen!

ELIS
Mich fasst aus Klüften ein gewaltiger Hauch . . .

TORBERN
Dir widert Landluft, Seeluft widert dir.

The Mine at Falun

What is it I must gain
And what the price that I must pay for it?
So here I stand, a seaman, Elis Fröbom.
An orphan too: if this should be the trap-door
Opening on Hell, and he the Devil's envoy,
And it should be my soul this one is after,
Then you, to whom I cling, beseeching you,
Give me a sign, and courage to resist!

Pause

If I compelled my senses to deny it,
Still my own tongue would fight against my will,
And let it out: something is changing me!

He feels himself

Whatever it may be, I have no choice!
My knees are leaden . . .

TORBERN

Since they feel the pull
To plumb the depths.

ELIS

The clouds above, the trees,
Are growing dim . . .

TORBERN

Your eyes seek greater beauty!

ELIS

A mighty breath from chasms seizes me . . .

TORBERN

Land air revolts you, and the sea air too.

[327]

Hugo von Hofmannsthal

ELIS

Der Boden wankt!

Klammert sich an den Busch.

TORBERN

Steh! Seemann, schwindelt dich?

ELIS

schon im Versinken

Ich sinke ja! es nimmt mich ja! ich muss!

Er versinkt völlig.

Rasche Verwandlung.

Im Innern des Berges. Ein nicht sehr grosser Raum, rechteckig, dessen Wände aus dunklem, fast schwarzem Silber. Zwischen Pfeilern rechts ein Ausgang, von Finsternis völlig verhangen, zu dem drei runde Stufen aufsteigen. Die Decke flach gewölbt. Alles aus dem gleichen, prunkvoll finsteren Stoff gebildet.

ELIS

steht mit dem Rücken an die linke Seitenwand gelehnt, die Augen weit aufgerissen; das Weiss seiner Augen ist im Anfang das einzige Helle in dem finsteren Raum, auf dem die Schwere undurchdringlicher Wände lastet

Ich hab geträumt! Jetzt lieg ich wach! Ich lieg
In meiner Koje. Nein, ich steh. Ich bin
Ganz angezogen. Hier ist Hartes: Stein.
So bin ich blind! Ich fiel: doch schmerzt mich nichts.
Ich fiel endlos durch rötlich schwarze Schlünde.
Ich bin nicht blind. Ich sehe meine Hände!
Ich bin allein in einem finstern Raum.
Nein, nicht allein! Da! da! da! da!

The Mine at Falun

ELIS

The ground is quaking!

Clings to the bush.

TORBERN

Are you giddy, seaman?

ELIS

sinking into the ground

I'm going down! It forces me! I must!

He vanishes.

The scene changes quickly.

The mountain's interior. A hall, not very large, square, whose walls are of silver that is almost black. An exit, right, between pillars completely veiled in darkness, with three steps leading up to it. The ceiling gently vaulted. All made of the same splendidly gloomy material.

ELIS

stands leaning against the left wall, his eyes wide open; at first the white of his eyes is the only bright thing in the dark scene, which conveys a sense of impenetrable walls weighing down on it

I dreamed. And now I lie awake. I lie
In my own cabin. No, I stand. I'm wearing
My working clothes. This stuff is solid—rock.
That means I'm blind. I fell. But feel no pain.
I fell unendingly through reddish blackness.
No, I'm not blind. For I can see my hands.
I'm all alone in a dark room. But no,
I'm not alone. There! there! and there!

[329]

Hugo von Hofmannsthal

Die Bergkönigin ist zwischen den finstern Pfeilern rechts hervorgetreten und steht auf der obersten der drei dunklen Stufen. Vom Scheitel bis zur Sohle ist sie in ein schleierhaftes Gewebe gehüllt, dem ein sanfter Glanz, das gedämpfte Leuchten ihres Körpers, entströmt. Am stärksten leuchtet ihr Scheitel, wo ein fast glühender Reif in funkelndem Haar den Schleier zusammenhält. Die lautlose Gestalt, die unmerklich hebt wie eine hochstielige Blume, strömt in den ganzen Raum eine mässige Helle aus, und die finstern Silberwände blinken manchmal auf.

ELIS
auf die Gestalt hinstarrend

Ich träum
Und träum nur, ich bin wach.

KÖNIGIN
Nein, Elis Fröbom,
Nun träumst du nicht.

ELIS
Es spricht zu mir.

KÖNIGIN *ohne sich zu regen*
Er meint,
Er liegt im Traum. Bring ihm zu trinken, Agmahd.

Der Knabe Agmahd kommt lautlos die Stufen herab. Er ist völlig schwarz gekleidet. Sein Kopf ist hell, mit weichem blondem Haar. Er hat meergrüne Augen, die seltsam ins Leere zu starren scheinen. Er trägt auf silberner Schüssel einen silbernen Becher, aus dem schwaches Leuchten steigt. Lautlos gleitet er auf Elis zu und bleibt vor ihm stehen, den Becher aufwartend.

[330]

The Mine at Falun

*The Queen of the Mountain has emerged from the dark
pillars on the right and stands on the third of the dark steps.
She is draped from head to foot in a veil-like material, from
which a faint glow, the muted gleam of her body, radiates.
The top of her head gleams most brightly of all, where an
almost glowing fillet fastens the veil to her sparkling hair.
The silent figure that sways imperceptibly like a flower on a
long stalk, fills the whole room with a dim light, and the
dark silver walls flash from time to time.*

ELIS

staring at the apparition

I dream,
And only dream that I'm awake.

QUEEN

No, Elis,
Now you have ceased to dream.

ELIS

It speaks to me.

QUEEN *motionless*

He thinks he's dreaming. Agmahd, a drink for him.

*The boy Agmahd comes noiselessly down the steps. He is
clothed entirely in black. His head is bright, with soft, fair
hair. His eyes are sea-green, and they seem to stare strangely
into the void. He carries a silver goblet on a silver dish, which
emits a faint gleam. He glides towards Elis without a sound,
stands before him, and proffers the goblet.*

Hugo von Hofmannsthal

ELIS

Du liebliches Gesicht, wo kommst du her?
Lass mich dein Haar anrühren! Kennst du mich
Nich mehr? Ich bins, der bei dir lag, so oft, so oft,
Dort bei den Palmen, dort am stillen Fluss.
Weisst dus nicht mehr? wie ich dich lehrte, dich
Zu spiegeln hier in meinen beiden Augen,
Und wie ich mir dein Zeichen in den Arm
Einschnitt? Sieh mich doch an, weisst du nichts mehr?
Wie? Trinken soll ich, weil die dort es will.

Er nimmt den Becher und trinkt

Es glüht und schäumt und schüttert durch mein Innres hin.
Bieg mir dein Antlitz her! Verfärbst du dich?
Wie anders scheinst du nun! Du bist kein Mädchen . . .
Du bist es, du Ertrunkner, lieber, lieber!
Nicht wahr, wir waren Freunde! Dass du starbest!
Wir zogen dich heraus, da lagest du:
Dein Leib war hell und kühl wie Elfenbein:
Ich kaufte ein geweihtes Licht und sass
Die ganze Nacht bei dir, es drückte mich,
Dass ich nicht weinen konnte, und ich sah dich an.
Kommst du jetzt, mir das danken? Bleib doch hier!
Was schwankst du fort? Lass mich nicht hier allein.

Der Knabe Agmahd hat sich von ihm entfernt, ist plötzlich
im Dunkel der Wände wie verloschen.

ELIS

Und du! Du bebst! Bebst du vor Ungeduld?
Sinnst du auf meinen Tod? Du! du!

KÖNIGIN
                              Ich acht auf dich.

The Mine at Falun

ELIS

Where have you come from, lovely apparition?
Wait, let me touch your hair. Don't you remember
Me who so often lay beside you, often
Under the palm-trees, down by the quiet river?
Have you forgotten how I taught you then
To see your mirror image in these eyes,
And how I carved your sign into this arm?
Look at me now. Have you forgotten me?—
But I must drink, because it is her will.

He takes the goblet and drinks

It glows and foams and quivering pours through me.
Come, let me see your face. Do you turn pale?
How different you seem now. You are no girl . . .
Oh, it is you, the drowned, my dear, dear friend!
Were we not friends? Oh, that you had to die!
We pulled your body out, and there you lay
Your body bright and cool as ivory.
I bought a holy candle and watched by you
The whole night long, and felt so miserable
Because I could not weep, and looked at you.
Is it to thank me for it you have come?
No, stay with me. Don't leave me here alone.

*The boy Agmahd has moved away and vanished, as though
extinguished in the darkness of the walls.*

ELIS

And *you* are trembling. Is it with impatience?
Is it my death you scheme? You—you?

QUEEN

I'm watching you.

[333]

Hugo von Hofmannsthal

ELIS

Mir grauts vor dir.

KÖNIGIN

Warum? Du kennst mich nicht!

Sie wirft mit einer ungeduldigen Bewegung die Arme nach rückwärts und faltet die Hände im Nacken, so dass die weiten Ärmel zurücksinken und die wundervollen Hände sichtbar werden.

ELIS

Den Händen, die du hast, entblüht ein Glanz,
Mir ist, als trät mein Blut aus mir ins Freie,
Wenn ich hinseh.

KÖNIGIN

streckt die Rechte aus

Tritt her und rühr sie an.

ELIS *unbeweglich an seinem Platz*

Ich kann nicht. Wir sind nicht aus einer Welt.
Ich kanns nicht fassen, dass ich hier steh, ich!
Warum denn ich? Droben sind Tausende!
Warum denn ich? Mich schauderts bis ins Mark.

KÖNIGIN

Und ich hab mich so lang nach dir gesehnt.
Wohl hundert Jahr. Was zuckst du? Grauts dich so?
Sieh, ich kann doch für dich nicht fremder sein,
Nicht unbegreiflicher als du für mich.
Mich schauderts nicht. Und glaub mir, manches, was ich
                                                    [weiss
Von euch da droben, ist wohl schauerlich.

[334]

The Mine at Falun

ELIS

You frighten me.

QUEEN

But why? You do not know me.

*With an impatient movement she throws back her arms and
folds her hands behind her neck, so that her wide sleeves fall
back and her marvellous hands are seen.*

ELIS

A radiance, like a bloom, your hands emit.
I feel as though my blood flowed out from me,
Released, when I look there.

QUEEN

holding out her right hand

Come close and touch it.

ELIS *motionless in his place*

I cannot. We are not of the same world.
I cannot fathom it, that *I* stand here,
I, of the thousands in the world above,
I, of all men. It makes my marrow creep.

QUEEN

And I have yearned for you so very long—
A hundred years it seems. Why do you quiver?
Truly, I cannot be more strange to you,
Incomprehensible, than you to me.
I feel no dread; and yet, believe me, much
Of what I know about your kind is gruesome.

[335]

Hugo von Hofmannsthal

Ich weiss, ihr kennt das Angesicht des Wesens,
Das euch geboren hat. Ihr nennt es «Mutter,»
Wohnt unter einem Dach mit ihm, berührt es!
Das macht mich grauen, wenn ichs denken soll.
Ich weiss, ihr schlummert niemals lang, doch wenn
Ihr euch hinlegt zu einem langen Schlaf,
So seid ihrs schon nicht mehr: der Erdengrund,
Der mich mit klingendem Gehäus umschliesst,
Euch löst er eure Glieder auseinander,
Und Bäume wachsen auf aus eurer Brust,
Und Korn schlägt seine Wurzeln euch im Aug.
Und die dann droben leben, die ernährt,
Was also aufkeimt aus der Brüder Leib.
Mich dünkt, ich stürb vor Graun, müsst ich so leben
Hervor aus einem Leib, hinab zu Leibern.
Und wenn ich eurer einen atmen seh,
Werd ichs nicht los, mir ist, als müsst an ihm
Noch hängen Ungewordnes und Verwestes,
Als wär er nie allein, wo er auch geht und steht.
Und dennoch lieb ich dich und will dich halten!

Ringt ungeduldig die Hände

Graut dir, dass ich schon war, bevor du warst?
Macht dich das zornig, dass ich schlafen kann,
So lang und rein und tief? Dass ich allein bin,
Nur spielend mit Geschöpfen, die mir dienen?
Gib mir doch Antwort, steh nicht stumm und hart!
Sieh: euch da droben flutet ohne Halt
Die Zeit vorüber, doch mir ists gegeben,

The Mine at Falun

I know, you look upon that creature's face
From whom you issued forth. You call it "Mother,"
Live under the same roof with it, and touch it!
To think of that, fills me with dread and horror.
I know you never sleep for long, but when
You do lie down to seek unbroken sleep
You are no longer you: the depth of earth,
That like a resonant shell encloses me,
Dissolves your limbs, estranged from one another,
And from your breast great trees rise up, and corn
Strikes roots within the hollows of your eyes.
And those who live above are nourished by
This crop that's sprouting from their brothers' bodies.
I think I'd die of horror if my life
Were but this battening of flesh on flesh,
This growing out of bodies, into bodies.
And when I look at one of you, see him breathe,
I cannot help it, but I feel as if
Something that's not yet formed and then again
Something that's putrefied attached to him,
As if he never were himself alone.
And yet I love you, long to keep you here!

Wringing her hands impatiently

Is it because I was before you were
That you feel dread? And does it make you angry
That I can sleep a sleep so long and deep
And pure? Or that I'm utterly alone,
And only play with creatures here to serve me?
Come, answer me. Don't stand there hard and dumb!
Look! for you men up there time rushes by
Unceasing, but to me the power was given

[337]

Hugo von Hofmannsthal

In ihren lautlosen kristallnen Strom
Hinabzutauchen, ihrem Lauf entgegen
Und ihren heiligen Quellen zuzugleiten!
Heft nicht so dumpf den starren Blick auf mich!
Begreifst du nicht: das uralt heilige Gestern,
Ruf ich es auf, umgibts mich und wird Heut:
Und Dunkelndes und Funkelndes vergeht,
Und Längstversunknes blüht und glüht herein.

*Indem die Wand des Hintergrundes durchsichtig wird, tut
sich eine tiefe Landschaft auf. Über hellgelb leuchtende
Gewässer neigen sich ungeheure Bäume, bald von glühenden,
bald von zarten Farben. Im fernen Hintergrunde werfen
mächtige dunkle Abgründe und Felsenwände eimander
geheimnisvollen metallischen Schein zu.*

Und wieder tauch ich auf und lass dies alles
Hinunterrollen in die ewigen Tiefen!

*Indem sie so weiterspricht, ohne sich im geringsten zu wenden,
steht rückwärts wieder die finstere, dann und wann aufblin-
kende Wand von dunklem Silber.*

Ahnst du denn nicht, wie mächtig Geister sind,
Und bist doch einer! Wirst du immer bleicher?
Vielleicht ist dies Musik vor deinem Ohr!

*Schlägt in die Hände. Der alte Torbern steht plötzlich da, das
Gesicht ihr zugewendet, in dem von ihr ausgehenden Lichte
regungslos wie ein ehernes Standbild.*

Sprich zu ihm, Torbern. Hilf mir du, ihn fasssen!
Dich wird er hören, weil du auch ein Mensch.

TORBERN
Mich ekelt seine Dumpfheit. Königin,

The Mine at Falun

To plunge into its silent crystal course
And glide against the current to its holy sources!
But still you stare at me with unseeing eyes!
Try to grasp this: if I invoke the pristine
And holy yesterday, at once it comes.
Envelops me and has become today:
The darkling and the sparkling things are gone,
And things long past begin to blow and glow.

*As the wall in the background becomes transparent a deep
landscape opens up. Enormous trees overhang pale yellow,
shining waters, now assuming glowing colours, now delicate
shades. In the far background vast gloomy chasms and rock
faces exchange a mysterious metallic glint.*

Then I emerge again and at my word
All this rolls back into eternal depths!

*As she speaks on, without so much as turning her head, the
background changes again to the wall of dark silver, that
flashes now and again.*

Can you not sense how powerful spirits are,
Who are yourself a spirit? But still grow paler?
Perhaps this will be music in your ears!

*Claps her hands. Old Torbern suddenly stands there, his face
turned towards her, motionless as a statue in the radiance
emitted by her.*

Speak to him, Torbern. Help me to make him see.
He'll understand you, since you're human too.

TORBERN

His cloddishness revolts me. Rather tell me,

Ist dies das letztemal, dass ich dich sehe?

KÖNIGIN

Ich weiss nicht.

TORBERN

Wohl, ich weiss! Und er steht da,
Wo ich einst stand!

KÖNIGIN

Sprich nicht davon!
Sag ihm, wie über aller Menschen Lose
Dein Los anschwoll. Wie du verlernen durftest,
Zu messen dich mit ihrer Zeiten Mass.
Wie dir zu Dienst das wogende Gewässer
Vor deinen Füssen starrte, dich zu tragen.
Wie dich die Kraft, die in dir wuchs und wuchs,
Hin über Klüfte riss, wie ihre Sterne
Herniederstürzten, deinem Pfad zu leuchten.
Sag ihm . . .

ELIS

Nun, wie geschah dies, Torbern, wie?

TORBERN

Vom Anfang soll ich reden, nun das Ende
So nah? Entkräftend fassts mich an wie fahle Träume.
Es ist so lange her. Die nun im Sarge liegen,
Damals stand noch der Baum in jungem Saft,
Der später, später gab das Holz zu ihren Wiegen.
Verlernen durft ichs, mich mit ihrem Mass zu messen.
Verlernen durft ich alles, was sie meinen.
Die ganze Welt, die sie mit dumpfem Sinn

The Mine at Falun

Is this the last time I shall see you, Queen?

QUEEN

I do not know.

TORBERN

But *I* know. And he stands
Where I stood once!

QUEEN

But do not speak of it.
Tell him how greater than all men's destinies
Your destiny grew. How you had leave to unlearn
That temporal measure other men must keep.
How for your sake the billowing waters froze
To smooth rigidity, and bore your weight.
How the great strength that grew and grew in you
Swept you across abysses, how the stars
Came hurtling down to light you on your way.
Tell him . . .

ELIS

How did it come about, then, Torbern? How?

TORBERN

Am I to speak of the beginning, now
That the end is near? Oh, like desolate dreams
It all returns to me, and wearies me.
It was so long ago. Those in their coffins now—
Why, at the time that tree was but a sapling
Which later, later yielded wood to make their cradles.
This temporal measure I had leave to unlearn;
Leave to unlearn all that they think and say.

Aufbaun, brach mir in Stücke. Ob ein Mensch,
Ich ward ein Geist und redete mit Geistern.
Von ewiger Luft umwittert, ward ich schnell
Dem dumpf umgebend Menschlichen entfremdet:
Mir galt nicht nah, nicht fern: ich sah nur Leben.

Er tut einen tiefen Atemzug

Da droben waren welche, die mit Armen
Und Lippen klammernd als an einem Teil
Von ihrem Selbst an mir inbrünstig hingen:
Ich schüttelte sie weg von meiner Brust.
Mein Herz schwoll auf und redete bei Tag
Und Nacht mit den Abgründen und den Höhen,
Und meinem seligen Aug entblösste sich
Die Schwelle deines Reichs . . .

KÖNIGIN *schnell*

Nichts davon, Torbern,
Hier steht er ja und weiss nicht, wie ihm ist!
Nun geh.

TORBERN

Muss ich?

KÖNIGIN

Hast du noch nicht gelernt
Zu fühlen, was du musst?

TORBERN

So schwank ich denn im Kreis dem Anfang wieder zu,
Und so begegn ich dem, der nach mir kommt.

KÖNIGIN

Er wird dich rufen.

The Mine at Falun

All of that world which their dim minds construct
Collapsed and broke for me. Although a man,
A spirit I became and spoke with spirits.
Eternal air around me, quickly I
Became estranged from all that's dully human:
Nothing was near or far: all was sheer life.

He takes a deep breath

Up there dwelled such who with their arms and lips
Clung fast to me, as to a vital part
Of their own selves; frenziedly, wildly clung:
It was an easy thing to shake them off.
My heart grew full, and both by day and night
Held converse with the chasms and the heights,
And to my blissful eyes there was revealed
The threshold of your realm . . .

QUEEN *quickly*

No, Torbern, not of that!
Look, there he stands, all puzzled and perplexed!
Now leave us.

TORBERN

Must I?

QUEEN

Have you not yet learnt
To feel what you must do?

TORBERN

Well, in a circle then I'll stagger back
To where I started, meeting my successor.

QUEEN

He'll call you.

[343]

Hugo von Hofmannsthal

TORBERN

Mag er folgen,
Wo er mich schreiten sieht, doch stumm, mich ekelt
Gespräch der Menschen. Mag er sich von Zeichen
Zu Zeichen tasten, endlich trifft er her.
Und ich—er soll schnell kommen!—in mir flackerts
Und zuckts und will verlöschen! Jahre glitten
An meinen Wimpern ab wie leichter Duft
An Felsenwänden . . . und nun zehrt der Hauch
Von einer einzigen Nacht mit Wut an mir;
Und wo ich ruhe, mein ich schon zu sinken.

Er verschwindet.

ELIS

Ihn treibt ein ungeheurer Geist umher,
Er kam zu dir und durfte bei dir wohnen,
Die Jahre hatten ihm nichts an, er hing
An deinem Aug, an deinem Leib . . . Erbarm dich meiner:
Er trat heran, er durfte dich berühren,
Er! er! doch ich! wie ich?

KÖNIGIN
Du bist wie er.

ELIS

Die Stimme, die du hast, greift mir ins Innre.
Ich will mit dir sein können!

KÖNIGIN
Bist dus nicht?

ELIS

Dies Grauen . . .

KÖNIGIN
Wirfs von dir!

[344]

The Mine at Falun

TORBERN

Let him follow, then,
Where I must go, but silently; I loathe
The speech of men. And let him grope his way
From sign to sign; at last he will be here.
And I—let him come quickly—for in me
All flickers and dies down. Year after year
Has slipped from off my eyelids like faint fragrance
From walls of rock . . . and now the clinging breath
Of one sole night consumes me utterly;
And where I rest I fear that I shall perish.

He vanishes.

ELIS

A mighty spirit has him in its power.
He came to you and was allowed to live
With you, unscathed by time; allowed to adore
Your eyes, your body . . . Now have mercy on me:
He was admitted, was allowed to touch you.
He, he! But what of me, and why?

QUEEN

You are

As he is.

ELIS

Oh your voice, it grips my heart.
I wish I could be with you.

QUEEN

Are you not?

ELIS

This horror . . .

QUEEN

Cast it off!

[345]

Hugo von Hofmannsthal

ELIS

Wie konnt ich kommen?

KÖNIGIN

Fragst du aufs neu? Weil du ein Geist wie ich.
Dein Mund sprach mächtige Worte aus.

ELIS

Doch wann?

KÖNIGIN

Du sehntest dich herab, den Boden schlug
Dein Fuss, unwillig trugst du, zornig atmend,
Den Druck der irdischen Luft, dein Blick durchdrang
Die Niedrigkeit, dein Mund verschmähte sie,
Ein ungeheurer Strahl entglomm dem Aug,
Und das Gewürme floh, die Finsternis
Trat hinter sich, so wie sies tut vor mir!

ELIS

Wie kam es über mich!

KÖNIGIN

Es schläft in euch.
Doch ahnt ihrs nicht. Du warst zu Tod erstarrt,
Dein Mund verhangen, deine Augen öd.
Da trats in dir empor, und wie im Traum
Griffst du mit Aug und Mund nach Strahlendem,
Gebunden wie ein Kind, und doch ein Zauberer!
Und halb noch dunkel, halb wie Geister leuchtend,
Ergriffs dich, unbewusst herabzusteigen!
War dir, du fielest? war dir nicht, du flogest?
Und fühltest nicht, wie ich im Dunkel stand
Und bebte?

[346]

The Mine at Falun

ELIS

What brought me here?

QUEEN

You ask again? Because you are a spirit,
As I am. Powerful words your lips have uttered.

ELIS

But when?

QUEEN

Why, when you longed for the descent,
Stamped on the ground, unwilling to endure
The weight of earthly air, angrily breathed it,
Your glance saw through the vileness, your lips scorned it,
A mighty beam of light flashed from your eyes,
The crawling vermin fled, darkness gave way
And lifted from your path, as from my path!

ELIS

How it came over me!

QUEEN

It sleeps in men,
Only they do not know it. You were numb
As death, your lips were stifled, vacant your eyes.
Then it rose up in you, and, as though dreaming,
With eyes and mouth you sought that radiancy,
Dependent as a child, yet a magician!
And still half-dark, half-luminous as spirits,
It moved you to descend unknowingly!
Was it like falling? Not rather as though you flew?
And were you not aware that in the dark
I stood and quivered?

Hugo von Hofmannsthal

ELIS

So darf ich hingehn und dein Antlitz sehn?

KÖNIGIN

Tritt her!

ELIS

tritt zu ihr.

KÖNIGIN

*steigt die Stufen herab, ihm entgegen, hebt mit der Linken
den Schleier von ihrem Antlitz, so dass sein Gesicht, von
unten ihr entgegengehoben, ganz von ihrem Abglanz über-
flutet wird.*

ELIS

schreit auf

Ah!

Duckt sich, geblendet, gegen den Boden.

KÖNIGIN

*lässt den Schleier wieder zufallen, richtet sich auf, spricht
sanft*

Sinn ich auf deinen Tod? Wirst dus ertragen,
Mit mir zu sein? Wirst du die ganze Welt
Bei mir vergessen können?

ELIS

vor ihren Füssen, seiner Stimme nicht mächtig

Sprich langsamer. Dein Antlitz funkelt so
Vor meinen Sinnen!

KÖNIGIN

Elis!

[348]

The Mine at Falun

ELIS

Then I may go and look upon your face?

QUEEN

Come here!

ELIS

approaches her.

QUEEN

descends the steps to meet him, lifts the veil from her face with her left hand, so that his face, turned up to her, is bathed in her effulgence.

ELIS

cries out

Oh!

Turns his face to the ground, dazzled.

QUEEN

lets the veil fall again, draws herself up and says gently

Do I desire your death? Can you endure
To be with me? Oblivious of all the world
Because of me?

ELIS

at her feet, unable to control his voice

Oh, speak more slowly. All my being is dazed
With looking at you.

QUEEN

Elis!

[349]

Hugo von Hofmannsthal

ELIS

Wie?

KÖNIGIN

Merk auf!

Du darfst nicht bleiben.

ELIS

Wie?

KÖNIGIN

Du musst hinauf
Und wiederum herab. Komm bald! komm bald!
Du!

ELIS

schwach, völlig vor ihr liegend

Ich muss sterben, wenn du mich verhöhnst.

KÖNIGIN

Hör mich: es muss so sein.

ELIS

Wie?

KÖNIGIN

Hör mich, Lieber.
Ich darf dich noch nicht halten. Ich kann dir
Noch nicht gehören. Deine Sinne sind
Mit Sehnsucht vollgesogen noch nach denen
Da droben.

ELIS

Wie?

The Mine at Falun

ELIS

What?

QUEEN

Now listen!
You must not stay.

ELIS

Not stay?

QUEEN

You must go back
And then descend again. But soon, dear Elis,
But soon!

ELIS

weak, prostrate before her

No, if you mock me I shall die.

QUEEN

Listen: It must be.

ELIS

What?

QUEEN

Listen, my love.
I may not keep you yet, nor can be yours,
Because your senses are still steeped in longing
For those above.

ELIS

Above?

Hugo von Hofmannsthal

KÖNIGIN

Dir ist es nicht bewusst.
Doch hab ichs wohl gesehn. Der Knabe Agmahd,
Ein schwankend wesenlos Gebilde ists:
Ein Spiegel. Jedem zeigts, was heimlich ihm
Am Herzen ruht. Du stiessest sie von dir,
Die droben, aber etwas lebt von ihnen,
Noch etwas lebt in dir. Du musst hinauf . . .

ELIS *schwach*

Ja.

KÖNIGIN

Und ein Bergmann sein. In Einsamkeit,
Tief eingewühlt in Dunkel. Immer näher . . .

ELIS

Ja.

KÖNIGIN

Geh dem Alten nach, er weiss den Weg,
Ob widerwillig auch, er zeigt ihn dir.

ELIS

Ja.

KÖNIGIN

berührt ihm leise die Schulter

Auf, mein Zauberer!

ELIS

Weh, du wirst mir bleicher!

[352]

The Mine at Falun

QUEEN

You do not know it.
But I see it clearly. Now, that page-boy, Agmahd,
Is an amorphous, insubstantial thing:
A mirror; showing to each one the secrets
Deep in his heart. True, you rejected them,
Those up above, but some small part of them
Still lives in you. Therefore you must go back.

ELIS *feebly*

Yes.

QUEEN

And become a miner. Solitary,
Deep down, entombed in darkness. Ever closer . . .

ELIS

Yes.

QUEEN

Go where the old man went; he knows the way,
And, though reluctantly, will show it to you.

ELIS

Yes.

QUEEN

lightly touches his shoulder

Go now, my magician!

ELIS

Oh, you fade from me!

[353]

Hugo von Hofmannsthal

Die Gestalt der Königin wird undeutlicher, endlich unsichtbar.

Ich seh dich nicht! Erbarmen! Gib mir Antwort!
Sag noch ein einzig Wort zu mir!

STIMME DER KÖNIGIN
Komm bald!

Verwandlung. Die Szene wie zu Anfang des Aufzuges.

ELIS
*taucht aus dem Erdboden empor, liegend, mit geschlossenen
Augen. Es dunkelt. Die Fenster der Schenke, die nun geschlossen sind, blinken noch einmal auf, erblinden dann. Elis
schlägt die Augen auf, richtet sich jäh auf*

Dorthin! dorthin! Nun zeig den Weg! Wo bist du?

*Läuft ans Fenster der Schenke, schlägt daran, versucht hin-
einzusehen.*

FRAU JENSEN
aus der Schenke tretend

So kommt Ihr wieder? Nun, mir war nicht bang.

ELIS *ohne Atem*

Der Alte, wo?

FRAU JENSEN
Der da war, der? der Bettler?

ELIS
Ein Bettler, er, der Könige machen kann!
Weib, wo er ist?

[354]

The figure of the Queen becomes indistinct, then invisible.

I cannot see you. Answer me, take pity
On me and speak one single word!

> VOICE OF THE QUEEN
>> Come soon!

The scene changes. The inn, as at the beginning of the play.

> ELIS

rises from underground, lying down, his eyes closed. It is dusk. The windows of the inn, which are closed, are illumined briefly, then darken again. Elis opens his eyes, sits up with a jerk

That way, that way! Now guide me there! Where are you!

Runs to the window of the inn, beats on it, tries to look inside.

> MRS. JENSEN
>> *coming out of the inn*

Oh, so you're back. I can't say I was worried.

> ELIS *breathlessly*

The old man—where?

> MRS. JENSEN
>> That beggar, who loitered here?

> ELIS

Beggar indeed, a beggar who can make kings!
Woman, where is he?

Hugo von Hofmannsthal

FRAU JENSEN

Ja, was weiss ich?

ELIS

Vernichtung!

Besinnt sich

Hier, nehmt Euch selbst.

Wirft ein Geldstück hin

Und nun ist Eins zu sorgen.
Ich muss nach Falun.

FRAU JENSEN

Wos hinuntergeht
Ins Innere des Berges?

ELIS

Recht! Und das
Sogleich, eh diese Nacht zu Ende geht.

FRAU JENSEN

Wie wollt Ihr das?

ELIS

seine Geldkatze in der Hand

Ich reit ein Pferd zu Tod
Und kauf ein neues, wo das erste fiel.

FRAU JENSEN

Nicht in drei Tagen und dazu drei Nächten
Trägt Euch ein Saumtier durch die Pässe hin,
Zu Wasser aber . . .

[356]

The Mine at Falun

MRS. JENSEN

How should I know?

ELIS

Damnation!

Reflects

Here! Help yourself.

Throws down a coin

And now there's one thing more,
I have to go to Falun.

MRS. JENSEN

Where you go
Right down into the mountain?

ELIS

Yes. And now,
At once, before this night is over.

MRS. JENSEN

How will you get there?

ELIS

his purse in his hand

Ride a horse to death
And buy another where the first falls dead.

MRS. JENSEN

Not in three days and nights. No horse or mule
Would take you through the passes in that time.
By water, though . . .

Hugo von Hofmannsthal

ELIS

Also denn zu Wasser.
Hier wohnen Fischer, schaukelt doch ein Boot,
Des Menschen ist es wohl, der drinnen schläft:
Ich weck ihn denn!

FRAU JENSEN
hält ihn

Den rührt nicht an, der schläft nicht irdischen Schlaf:
Wo der liegt, ist die Schwelle schon zum Jenseits!

ELIS

Die will mein Fuss betreten: Er soll aufstehn
Und mir den Weg nicht sperren!

*Des Fischers Sohn richtet sich auf und tritt aus seinem Boot
ans Land.*

FRAU JENSEN
aufschreiend

Gott im Himmel!

Fliegt an des Fischers Haus

Alt-Fischer, Fischer-Mutter, Euer Sohn!

DER ALTE FISCHER
läuft heraus, reisst die Mütze vom Kopf.

SEINE FRAU
hinter ihm.

DER ALTE FISCHER

Mutter, Mutter, still!

[358]

The Mine at Falun

ELIS

All right, by water, then.
This is a fishing village, I can see a boat
Tug at its moorings, someone asleep inside it.
The owner, I suppose. I'll go and wake him!

MRS. JENSEN

holding him back

Don't touch that boy. He sleeps no earthly sleep;
The next world's threshold, that's where *he* is lying!

ELIS

And what I want to cross. He shall get up
And shall not bar my way!

*The Fisherman's Son rises and steps on to the shore from his
boat.*

MRS. JENSEN

crying out

Great God in Heaven!

Rushes to the Fisherman's cottage

Hey, fisherman! Fisherman's wife! Your son!

THE OLD FISHERMAN

running out, tears his cap from his head.

HIS WIFE

follows.

THE OLD FISHERMAN

Quiet, Mother, quiet!

[359]

Hugo von Hofmannsthal

DES FISCHERS SOHN

ein grosser, starker blondbärtiger Mann, geht ruhig auf Elis zu,
macht einen Kratzfuss, sagt

Das Schiff wär fertig, wenn der Herr jetzt will.

Fischer und Frau kommen von der Seite, betrachten den
Sohn mit scheuer Ehrfurcht.

DER ALTE FISCHER

nimmt mit gespreizten Fingern den Sohn bei der Hand, mit
zitternder Stimme

Mein Sohn, mit dir hat sich ein grosses Wunder
Begeben!

DER SOHN *ruhig*

      Mutter, führ den Vater weg:
Er hat schon trunken, eh die Sonne auf ist.
Ich hab nicht Zeit, ich muss den Fremden führen.
Nach Falun will der Herr!

DER ALTE FISCHER

          Mein Kind, erkennst
Denn nicht, die Sonn ist unter, Nacht bricht an!

DER SOHN

Lass, Vater, wir sind eilig, und der Landwind
Ist stark und gut. Grad hat er mir die Rah
So hinters Ohr geschlagen, wie zum Zeichen,
Dass ich mich nicht versäumen soll.

DER ALTE FISCHER *feierlich*

             Der Landwind,
Der ist verschwunden seit zehn Tagen, Sohn.

Ein starker Windstoss.

[360]

The Mine at Falun

THE FISHERMAN'S SON

a tall, sturdy man with fair hair and beard, walks calmly up to Elis, bows, and says

The boat is ready now, if you are, sir.

The Fisherman and his Wife approach from the side, look at their son with awe and reverence.

THE OLD FISHERMAN

seizing his Son's hand with outstretched fingers, in a trembling voice

My son, a mighty miracle has been wrought
In you.

THE SON *calmly*

    Come, Mother, take the old man home:
He's started drinking before the sun is up.
I have no time to waste, the stranger's waiting.
Falun is where he wants to go.

THE OLD FISHERMAN

                My child,
The sun has set, it's nightfall—can't you see?

THE SON

No matter, Father. Time is short and the land breeze
Steady and strong. Just now it brought the main yard
Down just behind my ear, as if to warn me
That I must waste no time.

THE OLD FISHERMAN *solemnly*

            No, son, the land breeze
Has not so much as stirred these last ten days.

A strong gust of wind.

Hugo von Hofmannsthal

DER SOHN

Und da sollt Abend sein!

DER ALTE FISCHER *erregt*

Mein Sohn, mein Sohn!

DER SOHN *zur Mutter*

So führ ihn weg! Er redet nicht Verstand.

Zu Elis, munter

Das ist der rechte Wind auf Falun zu.
Der Herr wird wohl zufrieden sein. Geh, Mutter,
Bring mir die Mütze noch. Gleich, Herr, sogleich!

*Er geht zum Schiff, tut noch die letzten Handgriffe.—Der
Wind wird stärker, der Himmel immer dunkler. Das Folgende
rufen die beiden einander zu, indem sie die Hände schall-
verstärkend an den Mund heben.—In der Ferne, über den
blauen Bergen, die nun nicht mehr sichtbar sind, fällt ein
Stern.*

ELIS

Du! du! Fiel nicht ein Stern?

DER JUNGE FISCHER

Ja, Herr, grad über Falun hin!

ELIS

Der tote Mann stand auf zu meinem Dienst,
Die Sterne stürzen, meinem Pfad zu leuchten,
Und wenn dies Boot zerscheitert unter mir:
Die grüne Woge starrt und wird mich tragen.
Mein Innres schaudert auf, und fort und fort
Gebierts in mir ihr funkelnd Antlitz wieder . . .
Und was mir widerführ, nun sterb ich nicht,
Denn dieser Welt Gesetz ist nicht auf mir.

Er springt ins Boot, das sogleich vor dem Wind liegt.

Der Vorhang fällt.

The Mine at Falun

THE SON

And there you stand and try to make me think
It's evening. Well, well.

THE OLD FISHERMAN *excited*

My son, my son!

THE SON *to his mother*

Take him away, then! The old man is raving.

To Elis, vivaciously

It's just the wind we need to get to Falun.
We shouldn't have much trouble, sir. Please, Mother,
Go in and get my cap. One moment, sir!

He goes to the boat, makes the last preparations. The wind grows stronger, the sky darker and darker. What follows is shouted by the two persons through their cupped hands. In the distance, above the blue mountains no longer visible, a shooting star falls.

ELIS

Hey, you! Did you see the star fall?

THE YOUNG FISHERMAN

Yes, sir. Just over Falun!

ELIS

This dead man rose again to serve me,
Stars hurtle down to light me on my way,
And if this boat should split before we've crossed,
Why, the green wave will freeze and bear my weight.
My senses quiver, and incessantly
Evoke new visions of her glittering face . . .
Whatever happens now, I cannot die,
Free of the law that rules this earthly life.

He jumps into the boat, which immediately takes the wind.

Curtain

[363]

THE MARRIAGE OF ZOBEIDE

Translated by

CHRISTOPHER MIDDLETON

DES KERKERMEISTERS TOCHTER: "Lieber Gott, wie verschieden sind Männer!"—*Altes englisches Trauerspiel "Palamon und Arcite"*

Die Hochzeit der Sobeide

DRAMATISCHES GEDICHT

EIN REICHER KAUFMANN

SOBEIDE, *seine junge Frau*

BACHTJAR, *der Juwelier, Sobeidens Vater*

SOBEIDENS MUTTER

SCHALNASSAR, *der Teppichhändler*

GANEM, *sein Sohn*

GÜLISTANE, *eines Schiffshauptmanns Witwe* ⎫

EIN ARMENISCHER SKLAVE ⎬ *im Hause Schalnassars*

EIN ALTER KAMELTREIBER ⎭

EIN GÄRTNER

SEINE FRAU

BAHRAM, *Diener des Kaufmanns*

EIN SCHULDNER DES SCHALNASSAR

*In einer alten Stadt im Königreich Persien.
Die Zeit ist der Abend und die Nacht nach dem Hochzeitsfest
des reichen Kaufmanns.*

[366]

The Marriage of Zobeide

A DRAMATIC POEM

A RICH MERCHANT

ZOBEIDE, *his young wife*

BAKTYAR, *the jeweller, Zobeide's father*

ZOBEIDE'S MOTHER

SHALNASSAR, *the carpet-dealer*

GANEM, *his son*

GULISTAN, *a sea-captain's widow* ⎫
AN ARMENIAN SLAVE   ⎬ *in Shalnassar's house*
AN OLD CAMEL-DRIVER   ⎭

A GARDENER

HIS WIFE

BAHRAM, *the merchant's servant*

A DEBTOR OF SHALNASSAR'S

Scene: an old town in the kingdom of Persia.
*Time: the evening and night after the wedding-feast of the
Rich Merchant.*

[367]

I

Das Schlafzimmer im Hause des reichen Kaufmanns. Rück-
wärts ein Alkoven mit dunklen Vorhängen. Links eine Tür,
rechts eine kleine Tür in den Garten und ein Fenster. Lichter.
Es treten auf: Der Kaufmann und sein alter Diener Bahram.

KAUFMANN

Bahram, gabst du gut acht auf meine Frau?

DIENER

Acht, inwiefern?

KAUFMANN

Sie ist nicht fröhlich, Bahram.

DIENER

Sie ist ein ernstes Mädchen. Und die Stunde
liegt schwer auch auf der leichtesten, bedenk.

KAUFMANN

Und auch die Andern: je mehr Lichter ich
befahl zu bringen, um so trüber hing
ein Schleier über dieser Hochzeitstafel.
Sie lächelten wie Masken, und ich fing
mitleidige und finstre Blicke auf,
die hin und wider flogen, und ihr Vater
versank zuweilen in ein düsteres Sinnen,
aus dem er selbst sich mit gezwungnem Lachen
aufschreckte.

DIENER

Herr, der allgemeine Stoff
der Menschen hält nicht gut den stillen Glanz

The Marriage of Zobeide

I

*The bedroom in the Rich Merchant's house. An alcove, in
the background, with dark curtains. Left, a door; right, a small
door leading into the garden, and a window. Lights. Enter
the Merchant and his old servant Bahram.*

MERCHANT

Bahram, did you observe her well, my wife?

SERVANT

But in what way?

MERCHANT

She is not happy, Bahram.

SERVANT

She is a serious girl. Moments like these
lie heavy, you must know, even on the frivolous.

MERCHANT

The others too: the more I asked for lights,
the darker grew the veil that seemed to hang
over the table of this marriage feast.
They smiled as only masks can smile; I caught
their glances flying dark and sympathetic
hither and thither; and her father, sometimes,
sank into a sombre meditation,
from which he was only able to rouse himself
with a forced laugh.

SERVANT

Sir, the common stuff
that men are made of does not well endure

von solchen Stunden. Wir sind nicht gewohnt
was andres, als nur mit den nächsten Dingen
uns abzuschleppen. Kommt ein solcher Tag,
so fühlen wir: still tut ein Tor sich auf,
daraus uns eine fremde, kühle Luft
anweht, und denken gleich ans kühle Grab.
Aus einem Spiegel sehen wir unser eignes
vergessenes Gesicht entgegenkommen
und sind dem Weinen näher als dem Lachen.

KAUFMANN
Sie nahm von keiner Speise, die du ihr
vorschnittest.

DIENER
                Herr, ihr mädchenhaftes Blut
hielt ihr die Kehle zugeschnürt; sie nahm
doch übrigens vom Obst.

KAUFMANN
                Ja, einen Kern!
ich habs gesehen, vom Granatapfel.

DIENER
Auf einmal auch besann sie sich, dass Wein,
wie flüssig Blut durchfunkelnd durch Kristall,
vor ihr stand, und sie hob den schönen Kelch
und trank ihn wie mit plötzlichem Entschluss
zur Hälfte aus, und Röte flog ihr in
die Wangen, und sie musste tief aufatmen.

KAUFMANN
Mir scheint, das war kein fröhlicher Entschluss,
so tut, wer selber sich betrügen will,
den Blick umwölken, weil der Weg ihn schaudert.

the radiance of such moments. We're accustomed
to dragging on as best we can with things
that are familiar. But on a day
like this we feel a door has softly opened,
through which a cool and alien atmosphere
breathes on us, and we think of the cool grave.
We see our own forgotten countenance
moving towards us from a mirror, and
we're nearer then to tears than we are to laughter.

MERCHANT

She took none of the dishes that you laid
and cut for her.

SERVANT

But, sir, her virginity
had made her feel a tightness in her throat;
she took some fruit, you know.

MERCHANT

A single kernel-fruit
from a pomegranate! One! That's all I saw.

SERVANT

And all at once she realized that wine,
like liquid blood that sparkled in the crystal,
stood there before her, and she took the cup,
the lovely cup, and suddenly resolved,
drank up the half of it, and blushes rose
into her cheek with her deep respiration.

MERCHANT

I think that was not a happy resolution.
This is the way of self-deceivers when
they veil their eyes for horror of what they do.

[371]

DIENER

Du quälst dich, Herr. So sind die Frauen nun.

KAUFMANN
im Zimmer herumschauend, lächelt

Auch einen Spiegel hast du her gestellt.

DIENER

Herr, du befahlst mirs selbst, der Spiegel ists
aus deiner Mutter Kammer, wie das andre.
Und selbst befahlst du mir, gerade den . . .

KAUFMANN

So? tat ich das? Dann wars ein Augenblick,
in dem ich klüger war als eben nun.
Ja, eine junge Frau braucht einen Spiegel.

DIENER

Nun geh ich noch, den Becher deiner Mutter
zu holen, mit dem kühlen Abendtrunk.

KAUFMANN

Ja, hol den Abendtrunk, geh, guter Bahram.

Bahram ab.

Du, Spiegel meiner Mutter, wohnt kein Schimmer
von ihrem blassen Lächeln drin und steigt
wie aus dem feuchten Spiegel eines Brunnens
empor? Ihr Lächeln war das matteste
und lieblichste, das ich gekannt, es glich
dem Flügelschlagen eines kleinen Vogels,
bevor er einschläft in der hohlen Hand.

The Marriage of Zobeide

SERVANT

Sir, you torment yourself. Women are like that.

MERCHANT

looking around the room, smiles

You've also placed a mirror here, I see.

SERVANT

Just as you told me, sir; that is the mirror
out of your mother's room, like the other things.
And you yourself insisted, that was the one . . .

MERCHANT

I? I insisted? That must have been a moment
when I was wiser than I am. Of course,
a young woman will require a mirror.

SERVANT

I shall go now and bring your mother's cup,
with the cool drink for the evening in it.

MERCHANT

Yes,
bring now my evening drink, good Bahram, go.

Exit Bahram.

You, mirror of my mother, does no trace
of her pale smile inhabit you and rise
as from the liquid mirror of a fountain?
Her smile, it was the faintest and the sweetest
that ever I have seen, her smile was like
the fluttering of the wings of a small bird
before it falls asleep in your hollow hand.

[373]

Hugo von Hofmannsthal

Vor dem Spiegel

Nein, nichts als Glas. Er stand zu lange leer.
Nur ein Gesicht, das lächelt nicht: das meine.
Mein Selbst, gesehen von den eignen Augen:
so inhaltslos, als würfen nur zwei Spiegel
das unbewusste Bild einander zu.
O könnte ich darüber weg! nur einen,
den kleinsten Augenblick darüber weg,
und wissen, wie das Innre ihres Blicks
mich nimmt! Bin ich für sie ein alter Mann?
Bin ich so jung, als manchesmal mich dünkt,
wenn ich in stiller Nacht in mich hinein
auf den gewundnen Lauf des Blutes horche?
Heisst das nicht jung sein, wenn so wenig Hartes
und Starres noch in meinem Wesen liegt?
Mich dünkt, dass meine Seele, aufgenährt
mit dünner, traumhafter, blutloser Nahrung,
so jung geblieben ist. Wie hätt ich sonst
dies schwankende Gefühl, ganz wie als Knabe,
und diese seltsame Beklommenheit
des Glücks, als müsst es jeden Augenblick
mir aus den Händen schlüpfen und zerrinnen
wie Schatten? Kann ein alter Mensch so sein?
Nein, alten Menschen ist die Welt ein hartes,
traumloses Ding; was ihre Hände halten,
das halten sie. Mich schauert diese Stunde
mit ihrem Inhalt an, kein junger König
kann trunkner dieses rätselhafte Wort
«Besitz» vernehmen, wenns die Luft ihm zuträgt!

Dem Fenster nah

Ihr schönen Sterne, seid ihr da, wie immer!
Aus meinem sterblichen, haltlosen Leib

The Marriage of Zobeide

Before the mirror

Nothing but glass. Too long it's been deserted.
Only a face that does not smile: my face.
My self that is beheld by its own eyes:
so substanceless it seems two mirrors throw
the unconscious image back and forth between them.
If I could penetrate beyond it! One,
one single tiny moment penetrate and find
how the interior of *her* glance receives me!
I may appear to her as an old man.
Am I as young as sometimes it would seem,
when in the quiet night I stand and hear
the labyrinthine flowing of my blood?
Does it not mean I'm young when in my being
there is so little that is hard and rigid?
To me it seems my soul has been so fed
on dreamlike, thin, and bloodless nourishment
that it is young still. How else could I know
this quavering of the heart, as in my boyhood,
and this most curious oppressiveness
of joy, as if at any given moment
it must escape my hands and melt away
like shadows? Can old men behave like this?
No, for the world to old men is a hard
and dreamless thing; and what their hands do hold,
they hold it firm. But what this moment holds
sets me atremble; no young king could hear
with drunker senses this mysterious word
"possession" so dispensed out of the air.

Near the window

O lovely stars, still you are there, as always!
To watch, out of my mortal vagrant flesh,

heraus dem Lauf von euch in kreisenden,
ewigen Bahnen zuzusehen, das war
die Kost, die meine Jahre leicht erhielt,
dass ich den Boden kaum mit meinen Füssen
zu treten glaubte. Bin ich wirklich welk
geworden, während meine Augen immer
an diesen goldnen hingen, die nicht welken?
Und hab ich aller stillen Pflanzen Art,
ihr Leben zu begreifen, ihre Glieder
gelernt, und wie sie anders auf den Bergen
und anders wieder nah am Wasser werden,
sich selber fast entfremdet, doch im tiefsten
sich selber treu; und konnte sicher sagen:
der geht es wohl, von reiner Luft genährt,
leicht spielt sie mit der Last der edlen Blätter,
der hat ein schlechter Grund und dumpfes Leben
den Halm verdickt, die Blätter aufgeschwemmt—
und mehr . . . und von mir selber weiss ich nichts,
und dicke Schalen legen sich ums Auge
und hemmen dieses Urteil . . .

Er geht hastig wieder vor den Spiegel

Leeres Werkzeug!
Auch überrumpelt lässt du nicht die Wahrheit,
wie Menschen oder Bücher doch zuweilen,
in einem Blitz erkennen.

DIENER
zurückkommend

Herr!

KAUFMANN
Was ist?

your moving through your circular eternal
courses was all the nourishment that made
my years lie easy on me, so that it seemed
my feet scarce touched the ground. Now can it be
that I have withered, even while my eyes
rested on these unwithering golden ones?
And I have learned the ways of all quiet plants,
to understand their lives, to know their bodies,
and how on mountains they grow otherwise,
and otherwise again by riversides,
almost estranged from their true selves, and yet
profoundly faithful to them; I could say:
this one is healthy, nourished by air that's pure,
it plays with the weight of its fine petals lightly;
a stifled life and barren soil have thickened
the stalk of that one, puffed its petals out,
and more . . . yet of myself I'm ignorant,
and heavy swathings hamper my sight and blot
all judgement out . . .

He walks quickly back to the mirror

      O empty, empty thing!
I take you by surprise but still you do not,
as men and books do sometimes, let the truth
be known as in a flash.

SERVANT
returning

Sir!

MERCHANT
   What's the matter?

Hugo von Hofmannsthal

DIENER

Die Gäste brechen auf. Dein Schwiegervater,
auch andre, haben schon nach dir gefragt.

KAUFMANN

Und meine Frau?

DIENER

Nimmt Abschied von den Eltern.

*Kaufmann steht einen Augenblick mit starrem Blick, dann
geht er mit starken Schritten durch die Tür links.
Diener folgt ihm.*

*Die Bühne bleibt eine kurze Zeit leer. Dann tritt der Kauf-
mann wieder ein, einen Leuchter tragend, den er auf den
Tisch neben den Becher mit dem Abendtrunk stellt. Hinter
ihm tritt Sobeide ein, von ihrem Vater und ihrer Mutter
geführt. Alle bleiben in der Mitte des Zimmers, etwas links,
stehen, der Kaufmann etwas abseits.*

*Sobeide löst sich sanft von den Eltern. Der Schleier hängt ihr
rückwärts herab. Sie trägt eine Perlenschnur im Haar und
eine grössere um den Hals.*

DER VATER

Ich hab von vielem Abschied nehmen müssen.
Dies ist das Schwerste. Meine gute Tochter,
das ist der Tag, den ich zu fürchten anfing,
als ich dich in der Wiege lächeln sah,
und der der Alp in meinen Träumen war.

Zum Kaufmann

Vergib mir das. Sie ist mehr als mein Kind.
Ich geb dir, was ich nicht benennen kann,
denn jeder Name fasst nur einen Teil—
sie aber war mir alles!

[378]

The Marriage of Zobeide

SERVANT

The guests are leaving now. Your father-in-law,
the others too, they have been asking for you.

MERCHANT

What of my wife?

SERVANT

She's making her farewells.

*The Merchant stands a moment with fixed gaze, then walks
with firm steps through the door, left. The Servant follows
him.*

*The stage is empty for a few moments, then the Merchant
returns, carrying a candelabrum, which he sets on the table
beside his evening drink. Behind him Zobeide enters led by
her Father and Mother. All stop in the middle of the room,
slightly to the left, the Merchant a little apart from the others.*

*Zobeide quietly separates herself from her parents. Her veil
hangs down her back. She has a string of pearls in her hair,
and a larger one round her neck.*

THE FATHER

I've taken leave of many things before.
Of all farewells, this is the hardest. O my daughter,
this is the day that I began to dread
when first I saw you smiling in your cradle,
and which in dreams has been my incubus.

To the Merchant

Forgive me. She is more than just my child.
In her I give you what I cannot name,
for every name fits but a part of her—
while she to me was all things!

[379]

Hugo von Hofmannsthal

SOBEIDE
Lieber Vater!
die Mutter bleibt bei dir.

DIE MUTTER *sanft*
O lass ihn doch:
er hat ganz recht, dass er mich übersieht;
ich bin ein Teil von seinem Selbst geworden:
was mich trifft, trifft ihn auch zugleich; doch was ich tu,
berührt ihn anders nicht, als wenn die Rechte
und Linke sich des gleichen Leibs begegnen.
Die Seele bleibt indes ein ewig saugend Kind
und drängt sich nach den lebensvollern Brüsten.
Leb wohl. Sei keine schlechte Frau als ich,
und keine minder glückliche. Dies Wort
schliesst alles ein.

SOBEIDE
Einschliessen ist das Wort!
In euer Schicksal war ich eingeschlossen:
nun tut das Leben dieses Mannes hier
die Pforten auf, und diesen Augenblick,
den einzgen, atme ich in freier Luft:
nicht eure mehr, und noch die Seine nicht.
Ich bitt euch, geht, ich fühl, dies Ungewohnte,
so ungewohnt wie Wein, hat grössre Kraft
und macht mich mein und sein und euer Dasein
mit andren Blicken ansehn, als mir ziemt.

Mühsam lächelnd

Ich bitt euch, seht mich nicht verwundert an:
mir gehn oft solche Dinge durch den Kopf,
nicht Traum, nicht Wirklichkeit. Ihr wisst, als Kind
war ich noch ärger. Und ist nicht der Tanz,

The Marriage of Zobeide

ZOBEIDE

Dearest father,
Mother is with you still.

THE MOTHER *softly*

O let him speak:
for he has every right to overlook me;
I have become a part of his own self:
all that can come my way, comes his way too; and yet
whatever I do cannot touch him more
than when the right hand of one body touches
the left of that same body. Yet, for sure,
the soul is ever a child that sucks and sucks,
forever seeking out life's fullest breasts.
God with you. Be no worse a woman than I,
and no less happy either. What I say
includes . . . all things.

ZOBEIDE

Includes—that is the word.
I was included in your destiny,
and now the life of this man here has flung
the gates wide open, and this is the moment,
the only moment that I breathe free air:
not your air now, nor yet the air that's his.
So go, please go; this strangeness that I feel,
as strange to me as wine, has a greater power
and makes me see my life and his and yours
with eyes I have no right to see them with.

Gives a strained smile

There is no need for you to be surprised:
often such things pass through my head, not dreams,
and not realities. When I was a child,
I was much worse, you know it. And is not the dance

[381]

den ich erfunden hab, auch solch ein Ding:
wo ich aus Fackelschein und tiefer Nacht
mir einen flüssigen Palast erschuf,
drin aufzutauchen, wie die Königinnen
des Feuers und des Meers im Märchen tun.

*Die Mutter hat indes dem Vater einen Blick zugeworfen und
ist lautlos zur Tür gegangen. Lautlos ist ihr der Vater gefolgt.
Nun stehen sie, Hand in Hand, in der Tür und verschwinden
im nächsten Augenblick.*

SOBEIDE
Geht ihr so leise! Wie? Und seid schon fort!

Sie wendet sich, geht schweigend, den Blick zu Boden.

DER KAUFMANN
*umfängt sie mit einem langen Blick, geht dann nach rück-
wärts, bleibt wieder unschlüssig stehen*

Willst du den Schleier nicht ablegen?

Sobeide schrickt auf, sieht sich zerstreut um.

KAUFMANN
deutet nach dem Spiegel

Dort.

*Sobeide bleibt stehen, löst mit mechanischen Bewegungen
den Schleier aus dem Haar.*

KAUFMANN
Es wird dir hier—in deinem Haus—vielleicht
im ersten Augenblick an manchem fehlen.
Dies Haus ist seit dem Tode meiner Mutter

that I invented, just this kind of thing:
when from the torches' gleaming and deep night
I made myself a water palace, there
to enter in, just like those queens of fire
and ocean queens that come in fairy tales.

*While she is speaking, her Mother has glanced towards her
Father, and has moved without a sound to the door. Without
a sound her Father too has followed. Now these two stand,
holding hands, in the door, and the next moment they vanish.*

ZOBEIDE

You go so quietly? And now you're gone!

She turns, walks in silence, her eyes down.

MERCHANT

*gazes at her with complete absorption, then, after a while,
retreats, stops again, irresolute*

Now would you like to take your veil off?

Zobeide, startled, looks distractedly about her.

MERCHANT

points to the mirror

There.

*Zobeide does not move, mechanically loosens the veil from
her hair.*

MERCHANT

Here, in your house, perhaps you'll find at first
that certain things you may require are missing.
This house has not provided for the needs

entwöhnt, dem Leben einer Frau zu dienen.
Auch trägt, was etwa an Geräten da ist,
kaum solchen Prunk an sich, womit ich gern
dich eingerahmt erblickte, doch mir schien
das nicht sehr schön, was jeder haben kann:
ich liess aus der gepressten Luft der stillen,
verschlossnen Schränke, die mir selbst den Atem
ergriff, wie Sandelholz im Heiligtum,
dies alles nehmen und zu deinem Dienst
in deine Kammer stellen, dort hinein,
woran vom Leben meiner Mutter etwas—
verzeih—für mich noch hängt. Mir war, ich könnte
dir damit etwas zeigen . . . Manchen Dingen
sind stumme Zeichen eingedrückt, womit
die Luft in stillen Stunden sich belädt
und etwas ins Bewusstsein gleiten lässt,
was nicht zu sagen war, auch nicht gesagt sein sollte.

Pause

Es tut mir weh, dich so zu sehn, betäubt
von diesen überladnen Stunden, die
kaum aufrecht gehen unter ihrer Last.
Es ist zu sagen, alles Gute kommt
auf eine unscheinbare, stille Art
in uns hinein, nicht so mit Prunk und Lärm.
Lang meint man, plötzlich werd es fern am Rand
des Himmels wie ein neues Land auftauchen:
das Leben, wie ein nie betretnes Land.
Doch bleibt die Ferne leer, allein die Augen
begreifen langsam da und dort die Spur,
und dass es rings ergossen ist, uns einschliesst,
uns trägt, und in uns ist, und nirgends nicht ist.
Ich rede Sachen, die dir wenig Freude

The Marriage of Zobeide

of any woman since my mother died.
Even those things which are here do not have
that splendour I would like to see all round you.
Yet I did not think those things beautiful
which any man can have: and I gave orders
that out of long-locked silent cabinets,
the scent of whose crushed air quite took my breath
like the odour of sandalwood in a sanctuary,
these things should be removed into your room,
to be of use to you, into your room
where something of my mother's life (forgive me)
still now remains. It seemed to me I could
in this way show you something . . . There are imprinted
on certain things dumb signs with which the air
in silent moments seems to charge itself,
slipping a something into consciousness
which cannot, even should not, be expressed.

Pause

It pains me so, to see you bewildered by
the gravity of this moment which can scarce
walk upright underneath its heavy burden.
I know that all that's good comes into us
in quiet and unobtrusive ways,
not with this show of splendour and commotion.
For long one thinks that suddenly far off
on the horizon that new land will loom—
life, like a country still to be explored.
You watch, there's nothing there, but then the eyes
slowly discern its traces, here and there,
and that life flows all round us and includes us,
bears us, is in us, and is absent nowhere.
The things I'm saying may not make you happy.

[385]

zu hören macht. Sie klingen wie Entsagung.
Bei Gott! mir klingen sie nicht so. Mein Kind,
nicht wie ein Bettler fühl ich mich vor dir,

Mit einem grossen Blick auf sie

wie schön dir auch der grosse Glanz der Jugend
vom Scheitel niederfliesst bis an die Sohlen . . .
Du weisst nicht viel von meinem Leben, hast
gerade nur ein Stück von seiner Schale
durch eine Hecke schimmern sehn im Schatten.
Ich wollt, du sähest in den Kern davon:
so völlig als den Boden untern Füssen,
hab ich Gemeines von mir abgetan.
Scheint dir das leicht, weil ich schon alt genug bin?
Freilich, mir sind auch Freunde schon gestorben,—
dir höchstens die Grosseltern,—viele Freunde,
und die noch leben, wo sind die zerstreut?
An ihnen hing der längst verlernte Schauer
der jungen Nächte, jener Abendstunden,
in denen eine unbestimmte Angst
mit einem ungeheuren, dumpfen Glück
sich mengte, und der Duft von jungem Haar
mit dunklem Wind, der von den Sternen kam.

. . . .

Der Glanz, der auf den bunten Städten lag,
der blaue Duft der Ferne, das ist weg,
ich fänd es nicht, wenn ich auch suchen ginge.
Allein im Innern, wenn ich rufe, kommts,
ergreift die Seele, und mir ist, es könnte
auch deine—

Er wechselt den Ton

Weisst du den Tag, an dem du tanzen musstest
vor deines Vaters Gästen, wie? Ein Lächeln

The Marriage of Zobeide

You hear a note of resignation in them.
By God! I cannot hear it. My dear child,
I do not feel a beggar when I'm beside you,

He gazes ardently at her

however beautifully youth's radiance
flows down ensheathing you from head to foot . . .
You know very little of my life, have glimpsed
only a single fragment of its skin,
shining as through a hedge, and in the shadow.
I want you now to see into its core:
as wholly as the firm ground underfoot
I have forsaken all common character.
Does that seem easy to you, since I am old?
I have of course lost friends, yes, friends, through death, but
you

at most your grandparents,—my many friends,
my friends still living, where are they scattered to?
With them I knew that long-forgotten trembling
of my young nights, and of those twilight hours
in which an indefinable terror mingled
with joy, enormous and ignorant joy,
and fragrance of young hair was mingled with
the wind that blew all sombre from the stars.

.   .   .   .

The radiance that lay upon bright cities,
the blue mist of the distance, these are gone,
I would not find them, even if I looked.
But deep within me, if I call, they come
and seize my soul; and I believed, perhaps,
also your soul—

He changes his tone

Do you remember the time you had to dance,
that time, before your father's guests? A smile

[387]

blieb immerfort auf deinen Lippen, schöner
als jedes Perlenband und trauriger
als meiner Mutter Lächeln, das du nie
gesehen hast. Der Tanz hat alle Schuld:
dies Lächeln und der Tanz, die beiden waren
verflochten wie die wundervollen Finger
traumhafter Möglichkeiten. Möchtest du,
sie wären nie gewesen, da sies sind,
die schuld sind, meine Frau, dass du hier stehst?

SOBEIDE
*in einem Ton, in welchem man hört, wie die Stimme
die Zähne berührt*

Befiehlst du, dass ich tanzen solle, oder
befiehlst du etwas andres?

KAUFMANN
Meine Frau,
wie sonderbar und wild sprichst du mit mir?

SOBEIDE
Wild? Hart, kann sein: mein Schicksal ist nicht weich.
Du redest wie ein guter Mensch, so sei
so gut und rede heute nicht mit mir!
Ich bin dein Ding, so nimm mich für dein Ding,
und lass mich wie ein Ding auch meinen Mund
vergraben tragen und nach innen reden!

*Sie weint lautlos, mit zusammengepressten Lippen, das
Gesicht gegen das Dunkel gewandt.*

KAUFMANN
So stille Tränen und so viele! Dies
ist nicht der Schauer, drin der Krampf der Jugend
sich löst. Hier ist ein Tieferes zu stillen
als angeborne Starrheit scheuer Seelen.

perpetually lay upon your lips,
more lovely than a necklace of pearls, more sad
than the sad smile of my mother you yourself
have never seen. To that dance all is due:
that smile, and then the dance, together joined
like marvellous fingers of dreamed possibility.
Would you prefer that they had never been,
whose fault it is, my wife, that you are here?

ZOBEIDE

her tone that of a voice touching the teeth

Do you command me now to dance, or do you
command some other thing of me?

MERCHANT

My wife,
how strangely, wildly you are speaking to me!

ZOBEIDE

Wild? Hard perhaps: my destiny's not soft.
You speak like a kind man, so then be kind
and do not speak to me today like this.
I am a thing: so take me as a thing;
and let me, like a thing, conceal my mouth,
and speak not otherwise than inwardly.

*She weeps soundlessly, with lips pressed together, her face
turned towards the darkness.*

MERCHANT

Such quiet tears, so many tears! And this
is not the shuddering in which the cramp
of youth dissolves. Here deeper things are silenced
than the natural stiffness of shy souls.

[389]

Hugo von Hofmannsthal

SOBEIDE

Herr, wenn du in der Nacht erwachst und mich
so weinen hörst aus meinem Schlaf heraus,
dann weck mich auf! Dann tu ich, was dein Recht
ist, mir zu wehren, denn dann träume ich
in deinem Bett von einem andren Mann
und sehne mich nach ihm, das ziemt mir nicht,
mich schaudert vor mir selber, es zu denken:
versprich mir, dass du mich dann wecken wirst!

Pause.

*Der Kaufmann schweigt: tiefe Erregung färbt sein Gesicht
dunkel.*

Du fragst nicht, wer es ist? Ist dirs so gleich?
Nein? Dein Gesicht ist dunkel, und dein Atem
geht schwer? So will ich selber dir es sagen:
du hast ihn hie und da bei uns gesehn,
sein Name ist Ganem—des Schalnassar Sohn,
des Teppichhändlers—und ich kannte ihn
drei Jahre lang. Doch nun seit einem Jahr
hab ich ihn nicht gesehn.
Dies sag ich dir, dies letzte geb ich preis,
weil ichs nicht leide, dass ein Bodensatz
von Heimlichkeit und Lüge in mir bleibt:
ob dus erführst, ist gleich: ich bin kein Becher,
für rein gekauft und giftger Grünspan drin,
der seinen Boden frisst—und dann, damit
du mir ersparst, in meinem Haus als Gast
ihn etwa oft zu sehn, denn das ertrüg ich schwer.

KAUFMANN
drohend, aber schnell von Zorn und Schmerz erstickt
Du! du hast . . . du hast . . .

Er schlägt die Hände vors Gesicht.

The Marriage of Zobeide

ZOBEIDE

Lord, if you wake up in the night and hear
that I am weeping, waken me, I beg you!
For then I shall be doing what you have
the right to stop me doing; in your bed
I shall be dreaming of another man
and longing for him; that I should not do,
I shudder at myself to think of it:
promise me then that you will waken me!

Pause

The Merchant is silent: his face darkens with deep emotion.

You do not ask me who it is? Do you care so little?
No? And your face is dark, you breathe as if
breath were a labour? Then I'll tell it you:
you've seen him, now and then, with us at home,
his name is Ganem, he is Shalnassar's son,
you know, the carpet-dealer, for three years
I've known him. Yet I have not seen him now
for one whole year.
I tell you this, surrender this last thing,
because I cannot endure that a residue
of secrecy and lies should remain in me:
I do not mind your knowing, I am no cup
bought as pure but poisoned with verdigris
that eats the metal—this I tell you now
that you may save me having to see him here,
a guest in my own house; I could not bear it.

MERCHANT

in a threatening tone which is quickly stifled by anger and pain
You! You have . . . you have . . .

He covers his face with his hands.

[391]

Hugo von Hofmannsthal

SOBEIDE

So weinst du auch an deinem Hochzeitstag?
Hab ich dir einen Traum verdorben? Sieh,
du sagst, ich bin so jung, und das, und das—

Zeigt auf Haar und Wangen

ist wirklich jung, doch innen bin ich müd,
so müd, es gibt kein Wort, das sagen kann,
wie müd und wie gealtert vor der Zeit.
Wir sind gleich alt, vielleicht bist du noch jünger.
Du hast mir im Gespräch einmal gesagt:
seitdem ich lebe, diese ganze Zeit
wär dir beinahe nur in deinen Gärten
dahingegangen und im stillen Turm,
den du gebaut, den Sternen nachzuschauen.
An diesem Tage hielt ich es in mir
zum erstenmal für denkbar, deinen Wunsch
und meines Vaters, das wars noch viel mehr,
ja . . . zu erfüllen. Denn mir schien, die Luft
im Haus bei dir müsst etwas Leichtes haben,
so leicht! so ohne Last! und die bei mir
war so beladen mit Erinnerung,
der luftige Leib schlafloser Nächte schwamm
darin umher, an allen Wänden hing
die Last der immer wieder durchgedachten,
verblassten, jetzt schon toten Möglichkeiten;
die Blicke meiner Eltern lagen immer
auf mir, ihr ganzes Leben . . . viel zu gut
verstand ich jedes Zucken ihrer Augen,
und über allem diesem war der Druck
von deinem Willen, der sich über mich
wie eine Decke schweren Schlafes legte.
Es war gemein, dass ich mich endlich gab:

The Marriage of Zobeide

ZOBEIDE

You too then weep upon your wedding-day?
And have I spoiled the dream you dreamed? But look,
you say I am so young, and this, and this

Points to her hair and cheeks

is surely young, but in me I am tired,
so tired there are no words could ever say
how tired I am, and old before my time.
Our ages are the same; you may be younger.
You said to me in conversation once:
since I have been alive, all these long years
had passed for you, almost, as you walked your garden,
and stood in the silent tower that you built
to watch the stars. That day, and not before,
I first believed, and secretly believed,
that your wish, and my father's, which was more . . .
might be fulfilled. It seemed to me the air
inside your house must have a levity,
such levity! Unburdened! While the air
around me was so thick with memories
that the airy body of my sleepless nights
swam round in it, there clung to every wall
the weight of possibilities I'd pondered
until they paled, and now are even dead;
my parents' eyes were always watching me,
their whole life in them, I understood too well
the tiniest agitation in those eyes,
and lying over all things was the load
and pressure of your will that had been spread
like a blanket of heavy sleep to cover me.
It was a common act to give myself:

ich such kein andres Wort, doch das Gemeine
ist stark, das ganze Leben voll davon:
wie konnt ichs unter meine Füsse bringen,
da ich darinnen war bis an den Hals?

KAUFMANN

So wie ein böser Alpdruck lag mein Wunsch
auf deiner Brust! so hassest du mich doch . . .

SOBEIDE

Ich hass dich nicht, ich hab zu hassen nicht
gelernt, vom Lieben nur den Anfang erst,
der brach dann ab, doch kann ich andre Dinge
schon besser, als: mit Lächeln, wie du weisst,
zu tanzen, wenn mir schwerer als ein Stein
das Herz drin hing, und jedem schweren Tag
entgegen, jedem Übel ins Gesicht
zu lächeln: alle Kraft von meiner Jugend
ging auf in diesem Lächeln, doch ich triebs
bis an das Ende, und nun steh ich da.

KAUFMANN

Dies alles hängt nur schattenhaft zusammen.

SOBEIDE

Wie dies zusammhängt, dass ich lächeln musste
und endlich deine Frau geworden bin?
Willst du das wissen? muss ich dir das sagen?
So weisst du, weil du reich bist, gar so wenig
vom Leben, hast nur Augen für die Sterne
und deine Blumen in erwärmten Häusern?
Merk, so hängt dies zusamm: arm war mein Vater,
nicht immer arm, viel schlimmer: arm geworden,
und vieler Leute Schuldner, doch am meisten

The Marriage of Zobeide

I'll seek no other word for it; but strong,
how strong is all that's common, life is filled with it.
How could I ever tread it underfoot
when I was standing deep and in the midst of it?

MERCHANT

So like an evil incubus my will
lay on your heart! You must have hated me . . .

ZOBEIDE

I do not hate you; I have never learned
to hate, have only begun to learn of love,
and that beginning stopped; but there are other things
I can do better; I can dance, as you know,
and smiling, when more heavy than a stone
my heart hung in me; I can smile at each
so heavy passing day, smile in the face
of every evil: all the power of my youth
passed out into that smile; and yet I went
on to the bitter end; and here I am.

MERCHANT

These things have only shadowy connections.

ZOBEIDE

You ask, can my forced smile then be connected
with this—that I have now become your wife?
You want to know? Must I be the one to tell you?
Do you then know so little, being rich,
about this life, have you eyes for the stars alone
and for the flowers you keep in heated houses?
I'll tell you then: my father, he was poor,
he had not always been so poor, but worse,
he had become poor, and had creditors,

der deine; und von meinem Lächeln lebte
die kummervolle Seele meines Vaters,
wie andrer Leute Herz von andren Lügen.
Die letzten Jahre, seit du uns besuchst,
da konnt ichs schon, vorher war meine Schulzeit.

KAUFMANN

Meine Frau geworden!
Sie hätt sich ebenso mit einer Schere
die Adern aufgetan und in ein Bad
mit ihrem Blut ihr Leben rinnen lassen,
wär das der Preis gewesen, ihren Vater
von seinem grossen Gläubiger zu lösen!
. . . So wird ein Wunsch erfüllt!

SOBEIDE

Nimms nicht so hart. Das Leben ist nun so.
Ich selber nehms schon wie im halben Traum.
Wie einer, wenn er krank ist, nicht mehr recht
vergleichen kann und nicht mehr sich entsinnen,
wie er am letzten Tag dies angesehen,
und was er dann gefürchtet und gehofft:
er hat den Blick von gestern schon nicht mehr . . .
so, wenn wir in die grosse Krankheit «Leben»
recht tief hineingekommen sind. Ich weiss
kaum selber mehr, wie stark ich manche Dinge
gefürchtet, andere wie sehr ersehnt,
und manches, was mir einfällt, ist mir so,
als wärs das Schicksal einer andern Frau,
grad etwas, das ich weiss, doch nicht das meine.
Schau, meine Art ist bitter, doch nicht schlimm:
war ich im ersten Augenblick zu wild,
so wird auch kein Betrug dabei sein, wenn ich

chiefly yourself; and his unhappy soul
lived on my smile, as the hearts of other men
live upon other lies. And in the years
that you paid visits to us, then I knew
the way to smile; before then were my schooldays.

MERCHANT

Now you become my wife!
She would have done much better to have taken
a pair of scissors, cut her veins, and let
her life run with her blood into a bath,
if that was to be the price she paid to free
her father from his chiefest creditor!
. . . So wishes are fulfilled!

ZOBEIDE

Please do not take it hard like this. It's life.
I take it as a kind of dream, myself.
Like one who, being ill, cannot compare
quite rightly, and who cannot remember how
he saw this thing or that the day before,
and what he then had feared, what he had hoped,
for he has lost the look of yesterday . . .
thus too when we have passed deep into the illness
that we call "life." I hardly know, myself,
how strongly I have feared particular things,
how strongly I have wanted other things,
and sometimes things that happen to me happen
as if they were the fate of another woman,
something I know of, but which is not mine.
I may be bitter, but I am not bad:
I may have been too wild, just at the first,
but I shall not deceive you, either, when

sanft sitzen werd und deinen Gärtnern zusehn.
Mein Kopf ist abgemüdet. Mir wird schwindlig,
wenn ich zwei Dinge in mir halten soll,
die miteinander streiten. Viel zu lang
hab ich das tuen müssen. Ich will Ruh!
Die gibst du mir, dafür bin ich dir dankbar.
Denk nicht, das wäre wenig: furchtbar schwach
ist alles, was auf zweifelhaftem Grund
aufwächst. Doch hier ist nichts als Sicherheit.

KAUFMANN

Und dieser Mensch?

SOBEIDE

Auch das nimm nicht so schwer.
Schwer wars zu nehmen, hätt ich dirs verschwiegen;
nun hab ichs hergegeben. Lass es nun!

KAUFMANN

Du bist nicht los von ihm!

SOBEIDE

Meinst du? Was heisst
denn «los»? Die Dinge haben keinen Halt,
als nur in unserm Willen, sie zu halten.
Das ist vorbei.

Handbewegung.

KAUFMANN *nach einer Pause*

Du warst ihm, was er dir?

Sobeide nickt.

Wie aber, wie nur denn ist dies gekommen,
dass dich zur Frau nicht er—

The Marriage of Zobeide

I quietly sit and watch your gardeners.
My head is quite tired out. And I grow giddy
when I must try to keep in it two things
which fight against each other. I have had
to do this far too long. It's peace I want!
You give me this, and I am grateful to you.
But do not think this is a little: all
that grows upon the soil of doubt is frail,
terribly frail. But here all things are sure.

MERCHANT

This other man?

ZOBEIDE
                    That need not burden you.
It would have been a burden if I had said
nothing about it to you; but I have.
So let it be.

MERCHANT
You are not free of him!

ZOBEIDE

You think I am not? "Free," what does it mean?
Things only have a foothold in our will
to hold them fast. It's finished.

She makes a gesture.

MERCHANT *after a silence*
                    Were you to him
just as he was to you?

                    Zobeide nods.

                    But how can it be
that you are not the wife—

[399]

Hugo von Hofmannsthal

SOBEIDE

Wir waren arm!
Nein, mehr als arm, du weisst. Sein Vater auch.
Auch arm. Dazu ein harter, düstrer Mensch,
wie meiner allzu weich, und auf ihm lastend,
so wie der meinige auf mir. Das Ganze
viel leichter zu erleben, als mit Worten
zu sagen. Alles ging durch Jahre hin.
Wir waren Kinder, als es anging, müde
am End wie Füllen, die man allzu früh
am Acker braucht vor schweren Erntewagen.

KAUFMANN

Es ist zu sagen: das kann nicht so sein,
das mit dem Vater. Diesen Schalnassar,
den Teppichhändler, kenn ich. Nun, es ist
ein alter Mensch; von ihm mag Gutes reden,
wer will, ich nicht. Ein schlechter alter Mensch!

SOBEIDE

Kann sein, gleichviel! Ihm ists der Vater eben.
Ich hab ihn nie gesehn. Er sieht ihn so.
Er nennt ihn krank, wird traurig, wenn er redet
von ihm. Deswegen hab ich ihn auch nie
gesehn, das heisst, seit meiner Kinderzeit,
und da nur hie und da am Fenster lehnen.

KAUFMANN

Doch gar nicht arm, nichts weniger als arm!

SOBEIDE
ihrer Sache völlig sicher, traurig lächelnd

Meinst du, dann stünd ich hier?

[400]

The Marriage of Zobeide

ZOBEIDE

We were so poor!
No, more than poor, you know it. And his father,
he too was poor, a hard, dark-minded man,
as mine was all too soft, who pressed upon him,
as mine too pressed on me. Yet everything
was easier to endure than it is to find
the words to speak of it. The years passed by.
We were just children when it started, tired
when it was finished, like young horses, used
when they're too young, on heavy harvest wagons.

MERCHANT

Surely it can't be true, what you have said
about his father. Shalnassar, I know him,
the carpet-dealer. He is old, of course;
let those who will, speak good of him, but I,
I cannot; he's an old and wicked man.

ZOBEIDE

Perhaps, but all the same, that is his father.
I have not met him, and I only know
what his son says of him. He says he's ill,
and saddens when he speaks of him. That's why
I have not seen him—only as a child,
when I saw him sometimes looking from his window.

MERCHANT

But he's not poor, he's anything but poor!

ZOBEIDE

completely certain that she is right, smiling sadly
If he was not, would I be standing here?

[401]

KAUFMANN

Und er?

SOBEIDE

Wie, er?

KAUFMANN

Er liess dich deutlich sehn,
dass ihm unmöglich schien, was er und du
durch Jahre wünschtet und lang möglich hieltet?

SOBEIDE

Da es unmöglich war! . . . und dann, zudem
«durch Jahre wünschtet»—alle diese Dinge
sind anders, und die Worte, die wir brauchen,
sind wieder anders. Hier ist dies gereift,
und hier vermodert. Augenblicke gibts,
die Wangen haben, brennend wie die Sonnen—
und irgendwo schwebt ein uneingestanden
Geständnis, irgendwo zergeht in Luft
der Widerhall von einem Ruf, der nie
gerufen wurde; irgend etwas flüstert:
«Ich gab mich ihm,» merk: in Gedanken! «gab»—
der nächste Augenblick schluckt alles ein,
so wie die Nacht den Blitz . . . Wie alles anfing
und endete? Nun so: ich tat die Lippen
nicht auf und bald auch meine Augenlider nicht,
und er—

KAUFMANN

Wie war denn er?

SOBEIDE

Mich dünkt, sehr vornehm.
Wie einer, der im Andern selbst sein Bild

MERCHANT

And he?

ZOBEIDE

What do you mean?

MERCHANT

He gave you to understand
quite clearly it was impossible, what you and he
for years had wanted and thought possible?

ZOBEIDE

Because it was impossible! . . . and then
"for years had wanted"—these are different,
quite different things, and the words we use for them
again are different. Here things grew ripe,
and here grew rotten. Moments come which have
cheeks that are hot and burn like suns—and somewhere
hovers an unconfessed confession, somewhere
the echo of a cry dies in the air, a cry
which was not uttered; something is whispering:
"I gave myself to him," but that is "gave" in thought—
all things are swallowed up by the next moment,
like lightning by the night. . . . How things began,
and ended? In this way: I did not open
my lips, then soon I did not open my eyes,
and he—

MERCHANT

Yes, how did he behave?

ZOBEIDE

Nobly, I think;
he behaved like a man who meant to destroy his image

zerstören will, dem Andern Schmerz zu sparen—
ganz ungleich, nicht so gütig mehr wie sonst
—die grösste Güte lag drin, so zu sein—,
zerrissen, voll von einem Spott, der ihm
im Innern weher tat vielleicht als mir,
wie ein Schauspieler manches Mal, so seltsam
voll Absicht. Andre Male wieder so
von meiner Zukunft redend, von der Zeit,
da ich mit einem Anderen—

KAUFMANN *heftig*

Mit mir?

SOBEIDE *kalt*

Mit irgendeinem Anderen vermählt,
so redend, wie er wusste, dass ich nie
ertragen würde, dass es sich gestalte.
So wenig, als er selbst es eine Stunde
ertrüge, denn er gab sich nur den Schein,
mein Wesen kennend, wissend, dass ich so
mit mindren Schmerzen mich losmachen würde,
sobald ich irr an ihm geworden wäre.
. . . .
Es war zu künstlich, aber welche Güte
lag drin.

KAUFMANN

Sehr grosse Güte, wenn es wirklich
nichts war, als nur ein angenommner Schein.

SOBEIDE *heftig*

Mein Mann, ich bitte, dieses eine bitt ich
von dir: verstöre unser Leben nicht:

within another to save the other pain—
but not consistently, not always kind—
his greatest kindness lay in his simply being—
but desperately, full of mockery
which hurt him more perhaps than it hurt me,
and sometimes like an actor, strangely full
of calm design. At other times again
speaking about my future and the day
that someone else should . . .

MERCHANT *violently*

Was that someone me?

ZOBEIDE *coldly*

That someone else should marry me, and speaking
as if he knew that I could never bear it.
As little even as he himself could bear it
a single hour, but pretending it all,
knowing my nature, knowing that I could
be free from him less painfully as soon
as I had found I had been mistaken in him.

.   .   .   .

It was too artificial, but what kindness
was in it all!

MERCHANT

Kindness indeed, if really
it was no more, no more than mere pretence.

ZOBEIDE *violently*

Husband, I ask you this one single thing,
no more; do not destroy our life together.

[405]

es ist noch blind und klein wie junge Vögel:
mit einer solchen Rede kannst dus töten!
Nicht eine schlechte Frau werd ich dir sein:
ich meine, langsam finde ich vielleicht
in andern Dingen etwas von dem Glück,
nach dem ich meine Hände streckte, meinend,
es wär ein Land ganz voll damit, die Luft,
der Boden! und man könnte dort hinein:
jetzt weiss ich schon, ich sollte nicht hinein . . .
Ich werde dann beinahe glücklich sein,
und alle Sehnsucht ohne Schmerz verteilt
an Gegenwart und an Vergangenheit
wie helle Sonne in den lichten Bäumen,
und wie ein leichter Himmel hinterm Garten
die Zukunft: leer, doch alles voller Licht . . .
Nur werden muss mans lassen:
jetzt ist noch alles voll Verworrenheit,
du musst mir helfen, das darf nicht geschehn,
dass du mit einem falschen Wort dies Leben
zu stark an mein vergangnes knüpfst: sie müssen
geschieden sein durch eine gläserne,
luftlose Mauer wie in einem Traum.

Am Fenster

Der Abend darf nicht kommen, der mich hier
an diesem Fenster fände ohne dich:
—schon nicht zu Haus zu sein, nicht aus dem Fenster
von meiner Mädchenkammer in die Nacht
hinauszuschaun, hat eine sonderbare,
gefährliche, verwirrende Gewalt:
als läg ich auf der Strasse, niemands eigen,
so meine Herrin, wie noch nie im Traum!
Ein Mädchenleben ist viel mehr beherrscht

The Marriage of Zobeide

It is still blind and small as young birds are:
speak once like this—and you will kill it quite!
I shall not be a bad wife, no, because
I think that slowly I shall find perhaps
in other things a little of that joy
for which I once held out my hands, convinced
there was a country full of it, the air,
and earth! that one could enter into it:
and now I know it was not mine to enter. . . .
Then I shall almost have my happiness,
and all my longing, painless, shall be shared
between the present and the time that's past
like a bright sun among the shining trees,
and like a weightless sky behind the garden,
the future: empty, but all filled with light. . . .
Only we *must* let these things grow:
everything now is full of this confusion,
and you must help me, do not let it happen
that a false word of yours should link this life
too closely with my life that's past: they must
be separated by a wall of glass,
an airless wall as in a dream.

At the window

That night
must never come which finds me all alone
standing beside this window here without you:
even to be no more at home, no more to look
into the night, out of my bedroom window,
has a strange, dangerous, bewildering power:
as if I lay on the street, belonging nowhere,
and my own mistress, as I had never dreamed!
The life a girl lives is far more oppressed

[407]

von einem Druck der Luft als du begreifst,
dem Freisein das Natürliche erscheint.
Der Abend darf nie kommen, wo ich hier
so stünde, aller Druck der schweren Schatten,
der Eltern Augen, alles hinter mir,
im dunklen Vorhang hinter mir verwühlt,
und diese Landschaft mit den goldnen Sternen,
dem schwachen Wind, den Büschen so vor mir!

Immer erregter

Der Abend darf nie kommen, wo ich dies
mit solchen Augen sähe, die mir sagten:
Hier liegt ein Weg, er schimmert weiss im Mond:
bevor der schwache Wind die nächste Wolke
dem Mond entgegentreibt, kann den ein Mensch
zu Ende laufen, zwischen Hecken hin,
dann aber einen Kreuzweg, einen Rain
im Schatten dann vom hohen Mais, zuletzt
in einem Garten! und dann hätt er schon
die Hand an einem Vorhang, hinter dem
ist alles: Küssen, Lachen, alles Glück
der Welt so durcheinander hingewirrt
wie Knäuel goldner Wolle, solches Glück,
davon ein Tropfen auf verbrannten Lippen
genügt, so leicht zu sein wie eine Flamme,
und gar nichts Schweres mehr zu sehen, nichts
mehr zu begreifen von der Hässlichkeit!

Fast schreiend

Der Abend darf nie kommen, der mit tausend
gelösten Zungen schreit: Warum denn nicht?
warum bist du ihn nicht in einer Nacht
gelaufen? Deine Füsse waren jung,

The Marriage of Zobeide

by the bare air than you can understand,
to whom your freedom seems quite natural.
No night must ever come to find me here
with all the pressure of the heavy shadows,
and of my parents' eyes, all that's behind me,
entangled in the curtains, dark behind me,
and this scene there, with all the golden stars,
the gentle wind, the bushes, like *this* before me!

Still more impassioned

The night must never come in which I look
upon these things with eyes that tell me: Here,
here is a white path, shimmering in the moonlight:
before the gentle wind can drive the closest
cloud towards the moon, one could take that path
and run to the end of it, between the hedges,
then to a crossroads, then across a ridge
enshadowed by the tall maize, finally
arriving in a garden! then his hand
is resting on a curtain, and behind this
everything is: kissing, laughter, the joys
of all the world in uttermost confusion,
like tanglements of golden wool, such joys
a single drop of them on ashen lips
is enough to make one light as a flame and see
no single heaviness anywhere and to know
not one more thing of ugliness!

Almost shrieking

The night
must never come that cries with a thousand tongues:
Why not? Why did you not run to him that night?
Your legs were young, your breath was strong, and why,

dein Atem stark genug, was hast du ihn
gespart, damit dir reichlich überbleibt,
in deine Kissen nachts hineinzuweinen?

*Sie kehrt dem Fenster den Rücken, klammert sich an den
Tisch, sinkt in sich zusammen und bleibt auf den Knien liegen, das Gesicht an den Tisch gedrückt, den Leib vom Weinen durchschüttert.*

Lange Pause

KAUFMANN

Und wenn ich dir die erste Tür auftäte,
die einzige verschlossne auf dem Weg?

*Er tuts; durch die geöffnete kleine Tür in den Garten rechts
fällt Mond herein.*

SOBEIDE
auf den Knien, beim Tisch

Bist du so grausam, in der ersten Stunde
ein abgeschmacktes Spiel aus meinem Weinen
zu machen, bist du so, mich recht zu höhnen?
so stolz darauf, dass du mich sicher hältst?

KAUFMANN
mit aller Beherrschung

Ich hätte sehr gewünscht, du hättest anders
gelernt von mir zu denken, doch dazu
ist jetzt nicht Zeit.
Dein Vater, wenns das ist, was dich so drückt,
dein Vater ist mir nichts mehr schuldig, vielmehr
ist zwischen mir und ihm seit kurzer Zeit
dergleichen abgemacht, wovon ihm Vorteil

why did you save it, keeping more than enough
with which to weep each night into your pillow?

*She turns her back on the window, grips the table with both
hands, sinks to her knees, where she remains, her face pressed
against the table, her body shaken by tears.*

Long pause

MERCHANT

And what if I were to open the first door
upon your way, the only one that's closed?

*He does so; through the small open door leading right, into
the garden, the moonlight falls.*

ZOBEIDE

on her knees, near the table

Are you so cruel that you begin to play,
so early, an absurd game with my tears?
Is *that* your way: to mock me utterly?
Are you so proud of having me for your own?

MERCHANT

making every effort to master his emotions

It would have brought me pleasure if you had learned
to think of me not in this way; but now
there is no time for it.
Your father, if it is this which oppresses you,
your father owes no debts to me, indeed
not long ago we made a contract which

und damit hoffentlich ein später Schimmer
von Freudigkeit erwächst.

Sie hat sich auf den Knien, zuhörend, ihm näher geschoben.

Du könntest also—
du kannst, ich meine, wenn es dieses war,
was dich am meisten lähmte, wenn du hier,
in einem—fremden Haus, den Mut des Lebens,
der dir verloren war, neu eingeatmet,
dich wie aus einem schweren Traum zur Hälfte
aufrichtest, und es diese Tür hier ist,
von der du fühlst, sie führt zum wachen Leben:
so geb ich dir vor Gott und diesen Sternen
den Urlaub, hinzugehn, wohin du willst.

SOBEIDE
immer auf den Knien

Wie?

KAUFMANN

Ich seh in dir so wenig meine Frau
als sonst in einem Mädchen, das, vor Sturm,
vor Räubern von der strasse, sich zu schützen
für kurz hier in mein Haus getreten wäre,
und spreche mir mein Recht ab über dich,
so wie mir keines zusteht über eine,
die solcher Zufall in mein Haus verschlüge.

SOBEIDE

Was sagst du da?

KAUFMANN
Ich sage, du bist frei,
durch diese Tür zu gehn, wohin du willst:
frei wie der Wind, die Biene und das Wasser.

[412]

should benefit him, even wake in him,
I hope, a gleam of happiness.

She has moved closer, listening, on her knees.

You could,
you can, I mean, if it was this which most
has crippled you, and also if you have
in this—strange house, breathed a new breath of life
that you had lost, and now can stand as after
a terrible dream half upright, and if this
door is the door you feel leads out to a life
of awakening, then before God and all these stars
I give you leave to go, wherever you will.

ZOBEIDE
still kneeling

I don't understand.

MERCHANT

I see in you my wife no more than I would
see her in any girl that, driven by a storm,
or chased by thieves, took refuge in my house,
for a short time, to shelter with me here,
and I renounce all right to you, because
I have no right over anyone who wanders,
lost, into my house, by a sheer accident.

ZOBEIDE

What is it you are saying?

MERCHANT
You are free
to walk out of this door, wherever you will,
free as the wind, and as a bee, and as water.

Hugo von Hofmannsthal

SOBEIDE *halb aufgerichtet*

Zu gehn?

KAUFMANN

Zu gehn.

SOBEIDE

Wohin ich will?

KAUFMANN

Wohin
du willst, zu welcher Zeit du willst.

SOBEIDE
noch immer betäubt, jetzt an der Tür

Jetzt?! hier?!

KAUFMANN

Jetzt, so wie später. Hier, wie anderswo.

SOBEIDE *zweifelnd*

Doch zu den Eltern nur?

KAUFMANN *in stärkerem Tone*

Wohin du willst.

SOBEIDE *zwischen Lachen und Weinen*

Das tust du mir? Das hab ich nie im Traum
gewagt zu denken, nie im tollsten Traum
wär ich auf meinen Knien mit dieser Bitte

Sie fällt vor ihm auf die Knie

zu dir gekrochen, um dein Lachen nicht

The Marriage of Zobeide

ZOBEIDE *half upright*

To go?

MERCHANT

To go.

ZOBEIDE

Wherever I will?

MERCHANT

Wherever
you will and when you choose.

ZOBEIDE

still only half-aware, now at the door

Now?! And here?!

MERCHANT

Now, or later. Here, or anywhere.

ZOBEIDE *doubting him*

But only to my parents?

MERCHANT *louder*

Wherever you will.

ZOBEIDE *between laughter and tears*

You do this to me? Never in my dreams
have I dared to think it, not in my wildest dreams
would I have crawled upon my knees to you

She falls on her knees before him

with this request, for fear of seeing you laugh

[415]

zu sehn bei solchem Wahnsinn . . . und du tusts,
du tust es! Du! Du guter, guter Mensch!

Er hebt sie sanft auf, sie steht verwirrt.

KAUFMANN
sich abwendend

Wann willst du gehen?

SOBEIDE
Jetzt! im Augenblick!
Oh, sei nicht zornig, denk nicht schlecht von mir!
Sag selber: kann ich denn die Nacht bei dir,
bei einem Fremden bleiben? muss ich nicht
sogleich zu ihm, gehör ich ihm denn nicht?
Wie darf sein Gut in einem fremden Haus
die Nacht verweilen, als wärs herrenlos?

KAUFMANN *bitter*

Gehörst ihm schon?

SOBEIDE
Herr, eine rechte Frau
ist niemals ohne Herrn: von ihrem Vater
nimmt sie der Gatte, dem gehört sie dann,
sei er lebendig oder in der Erde;
der nächste und der letzte ist der Tod.

KAUFMANN
So willst du nicht, zumindest bis zum Tag,
zurück zu deinen Eltern?

SOBEIDE
Nein, mein Lieber.
Das ist vorbei. Mein Weg ist nun einmal

at such a madness . . . yet you do it, do it,
you! O you are kind, you are kind to me!

Gently he lifts her up, she stands bewildered.

MERCHANT

turning away

When will you go?

ZOBEIDE

Now! This very moment!
O do not be angry, do not think ill of me!
Tell me yourself: could I spend the night with you,
who are a stranger? Must I not go at once
to him, for do I not belong to him?
How can his property stay overnight
in a strange house, as if it had no master?

MERCHANT *bitterly*

So you belong to him?

ZOBEIDE

Lord, a real woman is
never without a lord and master: from
her father she is taken by her husband,
and she belongs to him, if he live or die;
the next and final husband, he is death.

MERCHANT

You do not want, at least till morning comes,
to go back to your parents?

ZOBEIDE

No, my friend.
That now is finished. Once and for all my way

[417]

nicht der gemeine: diese Stunde trennt
mich völlig ab von mädchenhaften Dingen.
So lass mich ihn in dieser einen Nacht
auch bis ans Ende gehn, dass alles später
mir wie ein Traum erscheint, und ich mich nie
zu schämen brauch.

KAUFMANN
So geh!

SOBEIDE
Ich tu dir weh?

Kaufmann wendet sich ab.

SOBEIDE
Erlaub, dass ich aus diesem Becher trinke.

KAUFMANN
Er ist von meiner Mutter, nimm ihn dir.

SOBEIDE
Ich kann nicht, Herr. Doch trinken lass mich draus.

Sie trinkt.

KAUFMANN
Trink dies und sei dir nie im Leben not,
aus einem Becher deinen Durst zu löschen,
der minder rein als der.

SOBEIDE
Leb wohl.

KAUFMANN
Leb wohl.

[418]

is not the common one: this moment cuts
me off entirely from all girlish things.
So let me go my way in this one night,
even to the very end, that later all things
may be to me as in a dream, and I
need never be ashamed.

MERCHANT

Then go!

ZOBEIDE

Do I hurt you?

Merchant turns away.

ZOBEIDE

This cup, will you allow me to drink from it?

MERCHANT

It was my mother's. You may take it with you.

ZOBEIDE

I cannot, lord. But let me drink from it.

She drinks.

MERCHANT

Drink then, and may you never in your life
find any need to quench your thirst from a cup
that is less pure than this.

ZOBEIDE

Goodbye.

MERCHANT

Goodbye.

[419]

Hugo von Hofmannsthal

Sie ist schon auf der Schwelle.

Hast du nicht Furcht? Du bist noch nie allein
gegangen. Wir sind ausserhalb der Stadt.

SOBEIDE

Mein Lieber, mir ist über alle Furcht
und leichter, als noch je am hellen Tage.

Sie geht.

KAUFMANN
*nachdem er ihr lange nachgesehen, mit einer
schmerzlichen Bewegung*

Als zög jetzt etwas seine stillen Wurzeln
aus meiner Brust, ihr hinterdrein zu fliegen,
und in die leeren Höhlen träte Luft!

Vom Fenster wegtretend

Scheint sie mir nicht im Grund jetzt minder schön,
so hastig, gar so gierig, hinzulaufen,
wo sie kaum weiss, ob einer auf sie wartet!
Nein: ihre Jugend muss ich nur recht fassen,
ganz eins mit allem Schönen ist auch dies,
und diese Hast steht diesem Wesen so,
wie schönen Blumen ihre stummen Mienen.

Pause

Ich glaube, was ich tat, ist einer Art
mit dem, wie ich den Lauf der Welt erkenne:
Ich will nicht andere Gedanken haben,
wenn ich die hohen Sterne kreisen seh,
und andre, wenn ein junges Weib vor mir steht.
Was dort die Wahrheit, muss es hier auch sein.

The Marriage of Zobeide

She is already standing in the doorway.

Are you not afraid? You've never walked alone,
and here we are some distance from the town.

ZOBEIDE

My friend, now I have passed beyond all fear,
and feel a lightness, as if it were broad day.

She goes.

MERCHANT

*after looking for a long time in the direction in which she has
gone, with a pained gesture*

As if now something drew its silent roots
out of my heart to fly where she has flown,
and into the empty hollows crept the air.

Walking from the window

Is she not now, when all is said and done,
less beautiful to me, hasty, greedy to go
where she can hardly guess if she's expected?
No: I must only understand her youth,
that too is one with all that's beautiful,
and her being hasty suits just such a nature,
as beautiful flowers are suited by their dumb gestures.

Pause

What I have done, I think, is of one kind
with what I can recognize as the design of the world.
I do not want to think one thing when I watch
high stars that circle overhead and then
another thing when a young woman stands before me.
What is truth there must be truth also here.

[421]

Auch ist zu sagen, wenn es diese Frau,
wenn dieses Kind es nicht ertragen kann,
zwei Dinge gleichzeitig in sich zu halten,
von denen eins das andre Lügen straft,
soll ich es können, mit der Tat verleugnen,
was ich mit der Vernunft und dumpfer Ahnung
dem Ungeheuren abgelernt, das draussen
sich auftürmt von der Erde zu den Sternen?
Ich nenn es Leben, jenes Ungeheure,
und Leben ist auch dies, wer dürft es trennen?
Was ist denn Reifsein, wenn nicht: ein Gesetz
für sich und für die Sterne anerkennen!
Jetzt gab mir also mein Geschick den Wink,
so einsam fortzuleben, wie bis nun,
und—kommt einmal das Letzte, ohne Erben
und keine Hand in meiner Hand, zu sterben.

Verwandlung.

The Marriage of Zobeide

And even more: this woman, or this child,
if she cannot endure to hold in a single thought
two things of which the one belies the other,
should I be able, by an act, to deny
what I have learned by reason or dark supposition
from watching all that vastness there outside
that towers up from earth to the very stars?
I call it life, that vastness, and this too,
this too, is life, and who can dare divide it?
What then can ripeness be, but to be aware
that there's a single law for selves and stars!
Now therefore destiny gave me the sign,
to go on living, alone, as I've lived till now,
and—even if the end must come, if I,
with no inheritor, no hand in mine, must die.

Curtain

Hugo von Hofmannsthal

II

*Ein getäfelter Raum im Haus des Schalnassar. Links rück-
wärts kommt die Treppe herauf, rechts rückwärts steigt sie
empor, eng und steil. In Stockhöhe läuft eine Galerie aus
durchbrochenem Holzwerk mit Öffnungen, inneren Balko-
nen, um die ganze Bühne. Offene Ampeln. Links und rechts
vorne Türen mit Vorhängen. An der linken Wand eine nie-
drige Bank zum Sitzen, weiter rückwärts ein Tisch mit Sitzen.*

*Auf der Sitzbank neben der Tür links sitzt der alte Schal-
nassar, in seinen Mantel gewickelt. Vor ihm steht ein junger
Mensch, der verarmte Kaufmann.*

SCHALNASSAR
Wär ich so reich, als Ihr mich haltet—wahrlich,
ich bins nicht, weit davon entfernt, mein Lieber—,
ich könnt Euch dennoch diesen Aufschub nicht
gewähren, wirklich, Freund, um Euretwillen:
allzu nachsichtge Gläubiger sind, bei Gott,
des Schuldners Untergang.

DER SCHULDNER
Schalnassar, hört mich!

SCHALNASSAR
Nichts mehr! Ich kann nichts hören! Meine Taubheit
wächst immerfort mit Euren Reden. Geht!
Geht nur nach Haus: bedenkt, Euch einzuschränken:
Ich kenn Eur Haus, Ihr habt viel Ungeziefer,
Dienstboten mein ich. Drückt den Aufwand nieder,
den Eure Frau Euch macht: er schickt sich nicht
für Eure Lage. Was? ich bin nicht da,
Euch zu beraten! Geht nach Hause, sag ich.

The Marriage of Zobeide

II

A panelled room in Shalnassar's house. Left, towards the back of the stage, a flight of stairs ascends to it: right, towards the back of the stage, another flight of stairs ascends from it, narrow and steep. A gallery up in the three walls encircles the stage, with openings in the woodwork and built-in balconies. Open pendant lamps. Front, left and right, doors with curtains. Against the left-hand wall a low bench, further back a table with chairs.

On the bench beside the left-hand door old Shalnassar is sitting, wrapped in his cloak. In front of him stands a young man, an impoverished merchant.

SHALNASSAR

Were I as rich as you think I am—I am not,
naturally, no, far from it, my dear friend—
even then this respite is impossible,
really it is, my dear friend, for *your* sake:
all-too-considerate creditors are, by God,
their debtors' ruin.

THE DEBTOR

Listen, Shalnassar!

SHALNASSAR

Not another word! I cannot hear! My deafness
grows worse the more you speak. Now go, I say:
go home: plan to be less extravagant:
I know your household, you've got vermin there,
servants, I mean. Cut down your wife's expenses:
your situation does not warrant them.
What am I saying? I am not here to give
advice to you! Go home now, as I say.

Hugo von Hofmannsthal

DER SCHULDNER

Ich wollte schon, mein Herz lässt mich nicht gehn,
dies Herz, das so aufschwillt! Nach Haus! Mir ist
die Tür von meinem Haus schon so verhasst!
Ich kann nicht durch, dass nicht ein Gläubiger
den Weg mir sperrte.

SCHALNASSAR

Welch ein Narr wart Ihr!
Geht heim zu Eurer schönen Frau, so geht!
Geht hin! Setzt Kinder in die Welt! Verhungert!

*Klatscht in die Hände. Der armenische Sklave kommt die
Stiege herauf. Schalnassar flüstert mit ihm, ohne den andern
zu beachten.*

DER SCHULDNER

Nicht fünfzig Goldstück hab ich in der Welt!
Dienstboten, sagtet Ihr? Ein altes Weib,
die Wasser trägt, sonst nichts! Und die, wie lang noch?
Kein armer Teufel, den Almosen füttert,
ist elend dran wie ich: ich hab gekannt
die Süssigkeit des Reichtums: jede Nacht
hab ich geschlafen, und Zufriedenheit
war rings um meinen Kopf, und süss der Morgen.
Doch still! sie liebt mich noch, und mein Zusammenbruch
ist ganz vergoldet! Oh, sie ist mein Weib!

SCHALNASSAR

Ich bitt Euch, geht, ich muss die Lampen brennen,
solang Ihr hier herumsteht!

Zu dem armenischen Sklaven

Geh mit ihm.

Da sind die Schlüssel.

[426]

The Marriage of Zobeide

THE DEBTOR

I would have gone before, but my heart won't let me,
for it is bursting! Home! I cannot bear
the very sight of the door of my own house!
I cannot walk through it without some creditor
blocking my way.

SHALNASSAR

O what a fool you were!
Go home to your beautiful wife I say, go home!
Be off! Bring children into the world! And starve!

He claps his hands. The Armenian Slave comes up the stairs.
Shalnassar whispers to him, without looking at the Debtor.

THE DEBTOR

I've not a penny I can call my own!
Servants you say? Only an old old woman
to carry water, and how long will she last?
The poorest devil fed by charity
is better off than I: for I have known
the sweetness riches are: and every night
I've slept with satisfaction there to guard
my head, and sweet was morning when it came.
I'll speak no more of it: she loves me still,
my fall is golden! O, she is my wife!

SHALNASSAR

I ask you now to go; the lamps waste oil
as long as you're still here.

To the Armenian Slave

And you go with him.
The keys are here, take them.

[427]

Hugo von Hofmannsthal

DER SCHULDNER
seine Angst überwindend

Guter Schalnassar!
Ich wollt Euch nicht um einen Aufschub bitten!

SCHALNASSAR
Wie? meine Taubheit spiegelt mir was vor?

DER SCHULDNER
Nein, wirklich!

SCHALNASSAR
Sondern?

DER SCHULDNER
Um ein neues Darlehn!

SCHALNASSAR *wütend*
Was wollt Ihr?

DER SCHULDNER
Nein, ich will ja nicht, ich muss!
Du hast sie nie gesehn, du musst sie sehn!
Mein schweres Herz hört auf, so dumpf zu pochen
und hüpft vor Freude, wenn mein Aug sie sieht.

Immer erregter

Dies alles muss sich wenden! Ihre Glieder
sind für den Dienst der Zärtlichkeit geschaffen,
nicht für die wilden Klauen der Verzweiflung!
Sie kann nicht betteln gehn mit solchem Haar!
Ihr Mund ist ganz so stolz als süss: das Schicksal
will mich nur überlisten—doch ich lache—
wenn du sie sähest, alter Mann—

The Marriage of Zobeide

THE DEBTOR

overcoming his fear

Good Shalnassar!
I did not want to ask you for any respite!

SHALNASSAR

What? Has my deafness been deceiving me?

THE DEBTOR

Really I did not.

SHALNASSAR

What then?

THE DEBTOR

A new loan!

SHALNASSAR *furious*

Want what?!

THE DEBTOR

I do not *want* it, I *must* have it!
You have not ever seen her, but you must!
My heavy heart beats dull no longer but
it leaps for joy when my eyes rest on her.

Still more impassioned

Things must improve! Is not her body made
to serve affection, delicacy, sweetness,
not for the savage talons of despair?
She cannot beg, with hair like hers! Her mouth
is proud as it is sweet: and destiny
is trying to deceive me—but I laugh—
old man, if you could see her—

[429]

Hugo von Hofmannsthal

SCHALNASSAR

Das will ich!
Sagt ihr: der alte Mann, von dessen Gold
ihr junger Mann so abhängt—merkt Euch, sagt:
der gute alte Mann, der schwache Greis—,
verlangte, sie zu sehn. Sagt: alte Männer
sind kindisch: warum sollt es der nicht sein?
Doch ein Besuch ist wenig. Sagt ihr noch:
es ist beinah ein Grab, das sie besucht,
ein Grab, das grad noch atmet. Wollt Ihr das?

DER SCHULDNER

Ich hörte sagen, dass Ihr Euer Gold
anbetet wie was Heiliges, und zunächst dann
den Anblick von gequälten Menschen liebt
und Mienen, die den Schmerz der Seele spiegeln.
Doch seid Ihr alt, habt Söhne, und ich glaub nicht,
dass diese bösen Dinge wahr sind. Drum
will ich ihrs sagen, und wenn sie mich fragt,
wie mir das deucht, so will ich sagen: «Liebste,
nur wunderlich, nicht schlimm!»—Lebt wohl, doch lasst,
wenn Euer Wunsch gewährt ist, die Erfüllung
des meinen, Schalnassar, nicht lange anstehn!

Der Schuldner und der armenische Sklave gehen ab, die
Stiege hinab.

SCHALNASSAR

allein. Er steht auf, dehnt sich, scheint nun viel grösser

Ein süsser Narr ist das, ein süsser Schwätzer!
«Hört, alter Mann!»—«Ich bitt Euch, alter Mann!»
Ich hörte sagen, seine Frau ist schön
und hat so feuerfarbnes Haar, darin
die Hände, wenn sie wühlen, Glut und Wellen

[430]

The Marriage of Zobeide

SHALNASSAR

                                And I shall!
Tell her that the old man upon whose gold
her young man so depends—now listen: say:
the good old man, the very frail old man—,
asked, just to see her. Say: all old men are
childish: and surely *he* is just the same?
A visit—it's of small account. And say:
it's nothing but a grave that she will visit,
a grave just breathing still. Will you do this?

THE DEBTOR

I've heard men telling that you worship gold
like something that is holy, and that next
you like the sight of people being tortured,
the gestures made by souls when they're in pain.
But you are old, have sons, I don't believe
these wicked things are true. So I shall tell her,
and if she asks me what I think, I'll say:
"Dearest, he is eccentric, but not bad!"
Goodbye; but if your wishes are fulfilled
see that my own are not too long forgotten!

*The Debtor and the Armenian Slave leave, going down the
stairs.*

SHALNASSAR

alone. He stands up, stretches, seems now much taller

What a sweet fool that is, a sweet chatterbox!
"Listen, old man!"—"I ask you now, old man!"
I've heard it said his wife is beautiful,
and has fire-coloured hair, and when your hands
revel in it, it is as if they felt

[431]

zugleich zu spüren meinen. Kommt sie nicht,
so soll sie lernen, auf der nackten Streu
zu schlafen! . . .

        . . . Schlafenszeit wär nun für mich!
Man sagt, Genesne brauchen langen Schlaf.
Allein, bin ich schon taub, so will ich taub sein
für solche Weisheit. Schlafen ist nichts andres
als voraus sterben. Ich will meine Nächte
zugiessen noch den Tagen, die mir bleiben.
Freigebig will ich sein, wos mir gefällt:
der Gülistane will ich heute abend
mehr schenken, als sie träumt. Dies gibt den Vorwand,
dass sie die Kammer tauscht und eine grössre
bezieht, die näher meiner. Wenn sies tut',
soll Saft von Nelken, Veilchen oder Rosen
ihr Bad sein, Gold und Bernstein soll sie trinken,
bis sich das Dach in tollem Schwindel dreht.

Er klatscht in die Hände, ein Sklave kommt, er geht links ab,
der Sklave folgt ihm.

Gülistane kommt die Treppe links rückwärts herauf, hinter
ihr eine alte Sklavin. Ganem beugt sich spähend oben aus
einer Nische vor, kommt die Treppe rechts rückwärts herab.

GANEM
nimmt sie bei der Hand

Mein Traum! wo kommst du her? Ich lag so lang
und lauerte.

    Die alte Sklavin steigt die Treppe hinauf.

GÜLISTANE
Ich? aus dem Bade steig ich
und geh in meine Kammer.

a glowing and a rolling all at once. But if
she does not come, then she will learn to sleep
on the bare straw! . . .
           . . . It's time I slept as well.
They say that convalescents need much sleep.
But if I'm deaf, I'll let this wisdom fall
upon deaf ears. Sleep is no more nor less
than dying in advance. I'll mix my nights
with the days that may still yet be left to me.
And I'll be generous, where I want to be:
I'll give my Gulistan tonight far more
than she has ever dreamed, so make a pretext
that she may change her room and use a larger one,
closer to mine. And when she does so, then
she'll bathe in oils of violet, carnation,
attar of roses, she'll drink amber and gold
until the ceiling whirls in a frenzy above her.

He claps his hands, a slave comes, he leaves, left, the slave
following him.

Gulistan comes up the stairs, left, behind her an old Slave-
Woman. Ganem peers out of a niche in the gallery, then
descends the stairs, right.

GANEM
takes her hand

My dream! Where have you been? I lay so long
and waited for you.

    The old Slave-Woman goes up the stairs, right.

GULISTAN
      I? I have just been swimming,
and am going to my room.

Hugo von Hofmannsthal

GANEM

Wie du funkelst
vom Bad!

GÜLISTANE

Mein Bad war flüssig glühndes Silber
vom Mond.

GANEM

Wär ich der Bäume einer, die dort stehn,
ich würf mein ganzes Laubwerk bebend ab
und spräng zu dir! O wär ich hier der Herr!

GÜLISTANE

Ja, wärest du! Dein Vater ist sehr wohl.
Er bat mich, heut zur Nacht mit ihm zu speisen.

GANEM

Verdammte Kunst, die dieses Blut erweckte,
das schon so nahe am Erstarren war.
Ich sah ihn diesen Morgen mit dir reden.
Was wars?

GÜLISTANE

Ich habs gesagt.

GANEM

Sag, wars nicht mehr? Du lügst! es war noch mehr!

GÜLISTANE

Er fragte—

GANEM

Was? Doch still, die Wände hören.

[434]

The Marriage of Zobeide

GANEM

But how you shine,
fresh from the water!

GULISTAN

Moonlight made me a bath
of liquid glowing silver.

GANEM

I should like to be
one of the trees there; then I should strip
my leafage off and leap into your arms! If only
I were the master here!

GULISTAN

But you are not.
Your father is very well now. I am going
to dine with him tonight, at his invitation.

GANEM

O damn the art that woke his blood when it
was almost frozen! I saw him this morning,
talking to you, what did he say?

GULISTAN

I've told you.

GANEM

No more than that? You're lying! He said more!

GULISTAN

He asked—

GANEM

What? But be quiet; the walls have ears.

[435]

Hugo von Hofmannsthal

Sie flüstert.

GANEM

Geliebtes!
Indes du redest, reift in mir ein Plan,
höchst wundervoll, merk auf! und so begründet:
er ist nur mehr der Schatten seines Selbst,
er steht noch drohend da, doch seine Füsse
sind Lehm. Sein Zorn ist Donner ohne Blitz,
und—merk wohl—all seine Begehrlichkeit
ist nichts als Prahlerei des Alters.

GÜLISTANE
          Nun,
was gründest du auf dies?

GANEM
          Die grösste Hoffnung.

Er flüstert.

GÜLISTANE

Allein dies Gift—
gesetzt, es gäbe eins mit solcher Wirkung:
dem Geist nur tödlich und dem Körper spurlos—
dies Gift verkauft dir niemand!

GANEM
          Nein, kein Mann,
doch eine Frau—

GÜLISTANE
Um welchen Preis?

[436]

The Marriage of Zobeide

She whispers to him.

GANEM

My love!
There is a plan shaping in my mind as you speak,
a marvellous one, listen: here is the basis:
he's only now a shadow of himself,
he stands and threatens there, and yet his feet
are clay. His wrath is thunder without lightning,
and—listen now—his appetite's no more
than an old man's swaggering.

GULISTAN

Well then, and what
do you build upon this basis?

GANEM

The highest hopes.

He whispers.

GULISTAN

But yet, this poison—
even if one exists, with these effects:
fatal to the spirit, but with no bodily trace—
no man will sell it you.

GANEM

No, not a man,
a woman will.

GULISTAN

Her price?

[437]

GANEM

Um den,
dass sie vermählt mich wähnt und zu besitzen
mich wähnt—nachher.

GÜLISTANE

Dies machst du keine glauben.

GANEM

Es gibt schon lange eine, die dies glaubt.

GÜLISTANE

Du lügst: gerade, sprachst du, wär der Plan gereift,
nun aber sagst du: lange gibts schon eine.

GANEM

Die gibts: ich hab in dieses Lügennetz
sie eingesponnen, eh ich recht gewusst,
zu welchem Ende. Heute ist mirs klar.

GÜLISTANE

Wer ists?

GANEM

Des ärmlichsten Pastetenbäckers
hinkende Tochter, in der letzten Gasse
des Schifferviertels.

GÜLISTANE

Wer?

GANEM

Was tut ein Name? Ihre Augen hingen

GANEM

Is simply this:
that she believes me married, and that I'll
belong to her—afterwards.

GULISTAN

You'll not find this woman.

GANEM

There's one who has believed this for some time.

GULISTAN

You're lying: for you said your plan had just
this minute taken shape; and now you say
this woman has believed this for some time.

GANEM

She has: I caught her in this net of lies
before I knew where it would lead me. Now
I know.

GULISTAN

Who is she?

GANEM

She's the crippled daughter
of the poorest pastrycook in the whole town,
in the last narrow street down by the harbour.

GULISTAN

But who?

GANEM

What's in a name? Her doglike eyes

so hündisch bang an mir, wenn ich vorbeiging:
es war von den Gesichtern, die mich reizen,
weil sie die Lüge so begierig trinken
und solche Träumereien aus sich spinnen!
Und so blieb ich dort stehn und sprach sie an.

GÜLISTANE

Und wer schafft ihr das Gift?

GANEM

Das tut ihr Vater,
indem ers dort verwahrt, von wo sies stiehlt.

GÜLISTANE

Wie? ein Pastetenbäcker?

GANEM

Doch sehr arm
und sehr geschickt,—jedoch für keinen Preis
von uns zu kaufen: denn er ist von denen,
die heimlich einen Teil der heiligen Bücher
verwerfen und von keiner Speise essen,
auf die von unsereinem Schatten fiel.
Ich geh zu ihr, indessen du mit ihm
zu Abend isst.

GÜLISTANE

So hat ein jedes sein Geschäft.

GANEM

Das meine aber soll dem deinigen
die Wiederholung sparen. Ich bin früh
zurück. Brauch einen Vorwand. Geh von ihm.
Denn träf ich dich mit ihm—

followed me timidly when I passed that way:
she had one of those faces which intrigue me
because they drink up lies with such a greed
and spin such nets of dreams out of themselves!
And so I stopped one day, and spoke to her.

GULISTAN

And who'll get her the poison?

GANEM

                   Her father will,
by keeping it in the place she'll steal it from.

GULISTAN

But how? A pastrycook?

GANEM

               Yes, but a poor
and very clever one,—although we could not
buy him at any price: he's one of those
who secretly deny some of the things
that are said in holy scripture, and eat no food
on which the shadow of one of us has fallen.
I'll go to her, when you have gone to him
for supper.

GULISTAN

       Then each one has his own business.

GANEM

But mine will mean yours needs no repetition.
I'll be back early. Use some pretext. Leave him.
For if I find you with him—

Hugo von Hofmannsthal

GÜLISTANE
hält ihm den Mund zu

O still, nur still!

GANEM
bezwungen

Wie kühl sind deine Hände, und wie glüht
zugleich dein Blut hindurch, du Zauberin!
Du hältst gefangen mich im tiefsten Turm
und fütterst mich um Mitternacht mit dem,
was deine Hunde übriglassen, schlägst mich,
lässt mich im Staube kriechen.

GÜLISTANE
Recht! und du?

GANEM
gebrochen von ihrem Blick

Und ich?

Sieht zu Boden

Nun eben Ganem heiss ich doch!
Ganem der Liebessklave!

Er sinkt vor ihr nieder, umschlingt ihre Füsse.

GÜLISTANE
Geh nur, geh!
Ich hör den Vater, geh! Ich heiss dich gehn!
Ich will nicht, dass man uns beisammen trifft!

GANEM
Ich hab ein eitles inhaltloses Lächeln,
das trefflich dient, ihm ins Gesicht zu sehn.

The Marriage of Zobeide

GULISTAN

puts her hand over his mouth

Quiet, be quiet!

GANEM

mastered by her glance

How cool your hands are, yet how the blood glows
that runs in them, enchantress! And I am
kept as your prisoner in the deepest dungeon,
at midnight fed by scraps your dogs have left,
you whip me, make me crawl in the dust.

GULISTAN

O true!

And you?

GANEM

crushed by her look

And me?

He looks at the ground

Well, Ganem is my name!
Ganem, the slave of love!

He sinks down and embraces her feet.

GULISTAN

But you must go!
I can hear your father, go! I tell you: go!
I do not want us to be seen together.

GANEM

I have a vague and vacant smile that's useful
when I'm compelled to look him in the face.

[443]

Gülistane geht die Treppe hinauf. Der armenische Sklave kommt von unten. Ganem wendet sich, rechts vorne abzugehen.

DER SKLAVE

War Gülistane hier?

Ganem zuckt die Achseln.

DER SKLAVE

Doch sprachst du eben.

GANEM

Mit meinem Hund!

DER SKLAVE

So find ich sie wohl hier.

Geht hinauf.

Die Bühne bleibt kurze Zeit leer, dann tritt von links Schalnassar auf mit drei Sklaven, die Geräte und Schmuck tragen. Er lässt alles an der linken Wand niederstellen, wo ein Tisch mit niedrigen Sitzen befindlich ist.

SCHALNASSAR

Hier legt dies her! hier dies! und tragt nun auf!

Er geht an die unterste Stufe der Treppe rechts.

Ah, der Genesne, sagt man, soll der Sonne
entgegengehn. Nun denn, ich steh schon hier,

Gülistane kommt die Treppe herab, er führt sie zu den Geschenken.

und weiss nichts mehr von Krankheit, als dass Perlen
ihr Werk sind und der Bernstein, wenn sie Muscheln

The Marriage of Zobeide

Gulistan goes up the stairs. The Armenian Slave comes up the other staircase. Ganem turns, moving towards the door, right.

SLAVE

Gulistan, was she here?

Ganem shrugs his shoulders.

SLAVE

But you were talking.

GANEM

Talking to my dog!

SLAVE

Then I shall find her here.

He goes up the stairs, right.

For a few moments the stage is empty, then Shalnassar enters, left, with three slaves who are carrying various objects and jewellery. He signals to them to put everything down by the left-hand wall, where there is a table with low chairs.

SHALNASSAR

This, put it here, and this, here! Now serve up!

He walks to the foot of the right-hand staircase.

Ah, don't they say the convalescent should
approach the sun? And now I'm standing here,

Gulistan comes down the stairs, he leads her to the presents.

and know no more of illness but that pearls
and amber are its work, when it selects

zu ihrem Sitz wählt oder Bäume. Wahrlich,
die liegen beide da! Und hier sind Vögel
der Seide recht lebendig eingewebt,
wenn dirs der Mühe wert, sie anzusehen.

GÜLISTANE

Dies ist zuviel.

SCHALNASSAR

Für einen Taubenschlag,
doch nicht für ein Gemach, das gross genug ist,
um unbetäubt den Duft von Rosenöl
zu tragen, den die Krüge hier ausatmen.

GÜLISTANE

Die wundervollen Krüge!

SCHALNASSAR

Der ist Onyx,
der Chrysopras, wie? nicht der Rede wert.
Für undurchdringlich gelten sie und lassen
den Duft so durch, als wär es morsches Holz.

GÜLISTANE

Wie dank ich dir?

Schalnassar versteht nicht.

Wie ich dir danken kann?

SCHALNASSAR

Indem du alles dies
vergeudest: diesen Tisch von Sandelholz
und Perlmutter brauch in kühlen Nächten
statt dürrer Zweige, dir das Bad zu wärmen,
und achte, wie das Feuer sprüht und duftet.

[446]

a shell or a tree for a dwelling. Now indeed,
these both are here! And here again are birds,
most living representations worked in the silk,
if you care, perhaps, to trouble yourself to look.

GULISTAN

This is too much.

SHALNASSAR

Too much, yes, for a dovecote,
but not for a room that's big enough for us
to bear without danger of intoxication
the perfume of attar of roses these jugs breathe.

GULISTAN

The jugs are wonderful.

SHALNASSAR

This one is onyx,
and that is chrysoprase; well? Trivial stuff.
Impermeable, they say, but the perfume flows
filtering through it, as if it were rotten wood.

GULISTAN

How can I thank you?

Shalnassar does not understand.

I said: how can I thank you?

SHALNASSAR

By taking all these things
and squandering them: this table of sandalwood
and mother-of-pearl, use it when cool nights come
instead of dry sticks when you heat your bath,
and notice how the fire smells sweet and sparkles.

[447]

Hugo von Hofmannsthal

Man hört unten einen Hund anschlagen, dann mehrere.

GÜLISTANE

Durchsichtige Gewebe!

Hebt sie empor.

SCHALNASSAR

Totes Zeug!
Ich bring dir einen Zwerg, der zwanzig Stimmen
von Menschen und von Tieren in sich hat.
Statt Papagein und Affen schenk ich dir
sehr sonderbare Menschen, Ausgeburten
von Bäumen, die sich mit der Luft vermählen.
Die singen nachts.

GÜLISTANE

Ich will dich küssen!

Das Anschlagen der Hunde wird stärker, scheint näher.

SCHALNASSAR

Sag, ob junge Männer besser
verstehn zu schenken?

GÜLISTANE

Was für Stümper sind die
in dieser Kunst, und welch ein Meister du!

*Der armenische Sklave kommt, zupft Schalnassar am Kleide,
flüstert.*

SCHALNASSAR

Ein Mädchen sagst du? wohl ein Weib, doch jung,
wie? ich versteh dich nicht!

[448]

The Marriage of Zobeide

A dog is heard barking below, then several dogs.

GULISTAN

And these transparent fabrics!

Holds them up.

SHALNASSAR

All dead stuff!
I'll bring to you a dwarf with twenty tongues
of men and beasts in him. Instead of parrots
and monkeys, I shall give you curious beings,
beings that were born of trees, who blend with air.
They sing at night.

GULISTAN

I want to kiss you!

The barking grows louder, seems closer.

SHALNASSAR

Do young men know better
how to give presents, well?

GULISTAN

But they are bunglers
in such an art; but you, you are a master!

*The Armenian Slave comes, tugs at Shalnassar's cloak, whis-
pers.*

SHALNASSAR

A girl, you say? Perhaps a woman—but young?
What? I don't understand.

[449]

Hugo von Hofmannsthal

GÜLISTANE

Von welchem Weib ist da die Rede, Liebster?

SCHALNASSAR

Von keinem. «Bleib,» sprach ich zu diesem da,
und du misshörtest mich.

Zum Sklaven

Sprich hier, und leise!

DER SKLAVE

Sie ist halbtot vor Angst, ein Wegelagrer
war hinter ihr: dann rissen sie die Hunde
zu Boden. Ohne Atem fragte sie:
«Ist dies Schalnassars Haus, des Teppichhändlers?»

SCHALNASSAR

Es ist des süssen Narren Weib. Er schickt sie!
Sei still!

Geht zu Gülistane, die eine Perlenschnur um den Hals legt

O schön! sie sind den Platz nicht wert!

Tritt wieder zu dem Sklaven.

DER SKLAVE

Sie redet auch von Ganem.

SCHALNASSAR

Meinem Sohn!
Gleichviel! Sag: ist sie schön?

DER SKLAVE

Mir schien sies.

The Marriage of Zobeide

GULISTAN

What woman are you speaking of, my love?

SHALNASSAR

None. What I said to him was "whom," and you
simply misheard it.

To the Slave

Now speak here, and softly!

THE SLAVE

She is half dead with fear, a thief on the road
was running after her: and then the dogs
brought her to the ground. She asked, breathless:
"Is this Shalnassar's house, the carpet-dealer's?"

SHALNASSAR

The sweet fool's wife. So he has sent her! Quiet!

Walks over to Gulistan who is putting on a pearl necklace

Beautiful, but O not fit to be hung there!

Walks back to the Slave.

THE SLAVE

She also speaks of Ganem.

SHALNASSAR

Of my son!
No matter: is she beautiful?

SLAVE

I thought so.

[451]

Hugo von Hofmannsthal

SCHALNASSAR

Wie?

DER SKLAVE

Allein entstellt von Angst.

GÜLISTANE

Geschäfte?

SCHALNASSAR

zu ihr

Keines,

als dir zu dienen.

Greift hin, ihr die Spange am Nacken zu schliessen; es gelingt
ihm nicht.

GÜLISTANE

Aber!

SCHALNASSAR

greift sich ans Auge

Eine Ader

sprang mir im Aug. Ich muss dich tanzen sehn,
dann saugt das Blut sich auf.

GÜLISTANE

Wie wunderlich!

SCHALNASSAR

Tus mir zulieb!

GÜLISTANE

Da muss ich mir mein Haar

aufstecken.

SHALNASSAR

What do you mean?

SLAVE

Her fear concealed it.

GULISTAN

Business?

SHALNASSAR

to her

None but to be of service to you.

He reaches out to fasten the clasp at the back of the neck, but does not succeed in doing so.

GULISTAN

No!

SHALNASSAR

quickly puts a hand over one eye

My eye! It's a burst vein—I must see you dance,
it will stop the blood.

GULISTAN

That's strange.

SHALNASSAR

Do me this favour!

GULISTAN

Then I must go and put my hair up.

[453]

Hugo von Hofmannsthal

SCHALNASSAR

Steck dirs auf! Ich kann nicht leben,
solang du dich verweilst.

Gülistane geht die Treppe hinauf.

Zum Sklaven

Führ sie herauf:
sag nichts als dies: hier stünde, den sie sucht.
Merk: den sie sucht, nicht mehr!

Geht auf und nieder, der Sklave ab.

So arglos ist kein Mensch, ich will nicht glauben,
dass es dergleichen Narren gibt! Was Wegelagrer!
Er schickt sie her, und was dem widerspricht,
ist aufgeschminkt.
Ich dachte nicht, dass diese Nacht dies bringt,
doch Gold treibt dieses alles aus dem Nichts!
Ich will sie hüten, wenn sie mir gefällt:
ihr eigner Mann soll ihr Gesicht nicht mehr
zu sehn bekommen! goldne Kettchen leg ich
um ihre Knöchel!
Ich will mit zweien hausen und sie zähmen,
dass sie in einem Reif wie Papageien
sich schaukeln.

*Der Sklave führt Sobeide die Treppe herauf. Sie ist verstört,
ihre Augen wie erweitert, ihr Haar zerrüttet, die Perlenschnüre herabgerissen. Sie trägt keinen Schleier mehr.*

SCHALNASSAR

Käm mein Sohn vor Ärger um!
Ei da! und wie sie sich verstellt und zittert!

Er winkt dem Sklaven, zu gehen.

SOBEIDE
sieht ihn angstvoll an

Bist du der Schalnassar?

The Marriage of Zobeide

SHALNASSAR

                   Go then;
but how shall I live as long as you're away?

Gulistan goes up the stairs.

To the Slave

Now bring her here. Say only this: the man
for whom she is looking is waiting for her. Now:
the man for whom she is looking, say no more.

Walks up and down; the Slave goes.

Can a man be so artless? It's incredible
that there can be such fools! What? Thieves on the road?
He sent her here; and all that contradicts this,
is got-up nonsense.
I did not think tonight would bring me this,
but gold commands all things out of the emptiness!
I'll keep her, if I take a liking to her;
her husband shall not see her face again!
And I'll put chains of gold around her ankles.
And I'll live together with the two of them,
tame them, train them both to swing in hoops,
like parrots.

*The Slave leads Zobeide up the stairs. She is frantic, her eyes
seem enlarged, her hair in disorder, the pearl necklace gone.
She is no longer wearing a veil.*

And if my son were to die of chagrin.
Ah, now! How she dissembles, how she shivers!

He signals the Slave to go.

ZOBEIDE

looks at him timorously

Can you be Shalnassar?

[455]

Hugo von Hofmannsthal

SCHALNASSAR

Ja. Und dein Mann—

SOBEIDE

Mein Mann? wie weisst du das? bin ich denn nicht
gerade jetzt . . . war alles nicht heut nacht? . . .
Wie . . . oder du errätst?

SCHALNASSAR

So neckisch rede
mit einem jungen Affen. Ich bin alt
und weiss, wie viel ich Macht hab über Euch.

SOBEIDE

Wohl hast du Macht, doch wirst du sie nicht brauchen,
mir wehzutun.

SCHALNASSAR

Nein, beim wahrhaftgen Licht!
Doch ich bin nicht geschaffen, süss zu reden,
noch viel zu reden.
Beflissne Schmeichelei liegt hinter mir:
der Mund, der einer Frucht den Saft aussaugt,
ist stumm. Und dies ist das Geschäft des Herbstes.
Mag immerhin der Frühling süsser duften,
der Herbst verlacht den Frühling! Sieh nicht so
auf meine Hand. Weil sie voll Adern ist,
Gerank, darin der Lebenssaft erstarrt,—
oh, sie ergreift dich noch und kann dich halten!
Schon weh! ich wills mit einer Perlenschnur
umwickeln, komm!

Will sie fortziehen.

[456]

The Marriage of Zobeide

SHALNASSAR

Yes. And your husband—

ZOBEIDE

My husband? How do you know of this? It was
only just now that I . . . surely it was tonight? . . .
Or, or have you guessed?

SHALNASSAR

Speak in that teasing way
to some young monkey. I am old and know
how great is the power that I have over you.

ZOBEIDE

Yes, you have power, but you will not use it
to cause me pain.

SHALNASSAR

No, no by the light of heaven!
Yet it is not my way to speak with sweetness,
nor to speak much.
I've put all careful flattery behind me:
the mouth which sucks the juice out of a fruit
is dumb. And this is the occupation of Autumn.
However Spring may have a greater fragrance,
yet Autumn laughs at Spring! O no, you need not
stare at my hand. Because it is full of veins,
like tendrils with life's sap run dry in them—
O but my hand can grasp you still, and hold you!
There now, I'm sorry! Come, let me wrap it with
this string of pearls!

Tries to draw her away.

[457]

Hugo von Hofmannsthal

SOBEIDE

macht sich los

Erbarm dich meiner, du, mein armer Kopf
ist ganz zerrüttet! Redest du mit mir?
Sag, du bist trunken oder willst mich narren!
Weisst du denn, wer ich bin? Doch ja, du sprachest
von meinem Mann! Heut war mein Hochzeitstag!
Weisst du das? Heut! wie ich mit ihm allein war,
mit meinem Mann, da kam es über mich,
ich weinte laut, und wie er fragte, dann
erhob ich meine Stimme gegen ihn
und sagte ihm von Ganem, deinem Sohn,
alles! ich sag dir später, wie es war.
Jetzt weiss ichs nicht. Nur dies: er hat die Tür
mir aufgetan, in Güte, nicht im Zorn,
und mir gesagt: ich bin nicht seine Frau:
ich kann hingehen, wo ich will.—So geh
und hol mir Ganem! geh und hol ihn mir!

SCHALNASSAR

greift zornig in seinen Bart

Verdammtes Blendwerk! welcher Teufel liess dich ein?

SOBEIDE

Die Tochter Bachtjars bin ich, lieber Herr,
des Juweliers.

SCHALNASSAR

klatscht in die Hände, der Sklave kommt

Ruf Ganem!

SOBEIDE

unwillkürlich laut

Ruf ihn her!

[458]

The Marriage of Zobeide

ZOBEIDE

frees herself

Have pity on me, I am quite deranged,
O my poor head! Are you speaking to me now?
Are you drunk, or are you making a fool of me?
Do you know who I am? Of course, you spoke
about my husband! Today was my wedding day.
Do you know that? Today! Alone with him,
alone with my husband, something came over me,
I wept aloud, and when he questioned me
I lifted up my voice against him, told him,
told him of Ganem, everything, your son!
I'll tell you later how it came to be.
Now I no longer know. But this: he opened
the door to me, in kindness, not in anger,
and said to me: that I was not his wife:
that I could go wherever I will.—Now go
and fetch me Ganem! Ganem: bring him here!

SHALNASSAR

tugs angrily at his beard

What damnable deceit! What devil let you in?

ZOBEIDE

I'm Baktyar's daughter, sir, the jeweller's.

SHALNASSAR

claps his hands, the Slave comes

Tell Ganem to come here!

ZOBEIDE

shouts, involuntarily

Tell him to come!

[459]

Hugo von Hofmannsthal

SCHALNASSAR *zum Sklaven*

Hinauf die Mahlzeit! Ist der Zwerg bereit?

DER SKLAVE
Er wird gefüttert; wenn er hungrig ist, ˌ
ist er zu boshaft.

SCHALNASSAR
Gut, dies will ich ansehn.

Geht mit dem Sklaven links vorne ab.

SOBEIDE *allein*

Nun bin ich hier. Wie, fängt das Glück so an?
Ja, dies hat kommen müssen, diese Farben
kenn ich aus meinen Träumen, so gemischt.
Aus Bechern trinken wir, die uns ein Kind,
durch Blumenkränze mit den Augen leuchtend,
hinhält—doch aus den Wipfeln eines Baumes,
da fallen schwarze Tropfen in den Becher
und mischen Nacht und Tod in unsern Trunk.

Sie setzt sich auf die Bank

In alles, was wir tuen, ist die Nacht
vermengt, selbst unser Aug hat was davon:
das Schillernde in unseren Geweben
ist nur ein Einschlag, seine wahren Fäden
sind Nacht.
Der Tod ist überall: mit unsern Blicken
und unsern Worten decken wir ihn zu,
und wie die Kinder, wenn sie was verstecken
im Spiel, vergessen wir sogleich, dass wirs
nur selber sind, die ihn vor uns verstecken.
Oh, wenn wir Kinder haben, müssen sie
das alles lange, lange nicht begreifen.

[460]

The Marriage of Zobeide

SHALNASSAR *to the Slave*

Now serve the meal up. Is the dwarf quite ready?

THE SLAVE

They're feeding him, he's far too malicious
when he is hungry.

SHALNASSAR

Good, then I'll come and watch him.

He leaves with the Slave, left, front.

ZOBEIDE *alone*

Now here I am. Can happiness so begin?
Yes, for this had to be, out of my dreams
I know these very colours, how they are mixed.
We drink from cups held out to us by a child
whose eyes shine through the garlands, but there fall
down from the trees black drops into our cups
and mingle night and death with what we drink.

She sits down on the bench

The night is mixed with everything we do,
even our eyes have something of it in them:
our fabrics shine, and yet that shining comes
from an element infused, and its true colour
is night.
Death, it is everywhere: with words, with glances,
we try to cover it as best we can,
like children at their playing, who have hidden
something or other, we at once forget
it is ourselves alone who hide death from us.
O if we have children, they must be
protected long, long from discovering this.

[461]

Hugo von Hofmannsthal

Ich habs zu früh gewusst. Die schlimmen Bilder
sind immerfort in mir: sie sitzen immer
in mir wie Turteltauben in den Büschen
und schwärmen gleich hervor.

Sie sieht auf

Doch nun wird Ganem kommen! Wenn mein Herz
nur nicht mein ganzes Blut so in sich presste.
Ich bin zum Sterben müd. Ich könnte schlafen.

Mit mühsamer Lebhaftigkeit

Ganem wird kommen! dann ist alles gut!

*Sie atmet den Duft von Rosenöl und wird die kostbaren Dinge
gewahr*

Wie alles dies hier duftet! wie es funkelt!

Mit erschrockenem Staunen

Und da! Weh mir, dies ist des Reichtums Haus,
blödsinnige, belogne Augen, seht!

Sie erinnert sich fieberhaft

Und dieser Alte wollte Perlenschnüre
mir um die Hände winden: sie sind reich!
und "arm" war seines Mundes zweites Wort!
So log er, log nicht einmal, hundertmal!
ich sah sein Lächeln, wenn er log, ich fühls,
es würgt mich hier!

Sie sucht sich zu beruhigen

Oh! wenn er log—es gibt dergleichen Dinge,
die eine Seele zwingen! und sein Vater—
ich hab um meinen Vater viel getan!—

The Marriage of Zobeide

I knew it all too young. The wicked images
remain within me constantly, there they sit
like turtle-doves in bushes, and they swarm
suddenly out of me.

She looks up

But Ganem will be coming! O that my heart
would not cram all my blood so into itself.
I'm tired to death. And I would like to sleep.

With laboured animation

Ganem will come! Then all things will be well!

*She notices the scent of attar of roses, and sees the precious
things*

What fragrance there is here! How these things shine!

With horrified astonishment

And here! O grief, this is a rich man's house,
O foolish credulous eyes, just look at these things!

She remembers feverishly

And that old man wanted to wrap a necklace
of pearls around my hands: so they are rich!
And "poor" was every second word in his mouth!
So then he lied, not once, but a hundred times!
I saw him smiling as he lied, I feel it,
choking me now!

She tries to calm herself

O if he lied—there are things of that kind
which force and compel a soul! and then his father—
and for my father I have done so much!—

[463]

sein Vater dies? dies würgt mich noch viel mehr!
mutloses Herz, er kommt, und irgend etwas
enthüllt sich, alles dies begreif ich dann,
begreif ich dann—

Sie hört Schritte, blickt wild umher, dann angstvoll

Komm! lass mich nicht allein!

*Gülistane und eine alte Dienerin steigen die Treppe herab
und gehen zu den Geschenken bei dem Tisch.*

SOBEIDE *auffahrend*

Ganem! bist du es nicht?

GÜLISTANE *halblaut*

Sie ist verrückt.

*Sie lädt der Sklavin die Geschenke eines nach dem anderen
auf die Arme.*

SOBEIDE

steht in einiger Entfernung von ihr

Nein, Fräulein, nicht verrückt. Seid nur nicht bös.
Die Hunde sind mir nach! zuerst ein Mensch!
Ich bin fast tot vor Angst! Er ist mein Freund,
er wird Euch sagen, wer ich bin. Ihr wisst nicht,
was Angst aus einem Menschen machen kann.
Sagt, Fräulein, fürchten wir uns denn nicht alle
selbst vor Betrunknen? und der war ein Mörder!
Ich bin nicht mutig, und ich hab ihn doch
mit einer Lüge, die mir wie der Blitz
in meinen armen Kopf gefahren ist,
für eine Weile weggehalten—dann
ist er gekommen, seine Hände waren
schon da! Habt Mitleid mit mir, seid nicht zornig.
Ihr sitzt da an dem schönen Tisch mit Lichtern,
ich stör euch auf. Doch seid ihr seine Freunde,

his father this? This chokes me now still more!
O craven heart, he will be coming, soon
something will be revealed, then I shall understand,
shall understand.

She hears footsteps, looks wildly about her, then, timorously

Come, do not leave me alone!

*Gulistan and an old servant-woman come down the stairs
and walk across to the presents on the table.*

ZOBEIDE *passionately*

Ganem? Isn't it you?

GULISTAN *half aloud*

She must be mad.

*She heaps the presents up, one by one, in the old woman's
arms.*

ZOBEIDE

standing some distance from her

No, I am not mad. Do not be angry.
The dogs are after me! Before them it was a man!
I'm almost dead with fear! He is my friend,
and he will tell you who I am. You do not know
what fear can make out of a human being.
Tell me, are we not all alike afraid
of a drunken man? And he was a murderer!
I am not brave, yet for a while I kept him
off with a lie that came into my poor head
like a flash of lightning, but then, on he came,
his hands were at me! Have pity, do not be angry.
There you sit, with lights, at your beautiful table,
I am disturbing you. But if you are his friends,

er wird euch alles sagen. Und dann später,
wenn wir uns sehn und Ihr mich besser kennt,
dann lachen wir zusammen noch darüber.

Schaudernd

Jetzt könnt ich noch nicht lachen!

GÜLISTANE
sich zu ihr umwendend

Wer ist dein Freund? wer wird uns alles sagen?

SOBEIDE *arglos freundlich*

Ei, Ganem.

GÜLISTANE

Was hast du hier für ein Geschäft?

SOBEIDE
tritt näher, sieht sie starr an

Wie, bist du nicht die Witwe
Kamkars, des Schiffshauptmanns?

GÜLISTANE

Und du die Tochter
Bachtjars, des Juweliers?

Sie betrachten einander aufmerksam.

SOBEIDE

Es ist lang her,
dass wir einander sahn.

GÜLISTANE

Was kommst du, hier
zu tun?

SOBEIDE

So lebst du hier?—Ich komm den Ganem

Stockend

he'll explain everything. And then afterwards,
when we meet again and you may know me better,
then we shall laugh about it all together.

Shuddering

But now I could not laugh!

GULISTAN

turning to her

Who is your friend? Who will explain it all?

ZOBEIDE *ingenuous, friendly*

O, Ganem.

GULISTAN

What is your business here?

ZOBEIDE

walks closer, looks rigidly at her

Aren't you the widow
of Captain Kamkar?

GULISTAN

And aren't you the daughter
of Baktyar, the jeweller?

They study each other.

ZOBEIDE

We have not met
for a long time.

GULISTAN

And why have you come here?

ZOBEIDE

But do you live here?—I have come for Ganem—

Hesitantly

[467]

um ein Ding fragen—dran sehr vieles hängt
—für meinen Vater—

GÜLISTANE
Hast ihn lange nicht

gesehn, den Ganem?

SOBEIDE
Fast ein Jahr ist das.
Dass Kamkar starb, dein Mann, ist nun vier Jahr.
Ich weiss den Tag. Und wie lang lebst du hier?

GÜLISTANE
Verwandte sinds zu mir. Was kümmerts dich,
wie lang. Zwar, eben drum: nun seit drei Jahren.

Sobeide schweigt.

GÜLISTANE *zu der Sklavin*

Sieh zu, dass nichts hinunterfällt! Die Matten
hast du?

Zu Sobeide

Kann sein, wenn eine liegen bliebe
und Ganem fände sie, es fiel ihm ein,
die Wange drauf zu betten, weil mein Fuss
darauf geruht, und was du dann auch redest,
so wär er taub für deine Sache! Fänd er
vielleicht die Nadel, die aus meinem Haar
gefallen ist und etwa danach duftet:
er säh dich nicht, so hingen seine Sinne
an dieser Nadel.

Zu der Sklavin

Geh, heb sie mir auf!
Ei, bück dich doch!

Sie stösst die Sklavin, Sobeide bückt sich schnell und hält der

[468]

to ask him something,—it is very important,
—on behalf of my father—

GULISTAN

Is it long then since
you saw him, Ganem?

ZOBEIDE

It is nearly a year.
And it is four years since the death of Kamkar.
I know it to the day. You've been here long?

GULISTAN

They're relatives of mine. Why should you care
how long? But all the better: it's three years.

Zobeide says nothing.

GULISTAN *to the Slave-Woman*

Do not drop anything, be careful, and the mats,
have you got them?

To Zobeide

If one were dropped, you see,
and Ganem found it, it might occur to him
to use it as a pillow, since my foot
had rested on it; whatever you might say,
he would be deaf to you! And if he found
perhaps a pin that had fallen from my hair
and carried still the scent of it, a little,
he would not notice you, because his senses
would cling to that needle.

To the Slave-Woman

Go on, pick them up!
Down, you old wretch!

She kicks the Slave-Woman, Zobeide stoops quickly and holds

Sklavin die Nadel hin. Gülistane nimmt ihr die Nadel aus der Hand und sticht nach Sobeide.

SOBEIDE
Weh, warum stichst du mich?

GÜLISTANE
Damit ich dir zuvorkomm, kleine Schlange,
geh, dein Gesicht ist solch ein eitles Nichts,
man sieht dir an, was du verbergen willst.
Geh wieder heim, ich rate dir.

Zu der Sklavin

Du komm
und schlepp, soviel du kannst.

Zu Sobeide

Was mein ist, merk,
das halte ich und wahr es mir vor Dieben!

Sie geht mit der Sklavin die Treppe hinauf.

SOBEIDE *allein*

Was bleibt mir nun? Wie kann das noch gut werden,
was so beginnt? Nein, nein, mein Schicksal will
mich prüfen! Was soll dieses Weib ihm sein?
Dies ist nicht Liebe, dies ist Lust, ein Ding,
das Männern nötig ist zu ihrem Leben.

Fieberhaft hastig

Er kommt und wirft dies ab mit einem Wort
und lacht mich aus. Steht auf, Erinnrungen!
jetzt oder nie bedarf ich eurer! weh,
dass ich euch rufen muss in dieser Stunde!
Kommt keine seiner Mienen mir zurück?
kein unzweideutig Wort? ah, Worte, Mienen,
aus Luft gewobner Trug! ein schweres Herz

the needle out to the Slave. Gulistan snatches it from her
and stabs at Zobeide with it.

ZOBEIDE

Ah! Why do you do that?

GULISTAN

To show you, little snake, that I come first;
go home, you've got a silly, empty face,
it's plain what you have got to hide. Go home,
that's my advice to you.

To the Slave-Woman

And you, come now,
carry as much as you can.

To Zobeide

I keep what's mine,
I keep it, I'll not let it go to thieves!

She goes up the stairs with the Slave-Woman.

ZOBEIDE *alone*

Now what can I do? What good can come of things
that start like this? No, no, this is a trial
my destiny has set me. What can this woman mean
to him? This is not love, but lust, a thing
that men find necessary to the lives they live.

Feverishly quickly

He's coming, and he'll change it with one word,
laughing at me. Rise up now, memories,
now I require you, now or never! O
that I should have to summon you in this hour!
Can I recall none of the ways he looked at me?
No unambiguous word? Ah, words and looks,
a fabric made of air! A heavy heart

[471]

hängt sich an euch, und ihr zerreisst wie Spinnweb.
Fahr hin, Erinnerung, ich hab mein Leben
heut hinter mich geworfen, und ich steh
auf einer Kugel, die ins Ungewisse rollt!

Immer erregter

Ganem wird kommen, ja, sein erstes Wort
zerreisst die Schlinge, die mich würgen will;
er kommt und nimmt mich in den Arm—ich triefe
von Schreck und Graun anstatt von Duft und Salben—
ich schweig von allem, ich häng mich an ihn
und trink die Worte ihm vom Mund. Sein erstes,
sein erstes Wort wird alle Angst betäuben . . .
er lächelt alle Zweifel weg . . . er scheucht . . .
wenn aber nicht? . . . ich will nicht denken! will nicht!

Ganem kommt die Treppe herauf.

SOBEIDE
schreit auf

Ganem!

*Sie läuft auf ihn zu, befühlt seine Haare, sein Gesicht, fällt
vor ihm nieder, drückt den Kopf an ihn, zwischen krampf-
haftem Lachen und Weinen.*

Hier bin ich! nimm mich, nimm mich! halt mich fest!
Sei gut zu mir! Du weisst ja alles nicht!
Ich kann noch nicht . . . Wie schaust du mich denn an?

*Sie steht wieder auf, tritt zurück, sieht ihn mit entsetzlicher
Spannung an.*

GANEM
bleibt vor ihr stehen

Du?

seeks your support, and you break up like cobwebs.
Now leave me, memory; I've put my life
today behind me, and I stand upon
a rolling sphere that travels into the unknown!

Still more impassioned

Ganem will come, yes, the first word he speaks
will cut the coil that threatens to choke me now;
he'll come and take me in his arms—I'm wet
with dread and horror instead of fragrances—
I shall say nothing, I will cling to him
and drink up every word he utters. His first,
his very first word will deaden all my fear . . .
he'll smile all doubt away and he will banish . . .
but if he does not? No, I can't bear to think it . . . !

Ganem comes up the stairs.

ZOBEIDE

cries out

Ganem!

She runs to him, feels his hair, his face, falls at his feet and presses her head against them, laughing and weeping convulsively.

Here I am! Take me! Take me! Hold me in your arms!
Be kind to me! You don't know everything!
I can't yet . . . Why do you look at me like this?

She stands up again, steps back, looks at him with a terrible tension.

GANEM

stands quite still before her

You?

Hugo von Hofmannsthal

SOBEIDE *in fliegender Eile*

Ich gehör dir, Ganem! ich bin dein!
Frag mich jetzt nicht, wie dies gekommen ist:
dies ist der Kern von einem Labyrinth,
wir stehn nun einmal hier! Sieh mich doch an!
Er selber hat mich freigegeben! er . . .
mein Mann. Was wechselt dein Gesicht jetzt so?

GANEM

Um gar nichts. Tritt hierher, man hört uns etwa—

SOBEIDE

Ich fühl, es ist an meinem Wesen etwas,
das dir missfällt. Warum verbirgst du mirs?

GANEM

Was willst du?

SOBEIDE

    Ich will nichts, als dir gefallen.
Hab Nachsicht mit mir. Sag, worin ich fehle:
ich will so folgsam sein! war ich zu kühn?
Siehst du, es ist nicht meine Art: mir ist,
als hätt mich diese Nacht mit ihren Fäusten
gepackt und hergeworfen, ja, mir schaudert
vor allem, was ich dort vermocht zu reden,
und dass ich dann vermocht, den Weg zu gehn.
Missfällt dir, dass ichs konnte?

GANEM

    Warum weinst du?

SOBEIDE

Du hast die Macht, mich so veränderlich

The Marriage of Zobeide

ZOBEIDE *very quickly*

Ganem, I belong to you, I'm yours!
Don't ask me now how this has come to be:
this is the centre of a labyrinth,
once and for all we're here! Please look at me!
My husband set me free himself, my husband!
Why do you look at me so differently?

GANEM

No reason. But come here, people may hear us—

ZOBEIDE

I feel that there is something in my manner
which does not please you. Why do you hide it from me?

GANEM

What do you want?

ZOBEIDE

Only for you to like me.
O be considerate. What is wrong with me?
I will obey you! Was I too tempestuous?
But look, I'm not like that; it's that I feel
this night has seized me in its hands and hurled me
into this house, yes, and now I shudder
to think of what I managed then to say
and that I managed to take the path I spoke of.
You think I was wrong to do so?

GANEM

Why are you crying?

ZOBEIDE

You have the power to make me so changeable.

[475]

zu machen. Ich muss lachen oder weinen,
erröten und erblassen, wie dus willst.

Ganem küsst sie.

SOBEIDE

Wenn du mich küssest, sieh mich anders an!
Nein. Ich bin deine Magd. Tu, wie du willst.
Lass mich hier lehnen. Ich will sein wie Lehm
in deinen Händen und an nichts mehr denken.
Was runzelst du die Stirn?

GANEM

Weil du nun bald schon
nach Hause musst. Was lächelst du?

SOBEIDE

Ich weiss doch,
du willst mich nur versuchen.

GANEM

Nein, wahrhaftig,
da irrst du dich. Was meinst du denn? Ich kann dich
nicht hier behalten. Sag mir, ist dein Mann
denn über Land gereist, dass du nicht Furcht hast?

SOBEIDE

Ich bitte, hör nun auf, ich kann nicht lachen!

GANEM

Nein, ganz im Ernst: wann soll ich zu dir kommen?

SOBEIDE

Zu mir, wozu? Du siehst, ich bin doch hier:

Laugh I must, or weep, go pale or blush,
just as you will.

Ganem kisses her.

ZOBEIDE

Look different when you kiss me!
No. For I am your servant. Do as you will.
Let me lean here. I'll be like clay in your hands,
and think of nothing now. Why are you frowning?

GANEM

Because you must soon be going home. You smile?

ZOBEIDE

I know, you're simply trying to tempt me.

GANEM

No.
There you are wrong. What are you thinking of?
I cannot keep you here. Your husband, has he
left on a journey, to make you so unafraid?

ZOBEIDE

O stop, please stop; I cannot laugh.

GANEM

But seriously:
When do you think that I could come to you?

ZOBEIDE

Come to me, why? I am already here:

[477]

Sieh, hier zu deinen Füssen setz ich mich:
ich hab sonst kein Daheim als wie die Streu
zur Seite deinem Hund, wenn du mich sonst
nicht betten willst. Und niemand wird mich holen!

Er hebt sie auf.

GANEM
klatscht vergnügt in die Hände

Vortrefflich! wie du dich verstellen kannst,
wos die Gelegenheit erheischt! bei Gott,
es steht dir prächtig! und es soll uns nützen!
Jetzt wirds am freien Spielraum nicht mehr fehlen,
uns furchtlos unsrer Lust zu überlassen—
Wann soll ich zu dir kommen?

SOBEIDE
zurücktretend

Ich bin wahnsinnig!
mein Kopf ist schuld, dass ich dich andre Worte,
als du in Wahrheit redest, reden höre!
Ganem, so hilf mir! hab Geduld mit mir!
Was ist heut für ein Tag?

GANEM
Wozu das jetzt!

SOBEIDE
Es bleibt nicht so, es ist nur von der Angst,
und weil ich in der einen Nacht zuviel
hab fühlen müssen, das hat mich zerrüttet.
Heut war mein Hochzeitstag: wie ich allein war
mit meinem Mann, hab ich geweint und ihm
gesagt, es ist um dich: er hat die Tür
mir aufgetan.—

[478]

look, I'll sit down, here, down at your feet:
I have no other home but on the straw
beside your dog, unless you find for me
some other bed. And no one will come to fetch me.

He raises her up.

GANEM

claps his hands for joy

Marvellous, how you can act a part, dissemble
where the occasion calls for it! By God,
it suits you wonderfully, and should be useful!
Now we'll no longer be without liberty
to give ourselves to our pleasure without fear—
when shall I come to you?

ZOBEIDE

drawing back

       I have gone mad!
My head must be at fault to make me hear
words that you do not really speak at all!
Ganem, please help me! Please be patient with me!
What day is it?

GANEM

Why such a question now!

ZOBEIDE

It will all change, it only comes from fear,
and from my having had in a single night
to feel too much; I am utterly bewildered.
Today was my wedding-day; when I was alone
with him, my husband, I wept and told him that
it was for you. And then he went to the door
and opened it.

[479]

Hugo von Hofmannsthal

GANEM

Ich wett, er hat die Fallsucht
und wollte frische Luft. Du bist zu närrisch!
Lass mich dein Haar auflösen und dich küssen.
Dann aber schnell nach Haus: was später kommt,
soll besser werden als der Anfang heute!

Er will sie an sich ziehen.

SOBEIDE

macht sich los, tritt zurück

Ganem! er hat die Tür mir aufgetan
und mir gesagt, ich bin nicht seine Frau,
ich kann hingehen, wo ich will . . . der Vater
ist los von seinen Schulden . . . und mich lässt er
hingehen, wo ich will . . . zu dir, zu dir!

Sie bricht in Schluchzen aus

Ich lief, da war der Mensch, der mir den Schmuck
wegnahm und mich umbringen wollte—dann
die Hunde—

Mit dem Ausdruck kläglicher Verlassenheit

und jetzt bin ich hier, bei dir!

GANEM

unaufmerksam, nach rückwärts horchend

Mir ist, ich hör Musik! hörst dus nicht auch—
von unten?

SOBEIDE

Dein Gesicht und noch etwas,
Ganem, erfüllen mich mit grosser Angst—
Hör nicht auf dies, hör mich! hör mich, ich bitte!

[480]

The Marriage of Zobeide

GANEM

I'll wager he's epileptic
and wanted some fresh air! Sweet fool you are!
Let me untie your hair, then let me kiss you.
But, after, you run home: later it all
will turn out better than today's beginning!

He tries to draw her towards him.

ZOBEIDE

frees herself, takes a step back

Ganem! He opened the door to me and said:
I am his wife no longer, I can go
wherever I will . . . my father is free of debt . . .
and he has let me go, wherever I will . . .
to you! to you!

She begins to sob

I ran, then there was a man
who snatched my pearls and tried to kill me—then
the dogs—

With an expression of pathetic forsakenness

and now I'm here, I'm here with you!

GANEM

inattentive, listening behind him

I thought I heard some music. Can you hear it—
from down below?

ZOBEIDE

Your face and something else
fill me with unspeakable terror, Ganem—
Do not listen to that, but to me, to me!

[481]

Hugo von Hofmannsthal

Hör mich, die deinem Blick mit offner Seele
daliegt, die ihres Blutes Flut und Ebbe
vom Wechsel deines Angesichts empfängt:
du hast mich einst geliebt—dies, scheint mir, ist vorbei—
Was dann geschah, ist meine Schuld allein:
dein Glanz schwoll an in meinem trüben Sinn
wie Mond im Dunst——

> *Ganem horcht nach rückwärts.*

SOBEIDE *immer wilder*

      Gesetzt, ich war dir nichts:
warum dann logst du? wenn ich dir was war,
warum hast du gelogen? Sprich zu mir—
Bin ich dir nicht der Antwort wert?

> *Sonderbare Musik draussen und Stimmen.*

GANEM

      Bei Gott,
es ist des Alten Stimme und die ihre!

*Die Treppe herunter kommt ein flötenspielender Zwerg und
ein weibisch aussehender Sklave, der eine Laute spielt, voraus
andere mit Lichtern, dann Schalnassar, auf Gülistane ge-
stützt, zuletzt ein Verschnittener, mit einer Peitsche im Gürtel.
Gülistane macht sich los, tritt nach vorne, scheinbar auf dem
Boden etwas suchend, die anderen kommen auch nach vorne.
Die Musik verstummt.*

GÜLISTANE *über die Schulter, zu Schalnassar*

Mir fehlt ein Büchslein, ganz von dunklem Onyx,
mit Salbe voll. Bist du noch immer da,
du Tochter Bachtjars! Auf, und bück dich doch,
ob dus nicht finden kannst!

The Marriage of Zobeide

Listen to me; my soul is lying open
before your eyes, receiving from the change
of your expression the ebb and flow of my blood:
you loved me once—it seems that now is past—
What happened then was my fault, mine alone:
you were a radiance growing in my dark senses
like moonlight in the mist—

Ganem listens behind him.

ZOBEIDE *more and more wildly*
                    I may have been nothing to you:
but why did you lie? If I meant something to you,
why did you lie to me? O speak to me—
Am I not worth an answer?

Strange music outside, and voices.

GANEM
                O my God,
that is the old man's voice, and her voice too!

*Down the stairs come a dwarf playing a flute and an epicene
slave playing a lute, others in front of them carrying lights,
then Shalnassar, on Gulistan's arm, finally a eunuch with a
whip in his belt. Gulistan leaves the others, walks forward,
apparently looking for something on the floor; the others also
walk forward. The music stops.*

GULISTAN *over her shoulder, to Shalnassar*

I've lost a little box, made of dark onyx,
there's ointment in it. Are you then still here,
you, Baktyar's daughter? Down on your knees now,
and see if you can find it!

[483]

Sobeide schweigt, sieht auf Ganem.

SCHALNASSAR

      So lass und komm!
ich schenk dir hundert andre.

GÜLISTANE

      Doch die Salbe
war ein Geheimnis!

GANEM *dicht bei Gülistane*

    Wozu soll der Aufzug?

SCHALNASSAR

Was kommst du nicht? wer alt ist, kann nicht warten!
Und ihr voran! macht Lärm und tragt die Lichter!
Betrinkt euch: was hat Nacht mit Schlaf zu tun!
Voran bis an die Tür, dort bleibt zurück!

Die Sklaven stellen sich wieder in Ordnung.

GANEM *wütend*

Was Tür? an welche Tür?

SCHALNASSAR
zu Gülistane, die sich an ihn lehnt

     Antwort ich ihm?
Es ist, um dir zu schmeicheln! Tu ichs nicht,
geschiehts, um dir zu zeigen, dass mein Glück
der Schmeichelei des Neides nicht bedarf.

GANEM *zu Gülistane*

Sag nein! sag, dass er lügt!

[484]

The Marriage of Zobeide

Zobeide says nothing, looks at Ganem.

SHALNASSAR

        Leave it, and come:
I'll give you a hundred others.

GULISTAN

          But the ointment,
it was a secret!

GANEM *close to Gulistan*

What's all this pageantry?

SHALNASSAR

Why aren't you coming? Old men can't wait, you know.
And you in front there, make a noise, bring lights!
Get drunk; for what has night to do with sleep!
On, till you reach the door, then stop!

The Slaves line up again.

GANEM *infuriated*

            Which door?
Which door?

SHALNASSAR

to Gulistan, who is leaning on his arm

    Well, my dear, shall I answer him?
If so, only to flatter you! If not,
only to show you that my happiness
is not in need of jealous flattery.

GANEM *to Gulistan*

Say no! Say that he's lying!

[485]

Hugo von Hofmannsthal

GÜLISTANE

Geh, guter Ganem,
und lass uns durch. Dein Vater ist genesen,
darüber freun wir uns. Was stehst du finster?
Man muss sich doch mit den Lebendgen freun,
solang sie leben.

Sieht ihm unter die Augen.

GANEM

reisst dem Verschnittenen die Peitsche weg

Wozu trägst du die Peitsche, altes Weib?
Stieb auseinander, krüppelhafte Narrheit!

*Er schlägt auf die Musiker und die Lichter ein, wirft dann die
Peitsche weg.*

Schamlose Lichter, aus! und du, zu Bett,
geschwollner Leib! ihr, aufgeblähte Adern!
ihr, rote Augen! du, verfaulter Mund!
fort in ein ungesellig Bett! und Nacht,
lautlose Nacht statt unverschämter Fackeln
und frecher Pfeifen!

Er weist den Alten hinaus.

SCHALNASSAR

bückt sich mühsam um die Peitsche

Mir die Peitsche, mir!

SOBEIDE

schreit auf

Sein Vater! beide, um das Weib! die beiden!

GÜLISTANE

windet dem Alten die Peitsche aus der Hand

Geh selber doch zu Bett, jähzorniger Ganem,

The Marriage of Zobeide

GULISTAN

Leave us, Ganem,
and let us through. Your father is quite cured,
and we are glad of it. What's this dark look?
You know one must be happy with the living,
as long as they're alive.

She looks at him, but below the eyes.

GANEM

snatches the whip from the eunuch

What can you do, old woman, with a whip?
Away with you, you crippled fools, get out!

*He strikes at the musicians and the lights, then throws the
whip away.*

Out, shameless lights! And you, to bed,
you bag-fleshed body, bloated veins, red eyes,
you rotten mouth, off to your solitary bed!
And night, let there be soundless night, not these
frivolous lanterns, flippant pipes!

He turns the old man out.

SHALNASSAR

stoops with an effort to seize the whip

Give me the whip!

ZOBEIDE

screams

His father, both, that woman! Both of them!

GULISTAN

makes the old man let go of the whip

You go to bed yourself, and cool your temper,

[487]

und lass beisammen, was beisamm sein will!
Schilt deinen Vater nicht! Ein alter Mann
weiss richtiger zu schätzen, und ist treuer
als eitle Jugend. Hast du nicht Gesellschaft?
Des Bachtjar Tochter steht doch da im Dunkeln:
ich hab oft sagen hören, sie wär schön.
Auch weiss ich wohl, du warst verliebt in sie.
Nun gute Nacht.

Sie wenden sich alle zum Gehen.

GANEM *wild*

Geh nicht mit ihm!

GÜLISTANE *über die Schulter zurück*

Ich geh,
wohin mein Herz mich heisst.

GANEM *flehend*

Geh nicht mit ihm!

GÜLISTANE

Ei, lass uns durch! auch morgen ist ein Tag.

GANEM
an der Treppe vor ihr liegend

Geh nicht mit ihm!

GÜLISTANE
umgewandt

Du Tochter Bachtjars,
so halt ihn doch! ich will ihn nicht! ich trete
mit meinem Fuss nach seinen Händen! Du!

[488]

and leave together those that want to be!
Don't dare abuse your father! An old man
knows better what is good, and is more loyal,
than arrogant youth. I thought you had company!
There's Baktyar's daughter standing in the dark:
I've often heard it said she's beautiful.
Also I know you were in love with her.
Good night then.

All turn to go.

GANEM *wildly*

Don't go with him!

GULISTAN *over her shoulder*

          I am going
where my heart tells me to.

GANEM *imploring*

Don't go with him!

GULISTAN

O let us pass! Tomorrow's another day.

GANEM

prostrate on the stairs in front of her

Don't go with him!

GULISTAN

turns

     You, daughter of Baktyar,
you keep him, I don't want him, look, I'll stamp
my foot upon his hands, you see? You see?

[489]

Hugo von Hofmannsthal

SOBEIDE *wie von Sinnen*

Ja! ja! wir wollen einen Reigen tanzen!
Gib mir die Hand! und ihm! und ich dem Alten!
Wir wollen unser Haar auflösen: welche
das längre Haar hat, soll den Jungen haben
für heut—und morgen wieder umgekehrt!
Gemeinheit hat den Thron! die Lügen triefen
vom menschlichen Gesicht wie Gift vom Molch!
Ich will mein Teil von eurer Lustigkeit!
  Zu Ganem, der den Hinaufsteigenden zornig nachsieht

Hinauf! stiehl sie dem Vater aus dem Bett,
würg ihn im Schlaf: ein Trunkner wehrt sich nicht!
Ich seh dirs an: du stirbst, mit ihr zu liegen!
Wenn du sie satt bist oder wechseln willst,
dann komm zu mir, wir wollen leise gehn,
mein alter Mann hat keinen tiefen Schlaf,
nicht so wie die, die dies anhören können
und schlafengehn dabei!
          Sie wirft sich zu Boden
          Ich will dies ganze Haus
aufheulen aus dem Schlaf mit Schmach und Zorn
und Jammer . . .
          Sie liegt stöhnend
          . . . Oh, dich hab ich so geliebt,
und du zertrittst mich so!
Ein alter Sklave zeigt sich rückwärts, löscht die Lichter aus,
          isst eine herabgefallene Frucht.

GANEM
schlägt jähzornig in die Hände

Auf! schafft sie fort! hier ist ein Weib, das schreit.
Ich kenn sie kaum! sie sagt, es ist um mich!

[490]

The Marriage of Zobeide

ZOBEIDE *as if out of her mind*

Yes! Yes! Let us all dance together!
Give me your hand, and one to him, mine to the old man!
And we'll untie our hair: whoever has
the longest hair shall have the younger man,
today, for today, tomorrow we'll make a change!
Let common lust be king! The human face
will drip its lies like salamander's poison!
I want my share of all the fun you have!

To Ganem, who is looking angrily towards the others as they
proceed up the stairs

Get up and snatch her from your father's bed,
strangle him in his sleep, drunk and helpless!
I see it in your face: you're dying to sleep with her!
When you have had enough of her and want a change,
then come to me, we must be quiet, because
my husband's old and has a lightish sleep,
not sleep like those who hear the things I'm saying
and still can sleep!

She throws herself to the floor

       I want to howl this house
out of its sleep with horrible words and anger
and lamentation.

She lies groaning

       O I have loved you so much,
and yet you trample on me.

An Old Slave appears at the back of the stage and puts out
the lights; he picks up a fruit that has fallen down, and bites it.

GANEM

claps his hands angrily

Here! Take her away! This screaming woman!
I hardly know her! She says it's all for me!

[491]

Ihr Vater wollte sie dem reichen Mann
verkuppeln, aber sie verdreht das Ganze
und sagt, ihr Mann wär auch ein solcher Kuppler,
und der ist nur ein Narr, soviel mich dünkt.

Er tritt nahe an sie heran, mitleidig spöttisch

Ihr seid doch allzu gläubig. Doch daran
ist eure Art mehr schuld als unsre Kunst.
Nein, steh nur auf, ich will dich nicht mehr ärgern.

SOBEIDE
richtet sich auf, ihre Stimme ist hart

So war an allem nichts, und hinter allem
ist nichts. Von allem dem werd ich nicht rein:
was heut in mich kam, kann nicht mehr heraus.
Aus anderen vielleicht. Ich bin zu müd.

Sie steht

Fort, fort! ich weiss, wohin ich geh! nur hier
hinaus!

Der alte Sklave ist langsam die Stiege hinabgegangen.

GANEM
Ich halt dich nicht. Allein den Weg—
wirst du den finden? Zwar, du fandest ihn . . .

SOBEIDE
Den Weg! den gleichen Weg!

Sie schaudert

Der alte Mann
soll mit mir gehn. Ich hab nicht Furcht, ich will
nur nicht allein sein: erst bis wieder Tag ist—

[492]

The Marriage of Zobeide

Her father wanted to sell her off to a man
with money, but she's turned it upside down
and says her husband was the go-between;
in any case it seems he's just a fool.

He walks closer to her, with mocking sympathy

You're all of you too credulous. The fault
lies more in your own natures than our art.
No, just stand up, I'll not annoy you now.

ZOBEIDE

raises herself, her voice is hard

So it meant nothing and behind it all
stands nothing. Nothing now shall make me pure:
what entered me today will never leave me.
It may leave others. But I am too tired.

She stands up

Let me out, let me out! I know where I am going,
but let me out of here!

The Old Slave has gone slowly down the stairs.

GANEM

I'll not detain you.
But will you find the way?—You found it once . . .

ZOBEIDE

The way! The same way as before!

She shudders

Then let
the old man come with me. I'm not afraid,
but do not want to be alone: till the night is past—

[493]

Ganem geht nach rückwärts, holt den alten Sklaven zurück.

SOBEIDE

Mir ist, ich trüg ein Kleid, daran die Pest
und grauenvolle Spur von Trunkenheit
und wilden Nächten klebte, und ich brächte
es nicht herunter als mit meinem Leib zugleich.
Jetzt muss ich sterben, dann ist alles gut.
Doch schnell, bevor dies schattenhafte Denken
an meinen Vater wieder Blut gewinnt:
sonst wird es stark und zieht mich noch zurück,
und ich muss weitergehn in meinem Leib.

GANEM
führt den Alten langsam vor

Merk auf. Dies ist des reichen Chorab Frau.
Verstehst du mich?

DER ALTE
nickt

Des reichen!

GANEM
 Wohl. Die sollst du
begleiten.

DER ALTE
 Wie?

GANEM
 Du sollst den Weg sie führen
bis an ihr Haus.

Der Alte nickt.

[494]

The Marriage of Zobeide

Ganem goes back, fetches the Old Slave.

ZOBEIDE

I feel as if my dress were daubed with pestilence
and foul remains of drunkenness and nights
passed in wild orgy, and cannot take it off
except by taking off my body with it.
Now I must die, then all things shall be well.
But quickly, before these shadowy thoughts I have
about my father take on a body again:
then they would be too strong, and drag me back,
and I must walk in this flesh, just as before.

GANEM

slowly leads the old man forward

Now listen. This is the wife of the rich man, Korab.
You understand?

OLD MAN

nods

The rich man!

GANEM

Good. And you
must go with her.

OLD MAN

What?

GANEM

Guide her all the way,
As far as her house.

The Old Man nods.

SOBEIDE

Bis an die Gartenmauer.
Von dort weiss ich allein, wohin ich soll.
Will er das tun? Ich dank dir. Das ist gut,
sehr gut. Komm, alter Mann, ich geh mit dir.

GANEM

Geht hier den Gang, der Alte weiss den Weg.

SOBEIDE

Er weiss ihn, das ist gut, sehr gut. Wir gehn.

*Sie gehen durch die Tür rechts ab. Ganem wendet sich, die
Treppe hinaufzugehen.*

Verwandlung.

The Marriage of Zobeide

ZOBEIDE

As far as the garden wall.
From there I can find the way I have to take.
Will he do this? I thank you. That is good,
yes, good. Come then, old man, I'll go with you.

GANEM

Go down this passage. He will know the way.

ZOBEIDE

He knows it, good, yes, good. Then let us go.

They leave by the door on the right. Ganem turns to go up the stairs.

Curtain

Hugo von Hofmannsthal

III

Der Garten des reichen Kaufmanns. Von vorne rechts läuft die hohe Gartenmauer nach links rückwärts. In ihr ist ein kleines vergittertes Pförtchen, zu dem Stufen führen. Links verläuft sich ein gewundener Weg zwischen Bäumen. Es ist früher Morgen. Die Büsche sind mit Blüten beladen und die Wiesen stehen voller Blumen. Im Vordergrund sind der Gärtner und seine Frau beschäftigt, zarte blühende Sträucher aus einer offenen Trage zu nehmen und im ausgegrabenen Boden umzusetzen.

DER GÄRTNER
Dort kommen schon die andern. Nein, das ist
ein einzelner . . . der Herr!

DIE FRAU
            Der Herr? am Morgen
nach seiner Hochzeit vor der Sonne auf,
im Garten und allein. Das ist kein Mann
wie andre Männer.

DER GÄRTNER
Schweig. Er kommt hierher.

DER KAUFMANN
tritt langsam von links her auf

Die Stunde, wo die Sonne noch nicht auf ist
und alle Zweige in dem toten Licht
dahängen ohne Glanz, ist fürchterlich.
Mir ist, als säh ich diese ganze Welt
zurückgestrahlt von einem grauenhaft
entseelten Spiegel, öde wie mein innres Auge!

The Marriage of Zobeide

III

The garden of the Rich Merchant. The high garden wall recedes from front, right, towards the left. There is a small ornamental iron-work gate in it, to which steps lead. Left, a twisting path runs between trees. It is early morning. The bushes are crowded with blossoms, the grass is thick with flowers. In the front, the Gardener and his Wife are busy transferring delicate shrubs from an open box into the freshly dug soil.

GARDENER

Here come the others. No, it's a man, alone;
the master!

HIS WIFE

Him? After his wedding-day,
up in the morning, before the sun has risen,
alone and in the garden. He's not a man
like other men.

GARDENER

He's coming here. Be quiet.

MERCHANT

walks slowly from left

This hour, in which the sun has not yet risen,
and all the boughs hang in the dead light,
where no radiance touches them, is terrible.
It is as if I saw the world, all of it,
reflected in a glass made horribly lifeless,
and null and void as my own inner eye.

[499]

Hugo von Hofmannsthal

O welkten alle Blumen! wär mein Garten
ein giftiger Morast, ganz ausgefüllt
mit den verfaulten Leibern seiner Bäume!
und meiner mitten drunter!

*Er zerpflückt einen blühenden Zweig, dann hält er inne und
lässt ihn fallen.*

Ei, ein Geck!
ein alter Geck, so alt als melancholisch,
so lächerlich als alt! ich will mich setzen
und Kränze winden und ins Wasser weinen!

*Er geht ein paar Schritte weiter, fährt wie unwillkürlich mit
der Hand nach dem Herzen.*

O wie ist dies von Glas, und wie der Finger,
mit dem das Schicksal daran pocht, von Eisen!
Die Jahre setzen keine Ringe an
und legen keine Panzer hier herum.

*Er geht wieder ein paar Schritte, stösst dabei auf den Gärtner,
der seinen Strohhut abnimmt; fährt aus seinen Gedanken auf,
sieht den Gärtner fragend an.*

DER GÄRTNER
Dein Diener Scheriar, Herr, der dritte Gärtner.

DER KAUFMANN
Wie? Scheriar, wohl. Und diese ist dein Weib?

DER GÄRTNER

Ja, Herr.

DER KAUFMANN
Allein sie ist um vieles jünger

The Marriage of Zobeide

If all the flowers could wither! If my garden
were a poisonous morass, full to the brim
with the putrescent bodies of its trees!
And mine among them!

*He breaks off a branch with blossoms on it, then stops, and
lets it fall.*

Ah, a coxcomb and
an old one too, as old as melancholy,
as ridiculous as old. I shall sit down
and make a garland and weep into the water!

*He walks a few steps further, then suddenly, as if involun-
tarily, puts his hand to his heart.*

O how my heart is glass and how the fingers
with which fate drums on it are iron. The years
have put no rings on them, nor steeled it hard.

*He takes a few more steps, so comes upon the Gardener, who
doffs his straw-hat; this shakes him out of his pensiveness, he
looks at the Gardener questioningly.*

GARDENER

The third gardener, sir, your servant Sheriar.

MERCHANT

What? Sheriar, of course. This is your wife?

GARDENER

That's right, sir.

MERCHANT

But she is by many years

wie du. Und einmal kamst du zu mir klagen,
dass sie mit einem Burschen—welcher wars?

DER GÄRTNER
Der Eseltreiber wars.

DER KAUFMANN
Da jagt ich den
aus meinem Dienst, und sie lief dir davon.

DER GÄRTNER
sich verneigend

Du kennst die Wege aller heiligen Sterne,
doch du erinnerst dich der Raupe auch,
die einmal neben deinen Füssen kroch.
Es ist so, Herr. Doch kam sie mir zurück
und lebt seitdem mit mir.

DER KAUFMANN
Und lebt mit dir!
Der Bursche schlug sie wohl! Du aber nicht!

Er wendet sich ab, sein Ton wird bitter

Wir wollen uns nur zueinander setzen
ins Gras, und eins dem andern die Geschichte
erzählen! Lebt mit ihr! er hat sie doch!
Besitz ist alles! Welch ein Narr ist das,
der das Gemeine schmäht, da doch das Leben
gemacht ist aus Gemeinem durch und durch!

Er geht mit starken Schritten rechts vorne weg.

DIE FRAU *zum Gärtner*

Was hat er dir gesagt?

younger than you. Once you complained to me
that she had gone with a young man; now, which was it?

GARDENER

The donkey-boy.

MERCHANT

And so I turned him out.
He left my service; and she ran away.

GARDENER
bows his head

You know the courses of the holy stars,
yet you do not forget the caterpillar
that once upon a time crept past your shoe.
Yes, you are right. But she came back to me,
and has stayed ever since.

MERCHANT

And she has stayed ever since!
Perhaps he beat her! You would not do that.

He turns, his tone becomes bitter

So let us sit down on the grass and tell
our stories to each other. Stayed ever since!
He has her! To possess is all. O fool,
whoever scorns what's common, seeing that life
consists of what is common, through and through.

He walks firmly away, right, front.

WIFE *to the* Gardener

What did he say to you?

[503]

Hugo von Hofmannsthal

DER GÄRTNER
Nichts, nichts.

*Sobeide und der Kameltreiber erscheinen an dem Gitter-
türchen.*

DIE FRAU
Du, weisst du was?

Näher kommend

Schau! dort
die Frau! das ist die junge Frau
des Herrn! schau, wie verstört sie aussieht.

DER GÄRTNER
Kümmer dich
um deine Sach!

DIE FRAU
Schau, sie ist ohne Schleier,
und wer bei ihr ist. Schau. Das ist doch keiner
von unsern Dienern, sag?

DER GÄRTNER
Ich weiss nicht.

*Sobeide streckt ihren Arm durch das Gitter, nach dem Schloss
suchend.*

DIE FRAU
Du!
Sie will herein. Hast du den Schlüssel?

DER GÄRTNER
aufschauend

Wohl,
den hab ich, und da sie die Herrin ist,
so dient man ihr, eh sie den Mund auftut.

The Marriage of Zobeide

GARDENER

O nothing, nothing.

Zobeide and the Camel-Driver appear at the gate.

WIFE

Now there's a thing.

Comes nearer

Look! Over there—the woman!
That's the master's young wife.
Look, but she seems most terribly bewildered.

GARDENER

You mind your own business.

WIFE

Look, she's lost her veil,
and who's that with her? Look, surely that's not
one of the servants?

GARDENER

I don't know.

*Zobeide puts her arms through the iron-work, reaching for
the lock.*

WIFE

And now!
She's trying to get in. You've got the key?

GARDENER

looking up

Yes, I have got it, and since she is the mistress
we must not wait until she calls for us.

[505]

Hugo von Hofmannsthal

Er geht hin und sperrt auf. Sobeide tritt ein, hinter ihr der Alte. Der Gärtner sperrt wieder zu. Sobeide geht mit verlorenem Blick nach vorne, der Alte hinter ihr. Der Gärtner geht an ihr vorbei, nimmt den Strohhut ab, will wieder an seine Arbeit. Die Frau steht ein paar Schritte rückwärts, biegt neugierig das Buschwerk auseinander.

SOBEIDE

Sag, hier ganz nah ist doch der Teich, nicht wahr,
der grosse Teich, an dem die Weiden stehen?

DER GÄRTNER
nach rechts hin zeigend

Hier unten liegt er, Frau, du musst ihn sehen.
Soll ich dich führen?

SOBEIDE *heftig abwehrend*

Nein, nein, geh nur, geh!

*Sie will rechts abgehen, da hält sie der Alte am Kleid zurück.
Sie wendet sich um.*

*Der Alte hält bettelnd die Hand hin, zieht sie verlegen gleich
wieder zurück.*

SOBEIDE

Was?

DER ALTE
Du bist nun daheim, ich geh zurück.

SOBEIDE

Ja, und ich hab dir deinen Schlaf gestohlen
und geb dir nichts dafür. Und du bist alt

[506]

The Marriage of Zobeide

He walks over and opens the gate. Zobeide comes in, behind her the Old Man. The Gardener shuts the gate. Zobeide walks forward with a lost and vacant look, the Old Man behind her. The Gardener passes her, doffs his straw-hat, and is about to return to his work. His Wife is standing a few paces back, she parts the bushes and peers out inquisitively.

ZOBEIDE

Tell me, is there a pond quite near this place,
the big pond, with willows growing beside it?

GARDENER

pointing to the right

It is down there, my lady, you can't miss it.
Shall I show you?

ZOBEIDE *impulsively*

No! No, I'll go alone!

She is about to walk to the right when the Old Man tugs at her sleeve. She turns.

The Old Man holds out a begging hand, but withdraws it at once with embarrassment.

ZOBEIDE

What is it?

OLD MAN

Now you're home, I'll go my way.

ZOBEIDE

Yes, and I have stolen your sleep from you,
and give you nothing in return. You are old

[507]

und arm. Allein ich hab nichts, nichts, gar nichts!
So arm wie ich, war auch kein Bettler je.

Der Alte verzieht sein Gesicht zum Lachen, hält wiederum
seine Hand hin.

SOBEIDE

sieht ratlos umher, fährt sich mit der Hand ins Haar, spürt
ihre Ohrgehänge von Perlen, macht eines los, dann das
andere, gibt sie ihm.

Da nimm, da nimm und geh!

DER ALTE
schüttelt den Kopf

O nein, o nein!

SOBEIDE *qualvoll eilig*

Ich geb sie gern, geh, geh!

Will weg.

DER ALTE
hält die Ohrgehänge in der Hand

Nimm sie zurück. Gib mir ein kleines Stück Geld!
Ich bin ein armer Narr. Sie kämen her,
Schalnassar und die andern, über mich
und nähmen mir die Perlen. Ich bin alt
und solch ein Bettler! Dies wär nur mein Unglück!

SOBEIDE

Ich hab nichts andres. Komm heute abend wieder
und bring sie hier dem Herrn, er ist mein Mann,
er gibt dir Geld dafür.

and poor. But I have nothing, I have nothing!
No beggar was ever as poor as I am now.

The Old Man screws up his face to laugh, holds out his hand
again.

ZOBEIDE

looks around desperately, runs her hand through her hair,
feels her pearl ear-rings, takes them off, one by one, and gives
them to him.

There, take them, take them, and go home.

OLD MAN
shakes his head

O no, O no!

ZOBEIDE *agonized, quickly*

You're welcome to them; now go home!

Is about to go.

OLD MAN
holds the ear-rings in his hand

But take them back! Give me a small gold piece.
I am a poor fool. They would come, the others,
and Shalnassar, hit me, and take the pearls. I'm old,
and a poor beggar. These might bring me harm!

ZOBEIDE

I've nothing else. But come again this evening,
and bring them to the master, he's my husband,
he'll give you money for them.

[509]

Hugo von Hofmannsthal

DER ALTE

Bist du auch hier?

SOBEIDE

Frag nur nach ihm, jetzt geh und lass mich gehn!

Will weg.

DER ALTE

sie zurückhaltend

O wenn er gut ist, bitt ihn du für mich,
dass er mich in sein Haus nimmt: er ist reich
und hat so viel Gesinde. Ich bin fleissig,
brauch wenig Schlaf. Doch in Schalnassars Haus
hungert mich abends immer so. Ich will—

SOBEIDE

sich losmachend

Wenn du heut abend kommst, so sprich zu ihm:
ich liess ihn bitten, dass er dirs erfüllt.
Nun geh, ich bitte dich, ich hab nicht Zeit.

*Der Alte geht gegen die kleine Türe, bleibt aber im Gebüsch
stehen. Die Gärtnersfrau hat sich von links Sobeiden genä-
hert. Sobeide geht ein paar Schritte, dann lässt sie den leeren
Blick umherschweifen, schlägt sich an die Stirn, als ob sie
etwas vergessen hätte. Sie bleibt plötzlich vor der Gärtnersfrau
stehen, sieht diese verloren an, dann fragt sie hastig*

Der Teich ist dort? wie? dort? der Teich?

Zeigt nach links.

The Marriage of Zobeide

OLD MAN

Will you be there?

ZOBEIDE

Just ask for him; now go, leave me alone!

Is about to go.

OLD MAN

holding her back

O if he's good, then ask him, for my sake,
to take me into his house: for he is rich
and has so many servants. I work well,
need little sleep. But in Shalnassar's house
I'm always hungry in the evening. I'll—

ZOBEIDE

freeing herself

When you see him this evening, say to him:
It was my wish that he should take you in.
Now go, I ask you, I have no time to spare.

*The Old Man walks towards the small gate, but remains
standing among the bushes. The Gardener's Wife has approached Zobeide from the left. Zobeide walks a few paces,
then gazes around vacantly, strikes her forehead with her
hand, as if she has forgotten something. Suddenly she stops
in front of the Gardener's Wife, looks at her absently, then
asks quickly*

The pond is over there? Over there? The pond?

Points to the left.

Hugo von Hofmannsthal

DIE FRAU

Nein, hier.

Zeigt nach rechts

Hier diesen Weg hinab. Er biegt sich dort.
Du willst den Herrn einholen? er geht langsam:
wenn du zum Kreuzweg kommst, wirst du ihn sehn.
Du kannst ihn nicht verfehlen.

SOBEIDE *noch verstörter*

Ich, den Herrn?

DIE FRAU

Ei ja, du suchst ihn doch?

SOBEIDE

Ich, ihn?—Ja, ja,
ich—geh—dann—hin.

*Ihr Blick schweift angstvoll umher, haftet plötzlich auf einem
unsichtbaren Ziel links rückwärts*

Der Turm! Er ist verschlossen?

DIE FRAU

Der Turm?

SOBEIDE

Die Stiege, ja, zum Turm?

DIE FRAU

O nein!
Der Turm ist nie verschlossen. Auch zur Nacht nicht.
Weisst du das nicht?

SOBEIDE

Ei, ja.

[512]

The Marriage of Zobeide

WIFE

No, here, go down this path.

Points to the right

You come to a turning.
You want to catch the master up? He walks
slowly: and at the crossroads you should find him.
You cannot miss him then.

ZOBEIDE *still more bewildered*

I? The master?

WIFE

Of course; you're looking for him, aren't you?

ZOBEIDE

I?

Him? Yes, yes, then—I'll—go—there.
Her eyes wander timorously, to fasten suddenly on an invisible
object offstage, back, left.

The tower!

Is the tower locked?

WIFE

The tower?

ZOBEIDE

And the stair

that leads up to it?

WIFE

No, it's never locked.
Not even at night. You didn't know?

ZOBEIDE

I knew.

Hugo von Hofmannsthal

DIE FRAU

Willst du hinaufgehn?

SOBEIDE
mühsam lächelnd

Nein, nein, jetzt nicht. Vielleicht ein andermal.

Lächelnd, mit einer freundlichen Handbewegung

Geh nur. Geh, geh.

Allein

Der Turm! der Turm!
Und schnell. Er kommt von dort. Gleich ists zu spät.

*Sie sieht sich spähend um, geht erst langsam nach links, läuft
dann durchs Gebüsch. Der Alte, der sie aufmerksam beob-
achtet hat, folgt ihr langsam.*

DER GÄRTNER
ist mit seiner Arbeit fertig

Komm her und hilf mir tragen.

DIE FRAU
Ei, ja, gleich.

Sie nehmen die Trage auf und tragen sie weiter nach rechts.

DER KAUFMANN
tritt von rechts auf

Ich hab sie so geliebt! wie gleicht das Leben
betrügerischen Träumen! Heute, hier
und immer hätt ich sie besessen! ich!
Besitz ist alles! langsame Gewalt,

The Marriage of Zobeide

WIFE

You want to go there?

ZOBEIDE

smiles with an effort

No, not now, perhaps
another time.

Smiling, with a friendly gesture of the hand

You must be going!

Alone

The tower!
Quickly. He'll come. Before it is too late.

*She looks around, then walks slowly left, then begins to run,
through the bushes. The Old Man, who has been watching
her closely, follows her slowly.*

GARDENER

has finished his work

Come now, and help me carry this.

WIFE

I'm coming.

They take up the box and carry it towards the right.

MERCHANT

enters from the right

I loved her so much! How like deceptive dreams
life is! Today, and here, always I could have had her!
I! To possess is all! A gradual power

[515]

einsickernd durch die unsichtbaren Spalten
der Seele, nährt die wundervolle Lampe
im Innern, und bald bricht aus solchen Augen
ein mächtiges und süssres Licht als Mond.
Ich hab sie so geliebt! ich will sie sehn,
noch einmal sehn. Mein Aug sieht nichts als Tod:
die Blumen welken sehends wie die Kerzen,
wenn sie ins Laufen kommen, alles stirbt,
und alles stirbt vergeblich, denn sie ist
nicht da—

Der alte Kameltreiber kommt von links her über die Bühne
auf den Gärtner zugelaufen und zeigt diesem etwas, das links
in einiger Entfernung und in der Höhe vorzugehen scheint,
der Gärtner macht die Frau aufmerksam, alle sehen hin.

DER KAUFMANN
wird dies plötzlich gewahr, folgt mit den Blicken der gleichen
Richtung, wird totenblass

Gott, Gott! gebt Antwort! da! da! da!
die Frau! da! auf dem Turm! sie beugt sich vor!
was beugt sie sich so vor? schaut hin! schaut hin!

Die Frau schreit auf und schlägt die Hände vors Gesicht.

DER GÄRTNER
läuft nach links, sieht hin, ruft zurück

Sie lebt und regt sich! Herr! komm diesen Weg!

Der Kaufmann läuft hin. Die Frau hinter ihm.

Gleich darauf bringen der Kaufmann, der Gärtner und die
Frau Sobeide getragen, lassen sie im Gras nieder. Der Gärtner
legt sein Oberkleid ab und schiebt es ihr unter den Kopf. Der
alte Kameltreiber steht in einiger Entfernung.

seeps through the soul's invisible crannies, feeds
the miraculous lamp in the inner being, and soon
out of such eyes there breaks a greater and
a sweeter light than the light of the moon itself.
I loved her so much! I want to see her now,
see her once more. My eyes see only death:
the flowers seem to fade, like so many candles
when they melt away, and everything is dying,
and all things die in vain, for she's not here—

*The old Camel-Driver runs from the left across the stage to
the Gardener and points out something to him which seems
to be taking place to the left at some distance and at some
height; the Gardener calls his Wife's attention to it, and they
all watch.*

MERCHANT
*suddenly realizes this, looks in the same direction, goes deathly
pale*

God! God! Answer me! There! There! There!
My wife! Up in the tower! She's leaning over!
Why is she leaning over? Look, O look!

*The Gardener's Wife screams and covers her face with her
hands.*

GARDENER
runs left, looks, calls back

She's still alive, she's moving! Sir, come here!

The Merchant runs after him, the Wife following.

*Immediately the Merchant, the Gardener, and the Wife re-
turn, carrying Zobeide; they place her on the grass, the Gardener takes off his smock and pushes it under her head. The
old Camel-Driver is standing some distance away.*

[517]

Hugo von Hofmannsthal

DER KAUFMANN *auf den Knien*

Du atmest! Du wirst leben, du musst leben!
Du bist zu schön, zu sterben!

SOBEIDE
schlägt die Augen auf

Lass! ich muss sterben; still, ich weiss es gut.
Mein Lieber, still, ich bitte. Ich hab nicht
gedacht, dich noch zu sehn—
Ich hab dir abzubitten.

DER KAUFMANN *zärtlich*

Du!

SOBEIDE
Nicht dies!
Dies musste sein.—Von früher, heute nacht:
ich war mit dir, wie's keiner Frau geziemt zu sein:
ich tat mit meinem ganzen Schicksal so,
wie ichs beim Tanzen tu mit meinen Schleiern:
mit eitlen Händen rührt ich an mein Selbst.
Sprich nicht! versteh mich!

DER KAUFMANN
Was geschah dir—dann?

SOBEIDE
Nicht fragen, was geschah; nicht fragen, bitte.
Ich war schon vorher müd, und so am Ende!
Nun ist es leicht. Du bist so gut, ich will
dir noch was sagen: merk nur auf. Die Eltern—

The Marriage of Zobeide

MERCHANT *on his knees*

You're breathing! You will live, O you must live!
You are too beautiful to die.

ZOBEIDE

opens her eyes

Don't. I must die; don't speak, for I know it.
My dear, don't speak, I implore you. I did not think
that I would see you again—
I must ask you to forgive me.

MERCHANT *gently*

You!

ZOBEIDE

                                        But not for this.
This had to be. No, I mean earlier,
last night: I behaved as no woman ought to behave:
I did with my whole destiny what I
do with my veils when I dance: with hands too vain
I touched upon myself. O do not speak.
But try to understand.

MERCHANT

What happened—then?

ZOBEIDE

Don't ask me what has happened, please, don't ask.
Even before, I was so tired—exhausted!
Now it is easy. You are so kind; there's one
more thing I want to say: my parents, listen,

[519]

du weisst ja, wie sie sind—du musst sie nehmen:
ganz zu dir nehmen.

DER KAUFMANN
Ja, doch du wirst leben.

SOBEIDE
Nein, sag das nicht: merk auf: ich möchte manches
noch sagen. Ja, da ist ein alter Mann.
Der ist sehr arm: den nimm auch in dein Haus
um meinetwillen.

DER KAUFMANN
Nun bleibst du bei mir:
ich will erraten, was du willst: so leise
du atmest, will ich doch die Harfe sein,
die jedem Hauch mit Harmonie antwortet,
bis du dich langweilst und sie schweigen heisst.

SOBEIDE
Lass solche Worte: mir ist schwindlig und
sie flimmern vor den Augen. Klag nicht viel,
ich bitte dich. Wenn ich jetzt leben bliebe,
verstümmelt wie ich bin, so könnt ich dir
kein Kind je zur Welt bringen, und mein Leib
wär hässlich anzusehn, und früher, weiss ich,
war ich zuweilen schön. Das könntest du
nur schwer ertragen und vor mir verbergen.
Allein ich werde ja gleich sterben, Lieber.
Dies ist so seltsam: unsre Seele lebt in uns
wie ein gefangner Vogel. Wenn der Käfig
zerschlagen wird, so ist sie frei. Nein, nein,
du darfst nicht lächeln: nein, ich fühl es so;
es ist so. Sieh, die Blumen wissens auch

you know just how they are—please take them to you:
take them entirely to you.

MERCHANT

Yes, but you'll live.

ZOBEIDE

No, do not say it: listen: there is more
that I would like to say. Yes, there's an old man.
He's very poor: take him too into your house,
for my sake.

MERCHANT

Now I know you'll stay with me:
I'll guess what it is you want: however quietly
you breathe, I'll be the harp and give reply,
to every breath you breathe, with harmony,
till you are tired of it and ask for silence.

ZOBEIDE

Please, do not say such things. I am so giddy and
the words flicker before my eyes. And please,
do not mourn much. If I were now to live,
crippled as I am, then I could never bear
your children, no, and my body would be
ugly to look upon, and before, you know,
sometimes I was beautiful. You'd find it
difficult to endure and to hide your feelings.
But in a moment I shall die, my love.
This is so curious: our soul lives in us
like an imprisoned bird. And when the cage
breaks, then the bird is free. No, do not smile:
you may not, no, I feel these things are true;
they *are* true. Look, the flowers also know it,

[521]

und starren so vor Glanz, seit ich es weiss.
Kannst du es nicht verstehen? merk auf.

Pause

Du bist noch da und ich auch immer noch?
Jetzt seh ich dein Gesicht, so wie ichs nie
gesehn hab. Bist dus denn, du, mein Mann?

DER KAUFMANN

Mein Kind!

SOBEIDE

Aus deinen Augen lehnt sich so
die Seele! und die Worte, die du redest, zucken
noch in der Luft, weil dir das Herz so zuckt,
aus dem sie kommen. Weine nicht, ich kanns
nicht sehn, weil ich dich nun so liebhab. Lass
mich deine Augen sehn zuletzt. Wir hätten lang
zusammen sein und Kinder haben sollen,
nun ist es schrecklich—für die Eltern!

Sie stirbt.

DER KAUFMANN
halb gebückt

So lautlos fällt ein Stern. Mich dünkt, ihr Herz
war mit der Welt nicht fest verbunden. Nichts
bleibt mir von ihr als dieser Blick, des Ende
getaucht schon war in starrendes Vergessen,
und Worte, die der falsche Hauch des Lebens
noch im Entfliehen trüglich schwellen liess,
so wie der Wind, eh er sich schlafen legt
zum Trug die Segel bläht wie nie zuvor.

[522]

and stiffen so, with a radiance, since I know it.
Perhaps you understand? Just look at them.

Pause

Are you still there, and am I too still here?
Now I can see your face as I've never seen it
before. Is it really you, you, my husband?

MERCHANT

My child!

ZOBEIDE

The soul looks down out of your eyes!
And the words you speak still tremble in the air,
because the heart from which they come is trembling.
O do not cry, I do not want to see it,
because I love you now so much. I want
your eyes to be the last thing that I see.
We should have lived long years together, and had children,
now it is terrible—for my dear parents!

She dies.

MERCHANT

half crouching over her

A star might fall as silently. It seems
her heart had never taken root in this world.
Nothing of her remains to me but this look,
whose ending was dipped already in icy oblivion,
and words remain, which the false breath of life
made wrongly swollen even as it fled away,
just as the wind, before it sleeps, puffs out
the sails, deceiving, stronger than ever before.

[523]

Hugo von Hofmannsthal

Er erhebt sich

Ja, hebt sie auf. So bitter ist dies Leben:
ihr ward ein Wunsch erfüllt: die eine Tür,
an der sie lag mit Sehnsucht und Verlangen,
ihr aufgetan—und so kam sie zurück
und trug den Tod sich heim, die abends ausgegangen
—wie Fischer, Sonn und Mond auf ihren Wangen,
den Fischzug rüsten—um ein grosses Glück.

Sie heben sie auf, den Leichnam hineinzutragen.

Der Vorhang fällt.

The Marriage of Zobeide

He stands up

Yes, lift her up. How bitter is this life:
her wishes were fulfilled: the only door
that she had sought with longing and desire
was opened to her—so she has returned,
bringing her death home with her, who went forth
one evening, like the fishermen that dress,
with sun and moon ashine upon their faces,
their seaward fleet—to find great happiness.

They lift up her body and carry it into the house.

The curtain falls.

PROLOGUE
TO THE "ANTIGONE"
OF SOPHOCLES

Translated by

CHRISTOPHER MIDDLETON

Vorspiel zur «Antigone» des Sophokles

*Auf dem Theater. Die Hauptdekoration (Palast des Kreon)
ist aufgestellt. Mitwirkende sind im Abgehen. Theaterarbei-
ter löschen die Lichter aus.*

*Erster und zweiter Student sind vorne. Der zweite schon im
Überrock, den Hut auf dem Kopf. Der erste barhaupt, einen
grossen dunkeln Mantel über den Arm geschlagen.*

ZWEITER STUDENT

Die Prob ist aus. Man geht. Was kommst du nicht?

ERSTER STUDENT

sieht in die Kulisse, welche die Tür des Palastes darstellt

Wart, ich will sehn, was dort im Dunkeln steht.

ZWEITER STUDENT

Wo denn?

ERSTER STUDENT

Dort in der Tür.

ZWEITER STUDENT

Ich sehe niemand.

Prologue to the "Antigone" of Sophocles

*A stage. The main set (Creon's Palace) is in position. Actors
are leaving. Stagehands are switching off the lights.*

*First and second student on the proscenium. The second
has already put on his overcoat and hat. The first, bareheaded,
carries a large dark cloak over his arm.*

SECOND STUDENT

Rehearsal's over. They're going. Why don't you come?

FIRST STUDENT

looks at the palace door in the wings

Wait, I must see what's there, standing in the dark.

SECOND STUDENT

Where?

FIRST STUDENT

There, in the door.

SECOND STUDENT

I can see no one.

[529]

Hugo von Hofmannsthal

ERSTER STUDENT

Niemand? Du siehst das nicht? Sie ist sehr biegsam
und klimmt in einem Schattenstreif empor.
Doch ihr Gewand—du siehst nicht, wie sichs regt?

ZWEITER STUDENT

Ja, doch, ich seh. Die Zugluft weht es an.

ERSTER STUDENT

Wen?

ZWEITER STUDENT

Das Gewand, das dort im Dunkeln hängt.

ERSTER STUDENT

Du siehst nur ein Gewand? Ich sehe mehr.

ZWEITER STUDENT

*schon rückwärts, indes auch alle übrigen abgegangen sind und
nur die rückwärtige Bühne noch von einem dürftigen Licht-
schein erhellt wird.*

Wilhelm, so komm!

ERSTER STUDENT

Ich komme.

Er zögert wiederum.

ZWEITER STUDENT

Man will schliessen!

*Verschwindet, indem er eine schwere, eisenbeschlagene Tür
hinter sich zuschlägt; es ist völlig finster.*

ERSTER STUDENT

Ich bin schon da.

[530]

Prologue to the "Antigone" of Sophocles

FIRST STUDENT

No one? You can't see it? Supple she is,
and climbing upward in a strip of shadow.
Surely you see her robe, and how it moves?

SECOND STUDENT

Yes, I can see, of course. Blown by the draught.

FIRST STUDENT

But who is it?

SECOND STUDENT

Just a robe, hanging in the dark.

FIRST STUDENT

Only a robe? I can see more than that.

SECOND STUDENT

*walks to the back of the stage—everyone else has gone, and
only the back of the stage is lit by a dim light.*

Come on then.

FIRST STUDENT

Coming.

He still lingers.

SECOND STUDENT

Quick, they want to close.

*He vanishes and a heavy iron-mounted door slams behind
him; it is now quite dark.*

FIRST STUDENT

I'm coming.

[531]

Hugo von Hofmannsthal

Will gehen.—Der Genius tritt aus der Tür des Palastes und
steigt langsam die Stufen herab. Er trägt ein flutendes Ge-
wand und eine tragische Maske vor dem Gesicht. Ein milchi-
ger, schimmernder Schein umgibt ihn.

ERSTER STUDENT *ausser sich*

Heinrich, es tritt hervor!
Heinrich, es schaut auf mich!

Dann halblaut, sich selber mit Lächeln beruhigend

Schauspielerin!

Der Genius bleibt vor ihm stehen; er trägt schöne Reifen um
die nackten Arme; in der Rechten hat er einen hohen Stab,
wie die Herolde.

STUDENT

Mein Fräulein, ich war ziemlich lächerlich,
vor Ihnen zu erschrecken. Zwar, es wird
nicht mehr probiert, und so ganz unvermutet . . .

Stockt, lächelt verlegen, wechselt den Ton

Ich bin ein Neuling, auch in dieser Welt,
wo Tag auf Nacht, und Höhle auf Palast,
ein künstliches Geschöpf dem andern folgt—

Stockt wiederum unter dem geheimnisvoll auf ihn gehefteten
Blick, tritt einen Schritt zurück, spricht mit gezwungener
Lebhaftigkeit

Es regt die Phantasie gewaltig auf:
das Nichtigste ist nicht geheimnislos,
man trägt sogar ein Etwas mit hinaus—

Muss wieder innehalten, findet gewaltsam den Übergang

Die Griechen, sie sind doch recht fern—doch Sie,
Sie tragen dies Gewand, als wärs das Ihre—
ja, Sie sind hier im Täuschenden zu Haus,

Prologue to the "Antigone" of Sophocles

Makes as if to leave. The Spirit steps from the palace door and slowly descends the stairs, wearing a flowing robe, with a tragic mask over its face. A milky shimmering light surrounds it.

FIRST STUDENT *beside himself*

Look, it's walking forward now!
And looking at me!

Then, quietly, calming himself with a smile

It must be an actress!

The Spirit stops just in front of him; it is wearing bracelets, exquisite ones; in the right hand a tall staff, like a herald.

STUDENT

Madame, it was ridiculous of me
to be afraid of you. But the rehearsal
is over and, well, so unexpectedly . . .

Stops, smiles with embarrassment, changes his tone

I am a newcomer, new to this world too,
where nighttime yields to day, palace to cave,
one artificial creature to the next—

Stops again with the mysterious gaze fastened on him, takes one step back, and speaks with a forced liveliness

It mightily excites imagination:
even the least thing has its mysteries,
something one even takes away with one—

Has to pause again, finds the connection, and blurts out

The Greeks, they're very far from us—but you,
you wear this robe as if it were your own—
yes, you are quite at home in pure illusion,

und das geheimnisvolle Element
umgibt und nährt Sie; wie beneidenswert!

*Nach einer Totenstille Pause; mit gewaltsamer Leichtfertig-
keit auf die Gestalt zutretend*

Sehr schöne Maske, deine Augen leuchten!
Sprich nicht, noch nicht, der Augenblick ist köstlich!
Geheimnis ist der Schönheit schönstes Kleid:
ihr solltet immer nur in Larven gehn,
und eur Gesicht sollt was Verborgnes sein
und sich dem Blick nur geben, der schon liebt.
Doch deine Hand, die lass mir; Hände sprechen!

Indem er die Hand berührt, fährt er blass und zitternd zurück

Ah! Du bist keine Frau! Du bist kein Mensch!
Du bist die fürchterliche Gegenwart
von etwas, das mein Fleisch sich kräuseln macht
wie Zunder. Warum muss mir das geschehn!

Sehr stark

Wie, oder bin ich hier, und das ist drüben?

Flüsternd

Ich träume nur. Hier rechts von meinem Bett
ist meine Uhr, und dort das Fenster, wo nur?
Ein weisses Linnen regt sich von der Wand,
da nahm ich es für eine Nachtgestalt,
die hier vor mich hertrat. Wo ist mein Bett?
So fest liegt es auf mir, ich meine, ich höre,
wie fingernd ihre Hand den Stab berührt.
Ich hab den Mut nicht, nur ein Aug zu drehn.
Phantom, geträumtes, du, Phantom, was willst du?

GENIUS
Mit welchem Namen da benennst du mich?

[534]

and the mysterious element surrounds you,
and nourishes you too; how enviable!

A deathly pause, then walks frivolously right up to the Spirit

Most beautiful of masks, your eyes are shining!
O do not speak yet, do not spoil this moment!
Beauty's most beautiful dress is mystery:
your kind should always wear a mask, no more,
your face should always be some hidden thing
and give itself only to eyes that love.
But let me have your hand; for hands can speak!

*The moment he touches the Spirit's hand he starts back, pale
and trembling*

Ah! You're not woman, nor any human thing!
You are the presence that most terrifies,
of something that makes my flesh wreathe up like smoke
from tinder. Why should this be what I feel?

Loudly

What is this? Am I here? And is that there?

Whispers

I'm only dreaming. Here to the right of my bed
there is my clock, and there the window. Where?
A white sheet moved, and left the wall behind,
I took it for a midnight apparition
that stood before me. Yet, where is my bed?
It seems so obvious I think I hear
its fingers shifting on the staff it carries.
I dare not turn a single eye that way.
What do you want, you phantom I have dreamed?

SPIRIT

What is that word that you have used to name me?

[535]

Hugo von Hofmannsthal

STUDENT

Von irgendwo Emporgestiegenes,
des Gegenwart mich kalt besessen macht!
Wandrer, an dessen Sohlen Staub nicht haftet!
Ich weiss, ich werd erwachen, werde liegen
hart neben meinem Bette an der Erde,
allein, und werde sprechen: Dies war nichts!
Doch gib mir eine Nachricht, gib ein Etwas!
Mich überkommt das Süsse an dem Wahnsinn!

GENIUS

Die ewig leben, senden mich an dich
mit einer schönen Botschaft.

STUDENT

Deine Stimme
—ich red mit ihm!—ist schön. Jedwede Botschaft
muss schön sein, die du bringst.
Denn deine Stimme ist mit Glück geschwellt
wie Segel eines Fahrzeugs fern am Himmel,
drin Liebende der ganzen Welt vergessen;
und deiner Stimme Schwebung ist gesegnet
so wie ein goldner Tag im Herbst, den Greise,
auf Mauern wandelnd zwischen Rebenlauben,
mit kühler Hand und reinem Auge segnen.
Dies alles hab ich schon einmal geträumt.
Doch war es nie so schön.—

GENIUS
den Stock auf den Boden stossend

Du träumest nicht:
Das eben ist die Botschaft, die ich bringe:
Mich musst du glauben, dass du sie verstehst.

Prologue to the "Antigone" of Sophocles

STUDENT

O being, risen from some unknown space,
whose presence freezes me, makes me possessed!
Wanderer, to whose foot no dust can cling!
I know I shall wake up, that I shall lie
hard by the side of my bed, and on the earth,
alone, and I shall say: But it was nothing!
Yet give me now a message, give me something,
now that the sweets of madness overwhelm me!

SPIRIT

The eternal ones have sent me down to you.
The news I bring is beautiful.

STUDENT

         Your voice
—I'm talking to it now!—is beautiful.
Say what you may, it must be beautiful,
because your voice is filled with happiness,
like sails on a far ship crossing the sky
with lovers in it, who've forgot the world;
also the tremor of your voice is blessed
like a gold day in autumn, which old men,
walking along the walls between the vine leaves,
bless with cool hands and with their shining eyes.
All this has come to me before in dreams,
but never so beautiful.

SPIRIT
strikes the ground with the staff

        You did not dream:
And that is just the message which I bring:
you must believe me, if you would understand it.

[537]

Hugo von Hofmannsthal

STUDENT

Dich glauben? wer bist du?

GENIUS

Und wer bist du?

STUDENT

Ich? ich? ich steh doch hier, ganz Wirklichkeit.
Dies ist die Bühne, eh probierten wir
ein griechisch Trauerspiel; die draussen gehn
und Türen schliessen, die sind meinesgleichen;
und draussen ist die Stadt mit vielen Strassen:
auf Viadukten dröhnen Züge hin
durch schwefelfarbne Luft hinaus ins Land;
dort stehen Wälder, und die suchen wir
zuweilen—doch umgibt uns hier wie dort
Geschick und schlummerlose Wirklichkeit,
und nichts ist leer—, wie fandest du den Raum,
aus deinem Drüben hier hereinzugleiten?
Wer grub dir mit den Händen diese Höhlung
in die lebendige Luft? was willst du hier?

GENIUS

Die ewig leben, senden mich an dich
mit ihrer Botschaft.

STUDENT

Du bist ein Phantom,
die Stätte hier hat dich gebrütet, dies
unsichre Licht, die trügerischen Wände,
die Legionen Träume, die hier nisten.
Schönes Gespenst, du bist die Ausgeburt
von einem sonderbaren Haus: hier geben
erbärmliche und sehr erhabne Träume
einander Stelldichein—

[538]

Prologue to the "Antigone" of Sophocles

STUDENT

Believe you? But who are you?

SPIRIT

Who are *you*?

STUDENT

I? Who am I? I stand here, and am real.
This is the stage, and we have been rehearsing
a Greek tragedy; those who move outside,
closing the doors, they are the same as I am;
and outside is the town, with many streets:
through sulphurous air across the viaducts
trains roar away into the open country;
there woods are, which from time to time we visit—
yet here, as there, a destiny surrounds us
and a reality that knows no sleep,
and nothing's void—how could you find the space
to slip from your Beyond to where we are?
Who with his hands has dug this cavity
you occupy in living air? What do you want?

SPIRIT

The eternal ones have sent me down to you,
bearing their message.

STUDENT

Phantom is what you are,
hatched by this unaccountable place, by this
uncertain light, by these deceptive walls,
the legions of the dreams which nest in it.
O beauteous ghost, you are the monster child
of a strange house: here wretched dreams keep tryst
with dreams that are sublime—

[539]

Hugo von Hofmannsthal

GENIUS

Und kehrst doch selber gern hierher zurück,
und rührest ungeheueren Geschicken
wieder und wieder an den Saum des Mantels
und nahmest in der Seele dumpfen Spiegel
des Königs Ödipus furchtbares Auge,
das rollende, voll Abgrund der Verblendung,
und später blutige, gebrochene.
Und kommest wiederum und drängest dich,
der schwesterlichsten Seele Schattenbild
zu sehen: hier heraus wird sie dir treten,
Antigone, und wie sie reden wird
und ihren Leib dem Tod entgegentragen
mit heiligem, gebundnem Schritt, da wird
die Kraft der Seele dir von ihren Lippen
entgegenschwirren und wird ihre Fesseln
um deine Seele legen, dass sie nackt,
so wie die Sklavin einem Siegeswagen,
mitfolgt und spricht: «Dies musste so geschehen.
So will ich tun, und will so sterben müssen.
Denn hier ist Wirklichkeit, und alles andre
ist Gleichnis und ein Spiel in einem Spiegel.»

STUDENT

Mir ist, dies könnte möglich sein, doch seh ichs
wie zwischen Dämpfen, und es hält nicht stand!

GENIUS

Erfass es nur. Dir bietet sich kein Festes.
So wie die Möwe auf dem Kamm der Wogen
so muss dein Geist ausruhn auf Fliehendem.
Durchsichtig ist sein Thron und rollt dahin.
Erfass es! sei nicht dumpf! lass dich erschüttern!

[540]

Prologue to the "Antigone" of Sophocles

SPIRIT

Yet you yourself return perpetually
and touch the hem of giant destinies here,
take into the clouded mirror of your soul
the terrible eye of Oedipus the King,
the rolling eye that dazzling chasms fill,
the eye that's later bloody, and is broken.
And come again and crowd around to see
the shadow image of the sister soul:
even from here she shall appear to you,
Antigone, and when she comes to speak
and bring her body into the charge of death
with holy rhythmic step, then from her lips
the pure power of her soul shall whirl towards you,
shackle your soul and make it follow, naked,
as naked slaves follow a conqueror's car,
and it will speak: "These things were bound to be.
My will it is to do this, so to die.
For here reality is, all other things
are parables and playings in a mirror."

STUDENT

All this is not impossible, yet I see it
as hedged by mists, and nothing solid there!

SPIRIT

Only but grasp it. No firm thing is offered.
And like the gull upon a crest of wave,
your mind must rest upon a flowing motion.
Transparent is its throne, and rolls away.
Grasp it, with senses live, and be astonished!

[541]

Hugo von Hofmannsthal

Von Gipfeln, die im Lichte ewig blühn,
warfs mich herab zu dir mit einer Botschaft:
Antigones erhabnem Schattenbild
schrei ich in der erneuten Todesstunde
voran und streue Ehrfurcht ringsumher.
Mit starken Händen greif ich in die Luft
und banne sie, dass sie gewaltig sich,
ein unsichtbarer Schoss des Schicksals, lagert,
ausstossend des Gemeinen dumpfen Dunst.
Ob Tausende sich drängen, Einsamkeit
der Wüste giesse ich um jedes Herz,
die Unruh hemm ich, heiss die Zeit stillstehn.

Stösst dröhnend seinen Stab auf den Boden

Was hier geschieht, ist ihr nicht untertan.

Hier hebt eine leise Musik an, die Rede zu begleiten.

STUDENT
Du atmest kühn und stark. Doch eine Maske
verhüllt mir dein Gesicht. Wie glaub ich dir?
Zweideutig ist ein so verhüllter Anblick:
die Maske, die du trägst, ist wundervoll—
allein dein Wesen scheint mir mehr, viel mehr!

Hingerissen

Begreif ichs ganz, wie würd ich wesentlich!

Müde, entmutigt zurücktretend

Dein Anblick wieder nährt nur Träumereien.

GENIUS
Ich sprach zu dir, du ahntest, ahntest recht:
zuck nicht umher nach neuer Offenbarung!

[542]

Prologue to the "Antigone" of Sophocles

From peaks which bloom perpetual in the light
I was sent down to you, bringing a message:
I go before sublime Antigone,
her shadow image, in her death's new hour,
and scatter awe and reverence all around.
I rummage in the air, strong-handed; I
invoke her to descend in all her glory,
a womb of destiny, invisible, to disperse
the common fogs that dull the minds of men.
Though thousands crowd around her, I infuse
each heart with solitude as in a desert,
I make time stop, all agitation cease.

Strikes a loud blow on the boards with the staff

What happens here is not within time's power.

Now quiet music begins, accompanying what is said.

STUDENT

Courage and strength speak with you. But a mask
conceals your face. How then can I believe you?
Such veilings make ambiguous what we see;
the mask you wear is, surely, wonderful—
yet what you are seems more to me, far more!

Rapturously

If I could grasp that, O how real I'd be!

Wearily, drawing back, discouraged

Yet when I look at you, I'm filled with dreams.

SPIRIT

I spoke to you, you guessed, and guessed aright:
No, do not fumble for fresh revelations!

[543]

Hugo von Hofmannsthal

Ergriff ich dich, was kümmerts dich, wodurch?
Ich rief dich auf, ich rührte dich, ich bin!
Die Maske aber darf dich nicht verstören:
es tragen die Geliebtesten der Menschen
vor dir ein maskenhaft Gesicht:
ein menschlich Aug erträgt nichts Wirkliches.
Verlarvt, der Herold eines Schattens, steh ich
vor dir—glaubst du an mich?

STUDENT
Ich möchte glauben.

Hier schwillt die Musik an.

GENIUS
So hauch ich deine beiden Augen an.

Der Student neigt sich der Gestalt, die ihn anhaucht. Dann läuft ein starker Schauder durch seinen Leib. Der Genius tritt von ihm weg und steigt langsam die Stufen zum Palast empor, zweimal sich umblickend. Der Student richtet sich auf. Er ist blass. Er wirft einen völlig veränderten Blick um sich. Hier bricht die Musik plötzlich ab.

STUDENT
Die Stufen dort sind fürchterlich! Dort sass
Ödipus, und von seinen Lippen troff
der Fluch und Blut von seinen beiden Augen!

Er richtet den Blick nach aufwärts

Die Last des Daches, unter dem sie lebten,
der alte Laios schon! Die Sonne drüber—
Der Himmel hart und funkelnd wie Metall.—
Ich möchte meinen Leib von hier wegschleppen!
Die grelle Sonne liegt wie festgenagelt

[544]

Prologue to the "Antigone" of Sophocles

If I have moved you, why should you plumb the cause?
I summoned you, I stirred you, and I am!
You have no need to let my mask perturb you:
even the dearest beings that you know,
they only let you see the masks they wear:
the eye of man cannot bear that which is real.
So with my mask, the herald of a shadow,
I stand before you. Do you believe in me?

STUDENT

I want to.

Music louder.

SPIRIT

Then I'll breathe upon your eyes.

The Student leans towards the Spirit, which breathes upon him. Then a great shudder runs through him. The Spirit turns and slowly mounts the stairs to the palace, looking back twice. The Student draws himself up. He is pale. He stares about him, looking utterly changed. The music suddenly stops.

STUDENT

Those stairs, how terrible they are. The King,
Oedipus sat there, on his lips the curse,
and blood was streaming out of both his eyes!

He looks up

The weight of that roof under which they lived,
even in Laios' time! Sun overhead—
the sky, adamant and shining like metal.—
I want to drag my body from this place!
The garish sun lies nailed before this door,

vor dieser Tür, und nichts bleibt mir verborgen!
Innen und aussen muss ich sehn und wissen.
Ein schwerer schwacher Lufthauch weht mich an,
darin ist Staubgeruch und böser Dunst
von etwas, das verwest. Das kommt von dort,

Scheu sich umsehend

dort drüben, wo auf offnem Feld ein Leichnam liegt.
Wenn nur ein starker Wind herkäme und
der Staub ihn ganz zudeckte, dort den Toten.
Er liegt. Wenn man von etwas trinken könnte
und ganz vergessen, dass das alles ist!
Ich höre drin im Haus welche umhergehn.
Du! kannst du denn nichts helfen? nichts abwenden?

Genius winkt verneinend und verschwindet in der Tür des Palastes.

STUDENT
ihm wild nachrufend

Zu welchem Amte hast du mich geweiht?
Wie hast du mir die Poren aufgetan?
Was für ein sehendes Geschöpf gemacht
aus mir? Warum muss ich Teilnehmer sein
an etwas Furchtbarem, das nun geschehn wird?
Mein Blick schwankt durch die schweren Mauern da,
so wie durch Wasser, und ich seh die Jungfrau
Antigone, das funkelnde Gefäss
des Schicksals,

Hier fängt die Musik wieder an und wird nun immer mächtiger.

sehe ihre schlanken Schultern,
das schlichte Haar, entgegen mir bewegt sich

and nothing, nothing now is hidden from me.
And I must see inward and outward things.
A heavy, feeble breath of air I feel,
the smell of dust in it, the evil vapour
of something going bad. It comes from there,

Looking round timidly

over there, where a corpse lies in a field.
If only the wind blew stronger, and the dust
covered him up entirely, that dead man.
He lies there. If only one could have a drink
and quite forget that all these things are so.
I can hear people moving in the house.
You, can't you help, can you avert—nothing?

*The Spirit makes a gesture of denial and vanishes through the
door into the palace.*

STUDENT

shouting wildly after it

O to what office have you consecrated me?
How made the pores of my flesh open wide?
What visionary creature have you made
of me? Why must I now participate
in the terrible thing that is about to happen?
My eyes, they waver through the thick walls there,
as if through water, and I see the girl,
Antigone, the luminous vehicle
of destiny.

The music starts again and grows gradually louder.

I see her slender shoulders,
and her neat hair, and now towards me moving

[547]

ihr Fuss und ihr Gewand, auf ihrer Stirn
sind sieben Zeichen des ganz nahen Todes!
Sie geht durch eine Ebbe. Links und rechts
tritt in durchsichtigen erstarrten Wogen
das Leben ehrfürchtig vor ihr zurück!

Ihm scheint die Erscheinung wirklich aus dem Dunkel des
Palastes entgegenzukommen. Der dunkle Mantel flattert um
seinen bewegten Leib wie eine Wolke. Die Musik hat die
Kraft des vollen Orchesters und ist hier schon in die eigentli-
che Ouvertüre übergegangen.

Dies strahlende Geschöpf ist keines Tages!
Sie hat einmal gesiegt und sieget fort.
Da ich sie sehe, kräuselt sich mein Fleisch
wie Zunder unter einem Feuerwind:
mein Unvergängliches rührt sich in mir:
aus den Geschöpfen tritt ihr tiefstes Wesen
heraus und kreiset funkelnd um mich her:
ich bin der schwesterlichen Seele nah,
ganz nah, die Zeit versank, von den Abgründen
des Lebens sind die Schleier weggezogen:
einwühlen muss ich mich in meinen Mantel,
eh mich die übermässigen Gesichte
erdrücken! Denn dem Hauch des Göttlichen
hält unser Leib nicht stand, und unser Denken
schmilzt hin und wird Musik!

Er sinkt, das Gesicht in seinem Mantel verborgen, auf die
Stufen des Palastes. Der Vorhang fällt und bleibt unten, bis
die Ouvertüre zu Ende gespielt ist.

her foot and mantle, and upon her brow
the seven signatures of her close death.
She walks within the ebb. To right and left
in stiff transparent waves all life recedes
in reverence before her.

*The apparition seems to him to be actually emerging from the
darkness of the palace. Around his animated body the dark
cloak floats like a cloud. The music swells to the volume of an
orchestra, having indeed begun the opening bars of the over-
ture.*

This dazzling creature does not belong to time!
Once she has conquered, conquer she will for ever.
When I see her, my flesh wreathes up like smoke
from tinder winds of fire have breathed upon:
in me the imperishable begins to stir:
out of the creatures steps their deepest being
and circles round me, dazzling, luminous:
I have approached near to the sister soul,
most near, and time subsided, from the abyss
of life the covering veils are torn away:
shrink I must, bury myself in my cloak,
or be overwhelmed by the excess of vision.
For the body cannot bear the exhalation
of the divine, and mind must melt away,
becoming music.

*He sinks down, his face hidden in his cloak, on the stairs up to
the palace. The curtain falls and stays lowered until the over-
ture is finished.*

NOTES

Biographical Note

H UGO VON HOFMANNSTHAL was born in Vienna on February
1, 1874, the only child of a family of Austrian, south
German-Jewish, and Lombard antecedents. When he entered
the University of Vienna, in 1892, he was already famous
as a poet—as "Loris," his *nom de plume*. Hofmannsthal first
studied law; after military service, in 1894–95, he turned to ro-
mance philology and took the Ph.D. in 1898. Nearly all of his
lyrical poetry was written during the nineties, as well as most of
the short lyrical plays later collected as "little dramas" (the most
famous is *Death and the Fool,* 1893) and a few tales and essays.
He married in 1901 and settled in Rodaun, a village near Vienna.
He had three children. Occasionally he travelled—the Continent;
England twice, briefly; Greece, Morocco, Sicily once. In 1899,
Hofmannsthal had begun to write for the stage. From about 1908
until his death, he collaborated with both the composer Richard
Strauss and the producer Max Reinhardt. His drama *Elektra*
(1904), an adaptation from Sophocles, became the libretto in
1909 of an opera of Strauss. There followed the operas *Der Rosen-
kavalier* (1911), *Ariadne in Naxos* (1912), *The Woman without
a Shadow* (1919), *The Egyptian Helen* (1928), and *Arabella*
(staged in 1933). Reinhardt produced Hofmannsthal's rendering
of *Oedipus Rex* (1909), his morality play *Everyman* (1911), and
his comedy *The Man Who Was Difficult* (1918). During all these
years Hofmannsthal continued to write essays. He began two
works of prose fiction: *Andreas* (1912–13) and *The Woman with-*

out a Shadow (1919); only the latter was completed. During the first World War, he dedicated his efforts to his country, imperial Austria, and after the war to the new Austrian republic and to the idea of the European community. He was the guiding spirit behind the Salzburg Festival; his *Everyman* became one of its central pieces. For the Festival he wrote the *Salzburg Great Theatre of the World* (1922); that and his last tragedy, *The Tower* (1925, second version, 1927), had their starting-points in plays of Calderón. Hofmannsthal died suddenly on July 15, 1929, at Rodaun.

H. S.

Textual Notes

INTRODUCTION. Several previously unpublished notes by Hofmannsthal have been quoted here; they were transcribed from
annotated books in Hofmannsthal's library, to which I have had
access by kind permission of the poet's son, Mr. Raimund von
Hofmannsthal.

The sources for most of the other quotations are named in
the introduction, and all the works referred to are to be found in
the fifteen-volume edition of Hofmannsthal's works edited by
Herbert Steiner and published by S. Fischer Verlag, Frankfurt
a/M. Where no such source is mentioned, the quotation is from
the diaries and notes included in Volume 15 of the above-named
edition. I am grateful to Mr. Rudolf Hirsch, of S. Fischer Verlag,
for having read and commented on the introduction.

The letters to the Austrian poet and philosopher Rudolf
Pannwitz (b. 1881) from which I have quoted on pp. liv–lv
were published by Herbert Steiner in *Mesa* (Lexington, Ky.),
autumn 1955. Rudolf Pannwitz's part of the correspondence has
not yet been published. The quotation on p. v is based on a
transcription made available to me by Hofmannsthal's widow, the
late Mrs. Gerty von Hofmannsthal.

The quotations from the *Collected Poems* and *Collected Plays*
of W. B. Yeats have been used by permission of Mrs. W. B. Yeats,
The Macmillan Company, New York, and Messrs. Macmillan &
Co. Ltd., London.

M. H.

[555]

Textual Notes

The following list gives in alphabetical order the translated titles of works of Hofmannsthal's mentioned in the introduction but not published in the present volume. Those marked with an asterisk are to appear, with other plays and librettos, in a projected volume of dramatic writings.

Der Abenteurer und die Sängerin: The Adventurer and the Singer
Die ägyptische Helena: The Egyptian Helen
Ariadne auf Naxos: Ariadne in Naxos
Die Betrachtungen, die geschnittenen Steine und die redenden Masken: The Reflections, the Cut Stones, and the Speaking Masks
Elektra: Electra
Die Frau im Fenster: The Woman in the Window
Die Frau ohne Schatten: The Woman without a Shadow
Gerechtigkeit: Righteousness
Das gerettete Venedig: Venice Preserv'd
Gespräch über Gedichte: Conversation on Poetry
Gestern: Yesterday
Das grosse Salzburger Welttheater: The Great Salzburg Theatre of the World
Jedermann: Everyman
Der Jüngling und die Spinne: The Youth and the Spider
Das Märchen der 672. Nacht: The Tale of the Six-Hundred-and-Seventy-Second Night
Ödipus and die Sphinx: Oedipus and the Sphinx
Der Schwierige: The Man Who Was Difficult
Der Tod des Tizian: Titian's Death
Der Turm: The Tower
Vor Tag: Before Day
Der weisse Fächer: The White Fan
Weltgeheimnis: World Secret

*

xv. All these essays by Loris are more ambiguous than it was possible to elaborate in a brief introduction. Francis Vielé-Griffin's poems, for example, are treated as journalism in verse; this poet, Hofmannsthal says obliquely, "has the very dangerous gift of expressing nearly all those things which he does not feel, and scarcely thinks, with a sophisticated, almost memorable, aptness." Hofmannsthal is critical even of Pater. *"Marius the Epicurean,"* he writes in his essay on Pater of 1894, "demonstrates the inadequacy of any attempt to base one's whole way of life on the aesthetic view."

xv. Stefan George: Born 1868 in Germany, died in 1933.

xx. *The Letter of Lord Chandos:* 1901 or 1902; see the translation by Tania and James Stern in the preceding volume of Hofmannsthal's *Selected Prose* (1952).

xxx. *Ad me Ipsum:* Hofmannsthal's private jottings on his own development as an artist; now included in the volume *Aufzeichnungen.*

xxxv. *Freud and Breuer:* The *Studies on Hysteria,* which Freud wrote jointly with Josef Breuer more than five years before *The Interpretation of Dreams,* are usually regarded as the starting-point of psycho-analysis.

xli. *Bachofen:* His *Das Mutterrecht* appeared in 1861. The passage quoted is from the *Gesammelte Werke,* Vol. III (Basel, 1948), p. 823.

xliv. ". . . *the loveliness/That has long faded . . .":* From Yeats's lyric *He Remembers Forgotten Beauty,* in *The Wind among the Reeds* (1899).

lv. *Hermann Broch:* For his interpretation of Hofmannsthal's development, see his introduction to the preceding volume of *Selected Prose.*

lxi. *Book of Friends:* Compiled from notebooks of 1917–22. For selections, see the preceding volume of *Selected Prose.*

Poems

The dates of composition of the poems, in approximate chronological order, are as follows: *An Experience, Prologue to "Anatol"* (1892); *World and Self, Shepherd Boy's Song, Idyll* (1893); *Stanzas in Terza Rima* (1894); *A Dream of Great Magic* (1895); *Ballad of the Outer Life, Many truly . . .* (1895?); *The Youth in the Landscape* (1895, 1896?); *Song of Life, Your face . . . , A Boy, Inscription, Infinite Time* (1896); *Verses on a Small Child, We went along a way . . .* (1897); *The Self-Controlled* (1897?); *The Emperor of China Speaks, In Memory of the Actor Mitterwurzer* (1897, 1898?);

Traveller's Song, Three Epigrams (1898); *The Old Man's Longing for Summer* (1907?).

The present selection is arranged for coherence and consistency. The lyrical poems form a group, the more didactic or epigrammatic form another, and the *Idyll* is placed last as a transition to the verse plays.

8/9. THE SELF-CONTROLLED. In tone, prosody, and theme, this poem is very close to the manner of Stefan George. The influence was reciprocal; several of George's poems contain echoes of poems by Hofmannsthal; one of his late poems, *Der Mensch und der Drud*, may owe something to Hofmannsthal's *Idyll*, unless a common debt to Mallarmé's *L'Après-midi d'un faune* explains the remarkable similarities.

28/29. STANZAS IN TERZA RIMA. *I, first line.* This line is ambiguous in German: *ihren Atem* could mean either "her breath" or "their breath," and has been construed either way. The translator's interpretation is supported by a parallel passage in Hofmannsthal's verse play *Gestern:*

> *Dies Gestern? des'sen Atem ich noch fühle*
> *Mit seines Abends feuchter, weicher Schwüle*

(This yesterday? whose breath I still feel with its evening's moist, gentle warmth)

The theme, in both cases, is transitoriness itself, not the passing of any specific event.

Stanza 3. In his essay on D'Annunzio of 1893, Hofmannsthal writes of "a woman like a malignant and dumb dog," and later: "It is very strange when someone finds the images of his vision of the world in such motionless things, considering that in life all glides and flows."

III (30/31). The little children and the moon in this poem may derive from illustrations in the books of Kate Greenaway, which Hofmannsthal read in his childhood. In an essay called *Englischer Stil* (1896) he writes of a performance by the Barrington sisters, and says that "one expects the moon to rise behind their yellow hair and childish shoulders, the oversize Japanese full moon, as in the picture-books of Kate Greenaway behind the five school-girls with yellow hair, baby bonnets and pink dresses." Kate Greenaway is also mentioned in an earlier autobiographical piece on Hofmannsthal's childhood to which he gave the English title "The Age of Innocence" (1893).

32/33. BALLAD OF THE OUTER LIFE. *Stanza 4.* The following passage occurs in Hofmannsthal's thesis on the poetic development of Victor Hugo, written in 1901 when Hofmannsthal intended to take up an academic career: "Once again the places lie here and there by the roadside, the inviting ones and the gloomy ones, the thriving and the decayed, and impress their natures, fused into one living whole with the strange sound of their names, deeply upon the child's imagination." These correspondences between Hofmannsthal's poems and prose works—even an academic thesis in this instance—are frequent and characteristic; his criticism, too, sprang from poetic empathy.

36/37. A DREAM OF GREAT MAGIC. *Stanza 11.* Compare the passage from the "Chandos Letter" quoted on p. xxxiv.
Stanza 14. A paraphrase of Paracelsus: "our spirit that does not dwell in us and sets its chair amidst the upper stars." Hofmannsthal entered the quotation in his journal on June 5, 1895. Compare his remarks on poetic inspiration quoted on p. xxxviii.

52/53. THE EMPEROR OF CHINA SPEAKS. The nucleus of this monologue seems to be Goethe's poem *Königlich Gebet,* which Hofmannsthal quoted and praised in a book review of 1896. Goethe's poem, written about 1775, begins as follows:

Ha, ich bin Herr der Welt, mich lieben
Die Edlen, die mir dienen.

(Hah, I am lord of the world, I am loved by the nobles who serve me) but ends with a prayer for humility.

60/61. PROLOGUE TO "ANATOL." Written for the first edition of Arthur Schnitzler's one-act play *Anatol.* This improvisation on eighteenth-century Vienna represents the young Hofmannsthal at his most mundane and his most pictorial. Though in a trochaic verse letter of the same year to his friend Richard Beer-Hofmann the poet says that the trochaic line is not his metre, he seems to have found it suitable for incidental and informal verse. The trochaic metre had been naturalized in Austria by Grillparzer, who took it over from the Spanish dramatists and used it in his plays as an alternative to iambic blank verse. Hofmannsthal is often regarded as Grillparzer's successor in Austrian literature.

66/67. IN MEMORY OF THE ACTOR MITTERWURZER. This is Anton Friedrich Mitterwurzer (1844–1897). The poem is one of three commemorative poems for actors written by Hofmannsthal; the others were for Hermann Müller and Josef Kainz. Hofmannsthal also wrote several prose tributes to actors and dancers, such as Eleonora Duse, Nijinsky, Ruth St. Denis, and Grete Wiesenthal. In all these pieces he stressed the impersonality of the great artist. "For this, I think, is what artists are for: that all the things that pass through their souls should receive a meaning and a soul," he wrote on Duse in 1892; and, in a later essay on mime ("On Pantomime," 1911): "A pure gesture is like a pure thought, stripped of the momentarily witty, the exclusively individual, the grotesquely characteristic. . . . In that way pure gestures reveal the true personality, and this apparent renunciation of individuality is more than amply compensated." The actor and the dancer are intimately bound up with one of Hofmannsthal's central concerns, the problem of identity. Kainz alone, of the three actors to whom Hofmannsthal wrote verse tributes, is credited with an individuality preserved intact despite his absorption in his various roles; and a prose piece on Eleonora Duse (1903) attributes the same distinction to her maturity.

72/73. IDYLL. *Arnold Böcklin* (1827–1901) was a Swiss painter of mythological subjects.

Verse Plays

92/93. DEATH AND THE FOOL (1893). Eugen d'Albert composed a violin solo to be played by Death in Max Reinhardt's Berlin production of the playlet in 1908.

129. *You said I had reminded you of things.* An allusion to a poem which Hofmannsthal addressed to Stefan George in December 1891:

> *Du hast mich an Dinge gemahnet,*
> *Die heimlich in mir sind,*
> *Du warst für die Saiten der Seele*
> *Der nächtige flüsternde Wind . . .*

(You reminded me of things that are in me secretly; for the strings of my soul you were the nocturnal whispering wind)

Cf. introduction, p. xx.

140/141. THE EMPEROR AND THE WITCH (1897). Hofmannsthal's choice of a Byzantine setting for this play is another remarkable link with the late work of W. B. Yeats.

224/225. THE LITTLE THEATRE OF THE WORLD (1897). Written at Varese in northern Italy during an exceptionally productive period. In the same letter in which Hofmannsthal told his father of its completion, he mentioned his sketches for what was to become *The Marriage of Zobeide.* In an earlier letter he called *The Little Theatre of the World* a "lyrical dialogic trifle."

227 ff. *The Poet's speech:* The vision of the warriors at the riverside recalls engravings by Marcantonio and Agostino Veneziano; and these, in turn, go back to a lost cartoon by Michelangelo, *The Battle of Cascina.*

235. *The Young Gentleman's speech:* The allusion at the beginning to the old man, identifiable as the previous speaker, constitutes one of the few obvious connections between the characters in this playlet. The "her" of the last two lines (p. 241) comes rather unexpectedly; one might construe it as another ambiguity— the German *ihr* could conceivably refer back to *Morgenfrühe,* "the early morning"—but it makes better sense to regard this character as the lover. Both in *The Emperor and the Witch* and *The Woman without a Shadow,* hunting is linked symbolically or psychologically with erotic passion.

261. *The Madman's speech: The night with a thousand lips . . .* In Goethe's early poem *Willkommen und Abschied* night peers with

"a hundred dark eyes" out of the bushes. Other passages in the speech recall the poems of Hölderlin's last phase before his madness, especially in their syntax. In the previous year Hofmannsthal's friend Raoul Richter had given him the two-volume edition of 1846 of Hölderlin's works, which were only then being rediscovered and re-edited.

266/267.   THE MINE AT FALUN (1899). The origin of the theme was a real event (cf. introduction, p. lv): the discovery of a miner's corpse in a silver mine near the Swedish town of Falun, in 1809. It had been preserved for fifty years, it is said, by the effect of acid. Upon Hebel's account of the discovery Hoffmann based his somewhat elaborated tale, upon which Hofmannsthal in turn based the play.

304.   *Ich bin herumgekommen.* The 1946 and 1952 editions of Hofmannsthal's *Gedichte und Lyrische Dramen* wrongly substitute "Ich bin heruntergekommen." Dr. Herbert Steiner, the editor of those volumes, has kindly drawn the translator's attention to this error, which will be corrected in subsequent editions of the text. Dr. Steiner read the proofs of the present selection and made many valuable suggestions and emendations, of which this is one.

366/367.   THE MARRIAGE OF ZOBEIDE. The motto is clearly from the tragedy by John Fletcher (printed 1634), written probably with Shakespeare's collaboration, though it has been impossible to trace a German translation of this play under the title *Palamon und Arcite.*